12/7/94

D0984598

The New Recording Studio Handbook

The New Recording Studio Handbook

by John M. Woram
and
Alan P. Kefauver

First Edition

ELAR Publishing Company Inc.
Commack, New York 11725
Copyright© 1989

Printed in the United States of America
Library of Congress Catalog Number 89-080009
ISBN Number 0-914130-04-8

Second Printing—1990

New illustrations by Hal Keith
Page layout by K&S Graphics, Island Park N.Y.

for my teachers
Harold Boxer and
Bob Pierce

Contents

The Basics

Transducers: Microphones And Loudspeakers

Signal Processing Devices

Analog Audio Recording Systems

Digital Audio Systems

Synchronization Systems

The Console

The Recording Process

INTRODUCTION

If anything is certain in professional audio, it is that it is a technology-intensive industry. Newer products all come to us as better, easier, and therefore more cost-effective.

As publisher/editor of db The Sound Engineering Magazine, everything new comes across our desks. Of course, not everything that is called *new-and-revolutionary* is just that. But with a magazine, there is always a new issue about to come out that will report on the real and the not real.

Books are different. Technical books have a finite life tied to the technology they serve, and this is true of The Recording Studio Handbook as well. Originally published in 1976 and updated in 1982, it was time to have a completely new edition.

Who was to re-write this classic textbook? We needed a knowledgeable authority who was totally *au courant* with the recording industry. Who better than an educator-engineer-musician named Alan P. Kefauver. He is the Director of Recording and Coordinator of the Recording Arts and Science Program at the Peabody Institute, itself world-prestigious (yet a part of John Hopkins University). As part of Hopkins, Peabody offers only full-degree matriculated recording and music programs.

Alan is a user of the older book, and aware of the dated materials in its later chapters. (In the early chapters, the Decibel and the needed basic math understandings, have, of course, not changed.)

Much of the equipment he writes about is installed in the school's studios, but Alan's working knowledge goes well beyond that since he remains active on the recording and music scenes not only in his native Baltimore, but on an international scale as well.

Creating a new book, even if it builds from so auspicious a past as this one, presents all-new problems if only because the publisher *is* in New York, while the author is in Maryland. New text had to be written and submitted, new illustrations (and some old ones) had to be coordinated.

Long lists of pictures and drawings needed from manufacturers were created and db Magazine Associate Editor Carol A. Lamb found herself with a Herculean job of doing just that. Last minute substitutions, new information culled from a November 1988 AES Convention, and so on, all fell to Carol.

Between the fax machines and the telephone, and several visits to us by Alan, a new book was born. We got to know Alan better; he got to know us better. But what truly came from this was a better new book. The final evidence is in your hands now—The New Recording Studio Handbook.

Larry Zide
February 1989
ELAR Publishing Co. Inc.
Commack NY

Preface

Since its first publication in 1976, *The Recording Studio Handbook*, by John Woram, has been the standard reference work against which other audio textbooks are measured. However, as we all know, things in the audio business do not stand still and even though the book was updated with several supplementary chapters in 1982, many changes have occurred since then. As an educator, I was hoping that someone would modernize this classic text. I was very surprised when I was the one asked to do the revision. Still, I said to myself, why not? The book is so well written that all I'll have to do is change a few pictures and supplement the information on digital systems to reflect the current standards.

Little did I know ......

A year and a half later, I am truly amazed at the changes that technology has created in our industry. I knew of these changes all along, but rewriting this book has pointed out to me how different the modern recording studio is from the studios of the not too distant past. And, five or so years from now, someone will look at my hard disk digital work station and wonder why I still keep that obsolete thing around. In an evolving industry such as this one, everyone is constantly upgrading their facilities and thought processes. These changes happen a little bit at a time, and as such, the impact of the larger cumulative change is often missed.

A great deal of this book is not new since much of the original information is still current. A loudspeaker is still a loudspeaker. I have tried not to remove any valid information, yet integrate the new material within the framework of the old. There are, however, several new sections. These address digital storage methods, console automation, and synchronization systems among other things. As examples, MIDI , DAT, PD and DASH are each discussed.

As the book grew to encompass these changes and additions, it became clear that something would have to go if an affordable selling price was to be maintained. Sorry to say, but the glossary would have pushed it over the edge. I hope to include a new comprehensive glossary in a future book.

I have attempted to update and revise *The Recording Studio Handbook* of 1976 into *The New Recording Studio Handbook* of 1989 without tampering with the style or intent. When I first read the book, shortly after it had been published, I was taken with its easy and readable treatment of what can be a dry and difficult subject. I hope that I have been able to maintain that character.

Alan P. Kefauver
Baltimore, Md.
January 1989

SECTION 1—INTRODUCTION

THE BASICS

In subsequent sections of this book, it has been assumed that the reader has at least a general acquaintance with the basics, that is to say, a general understanding of the decibel, and a good idea as to the nature of sound and how it reacts in air. The first section of this book has been prepared as either a primer or as a refresher for these first principles of recording.

I suspect that the average recording studio reader will not necessarily be enthralled by a brief discussion on the physics of sound waves, but would rather get to the point, and then be off to the more interesting aspects of the recording science. With that in mind, this section has been prepared to cover as briefly and succinctly as possible the basic minimum knowledge required.

Section I is not the most interesting part of the whole book, but it may be required reading in order for the reader to make the most sense out of the other sections that are to follow.

Obviously, it is beyond the scope of this book to more than scratch the surface on the subject of sound and acoustics. However, you can never know too much about the nature of the sounds we are trying to capture and accurately store. There are many excellent texts available on the nature of sound, and the reader is encouraged to pursue his or her interest at the local library.

Chapter 1

THE DECIBEL

The decibel (dB) is the commonly used unit for the measurement of sound levels. It is always abbreviated small "d" capital "B" since it stands for one-tenth (deci) of a Bel. The Bel is a rather large unit of measure to work with, hence the decibel. Sound, such as a jet aircraft taking off or a quiet sail on a placid lake can be measured with a sound level meter. We think of a jet taking off, which creates a noise level of around 130 dB, as very loud, and a peaceful sail, about 35 dB, as very quiet. The sound level meter usually measures sound levels between 0 dB and 140 dB or more. However, 0 dB is not the total absence of sound but is equated to our threshold of hearing. That is, the lowest sound pressure level that an average listener with good hearing can detect. This zero reference level corresponds to a sound pressure of 0.00002 dynes/cm^2. In terms of intensity, this is equivalent to 0.000000000001 watts/meter^2. Chapter 2 contains a detailed discussion on the sound level meter itself.

Even a place as quiet as an acoustically correct recording studio has a certain amount of background noise. The simple movement of air may be around 25 dB above our thresholds at some frequencies. Therefore, we can say that the ambient noise level is 25 dB greater than our reference level of 0 dB.

Anyone who has ever spent time with a tape recorder has surely noted that the readings on the VU meter are not necessarily related to the actual volume heard in the room. Even with the playback loudspeakers turned off the meters will still register if a signal is applied to the tape recorder. In fact, changing the listening level in the room will have no effect whatsoever on the meter readings. Furthermore, typical meter readings of –10 to +3 suggest that a different zero reference value is being used. Actually, there are two measuring systems where the decibel is commonly used.

The first measurement system, as in our jet plane, is as a measure of acoustic power. Here the decibel tells us how far above

3

the threshold of hearing these sounds are. Figure 1-1 shows the typical sound levels found in our everyday environment. The second measurement, our VU meter, tells us something about the electrical power flowing through the meter circuit. However, whenever power measurements are made, whether acoustical or electrical, the formula for the decibel is the same. That formula is:

$$dB = 10 \log \frac{P}{P_R}$$

where:
P = the power to be measured
P_R = the reference power

When measuring acoustic sound, the reference power P_R corresponds to the pressure produced by a sound at the threshold of hearing. This pressure level may be expressed in microbars, dynes/cm^2, watts/meter^2 or newtons/meter^2. The relationship between these different systems is :

0 dB = 0.0002 microbars = 0.0002 dynes/cm^2 = 0.00002 newtons/m^2 = 0.000000000001 watts/m^2
Therefore, 1 microbar = 1 dyne/cm^2 = 0.1 newton/m^2 or:
10 microbars = 10 dynes/cm^2 = 1 newton/m^2.

For electrical measurements, a different reference level will be chosen later in the chapter.

Logarithms

From the above formula, it should be clear that the decibel is defined in terms of logarithms (abbreviated log). Therefore, some comprehension of the mathematical significance of the log is essential to an understanding of the decibel. The reader who is completely familiar with logarithms may wish to skip ahead. Others may also wish to do so, but should avoid the temptation.

In Figure 1-2, several very simple multiplication problems are solved. To the right of each answer, there appears a shorthand notation, consisting of the number 10 followed by a superscript. In mathematics, this superscript is known as an exponent, and to help realize its significance, we may say that an exponent indicates how many times the number, 1, is to be multiplied by 10. In

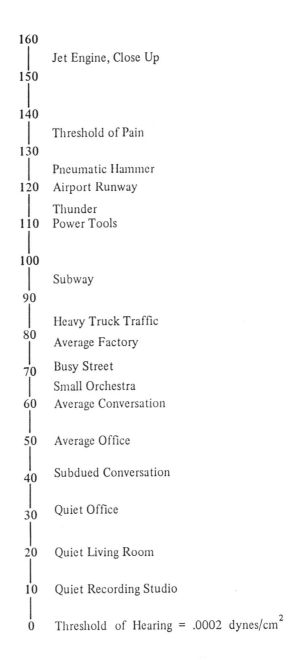

Figure 1-1. Typical sound pressure levels.

Problems	Answers
$1 =$	1, or, 10^0
$10 =$	10, or, 10^1
$10 \times 10 =$	100, or, 10^2
$10 \times 10 \times 10 =$	1,000, or, 10^3
$10 \times 10 \times 10 \times 10 =$	10,000, or, 10^4
$10 \times 10 \times 10 \times 10 \times 10 =$	100,000, or, 10^x (x=5)

Figure 1-2. A few simple multiplication problems solved.

the last problem, the exponent, x, is equal to 5, and is read as, "ten, raised to the fifth power," or simply, "ten to the fifth." The fact that $10^0 = 1$ may be difficult to understand. It may help to understand that 10^0 is not 1 multiplied by 10 at all, and so it remains simply 1. This explanation may not please the mathematicians, but it will enable us to get on with our introduction to the decibel with a minimum of pain.

We should also note that numbers less than 1 can be represented by powers of ten. For example:

$$0.1 \ = 10^{-1}$$
$$0.01 \ = 10^{-2}$$
$$0.001 = 10^{-3}$$

In fractional form, $0.001 = 1/1,000$ or, $1/10^3$, so, we may say that $0.001 = 1/10^3 = 10^{-3}./1 = 10^{-3}$ In other words, a power of ten in the denominator of a fraction may be moved to the numerator, simply changing the sign, in this case from plus to minus.

Often, a difficult fraction may be simplified by following this procedure. For example:

$$\frac{3,200,000}{0.004} = \frac{32 \times 10^5}{4 \times 10^{-3}} = \frac{32 \times 10^5 \times 10^3}{4} = \frac{32 \times 10^{5+3}}{4} = \frac{32 \times 10^8}{4} = 8 \times 10^8$$

Note that when powers of ten are to be multiplied, the exponents are merely added to find the product ($10^5 \times 10^3 = 10^{(5+3)} = 10^8$). Likewise, division may be accomplished by subtracting the exponents (10^5 divided by $10^3 = 10^{(5-3)} = 10^2$). The significance of this operation will be appreciated later in solving power and voltage equations in terms of decibels. For now, we may realize that cumbersome numbers become less so when converted to powers of ten. For example, the sound intensity at the threshold of hearing, stated earlier as 0.000000000001 watts/m^2 becomes simply 1 x 10^{-12} watts/m^2. A number such as 0.0000025 may be rewritten as 2.5 x 10^{-6}, or if it is more convenient, 25 x 10^{-7}. However, standard engineering notation uses exponents in a sequence of threes, such at 10^{-3}, 10^{-6}, 10^{-9}, 10^{-12}, etc. and 10^3, 10^6, 10^9, etc.

Now, if $1=10^0$, and $10 = 10^1$, it stands to reason that we should be able to represent any number between 1 and 10 by 10^x, with x equal to some value between 0 and 1. To find the value for x in a problem such as $3 = 10^x$, we will call this exponent a logarithm, and offer the following explanation.

The logarithm of a number is that power to which 10 must be raised (not multiplied) to equal the number.

The statement may appear to contradict what was just said about multiplying 1 by 10 a number of times. To help resolve the apparent contradiction, we may note that although the number 10 may indeed be simply multiplied by itself, say four times for example, (10^4 = 1 x 10 x 10 x 10 x 10 = 10,000), it is no simple matter to do the same thing 4.7 times. Yet, if 10^4 = 10,000, and 10^5 = 100,000, surely there must be value for $10^{4.7}$. To find the answer, something beyond simple multiplication is required. Returning to our sample problem, $3 = 10^x$, we may say that the log of 3 is x. The actual calculation of this, or any other log, is an involved calculation appreciated only by mathematicians, and the working recording engineer need not concern himself with the process, since logarithms are readily available with the push of a button on most serious calculators. A simplified log table is given here (Figure 1-3). It is important to comprehend the significance of the log, so that calculation of decibels will be clearly understood.

By studying the table of logs, we may notice several important characteristics of logs, which are really extensions of what was just pointed out about multiplying and dividing exponents. Since a log is an exponent:

When numbers are multiplied, the log of the product is equal to the sum of the logs of the numbers.

Number	Log	Number	Log	Number	Log
1	0.000	10	1.000	100	2.000
2	0.301	20	1.301	200	2.301
3	0.477	30	1.477	300	2.477
4	0.602	40	1.602	400	2.602
5	0.699	50	1.699	500	2.699
6	0.778	60	1.778	600	2.778
7	0.845	70	1.845	700	2.845
8	0.903	80	1.903	800	2.903
9	0.954	90	1.954	900	2.954
10	1.000	100	2.000	1,000	3.000

Figure 1-3 A simple table of logarithms.

$$\log\ (4 \times 5) = \log 4 + \log 5$$
$$\log 20 = \log 4 + \log 5$$
$$1.301 = 0.602 + 0.699$$
$$1.301 = 1.301$$

When numbers are divided, the log of the quotient is equal to the difference of the logs of the numbers.

$$\log\ (800/20) = \log 800 - \log 20$$
$$\log 40\quad = \log 800 - \ \log 20$$
$$1.602\quad = 2.903 - \ 1.301$$
$$1.602 = 1.602$$

A final point: note than when any number is doubled, the log increases by a constant amount: 0.301. When a number is multiplied by 10, its log increases by 1, and when a number is squared, its log is doubled.

Acoustic Power Measurements

If we know that our previously mentioned jet aircraft produces a sound intensity of 10 watts/m^2, the decibel level can be calculated from the previously described formula:

$$dB = 10 \log P/P_R = 10 \log 10^1/10^{-12} = 10 \log 10^{(1+12)} = 10 \log 10^{13}$$

$10 \times 13 = 130$ dB

where: $\qquad\qquad$ P = 10 watts/m^2 (the jet)

$\qquad\qquad\qquad$ P$_R$ = 10^{-12} watts/m^2 (the threshold of hearing)

The jet noise is therefore 130 dB above the threshold of hearing, or 10^{13} times as intense. Now although this certainly is not anyone's idea of soft, we probably don't think of a jet aircraft being 10,000,000,000,000 times the level of the threshold of hearing. Indeed, we may be surprised to realize that our ears are capable of responding to such an incredibly wide range of intensities.

The decibel notational system makes these large intensity ranges more manageable. As a matter of fact, the human ear responds psychoacoustically about the same way. For example, if one jet aircraft produces a sound level of 130 dB, what sort of acoustic horror awaits us in the presence of two such noises? Two jets will definitely sound louder than one, but not by as much as you might expect. The listener will probably note that the noise level has increased, but certainly it is nowhere near twice as loud as before.

Note that if one jet produces 10 watts/m^2, two would produce 20 watts/m^2. Or:

$$\text{NdB} = 10 \log 20 \ = 10 \log \frac{2 \times 10^1}{10^{-12}} = 10 \log \frac{[2 \times 10^{13}]}{10^{-12}} =$$

$$10 \, [\log 2 + \log 10^{13}] = 10 \, [0.301 + 13] = 10 \, [13.301] = 133.01 \text{ dB}$$

In other words, the two aircraft produce a sound that is only 3 dB above the noise of one of them. This dB value rather accurately parallels the listener's subjective impression of the increase in level. In fact, if we returned to a more normal monitoring environment and listened to a musical program, and were then instructed to turn up the volume control until the program was "twice as loud," the measured sound pressure level would likely be about ten times greater than before. Of course, this is merely an approximation, since the conception of change in listening level will vary somewhat from one person to another.

Inverse Square Law

As we have just seen, two jets are 3 dB louder than one jet. Now consider how the level in decibels would change if we double the distance that we are from the jet(s). One would suppose that the sound level would halve and that the level would be decreased by 3 dB. However, this is not the case. Let's see what happens as we move from, say, 100 feet in distance from our noise source to 200 feet away. At our original distance, the sound radiates equally into a sphere with a radius of 100 feet. This means that the sound is dispersed over an area of 125,664 square feet ($4\pi r^2$). When we move back to a distance of 200 feet, the sound is now radiating into an area of 502,655 square feet, or 4 times the original area. Since we know that doubling the sound power gives us a 3 dB increase in level, it makes sense that half the power level will cause a decrease of 3 dB, and that one-fourth the level (another halving) will give us a total decrease of 6 dB.

Since the constant level sound is radiating into a space that is four times as large as the original space, the sound power level will diminish by 6 dB. Simply stated, this means that every time we double the distance from the source of a sound in an open space, the level of the sound will drop 6 dB. And conversely, every time we halve the distance to the source of the sound, the sound level will rise 6 dB.

Electrical Power Measurements

In any electrical circuit, a certain amount of power is dissipated. For example, the power dissipated in a resistor may be found from the formula, $P = E^2/R$ or $P = I^2R$. Therefore, if we know the value of the resistance, and either the current, I, flowing through it or the voltage, E, across it, we may calculate the power. If the power then increases, we may calculate the difference in terms of decibels by comparing the new power with the old. For example, if the power dissipated in a resistor increases from 0.5 watts to 10 watts, the increase in decibels is found from the log of the ratio of the two powers, with the first value, 0.5 watts, used as the reference level.

$$NdB = 10 \log \frac{P}{P_R} = 10 \log \frac{10}{0.5} = 10 \log 20 = 10 \times 1.301 = 13.01 \text{ dB}$$

If we had wished, instead to calculate a decrease in dissipated power, the reference power would simply be placed in the numerator, and a negative sign would appear in the answer, to indicate a power loss.

In the recording studio, it is more convenient to work with voltage levels. This presents no problem, since power ratings are usually found only after the voltage has been measured anyway. And, since we invariably make all our measurements across the same resistance value, it may be eliminated from our calculations in the following manner.

Consider two different power values, P_a and P_b. Comparing them in terms of dB, $N_{dB} = 10 \log P_a/P_b$. But, since $P = E^2/R$, we may rewrite the formulas as:

$$10 \log \frac{E_a^2/R_a}{E_b^2/R_b}$$

Since the value of the resistance does not change, $R_a = R_b$, and the formula may be simplified to $10 \log E_a^2/E_b^2$, or to $20 \log E_a/E_b$. Now if we measure the voltage across the resistance at, say 6 volts, and later increase it to 12 volts, the dB increase is,

$$N_{dB} = 20 \log \frac{12}{6} = 20 \log 2 = 20 \times 0.301 = 6.02 \text{ dB}$$

Note that whereas a doubling of power gave us an increase of 3dB, a voltage doubling yields a 6 dB gain.

In the case of acoustic power measurements, there is a standard zero reference level. And although this zero reference level represents an extremely low value (the threshold of hearing), in the studio it is more convenient to use an electrical zero reference level equivalent to the voltage found across a resistance in a typical operating condition. This allows us to compare other voltages and note that they are so many decibels above or below our zero reference standard.

It may be confusing when discussing acoustical power and sound pressure level. It is important to note that sound pressure is a potential (E) analogous to voltage, where acoustical power is in watts (P). Therefore the $20 \log E/E_R$ formula is uses for calculating sound pressure level while the $10 \log P/P_R$ is used for acoustic power considerations.

The dBm

The voltage drop across a 600 ohm resistor through which 1 milliwatt (1×10^{-3}) of power is being dissipated is the standard studio zero reference level. Using the formula, $P = E^2/R$, we may discover that the zero reference voltage is 0.775 volts. Actually, the meters in the studio are voltmeters, but they are calibrated in decibels to enable us to make the kind of measurements that are most suited to audio signals. Although the range of voltages is nowhere near as great as the sound intensity variations cited earlier, the dB scale is still a most practical measuring system. Over the years, there have been other standard reference levels used. And so, to clarify the fact that our decibel measurements are made relative to 1 milliwatt across 600 ohms, the notation, dBm, is used. The m refers to the milliwatt reference power level.

Many regular voltmeters will also show a dB scale (Figure 1-4A) and upon inspection of the meter face, we may verify that 0 dB = 0.775 volts. However, it should be remembered that these dB scales are not dBm unless the measurements are being made across the 600 ohm line. Studio meters are usually permanently wired across the proper circuit values, but when using a bench-type voltmeter, there is no reason to suppose that all measurements are being made across 600 ohms. Of course, the voltage scale is accurate regardless of the resistance across which the measurement is being made, but if we were making our measurements across a 1,200 ohm resistor, we would have to use the following formula to determine the actual dBm value:

$$N_{dBm} = 10 \log \frac{E^2/R}{E^2_{ref}/R_{ref}}$$

When R_{ref} is less than R, the formula may be rewritten as:

$$N_{dBm} = 20 \log E/E_{ref} - 10 \log R/R_{ref}$$

E_{ref} and R_{ref} are the values of our standard zero reference level: 0.775 volts and 600 ohms. E is the voltage across the nonstandard resistance, and R is the value of that nonstandard resistance.

If we read an apparent 0 dBm (0.775 volts) across 1,200 ohms, the actual dBm value would be:

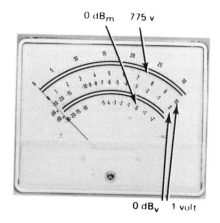

Figure 1-4B. A voltmeter with two dB scales:

0 dBm=0.775 volts (for use on 600-ohm lines.)

0 dBV=1 volt (for other dB measurements not referenced to 1 mw/600 ohms.) (Sennheiser RV-55, Sennheiser photo).

Figure 1-4A. A meter with both voltage and dB scales. The db level is the sum of the meter reading plus the dB value printed next to the rotary switch pointer.

$20 \log E/E_{ref}$ - $10 \log R/R_{ref}$ = $20 \log (0.775/0.775)$ –
$10 \log (1,200/600)$ = $20 \log 1$-$10 \log 2$ = 20×0 - $10 \times$
0.301 = -3.01 dBm = actual value in dBm

We may verify this by comparing the power dissipated across the zero reference standard with that dissipated across the 1,200 ohm resistance.

$P = E^2/R = (0.775)^2/600 = 1$ milliwatt
(in the zero reference standard)
$P = E^2/R = (0.775)^2/1,200 = 0.5$ milliwatt
(in the 1,200 ohm resistance)

Since the power across the 1,200 ohm resistance is half the reference power, the decibel value is down 3 dB, which confirms our previous calculation.

The dBV (1 volt reference level)

Decibel measurements are often made under conditions where a 600 ohm/1 milliwatt reference is inconvenient. For example, a certain acoustic pressure in front of a microphone may create an output level of –55 dBV. The dBV nomenclature indicates a zero reference level of 1 volt. If the microphone's output voltage is 0.0005 volts, its dBV output is:

$$N_{dBV} = -20 \log (1/0.0005) = -20 \log 2{,}000 = -20 \times 3.301 = 66.02 \text{ dBV}$$

Microphone output levels are discussed in greater detail in Chapter 3.

The dBv (0.775 volt reference level)

Some confusion arises from the fact that dBv measurements are frequently made with respect to a 0.775 volt reference level. Since 0.775 volts corresponds to 0 dBm, many voltmeters are calibrated so that 0.775 volts and 0 dB line up on the meter face, as shown in Figure 1-4A. Such meter faces generally contain the legend, "1mW., 600 ohms," reminding the user that the scale measures dBm only across a 600 ohm line. But since the meter is so often used under other circuit conditions, where the line impedance remains constant, though not at 600 ohms, there is little point in referring every reading back to a dBm value. In fact, in some cases the impedance of the circuit being measured may be unknown, making it impossible to calculate the actual dBm values. And so, the meter scale is simply read directly. Although readings thus made are not dBm, the arithmetic difference between any readings will be the same as if they were both converted to dBm via the formula given earlier.

This type of measurement is usually given in dBv, and the zero reference voltage may or may not be clearly specified. Generally, the nature of the measurement gives some clue as to the probable zero reference of 0.775 or 1 volt. Figure 1-4B shows a meter face containing both dB scales; 0 dBV = 1 volt, and 0 dBV = 0.775 volts.

The dBu (0.775 volt reference level)

Many electronic circuits now use what are called "active bridging" circuits, and a new reference standard is often used to define the relative level without regard to a standard impedance. The reference, once again, is 0.775 volt and the unit is called the dBu (u stands for units). The dBu allows us to use the decibel scale to make measurements in circuits without a 600 ohm reference. As mentioned about the dBV, readings thus made are not dBm, but again the arithmetic difference between any readings will be the same as if they were both (the reading and the reference) converted to dBm. The dBu and the dBv are often used interchangeably.

The Volume Indicator

So far, we have talked about studio meters in terms of decibels. However, when audio signals are being measured, the proper unit of measurement is usually the volume unit, or VU. The decibel has been defined as a ratio of powers, or perhaps voltages. As long as we are measuring a constant level, such as a 1,000 Hz reference tone, we may express the reading in dBm. On the other hand, an audio signal has a constantly changing level. Occasional peaks may be far above the average signal level, yet they do not contribute much to the listener's sensation of program loudness. The ear has a tendency to average the fluctuating program level in evaluating its subjective loudness. Thus, a program with a fairly constant, though moderate, level will be considered much louder than a low-level program with some recurring high-level peaks.

Equating this to the meter, we may note that a regular bench type voltmeter does a poor job of responding to the rapid level changes of an audio program. The meter ballistics are such that it is accurate only on steady-state tones. For audio measurements, a different meter movement has been designed. This is known as the volume indicator, and it is calibrated in volume units, or VU. When measuring steady-state tones, the volume indicator readings will correspond to those seen on a regular dBm calibrated voltmeter, yet on program measurements, the volume indicator will read somewhere between the average and peak values of the complex audio waveform. Volume indicator ballistics are designed so that the meter scale movement approximates the response of our ear; thus the meter does not register instantaneous peaks above the average level. In fact, the transient response of the human ear is limited by the reaction of the Staepedius muscle which is connected to the ear drum and the 3 small bones of the middle ear. The typical reaction time of this small muscle is about 300 milliseconds. Since our VU meter is calibrated to have a similar reaction times, this means that any signal having a peak value with a duration shorter than 300 ms will not be accurately metered. If the peaks are frequent, the meter will read somewhat higher than the average level, yet still below the actual peak level. The ballistics of the ASA (American Standards Association) standard volume indicator cause the meter to read 99 percent of its 100 percent deflection in 300 milliseconds. Its fall rate is the same as its rise time.

The fact that the volume indicator's reading corresponds to the listener's subjective impression of loudness makes it a valuable recording tool. However, it should be clearly understood that actual recorded levels are consistently higher than the meter readings. For example, the maximum-to-average ratio of program levels may be such that the volume indicator reads, say, 0 VU. But the instantaneous level that causes that 0 VU reading may be +10 dBm. Peak levels are often 9 to 10 dB above the average level seen on a standard VI meter.

Both in practice and in the literature on recording there is a tendency to refer to audio program measurements in decibels. Although there is surely little real danger in honoring this custom, the recording engineer should understand the difference between the decibel and the volume unit. The difference is particularly significant when high-level peaks are causing distortion, while the meter reading displays an apparently conservative recording level.

The Peak Reading Meter

The peak reading meter is more responsive to actual program peaks. Its ballistics are such that it will more accurately track the attacks of sudden high-level transient peaks. But since these peaks may be over just as suddenly as they occur, the movement is usually tailored to provide a more gradual fall-off, lest the rapid up and down movement prove to be too fast for the eye to follow. The standard peak reading meter has a rise time of 2.5 milliseconds followed by an exponential fall. Although many engineers use the loudness-related volume indicator, the peak reading meter gives a more accurate indication of what is actually being recorded. Since magnetic tape, as well as amplifiers, may be overloaded (and therefore distorted), by sudden bursts of high-level energy, some engineers prefer the peak reading meter, since it is more reliable in alerting the operator to potentially troublesome peaks that may escape the notice of the ear. Of course, a distorted amplifier will certainly be heard, but if the distortion takes the form of tape overload, it may not be noticed until the tape is played back later.

As noted earlier, the volume indicator and peak reading meter will read substantially the same on a sustained level program. This may cause the engineer to be too conservative with the record levels on program material such as organ music, which has very little peak information. However, with a program containing a significant number of high-level transients (for example, drums, tambourines, etc.), the peak reading meter may indicate levels 10 dBm or more above the volume indicator and can prevent the engineer from overloading the tape or amplifier.

Since the peak reading meter is not a volume indicator, it is correct to read it in decibels, rather than volume units.

Studio and Broadcast Reference Levels

Up until now, we have been talking about a zero reference level equal to 1 mW of power dissipated across a 600 ohm resistor. This value has no inherent significance—it is merely a mathematically convenient reference point. However, the assignment of handy reference points is one thing, and the design of efficient meter movements is quite another. Early on, it was found that due to the vagaries of meter construction, it was difficult to build a meter movement that would satisfactorily register 0 dBm (or 0 VU). Such a meter would have an impedance of less than 4,000 ohms, and would therefore load the circuit it was supposed to be measuring, causing inaccurate readings.

To negate the loading effect of the meter movement, a series resistor (empirically valued at 3,600 ohms) was inserted in the meter circuit. But now, although the meter no longer affected the circuit being measured, the presence of the series resistor caused the meter to read about 4 dBm lower, when measuring an actual 0 dBm. With the 3,600 ohm resistor in the meter circuit, when the meter did read 0 VU, the level would actually be +4 dBm. Rather than re-define the zero reference level, it was considered expedient to leave 0 dBm at 1 mW across 600 ohms, with the understanding that 4 dBm above this value would correspond to a zero reading on the volume indicator. Most, if not all, recording studio equipment now adheres to this 0 VU = +4 dBm conven-tion. However, the broadcast and telephone industries sometimes go one step further and define a zero reference of +8 dBm. This takes into account the higher output levels required for telephone lines, which play such an important part in broadcasting. This not a consistent policy, and the prudent engineer should be aware of which reference is in use. As may be noted in Figure 1-5, a standard volume indicator's meter face reads from –20 to +3. Therefore, if 0 VU = +4 dBm, the meter is capable of reading levels up to +3 VU = +7 dBm. For broadcast applications, an additional 4 dBm of attenuation is placed in the meter circuit, so that 0 VU = +8 dBm. Now, a meter reading of +3 VU signifies +11 dBm.

Many of the so called semi-professional and consumer tape re-corders use an output level of –10 dBm to correspond to a reading of 0 VU. Because of these conflicting zero reference levels, there is often some confusion about differences—if any—in recorded levels between studio, consumer, and broadcast tape recorders. It often comes as a surprise to learn that there is actually no differ-ence in recorded level, regardless of what level (–10, +4, +8, or whatever) has been defined as a zero reference.

For example, a standard test tape is used to align all machines, whether used in broadcast or recording studio work. For standard

Figure 1-5A. A typical volume indicator, calibrated in volume units (VU).

*Figure 1-5B. Two examples of peak reading meters. The meters on
the left contain 69 LEDs arranged in a vertical column. In the right
hand meters, a moving beam of light indicates the peak program level.*

operating level, the output level control is rotated until the meter
reads zero. Depending on the machine's meter circuit, this zero
will produce a level of either –10 dBm, +4 dBm or +8 dBm at the
machines output. Nevertheless, the input level—in this case from
the test tape—remains the same. Consequently, when the machines are placed in the record mode, the same input level applied
to both machines will cause identical meter readings. Of course, if
the actual output levels are compared, the studio and broadcast
machines will be louder. But this is because their playback amplifiers have been turned up to +4 dBm or +8 dBm respectively. In
any case, the input level, and therefore the level recorded on the

Figure 1-5C. A modern in-line recording console with plasma metering and switchable ballistics (Neve Series V photo).

tape, remains the same. Tape recorder alignment and operating levels will be discussed fully in Chapter 12.

Other Metering Standards

The Volume Indicator, reading in volume units (VU) is the most commonly used style of metering in the United States today, however, some form of peak metering is often found in conjunction. Peak metering, often called IEC (International Electrotechnical Commission) metering has several different standards in various parts of the world. The chart shown in Figure 1-5 compares these. The IEC Type I is often called DIN metering, while the IEC Type II is often referred to as Nordic metering. The Type III IEC metering is commonly called BBC (British Broadcasting Corporation) metering. The ballistics and standards for the VI (or VU) meter are shown for comparison. Note that not only do the ballistics (rise and fall response times) vary, but the O reference value (in dBm) varies as well.

	VU	BBC	IEC Type I	IEC Type II
Scale	–20VU to +3VU	Mk 1 to Mk 7	–50dB/+5dB	–36dB/+9dB
		(–12dB to +12dB)		
Rise Time	300ms to 0	100ms to Mk6	10ms to –1	10ms to –1
Fall Time	300ms to –20	2.85s to Mk1	13.3dB/sec	13.3dB/sec
Reference	0VU = +4dBu	Mk4 = 0dBu	0dB =+6dBu	0dB = 0dBu
1kHz Tone	(+4dBm) = 0VU	= Mk5	= –2dB	= +4dB

It is important for the engineer to understand thoroughly the type of meter in use. Only then can he or she be sure that what is being seen is what is actually the signal flowing in the circuit in question. Any of the above standards can be used effectively, and many engineers have a favorite type of metering that they prefer to use if given the choice.

The Decibel or Volume Unit in Equipment Specifications

In reading other chapters of this book, continuing reference is made to the decibel (dBm), with little or no further mention of the volume unit (VU). For example, we may read that a tape saturates at +10 dBm, or that an equalizer supplies a 6 dBm cut at 3,000 Hz. Since the effects of these variables are so often observed on volume indicators, it may seem contradictory to discuss them in terms of decibels. Although the volume unit is a measure of a complex audio waveform, for ease of measurement a steady tone is invariably used to determine equalizer performance or tape saturation. Therefore, the dBm becomes the correct unit of measurement. As an example, consider an equalizer set to give a boost at 1,000 Hz of +3 dB. When the equalizer is inserted, it might be expected that 1,000 Hz tones will now be higher by three volume units. However, if the 1,000 Hz tone is in the form of a sharp transient, the volume indicator may show little or no increase in reading, for the reasons discussed earlier. On the other hand, a sustained 1,000 Hz tone will be three volume units higher than before. Therefore, since the meter's response to the equalization change remains dependent on the nature of the program, it cannot be stated with certainty that a boost of +3 dB will always produce an increase of 3 VU. Consequently, these variables are specified in dBm, taking into account the steady-state conditions under which the measurements or calibrations were made.

CHAPTER 2

SOUND AND VIBRATION

SOUND

Simply stated, sounds are produced by mechanical vibrations. A vibrating object disturbs the molecules of air surrounding it, causing periodic vibrations in the air pressure. As the object vibrates back and forth, the pressure becomes alternately more, and then less, dense. These pressure compressions and rarefactions radiate away from the object as waves, eventually reaching the listener's ear, creating the sensation that we know as sound.

The classic example of a vibrating object is a taut length of string, which may be set into vibratory motion by striking it (as in the piano), plucking it (guitar), or by drawing a bow across it (violin). The rate of vibration is a function of the tension applied to the string as well as its length. In wind or brass instruments, the vibration is that of a column of air, and the vibration rate is regulated by changing the length of the air column. This is accomplished by opening and closing valves that change the length of the pipe (trumpet), or by keys that shorten the effective length of the column of air (clarinet).

Frequency and Range of Musical Instruments

When we say that a tone has a frequency of 440 Hertz (abbr. Hz), we mean that the device producing the tone or its air column is vibrating back and forth 440 times each second. Musical instruments do of course produce a wide range of frequencies, and a chart of the typical frequency ranges for various instruments is given in Figure 2-1. Note that the chart gives no information about the relative amplitude of the frequencies produced by the instruments. In most cases, the musician may vary the amplitude of each note played according to his or her taste.

Dynamic Range

The dynamic range of an instrument is a measure of the span between the quietist and loudest sounds it is capable of produc-

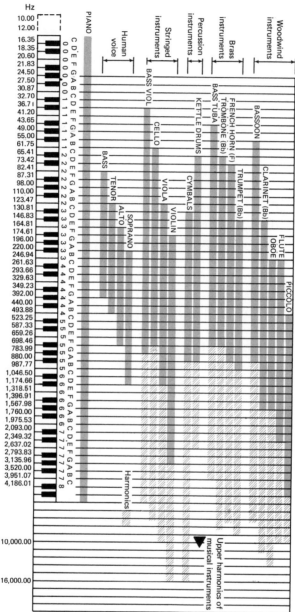

Figure 2-1. The frequency range of various musical instruments.

ing. Musically subjective terms such as pianissimo (very soft), mezzoforte (moderately loud), forte (loud), and fortissimo (very loud) are used to describe the relative intensity of the note produced.

The dynamic range of the human voice is quite broad—from a pianissimo whisper to a fortissimo shout—while the range of the harpsichord is practically zero, since each of its strings is plucked with the same amount of force, regardless of the strength with which the keys are struck. In fact, the harpsichord's successor, the pianoforte, or simply the piano, got its name in recognition of its wide dynamic range capability, as compared to its predecessor. The harder the key on a piano is struck, the more force is applied to the string and therefore the louder the note.

Frequency Response and Dynamic Range of Audio Equipment

Subjective terms such as piano and forte cannot be used to describe audio equipment. Although the equipment must be able to reproduce the dynamic range, measured in decibels, of whatever musical program is passing through it, its performance is evaluated in terms of frequency response also. The frequency response of a device is a measure of its relative amplitude at various frequencies within its range. Presumably, an amplifier will have a "flat" frequency response so that it supplies a gain of, say, 60 dB equally to all frequencies within its range plus or minus whatever dB tolerance from that "flat" response is specified.

In addition to a flat frequency response, an amplifier should not alter the full-scale dynamic range of the signal passing through it. However, this is not always possible since the dynamic range of some program material may exceed the dynamic range capabilities of an audio system or the capacity of the storage medium. This will be discussed in greater detail in Amplitude Domain Processing in Chapter 8.

Amplifier Bandwidth

The bandwidth of an amplifier, or any other audio device, is the range between the lowest and highest frequencies that are no more than 3 dB down in level. Figure 2-2 shows the frequency response of an amplifier with a flat response between 40 Hz and 10,000 Hz, and a 20 Hz to 20,000 Hz bandwidth. Note that the amplifier also passes frequencies below 20 Hz and above 20,000 Hz, but that these are considered as being outside the amplifier's bandwidth, since they are attenuated by more than 3 dB.

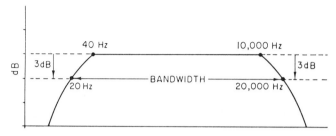

Figure 2-2. An amplifier with a "flat" frequency response between 40 Hz and 10,000 Hz and a bandwidth from 20 Hz to 20,000 Hz.

Frequency Response and Logarithms

As mentioned earlier, the listener's subjective response to loudness varies logarithmically. In a similar manner, our perception of the interval between any two frequencies depends on the relative location of those frequencies within the audio bandwidth. To a musician, a 220 Hz interval between the two tones of 220 Hz and 440 Hz is recognized as an octave (abbr. 8va). However, the same 220 Hz interval between 440 Hz and 660 Hz would be a perfect fifth in musical terms. An octave above an "A" of 440 Hz would be an "A" of 880 Hz. Therefore, we may define an octave as:

The interval between any two frequencies, f_1 and f_2, where $f_2 = 2f_1$.

We can see that as the frequency of f_1 increases, the arithmetic frequency interval within the octave grows larger. Yet to the ear, any octave relationship "sounds" the same as any other. By definition then, the ear's response to frequency is logarithmic.

Log Paper

If frequency response measurements are drawn on standard graph paper, as shown in Figure 2-3A, it will, for the reasons described before, be seen that each successive octave requires twice as much space as the one preceding it. A more satisfactory arrangement would allot an equal space to each octave, thus compensating for the ear's logarithmic response to frequency.

Log Paper is used for just this purpose, and may be prepared as shown in Figure 2-3B. Four equally spaced intervals, a-d, are drawn along the horizontal axis. The beginning of each interval is numerically labelled at twice the one before it (1, 2, 4, 8, 16).

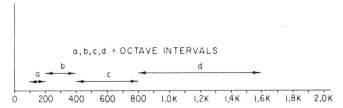

Figure 2-3A. When standard graph paper is used for frequency response data, each octave uses more space than the one preceding it.

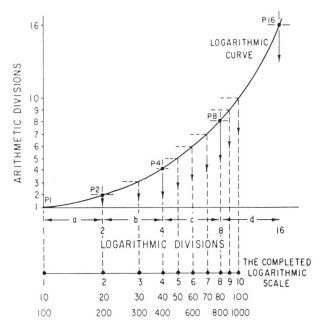

Figure 2-3B. A method of producing a logarithmic scale, so that each octave uses an equal amount of space.

The vertical axis is a simple arithmetic progression (1, 2, 3, 4,...16). Points are placed on the graph (P_1, P_2, P_4, P_8, P_{16}) at the intersections of lines drawn from corresponding numbers on both axes (1-1, 2-2, 4-4, 8-8, 16-16). A curve is drawn connecting the points. Now, lines from points 1 through 10 on the arithmetic axis are drawn to the curve, and then down (dashed lines) to complete the logarithmic scale. The 10 points on the logarithmic scale are labeled 1 through 10, or they may be labeled 10-100, 100-1,000, etc. If the scale is repeated several times as in Figure

27

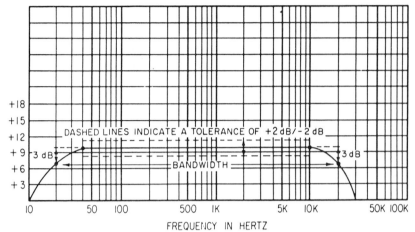

Figure 2-4. The frequency response of Figure 2-2 redrawn on logarithmic scale paper.

2-4, it may be seen that every octave now takes the same amount of space, regardless of its frequency interval.

The dB scale (vertical) is not drawn logarithmically since the dB itself takes into account the logarithmic sensitivity of the ear to loudness.

The Human Voice

Like the musical instrument and the audio amplifier, the human voice may be analyzed in terms of frequency, amplitude and bandwidth. Speech sounds are of course quite complex, and are not generally thought of as having a recognizable musical pitch. Some voices are deeper than others, but people do not speak in musical tones, since every spoken word produces energy at a great many frequencies simultaneously.

When the voice is analyzed, its "frequency response" is usually shown as an energy distribution curve, as in Figure 2-5. The curves show the relative amount of acoustic energy present at each frequency in a typical male and female voice. Sibilant sounds such as s, z, sh, and zh, produce a surprisingly large concentration of high level high frequency acoustic energy. Although the listener may not be distracted by an occasional sibilant peak, an amplifier may be driven into distortion producing a very unpleasant "spitty" and grainy sound if corrective measures are not taken. These measures too will be discussed in greater detail in Chapter 8.

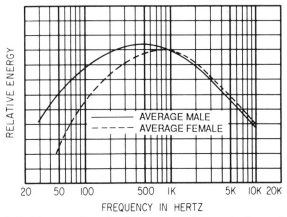

Figure 2-5. Energy distribution curves for typical speaking voices.

Wavelength of Sound in Air

As the vibrations from a musical instrument are transmitted through the air, we may calculate the physical length of one complete alternation of air pressure and call this the wavelength of that particular frequency. If we attach a pen to a vibrating object, and slide a piece of paper past it at a constant rate, the line traced on the paper will be a graphical representation of the vibration. If the vibration produces a pure tone; that is, a single frequency with no harmonics or overtones, the graph will show something called a sine wave. In Figure 2-6A, a sine wave is being produced by a tuning fork. If the paper were moving at the speed of sound, the physical length required for one complete oscillation to be drawn on the paper would correspond to the wavelength of the sine wave being measured. Since this is of course impractical, we may simply calculate the wavelength (abbr. λ) as:

$$\lambda = \frac{V}{F}$$

where:

(λ) = wavelength in feet (per cycle)

V = velocity of sound in air (feet per second)

F = frequency in Hertz (cycles per second)

From the formula, we see that wavelength is dependent not only on frequency, but on the velocity of sound in air. This has been measured to be 1,087 feet/second at a temperature of 32°F and increases about 1.1 feet/second for each degree in temperature.

Therefore, at a temperature of 70° F, the velocity of sound is approximately 1,130 feet/second. Putting this figure into our formula, we find that a frequency of 100 Hz has a wavelength of 1,130/100, or 11 feet 4 inches (11.3 ft.= 11 ft. 4 in.). If the temperature changes, the velocity—and therefore the wavelength—changes also. Figure 2-6B shows one complete cycle of a sine wave.

Wavelength on Tape

When any frequency is to be recorded on tape, the velocity is by no means the same or as constant as the speed of sound in air. Most tape recorders are capable of running at several speeds, and so the tape velocity may be halved or doubled, depending on the speed selected. In Figure 2-6A, the amount of paper taken up by one complete cycle depends on the speed at which the paper moves. Obviously, the slower the paper travels past the tuning fork, the less distance is used for each cycle and the smaller is the wavelength. And so it is with magnetic tape as it travels past the record head. The time it takes a wave to complete one complete oscillation is called its period and can be represented as:

$$P = \frac{1}{F}$$

where:

P = period in fractions of a second
F = frequency in Hertz (cycles/second)

If a 1,000 Hz sine wave is recorded and then played back at the same speed, each recorded cycle will have a period of one thousandth of a second and will be spread over whatever amount of tape passed the record head during that interval of time.

Later on, there would be no way to determine the frequency of the original sine wave *unless* we knew the speed at which the recording had been made. On playback, the frequency reproduced will depend on the speed at which the tape is moving. For example, at half speed, each cycle of a sine wave that was originally 1,000 Hz will now take two thousandths of a second to pass the playback head and the output will appear to be a 500 Hz tone.

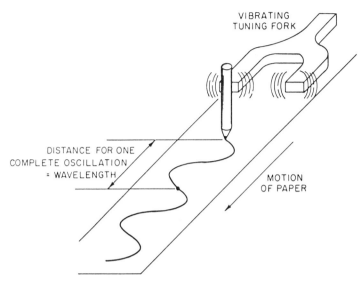

Figure 2-6A. A graph of the tuning fork's vibration is traced on the moving paper.

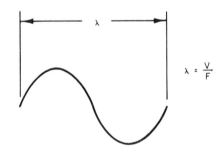

$\lambda = V/F$ λ = *Wavelength, in feet (per cycle)*
                   V = *Velocity of sound, in feet/second*
                   F = *Frequency of sound, in hertz (cycles/second)*

Figure 2-6B. One cycle of a sine wave.

The recorded wavelength remains unchanged, yet the frequency heard has dropped a full octave. Of course, an actual musical program played back at the wrong speed would be painfully obvious, but for the moment we are concerned with sine waves only. A sine wave with a recorded wavelength of one thousandth of an inch (1 mil) will produce the following frequencies:

31

7,500 Hz at a tape speed of 7.5 inches/second

15,000 Hz at a tape speed of 15 inches/second

30,000 Hz at a tape speed of 30 inches/second

In evaluating the performance of an analog tape recorder, references to playback frequency response are invariably made, since our primary concern is: How well does the machine reproduce the audio bandwidth? However, the playback head is actually responding to the wavelength on tape, and the frequency response depends on the "wavelength response" of the playback head, as well as the tape speed (velocity) selected.

Diffraction and Reflection

When a sound wave travels past an obstacle, a portion of the wave bends around the obstacle and moves off at an angle to the original straight line path. This is called diffraction and occurs when the wavelength of the sound is larger than the obstacle in its path. The phenomenon recalls the popular high school physics demonstration in which a beam of white light is made to pass through a prism, where it is dispersed into a rainbow of colors.

White light is a composite of energy of many different wavelengths, and as it passes through the prism, each wavelength—with its characteristic color—is refracted at a different angle. Now while energy passing through an object is refracted, when it travels past the object it is diffracted.

When the wavelength of the sound is shorter than the obstacle in its path, it is reflected and bounces off the object at an angle that is equal to the angle of approach—much like a mirror reflects light.

In either case, the result is the same; some of the energy is re-routed in a different direction, and the angle of deflection depends on the angle of incidence and the wavelength of the energy wave.

In the recording studio, diffraction and reflection are important considerations. A long wavelength (low frequency) may be bent (diffracted) almost completely around an obstacle in its path, while short wavelengths (high frequencies) will be reflected. Therefore, a listener (or microphone) in the shadow of the obstacle will hear a frequency distorted version of the original sound wave.

Sound and Hearing

In the chapter on decibels, we learned that the ear regularly encounters sound pressure levels between a very few dB and somewhat more than 110 dB. 0 dB was defined as the threshold of hearing. It should be pointed out that the actual sound pressure level at the threshold of hearing actually varies considerably, depending on the frequency of the sound. The ear is highly sensitive to frequencies between 3,000 Hz and 4,000 Hz, and less sensitive to frequencies outside this bandwidth.

For example, if a 3,500 Hz tone is heard at the threshold of hearing, the sound pressure level will be 0 dB (10^{-12} watts/m^2) as stated before. But, if the frequency of the tone is changed to 350 Hz (approximately 3 octaves and a major third below), the sound pressure level may have to be raised about 17 dB above this reference level in order for the average listener to detect the signal. At 35 Hz, the sound pressure level may have to be raised more than 50 dB in order for the signal to be heard.

Equal Loudness Contours

Therefore, our threshold of hearing is by no means constant over the entire range of audible frequencies. Figure 2-7A is a graph of the equal loudness contours as developed by Robinson and Dadson. Notice that the various contours are labeled in Phons, ranging from 0 to 130, and that at 1 kHz, the Phon rating corresponds to the sound pressure level in decibels. The Phon is a measure of "equal loudness." If we first listen to a 1,000 Hz tone measured at 50 dB sound pressure level, and then adjust another tone so that it appears to be just as loud, both tones are considered to have a loudness of 50 Phons, even though the measured sound pressure level of the second tone differs from the 50 dB level of the 1,000 Hz standard. The 0 Phon curve indicates the average listener's perception of equal loudness for frequencies determined to be at the threshold of hearing. This is often called the MAF or minimum audible field. As noted, low frequencies must be boosted considerably in sound pressure level in order to be heard, and frequencies above the maximum sensitivity area of

3 kHz to 4 kHz must also be boosted, though not to the same extent.

Notice also that although the equal loudness contours each follow the same general direction, there are significant differences in the ear's relative sensitivity at different listening levels. The sensitivity of the human ear is always greatest in that 3 kHz to 4 kHz region, and falls off as the frequency is lowered. However, in the 30 to 100 Phon range, there is again some increase in sensitivity as the frequency falls from 1,000 Hz to about 450 Hz, and then sensitivity again decreases until at the low end of the frequency spectrum the ear is at its least sensitive point.

The equal loudness contours are often referred to as the Fletcher-Munson curves, named after the two men who did early research in this area. The current version in Figure 2-7A show the recent revision of the curves by Robinson and Dadson.

The implications of the equal loudness contours should be clearly understood by every recording engineer. As the overall loudness level is changed, the ear's frequency response is significantly altered. Therefore, a frequency balance that is satisfactory at one listening level may not be so at another. Many engineers prefer a loud monitoring level, claiming that it allows them to hear every sound and nuance clearly. Later, when the level is reduced to a more normal loudness, there is inevitably some disappointment with the apparent lack of bass. Here, the equal loudness contours are working against the engineer.

For example, from Figure 2-7A, we see that at 120 Phons, the ear is 15 dB more sensitive to a 3,500 Hz signal than it is to a 1,000 Hz one. Below 1,000 Hz, the ear's sensitivity is uniform to about 200 Hz and then sensitivity falls off gradually. At 40 Phons, there is only a 7 dB sensitivity difference between 1,000 Hz and 3,500 Hz, and below 300 Hz, the sensitivity decreases rapidly. So, if a recording is balanced at 120 Phons, and then played back at 40 Phons, the bass will invariably sound weaker, and there will be a lack of "presence" in the 3,500 Hz area if these frequencies were attenuated earlier as a reaction to the ear's extreme sensitivity to them at 120 Phons.

The situation may be clarified somewhat if we invert the 120 and 40 Phon contours, as shown in Figure 2-7B. The curves now depict a graph of the ear's relative frequency response at 40 and 120 Phons. Now imagine that we added some equalization, while listening at 120 Phons, in order to create the apparently flat

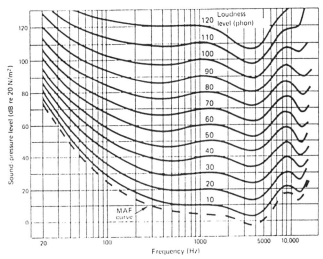

Figure 2.7A. Robinson and Dadson Loudness Contours. The contours illustrate the ear's sensitivity at various sound pressure levels relative to frequency. The MAF (Minimum Audible Frequency) curve defines the ear's minimum sensitivity.

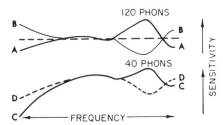

Figure 2-7B. The 120 and 40 Phon contours, inverted to compare the ear's relative sensitivity at these two listening levels.

A. The 120 Phon contour. Note the ear's extreme sensitivity in the 3,500 Hz area.

B. Equalization required to achieve an apparently flat-frequency response (dashed line) at a 120 Phon listening level.

C. The 40 Phon contour. Note the sharper fall-off in sensitivity at low frequencies.

D. The apparent frequency response at 40 Phons, as a result of the equalization that was added when listening at 120 Phons. Note the deficient bass and the lack of "presence" at 3,500 Hz.

frequency response shown by the dashed line. If we now observe the effect of this equalization on the 40 Phon contour, we arrive at the unsatisfactory frequency response shown in curve "D." The low frequency response has apparently fallen off, and there is also a pronounced fall-off in the 3 kHz to 4 kHz range.

It is an oversimplification to state that recordings should be monitored at the same loudness level at which they will be heard later on. Obviously, the engineer has no control over the record or CD buyer's listening habits, and cannot predict the level at which he will choose to listen to the finished product. However, the equal loudness contours do suggest that if studio monitoring levels are kept on the conservative side, there will be less disappointment later on. If the proper amount of bass is heard at lower listening levels, any subsequent level increase will bring with it an apparent bass boost. Generally, this is to be preferred over the opposite condition, where the bass apparently decreases from the ideal point as the level is dropped.

THE SOUND LEVEL METER

Although the recording engineer is concerned with the decibel primarily in terms of electrical power or voltage ratios, some understanding of the sound level meter is essential to good engineering practice.

Basically, a sound level meter consists of a microphone, an amplifier, and a meter calibrated in decibels. However, such a device may not be created by simply connecting any available microphone, amplifier and meter. In addition to a specially calibrated microphone, the sound level meter will contain several filters and "weighting" networks.

The filter networks allow the meter to respond to sound energy within various narrow bandwidths. For example, if the filter network was set at 1 kHz, sound (or noise) containing 1 kHz components could be measured, while the meter would be comparatively insensitive over the rest of the audio spectrum. This tunable feature allows the engineer to determine the frequency band which is contributing the greatest energy to the overall sound or noise level. Figure 2-8 is a photo of a high-quality sound level meter.

WEIGHTING NETWORKS

In addition to the filters just described, the sound level meter may contain additional filters called weighting networks. These weighting networks create a response in the meter that corre-

Figure 2-8. A sound level meter (Bruel and Kjaer 2230, B & K photo).

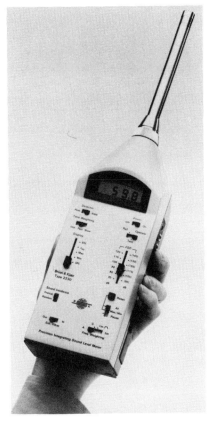

sponds to the ear's varying sensitivity at different loudness levels. As just described and shown by the Robinson and Dadson curves in Figure 2-7A, the ear is less sensitive to extreme high and low frequencies at lower listening levels. Therefore, at lower listening levels, noise in the low and high frequency regions would of course be less objectionable than the same amount of noise in the mid frequency area.

The "A," "B," and "C" weighting networks are filters which correspond to the sensitivity of the ear at listening levels of 40, 70 and 100 Phons, respectively. When making measurements at these levels, the insertion of the appropriate weighting network will therefore give a meter reading that is pretty much in accordance with what the listener subjectively hears.

Although noise level measurements of recording studio equipment are commonly made on a standard voltmeter, an "A" weighting net work is often inserted just before the meter input so that, as in sound level measurements, the reading conforms to

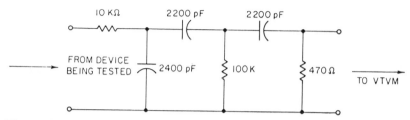

Figure 2-9A. Schematic. The network produces a 4 dB insertion loss.

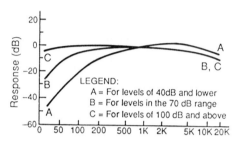

Figure 2-9B. The "A," "B," and "C" weighting curve.

LEGEND:
A = For levels of 40dB and lower
B = For levels in the 70 dB range
C = For levels of 100 dB and above

the subjective impression that the noise would make at low listening levels. Accordingly, noise specifications are frequently quoted at so many decibels, dBA. Or the level may be quoted in dBm, with the notation, "A Weighting." An "A" weighting network is shown in Figure 2-9A and the "A," "B," and "C" weighting curves are drawn in Figure 2-9B.

Perception of Direction

The ear is an extremely sensitive and complex device and as already mentioned, is capable of wide band frequency response and extended dynamic range. However, as responsive as the ear may be, one ear is limited in its ability to perceive the direction from where a sound originates. A single ear can determine pitch, loudness and even the character or timbre of a sound, but cannot tell us the location of that sound. For us to be able to localize a sound, we need two ears. It is the difference in the information received by these two ears that lets our brain tell us from where that sound source has originated. This binaural hearing uses the time of arrival differences and loudness differences between the left and right ear to determine the location of the sound.

If a single sound source is positioned directly in front of us, as in Figure 2-10A, the intensity or loudness will be the same at each ear, and the sound will arrive at each ear simultaneously. However, if a sound source is located to a position that is to the right of center (Figure 2-10B), because of the diffraction around

Figure 2-10. Sound originating from the center (A) will arrive at both ears at the same time, while sound from off center (B) will cause amplitude and time differences.

A   B

the head and the distance between our ears, the sound will arrive at the right ear before the left one. The sound will also be perceptually louder at the right ear than the left. These binaural cues are extremely important for our perception of direction and contribute to a good stereophonic recording as will be discussed in Chapter 4.

PHASE AND COHERENCE

In Figure 2-11A, various points along a sine wave are marked off in degrees. A second sine wave is drawn in Figure 2-11B. Although the two are of course identical in wave shape, amplitude and period (and therefore frequency) we may say that the second one has been shifted by 180° due to its relative position with respect to the first sine wave. Notice that as one sine wave reaches positive maximum amplitude (points "a"), the other reaches negative maximum amplitude. Both sine waves pass through zero amplitude at the same time (points "b"). If the two waves are combined graphically, as in Figure 2-11C, the resultant wave form will be a straight line, indicating zero amplitude. Since the waves are at all times equal in amplitude and opposite in polarity, they have cancelled each other out.

Figure 2-11. The combinations of two sine waves.

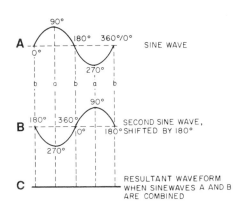

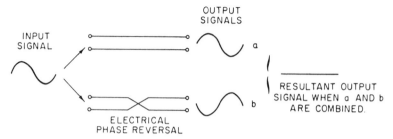

Figure 2-12. The effect of an electrical phase reversal.

A similar condition will occur electrically if audio signals of equal amplitude and opposite polarity are combined. This might happen to an audio signal that is passing through two different signal paths if there is a wiring reversal in one of the paths as shown in Figure 2-12. When the two are eventually combined, any signal common to both of them is cancelled out. The signals are said to be electrically out of phase.

An acoustic phase cancellation might occur if two microphones are positioned in such a way that one receives a positive pressure center at the same time that the other receives a negative one, as shown in Figure 2-13. This is a very real problem, which will be discussed in greater detail in the chapter on microphone applications.

Of course, actual program waveforms are considerably more complex than sine waves, and the relationship of one to another cannot really be measured as precisely as two sine waves of the same frequency. Phase relationships then become meaningless, and about all that can be said for the two waveforms shown in Figure 2-14 is that sometimes they are of the same polarity (+,+ or –,–) and other times they are not (+,– or –,+). Even when the

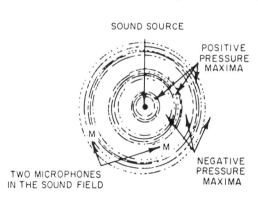

Figure 2-13. The acoustic phase reversal between the two microphones will cause a cancellation if their outputs are combined.

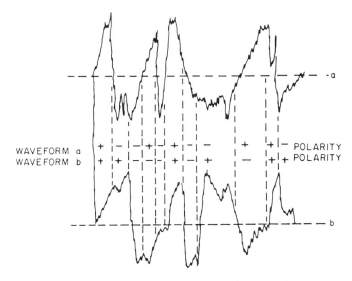

WAVEFORM a
WAVEFORM b

POLARITY
POLARITY

Figure 2-14. Two complex audio waveforms.

polarities are opposite, the wave forms do not cancel out, since their amplitudes are usually unequal. During those intervals when the waveforms are of the same polarity, they are said to be "coherent" and they interfere constructively; when the polarities are opposite, the waveforms are incoherent and interfere destructively.

When the same signal is applied to two signal paths, they are totally coherent since, regardless of the complexity of the waveforms, they are of course identical. But if one of the paths has an electrical phase reversal, the two signals become totally incoherent since they are at all times identical in amplitude and frequency yet opposite in polarity. As with the sine waves shifted by 180°, the totally incoherent wave forms will cancel out if combined. Of course, if two totally coherent waveforms are combined they will sum and show an increase of 3 dB in power as discussed in Chapter 1.

Signals from two different sources such as a guitar and a piano, will usually display a random coherence, since there is no signal component common to both signals unless they play exactly the same note at exactly the same time. An electrical phase reversal will have no effect on an eventual combination of the signals. However, if a signal from a center placed soloist is common to both sources, the phase reversal will cause it to cancel out when the signals are combined.

The Oscilloscope

The oscilloscope is an effective monitor of phase and coherency information. If a sine wave is applied to the scope's X axis input, a vertical line will be seen, as in Figure 2-15A. If the signal is instead applied to the Y axis input, a horizontal line will be seen, as in Figure 2-15B. In both cases, the length of the line is an indication of the amplitude of the applied signal.

If the sine wave is applied in phase to both signal inputs, a diagonal line will be seen as shown in Figure 2-15C. The angle of the line will indicate the relative amplitudes of the signal at both inputs. If the amplitudes are equal, the line will appear at a 45° angle, as seen in Figure 2-15C. If the amplitudes are unequal, the angle will change towards the vertical or the horizontal axis, depending on which amplitude is greater.

These displays are called lissajous patterns, and if there is an electrical phase reversal of 180° in one of the inputs, the slope of the diagonal line will be reversed (Figure 2-15D). If there is a phase incoherence of 90° between the two input signals, a perfect circle will be displayed, as seen in Figure 2-15E. These visual displays are a clear indication of any phase incoherence which might otherwise escape notice.

If complex audio waveforms are applied to both oscilloscope inputs, the coherent component will tend to produce a diagonal display in the in-phase direction, while the incoherent component will tend toward an out-of-phase display. The net resultant pattern will resemble those patterns shown in Figures 2-15 F, G, H. The general diagonal orientation of the display indicates the amount of coherency.

Most stereo programs contain a signal component that is common to both left and right. This is the phantom center-channel information which is heard equally from both speakers. Depending on the relative level of this center channel component, the oscilloscope pattern will take on an in-phase orientation, as in Figure 2-14 F. However, if an accidental phase reversal has occurred, the general orientation will be reversed, as in Figure 2-15H. This visual display will warn the engineer of a potentially troublesome condition which should be traced and corrected.

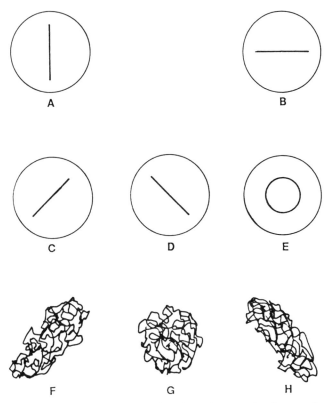

Figure 2-15. Oscilloscope patterns indicating phase and coherence between two signals.
A. Signal applied to Y axis input only generally signifies left track of a stereo program.
B. Signal applied to the X axis input only generally signifies right track.
C. Same signal applied to both inputs.
D. Same signal applied to both inputs but with a phase reversal in one input line.
E. Same signal applied to both inputs with a 90-degree phase relationship between them.
F. Stereo signal with a strong coherent component, resulting in an "in-phase" orientation.
G. Stereo signal with random coherency, resulting in a circular pattern with no noticeable diagonal orientation.
H. Stereo signal with a strong incoherent component, resulting in an "out-of-phase" orientation.

An accidental phase reversal, whether due to an improperly wired cable or an acoustical condition in the studio, may be difficult or impossible to detect by ear alone. In fact, it may actually enhance the sound by giving it a more spacious feeling. However, later on when the signals are combined during the mixdown process, the signals may cancel out almost completely. Therefore, the use of an oscilloscope or other suitable phase-response device as a visual monitor while recording cannot be overemphasized.

SECTION II

TRANSDUCERS: MICROPHONES AND LOUDSPEAKERS

Transducer:

1. A device actuated by power from one system and supplying power in the same or any other form to a second system.

2. A microphone or loudspeaker.

Modern recording studio practice is a curious mixture of art and science. The engineer who may describe the operating parameters of every integrated circuit in the studio to the "nth" dB, may be content to describe his favorite microphone as "warm." While demanding less than a fraction of a percent distortion from an equalizer, he may not care about the sensitivity rating of a new microphone, providing it is "clean" and sounds "right" to him. As for monitor speakers, he's apt to be more concerned with similar subjective value judgments than with the rated efficiency, radiation angles, and so forth.

Needless to say, these subjective evaluations are not much help to the beginning engineer who is trying hard to learn more about the science of recording. Yet, it is nearly impossible to avoid such descriptions of transducers in the recording studio.

Perhaps this avoidance of a more precise terminology is a necessary function of the transducing processes in the signal path from musical instrument to the listener. Along the way, many subtle changes take place. The microphone converts acoustic energy into mechanical, then electrical energy. The loudspeaker reverses the process, and at the end of the chain, the listener's ear converts acoustic energy into brain waves that are subjectively interpreted by the listener. Even in the control room, with the instrumentalists only a few feet away, the listener is several generations away from the actual musical event, and is actually evaluating the performance of the transducing system as well as the musical performance.

Personal taste, upbringing, and age are a very few of the factors that influence our musical taste and perception, and all these variables come into play when we evaluate what we hear in the control room. Another engineer will have another opinion, just as subjective, about the reproduced sound. One may prefer microphone *A* while another likes microphone *B*. If the monitor system is changed, opinions may change with it, and under no circumstances will there be unanimous agreement as to what sounds "right." Since microphones are easily changed and speakers are not, the listener tends sometimes to ignore the role of the speakers in his evaluation of the microphone. Yet a change in speakers will certainly influence one's preference in microphones.

Given the subjectivity of music, and the interdependence of one transducer on the other, definitive statements—especially on microphone technique—cannot easily be made. Nevertheless, a basic understanding of the more scientific aspects of both transducing systems will help the engineer develop his own personal recording technique.

Chapter 3 covers the basics of microphone theory, while Chapter 4 discusses some of the more general microphone techniques, which may be adapted or modified to suit the demands of everyday studio and concert recording practice. Chapter 5 concludes the section with a description of the loudspeaker and the enclosure in which it is placed, and also considers the interface between the speaker and the listening room.

CHAPTER 3

MICROPHONE DESIGN

At the heart of any microphone is its diaphragm, where acoustical energy is converted into an electrical signal as the membrane vibrates in response to the impinging sound wave. Microphones are commonly classified according to the manner in which this energy conversion takes place, and a description of the most popular classifications of studio microphones, Dynamic and Condenser, follows.

DYNAMIC MICROPHONES

Microphones in which an electrical signal is produced by the motion of a conductor within a magnetic field are classified as dynamic microphones. As you may remember from your Physics classes, when a magnet is moved up and down within a coil of wire a voltage is induced in the coil. If we were to pictorially represent the output of the coil, as in Figure 3-1, it would appear as a sine wave with the positive portion occurring as the magnet is plunged into the coil, and the negative portion registering as the magnet is withdrawn. The amplitude is dependent on the strength of the magnet and the number of turns in the coil of wire, while the frequency of the signal is controlled by how slow or fast the magnet is moved in and out of the coil. Obviously, the same is true if the coil moves and the magnet is stationary.

Dynamic Moving-Coil Microphones

In this type of microphone, a coil of wire is attached to the rear of the diaphragm, and the coil is suspended in a magnetic field as shown in Figure 3-2. As the diaphragm vibrates, so does the coil, and the magnetic field induces a voltage within the coil. The voltage is the electrical equivalent of the acoustical energy that caused the diaphragm to vibrate and is based on the following formula:

Figure 3-1. A magnet, moved up and down within a coil of wire, will produce a signal with both positive and negative components at the output of the coil.

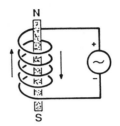

E = Blv

where:

E = the output signal, in volts

B = the fluxivity of the magnet, in gauss

l = the length of the coil, in feet

v = the velocity of the movement, in feet per second

Figure 3-3 shows two typical dynamic moving-coil microphones.

Dynamic Ribbon Microphones

In this type of dynamic microphone, a thin corrugated sheet, or "ribbon" of metal foil, takes the place of the diaphragm/moving coil combination. The ribbon is suspended within a magnetic field, and a small voltage is induced as the ribbon vibrates back and forth. The corrugations lend some structural strength to the ribbon which in early designs was quite delicate. Modern ribbon microphones however, are well suited to studio use and may be just as sturdy as their moving coil counterparts. A typical ribbon microphone is illustrated in Figure 3-4. Note that the ribbon microphone contains a built-in output transformer. The impedance of the ribbon is quite low, usually on the order of a fraction of an

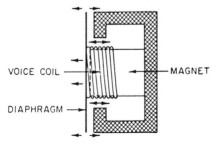

Figure 3-2. Cross sectional sketch of a dynamic moving-coil microphone.

VOICE COIL

MAGNET

DIAPHRAGM

*Figure 3-3. (A) Shure SM-58
(Shure Bros. photo), (B)
Electro-Voice RE-20
(Electro-Voice photo).*

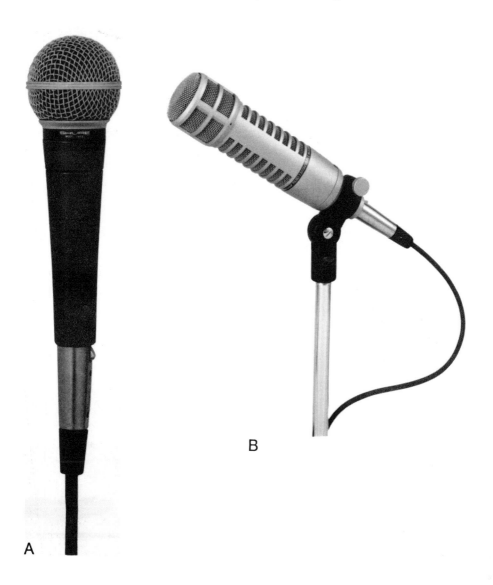

A

B

Figure 3-4. A studio ribbon microphone (Beyer M160, Beyer photo).

Figure 3-5. Close-up of a ribbon microphone with the protective cover removed (Beyer M260).

ohm, therefore, a transformer is required to raise the microphone's output impedance to a usable value. (Note: a possible source of confusion is the common studio practice of referring to moving coil microphones as "dynamics" while ribbons, which are also dynamic, are known simply as "ribbons.") Figure 3-5 shows a close-up of a ribbon microphone with the protective cover removed.

CONDENSER MICROPHONES

In the condenser microphone, the diaphragm is actually one of the plates of a capacitor. A capacitor is an electrical device capable of storing an electrical charge. (In earlier times, what we refer to today as a capacitor was known as a condenser. Hence the nomenclature "condenser microphone.") As the condenser microphone's diaphragm vibrates, the spacing between it and a stationary back plate varies, producing a changing capacitance. This change in capacitance causes an inverse proportional change in the applied voltage potential. This is shown in the following formula:

$$C = \frac{Q}{E}$$

where:
C = capacitance in farads
Q = charge in Coulombs
E = applied potential in Volts

A usable signal voltage is thus derived in conjunction with a pre-amplifier built into the microphone's case. The pre-amplifier is required since the capacitor's output and impedance must be converted to microphone level values. The pre-amplifier also requires a voltage supply and this is usually provided externally. The power supply furnishes a direct current polarizing voltage to the condenser/diaphragm plates, as well as supplying the necessary voltages for the transistors within the microphone's pre-amplifier. Figure 3-6 illustrates the built-in pre-amplifiers in several condenser microphones.

Electret Condenser Microphones

The electret condenser microphone has for its diaphragm two capacitor plates that have been permanently polarized by the manufacturer. Consequently, the diaphragm does not require an external power source, although a voltage supply is still needed for the transistors in the pre-amplifier. This voltage may be supplied by a simple battery, or provided from an external source.

RF Condenser Microphones

Some transistorized condenser microphones make use of a circuit that replaces the polarizing d.c. voltage with a radio frequency oscillator and a diode. Older versions of this type of condenser microphone were plagued with noise problems, however, improvements in this technology have recently produced some excellent models. This design now provides a very low noise

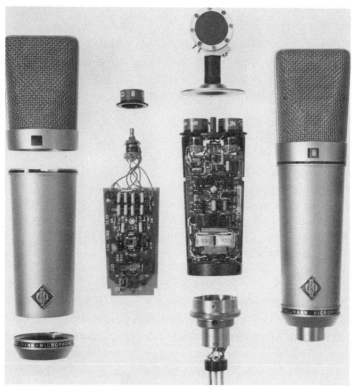

Figure 3-6A. Neumann U-87 (Gotham Audio photo).

Figure 3-6B. Neumann TLM-170 (Gotham Audio photo).

Figure 3-6C. AKG C-460B (AKG photo).

floor, and superior resistance to "popping" in high humidity conditions due to its extremely low output impedance. A power supply is necessary to provide voltages to the oscillator as well as to the built-in pre-amplifier. Because of its low noise, this type of microphone is quickly becoming accepted for digital recording.

Condenser Microphone Power Supplies

Like any pre-amplifier, the one within the microphone requires a power supply as noted above. In the case of older (and some new) tube-type condenser microphones, the power supply furnishes filament voltages as well as a polarizing voltage to the diaphragm. In the case of these tube-type condenser microphones, a special cable between the microphone and the power supply is required and contains extra conductors which carry the required voltages separate from the audio signal.

Today, however, most modern condenser microphones employ "phantom power" supply circuits, where both the audio and the d.c. supply voltage travel within the same conductors. The standard power supply in use today provides 48 volts d.c. to the microphone, and is usually found built into the recording console. The phantom circuit has greatly simplified recording set-ups, since now the engineer need not set up a separate power supply for each condenser microphone used. The condenser microphone will automatically draw the required power as soon as it is plugged in, while other non-condenser microphones should not be affected by the phantom power supply voltages.

If the recording console uses center-tapped microphone input transformers, the required 48-volt positive supply voltage may be applied as shown in Figure 3-7A. Since transformers do not pass d.c. from one winding to another, the only path for the supply voltage is through both conductors in the microphone cable, back toward the microphone. Within the microphone, another transformer, also center-tapped, passes the supply voltage to the pre-amplifier.

However, most consoles today utilize a non-center-tapped transformer configuration, or totally transformerless microphone pre-amplifier designs. It is now common practice to create an artificial center tap using two precision matched resistors, as shown in Figure 3-7B. Note that, on the return, the d.c. supply voltage goes to the negative side of the power supply leaving the a.c. audio signal free and clear. Thus it becomes doubly important that all microphone cables have their shields well-connected at both ends of the cable, since the shield must now provide this d.c. path back to the power supply, as well as fulfilling its primary purpose of shielding the signal leads against noise. Although a slight interruption in the shield may not make the cable unusable with dynamic microphones, it will prevent a phantom powered condenser microphone from properly functioning. Microphone cables are discussed in some detail at the end of this chapter (Balanced and Unbalanced Lines).

Formerly, power requirements often varied from one microphone manufacturer to the next. Today, however, this is seldom the case as most microphone manufacturers adhere to the DIN standard for the powering of condenser (capacitor) microphones. A typical circuit for powering multiple condenser microphones from one voltage source is shown in Figure 3-8. Of course, vacuum tube condenser microphones, whether vintage or modern, will still require filament voltage which is not available through phantom powering.

ACOUSTICAL SPECIFICATIONS

Directional Characteristics of Microphones

In any normal listening situation, we generally prefer to face the source of the sound which interests us. In fact, sounds originating from directly in front of us (called on-axis sound) may often be clearly heard despite the presence of loud distracting sounds in the surrounding but off-axis area. It seems that our brain allows us some flexibility in focusing on what it is we wish to hear, and with concentration we may be able to tune out other distracting sounds. This ability is greatly influenced by the relative direction from which the sound arrives. We find that we invariably attempt to face in the general direction of the sound to

Figure 3-7A. The phantom powering system is wired to the center tap of the console's input transformer.

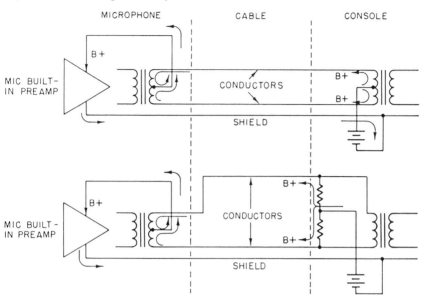

Figure 3-7B. An artificial center tap is created with two matched resistors.

which we are listening. For example, consider a concert performance by a large orchestra. A listener in the theater audience might have little trouble concentrating on a particular instrument within the ensemble, and a reasonable amount of distraction (air conditioning noises, outside traffic, and such) would be all but unheard, due to the listener's ability to concentrate on the music.

On the other hand, a single microphone in the audience will hear and pass along, every sound occurring within its range, without regard for the musical or non-musical significance of one sound over another. Obviously, the microphone does not enjoy the listener's ability to concentrate on the music alone. If a recording were made in this manner, the microphone would transmit both music and noise with equal facility as shown in Figure 3-9A.

Later on, when the playback lacks the visual cues that help the brain to concentrate, the listener will find it difficult or impossible to sort out the music from the noise, or to concentrate on an instrument which may have been clearly heard during the ac-

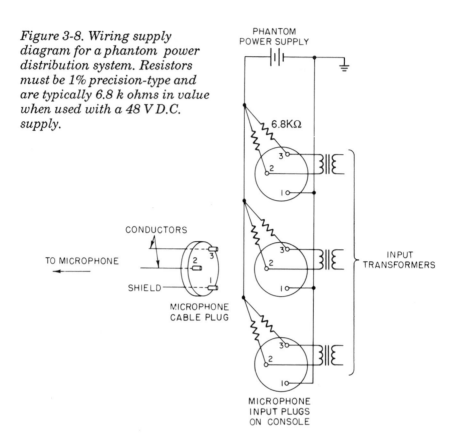

Figure 3-8. Wiring supply diagram for a phantom power distribution system. Resistors must be 1% precision-type and are typically 6.8 k ohms in value when used with a 48 V D.C. supply.

tual performance. And obviously, the recording engineer will have no control over anything but the overall recorded level of the total environment.

A dramatic improvement in perspective, if not control, may be realized by employing two microphones in an attempt to more closely simulate the effect of listening with two ears. Our brain perceives the placement of sound from this binaural effect. A person with only one ear can perceive pitch, loudness, and timbre, but will be unable to correctly determine the exact location of the source of the sound. (Our perception of direction was discussed in Chapter 2.) Yet two microphones have no more "brain power" than one, and some attempt must be made to separate, for the microphone's benefit, those sounds that are to be recorded from those that are not desired. To accomplish this, we might put the microphones very close to the sound source of interest as in Figure 3-9B, so that all other sounds are, from the microphone's view, drowned out by the sheer volume of the close-up instrument or voice. Even the most unwanted of noises, if very loud and close to one's ear, will mask all other sounds regardless of the listener's interest in them. Likewise, a microphone placed quite close to a musical instrument will not hear very much of anything else, wanted or not. This means that several microphones may be required to cover a large group, or even a small ensemble, if each microphone is placed close to an instrument or group of instruments.

In the case of a severe noise problem—and here "noise" may even mean the sound of other musical instruments—we may place certain instruments in isolation booths (Figure 3-9C) to acoustically protect them from being drowned out by other, much louder sound sources.

Another way to handle this situation is to take into consideration the actual design of the microphone. In any typical recording application, the microphone is no doubt placed so that the wanted sounds arrive on-axis, that is, from directly in front of the microphone. Presumably, unwanted sounds are off to the side or rear of the microphone (off-axis). A certain degree of insensitivity to these unwanted sounds may be designed into the microphone. It should be kept in mind, however, that the microphone's insensitivity has nothing to do with whether a sound is wanted or not, but is strictly a function of the angle from which the sound arrives.

Directional Sensitivity : The Omni-directional, Bi-directional, and Uni-directional Microphones.

A microphone may be classified as omni-directional, bi-directional (bi-radial), or uni-directional (cardioid) in nature, with these terms referring to the type of directional sensitivity that is inherent in its design. A brief description of each type of pattern follows.

Omni-directional (pressure) Microphones

A microphone that is equally sensitive to all sound sources, regardless of their relative direction, is known as an omni-directional microphone. Basically, the microphone consists of a diaphragm and a sealed enclosure, as shown in Figure 3-10. It is often also referred to as a pressure microphone, because it re-

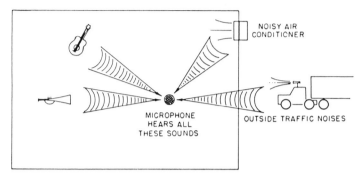

Figure 3-9A. A microphone in the middle of the room hears both wanted and unwanted sounds.

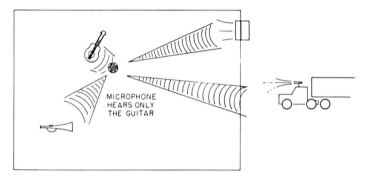

Figure 3-9B. A microphone placed very close-up hears the instrument directly in front of it, and most other sounds are considerably attenuated.

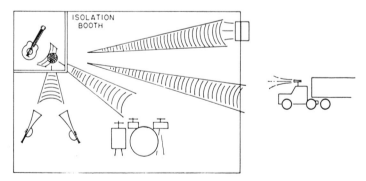

Figure 3-9C. In very noisy rooms, the isolation booth helps shield the microphone from unwanted sounds.

sponds to the instantaneous variations in air pressure caused by the sound wave. Since the microphone has no way of determining the location of the sound source causing the pressure variation, it responds with equal sensitivity to sounds (pressure variations) coming from all directions— hence the name omni-directional.

The microphone approximates the directional characteristics of the ear, which is likewise an omni-directional transducer. However, in the case of the ear, the head itself is somewhat of an acoustical obstruction to sounds arriving from certain off-axis locations. High frequencies in particular are better heard by the ear closest to the source producing them. In a similar manner, the casing of a physically large microphone may somewhat obstruct rear-originating sounds, causing a slight decrease in sensitivity. Once again, this will be most apparent at the higher frequencies.

Bi-directional (pressure gradient) Microphones

The bi-directional, or bi-radial microphone is equally sensitive to sounds originating from directly in front (0°) and from directly behind it (180°). It is least sensitive to sounds arriving from the sides (90° and 270°). This bi-directional characteristic is generally realized by leaving both sides of the diaphragm exposed, as shown in Figure 3-11. Thus, sounds may strike either the front or the rear of the diaphragm. This type of microphone is often referred to as a pressure gradient microphone, since the movement of the diaphragm is in response to the pressure gradient—that is, the difference in acoustic pressure between the front and rear of the diaphragm. Sounds that originate from the sides reach both the front and rear diaphragm at the same time and intensity. This creates a net pressure gradient, or difference, of zero, thus ex-

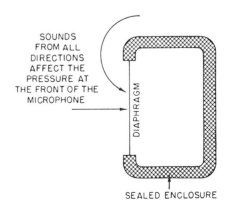

Figure 3-10. The omni-directional microphone.

59

plaining why this type of microphone is so highly insensitive at 90° and 270°. The bi-directional microphone is popularly called the figure-8 microphone since its pattern, as viewed from the top, resembles that number.

An important aspect of the bi-directional microphone is the electrical phase reversal between sounds arriving at its front and rear. To understand the significance of this, consider an instantaneous positive pressure wave striking the diaphragm. If the wave arrives from in front of the microphone, the diaphragm moves toward the rear, and a positive voltage is produced. If the instantaneous positive pressure wave was to simultaneously strike the rear of another bi-directional microphone, its diaphragm would move in the same relative direction (that is, away from the pressure wave). This would be toward the front of this microphone, and consequently, a negative voltage would be produced.

Although either voltage would constitute a usable audio signal, their equal and opposite polarities would cause a complete cancellation if their outputs were to be combined. In a like manner, a complex audio wave form that simultaneously reached the front and rear of two bi-directional microphones would be severely attenuated when the outputs of these microphones were combined, either while recording, or later on during a mixdown session. Therefore, when two bi-directional microphones are used, it is important to take into consideration this phase reversal and to make sure that no signal source is located between the rear of the bi-directional microphone and the front of another microphone, whether bi-directional or not. In practice, the attenuation is rarely total, especially if the individual frequency responses of the

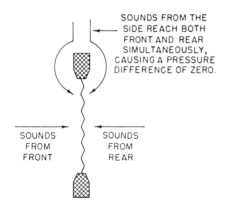

SOUNDS FROM THE SIDE REACH BOTH FRONT AND REAR SIMULTANEOUSLY, CAUSING A PRESSURE DIFFERENCE OF ZERO.

SOUNDS FROM FRONT

SOUNDS FROM REAR

Figure 3-11. The bi-directional microphone.

microphones are dissimilar. Characteristically, the combined output signal may sound thin or generally distorted in frequency response, as the two signals combine subtractively.

Uni-directional (Phase Shift) Microphones

A uni-directional microphone, usually referred to as a cardioid microphone, is most sensitive to sounds that originate from directly in front of it, that is at 0°, or what we consider on-axis. If the microphone is slowly rotated through a 360° arc, while its diaphragm remains at a constant distance from the source of the sound, its output level will continually decrease until the microphone is facing directly away from the source of the sound (180°). As the microphone continues to be rotated through this arc from 180° to 360°, its output level will increase until full level is reached once again at the on-axis point.

This fall off in sensitivity at the rear can be created by several methods. In single diaphragm microphones, this effect is generally the result of one, or a series of side or rear entry ports, as shown in Figures 3-12 and 3-13. The ports are arranged so that sounds originating from the rear can reach the diaphragm by two paths:

1) around the microphone to the front (P1) and,

2) through an entry port located at the rear of the diaphragm (P2).

If the two paths are of equal length, the pressure on both sides of the diaphragm will be the same causing no movement of the diaphragm, and therefore creating no output voltage. As such, the cardioid pattern microphone is also considered a pressure-gradient type. On the other hand, sounds arriving from the front (P3) must travel an extra distance to reach the rear of the diaphragm (P4). The phase shift caused by the difference in path lengths P3 and P4 causes a reinforcement of on-axis signals.

In dual diaphragm microphones this front-to-back sensitivity difference is caused by combining a pressure device with a pressure gradient type. This will be discussed in greater detail later in this chapter.

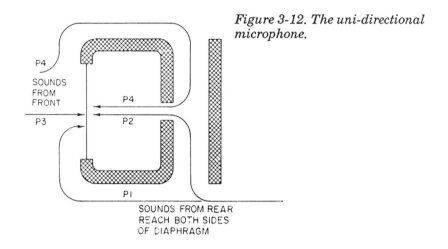

Figure 3-12. The uni-directional microphone.

Figure 3-13. The side- and rear-entry ports on two studio-quality uni-directional microphones (top—Electro-Voice RE-20, bottom—Sennheiser MKH-40. (E-V and Sennheiser photos.)

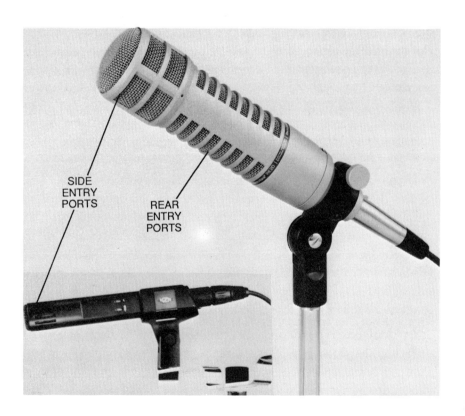

Microphone Polar Patterns

A polar pattern is a graph of a microphone's relative sensitivity to sounds that originate at various locations around it. Polar patterns for omni-directional, bi-directional, and cardioid microphones are shown in Figures 3-14 A, B, and C. In each case, the heavy line is the polar pattern itself, while the concentric circles indicate 5 dB decreasing increments of sensitivity. In a real polar plot of a specific microphone, there would be several pattern plots drawn on one graph, with each one representing a specific frequency. For simplicity, only one line is shown representing a frequency of 1000 Hz. Pattern with respect to frequency will be shown in greater detail later in this chapter.

The omni-directional polar pattern, in an ideal case, is simply a circle. This indicates that the microphone is equally sensitive to sounds originating from any direction. In practice, however, the omni-directional microphone will have a tendency to be slightly less sensitive to sounds originating from the rear since, as mentioned earlier, the case of the microphone itself may serve as somewhat of an acoustical barrier. This effect is noted by the slight flattening of the polar pattern in the vicinity of 180°, as shown in Figure 3-14A. In this area, the pattern almost touches the concentric circle marked 5 dB. This means that the microphone being measured is actually almost 5 dB less sensitive to sounds originating from that direction.

The bi-directional polar pattern shown in Figure 3-14B illustrates this microphone's equal sensitivity to sounds originating from the front and rear, as well as its insensitivity to sounds originating from 90° and 270° off-axis. As mentioned previously, the bi-directional microphone is popularly known as a figure-8, due to the characteristic shape of its polar pattern.

The uni-directional, or cardioid polar pattern is shown in Figure 3-14C. Notice that the polar pattern crosses the concentric circle at the 6 dB point, which is approximately 90°, and that at the rear (180°) it just touches the 25 dB circle. This means that sounds originating at these points will be attenuated by 6 dB and 25 dB respectively as compared to the same sound from on-axis or 0°. It is important to realize that in reality the practical cardioid microphone is certainly not totally deaf to off-axis sounds, but that these sounds are attenuated by a certain number of dB as the polar pattern indicates.

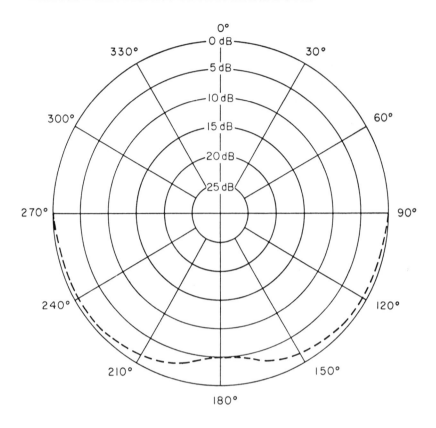

Figure 3-14A. The omni-directional polar pattern. The dashed line indicates a slight loss of sensitivity in the rear.

Somewhere between the polar pattern of the bi-directional or figure-8 microphone and the polar pattern of the cardioid or uni-directional microphone, a series of intermediate patterns may be derived in which the rear lobe of the figure-8 pattern becomes progressively smaller while the front lobe takes on a more car-dioid or wider shape. Although many of these patterns are purely mathematical models, several of them may be found in studio qu-ality microphones. The super-cardioid pattern, as shown in Fig-ure 3-15A, is often used as a viable alternative to the cardioid pattern. In Figure 3-15B, the super-cardioid is overlaid on a regu-lar cardioid pattern. It will be seen that the super-cardioid pat-tern is more sensitive to sounds originating from the rear, but somewhat less sensitive to side originating sounds than the car-dioid. The super-cardioid has two areas of minimum sensitivity.

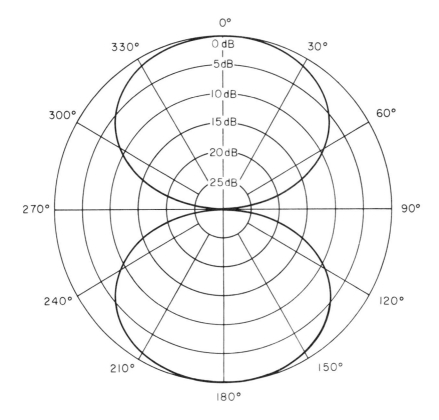

Figure 3-14B. The bi-directional polar pattern.

One at 126°, and the other at the reciprocal angle of 234°. An other polar pattern that may often be found is the hyper-cardioid. It is slightly less sensitive at the sides than the super-cardioid, but is yet more sensitive to sounds originating from 180°, as shown in Figure 3-16. Between the omni-directional polar pattern and the cardioid polar pattern is an intermediate pattern that is becoming more widely available, particularly on multi-pattern microphones. This so-called near-cardioid or wide-angle cardioid pattern is less sensitive to rear originating sounds than the omni, but more sensitive to sounds originating from the sides than the cardioid pattern.

The polar pattern for an interference or so-called shotgun microphone generally resembles a flattened out front lobe with a series of very small rear lobes, as shown in Figure 3-17A. The

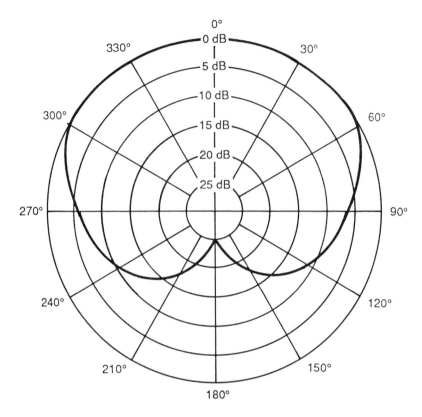

Figure 3-14C. The uni-directional (cardioid) polar pattern.

microphone consists of a long tube with many open ports along the full length as shown in Figure 3-17B. Sounds originating from the front enter the microphone unobstructed, while sounds arriving from the sides are "interfered" with and phase cancelled. The more off-axis the sounds, the greater the cancellation. This microphone is not used very often in recording studios, but may be a valuable tool on remote sessions when it is impossible to place a cardioid or other microphone close to the source of the sound. It is widely used in television studios and on movie sets, where it is important that the microphone not be seen in the picture.

Figure 3-20C gives a comparison of several important parameters for the various patterns that have been discussed.

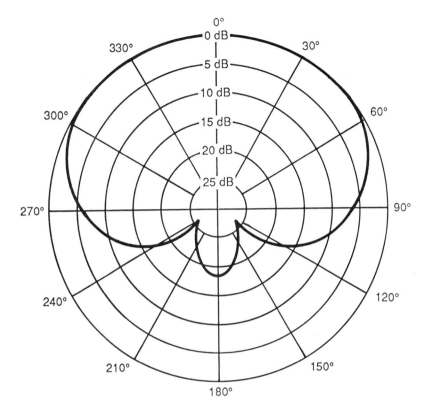

Figure 3-15A. The super-cardioid polar pattern.

Multi-Pattern Microphones

Many studio grade microphones have the ability to produce more than one polar pattern. This flexibility allows a microphone to perform well in a multitude of conditions. The most common method of accomplishing this is to build a microphone with two diaphragms.

One of the methods used in this dual-diaphragm design takes advantage of the fact that two cardioid patterns may be combined to produce either a bi-directional pattern or an omni-directional one. Figure 3-18 is a simplified illustration of this principle, where two diaphragms D1 and D2 are on either side of a common back plate. Each diaphragm used alone will produce a cardioid

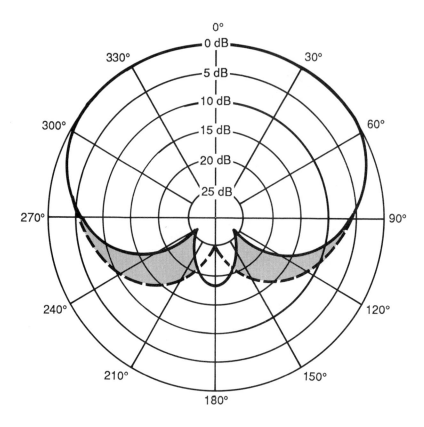

Figure 3-15B. A comparison of cardioid and super-cardioid polar patterns.

pattern. With the pattern selector switch in position 1, only one diaphragm, D1, is in use, and the microphone functions as a simple cardioid microphone. In position 2, the second diaphragm, D2, is also energized, and the two cardioid patterns combine to produce the omni-directional polar pattern as shown in Figure 3-19A. With the switch in position 3, the polarity of diaphragm D2 is reversed, and the opposing polarities cause a cancellation in the areas where the two patterns overlap. The result is a bi-directional pattern as shown in Figure 3-19B. When the pattern switch is in position 4, the second diaphragm is still negatively polarized, yet the resistor, R, drops the polarizing voltage some-what. Consequently, although D2 still yields a cardioid pattern, it is somewhat smaller than the D1 pattern, and their combination yields the intermediate pattern shown in Figure 3-19C. The size

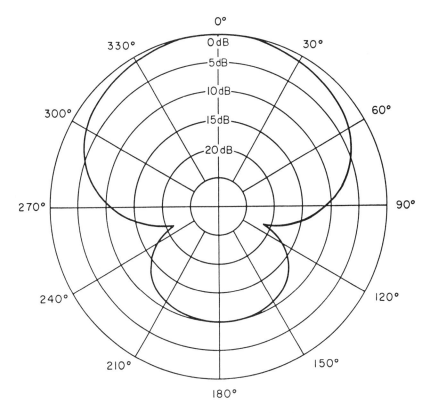

Figure 3-16. The hyper-cardioid polar pattern.

of the rear lobe depends on the actual value of R. If R=0, the pattern would be fully bi-directional, the equivalent of the pattern switch being in position 3. If R=∞ (open circuit), the pattern becomes cardioid again, since the second diaphragm is out of the circuit.

Another type of dual diaphragm multi-pattern microphone uses a fixed back plate and two diaphragms. This type of capsule is often called a Braunmühl-Weber capsule. In this capsule, the back plate is perforated and by varying the electrical potential on the two diaphragms, a variety of patterns can be produced. If the polarity on both diaphragms is positive, a pressure device is formed, responding equally to sounds from all directions. When the polarity of the rear diaphragm is changed to negative, a pressure gradient can be produced. And by combining the two, the

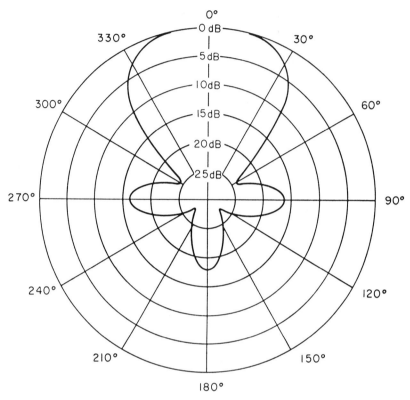

Figure 3-17A. A typical "shotgun" polar pattern.

Figure 3-17B. A modern ultra-directional or "shotgun" microphone.

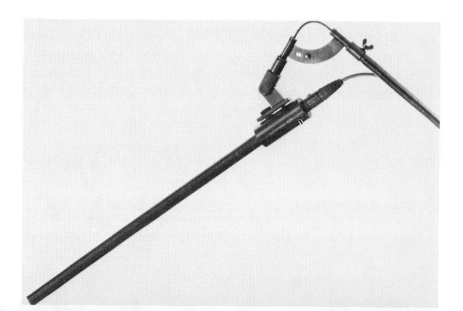

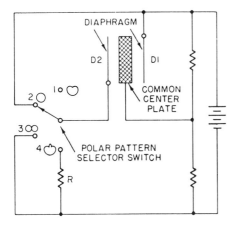

Figure 3-18. A dual diaphragm condenser microphone.
Position 1. Cardioid pattern.
Position 2. Omni-directional pattern.
Position 3. Bi-directional pattern.
Position 4. Intermediate (hyper- or super-cardioid) pattern.

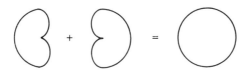

Figure 3-19A. Two cardioid patterns, added to create an omni-directional polar pattern.

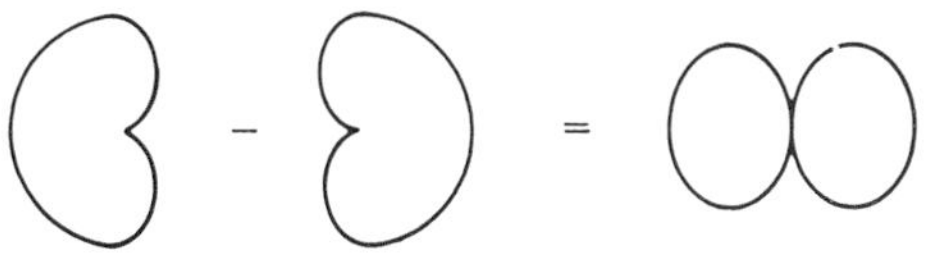

Figure 3-19B. Two cardioid patterns, subtracted to create a bi-directional polar pattern.

Figure 3-19C. Two unequal cardioid patterns, subtracted to create a super-cardioid pattern.

cardioid pattern can be derived. Figure 3-20A shows the patterns resulting from combining various amounts of the omni-directional and figure-8 patterns, while Figure 3-20B shows the circuit diagram for such a capsule.

In some multi-pattern condenser microphone systems, the pattern selector is replaced by a potentiometer, allowing a variable polarizing voltage to be supplied to the diaphragms. In this way, the microphone's polar pattern is continuously variable from bi-directional to omni-directional, with infinite intermediate patterns. Often, in the case of stereophonic microphones (which will be discussed in Chapter 4), this continuously variable potentiometer is remotely located. This allows the polar pattern of the microphone capsules to be changed without having to go to the microphone itself to do so. This is a great convenience when the microphone is located high in the air, or at the end of a long boom. Figure 3-21A shows a microphone with a built-in four position pattern selecting switch, while Figure 3-21B pictures a continuously variable pattern control for remote locations.

In another version of the multi-pattern microphone, variations in the polar pattern are realized by changing the diaphragm enclosure. These multi-pattern single diaphragm microphones have a variety of different capsules available for use on a common pre-amplifier body. A typical system would comprise an omni-directional capsule, a cardioid capsule, a figure-8 capsule and a preamplifier body. A microphone capsule of this type is shown in Figure 3-22. The figure-8 capsule picks up sound radially or at a 90° angle to the body of the microphone, while both the omni and the cardioid capsules pick up axially or parallel to the microphone body.

Some microphones use two diaphragms for a different reason. These single pattern dual diaphragm microphones use one diaphragm or capsule for low frequency pickup and the other for high frequencies, just as many loud speakers utilize two drivers—a woofer and a tweeter—to cover the complete audio spectrum. This type of microphone is illustrated in Figure 3-23. The high frequency system is physically small, while the low frequency system is approximately double that in size. A crossover frequency is determined that will allow each diaphragm to deliver signal from its optimum frequency range only. The two signals are then combined producing a single wide band output.

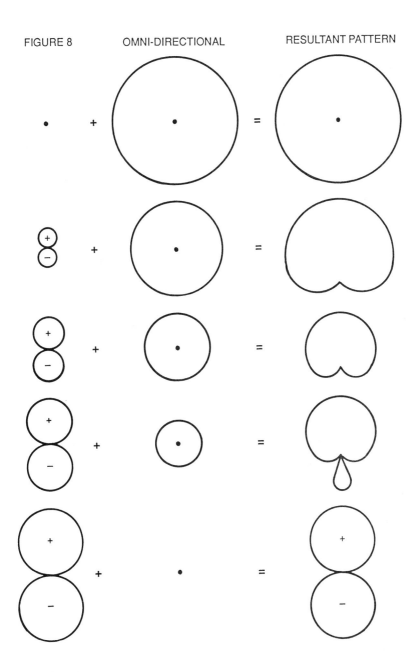

Figure 3-20A. Patterns resulting from combining a pressure device (omni) with a pressure gradient (figure 8.)

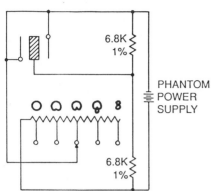

Figure 3-20B. A circuit diagram for a multiple pattern condenser microphone using a Braunmühl-Weber type capsule.

Figure 3-20C. A table of microphone pattern characteristics.

CHARACTERISTIC	OMNI-DIRECTIONAL	CARDIOID	SUPER-CARDIOID	HYPER-CARDIOID	BIDIRECTIONAL
Polar response pattern					
Polar equation	1	$.5 + .5 \cos\theta$	$\dfrac{.375 +}{.625 \cos\theta}$	$.25 + .75 \cos\theta$	$\cos\theta$
Pickup ARC 3 dB down (1)	—	131°	115°	105°	90°
Pickup ARC 6 dB down	—	180°	156°	141°	120°
Relative output at 90° dB	0	−6	−8.6	−12	−∞
Relative output at 180° dB	0	−∞	−11.7	−6	0
Angle at which output = 0	—	180°	126°	110°	90°
Random energy efficiency (REE)	1 0dB	.333 −4.8dB	.268 −5.7dB (2)	.250 −6.0dB (3)	.333 −4.8dB
Distance factor (DF)	1	1.7	1.9	2	1.7

NOTE:

1 = Drawn shaded on polar pattern

2 = Maximum front-to-total random energy efficiency for a first order cardioid

3 = Minimum random energy efficiency for a first order cardioid

Figure 3-21A. A dual-diaphragm condenser microphone with a built-in four-position pattern selector (AKG C414EB P48).

Figure 3-21B. Potentiometers mounted in a separate enclosure provide remote and variable pattern selection (Neumann C48i).

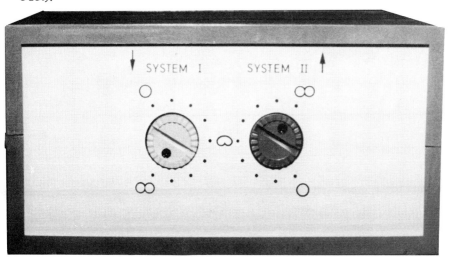

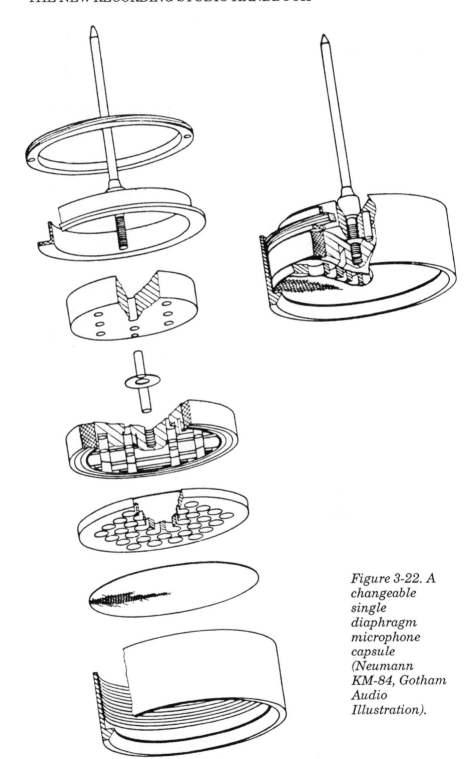

Figure 3-22. A changeable single diaphragm microphone capsule (Neumann KM-84, Gotham Audio Illustration).

Figure 3-23. A dual-capsule single-pattern condenser microphone (Sanken CU-41, Sanken photo).

MEASURING MICROPHONE POLAR RESPONSE

A microphone's polar response is measured by rotating the microphone through a 360° arc while keeping the sound source fixed, both in level and location. The measurements are made within an anechoic chamber, so that there will be no reflections from nearby surfaces to influence the off-axis response. The microphone is set up so that as it rotates, its diaphragm remains at a constant distance from the sound source, as shown in Figure 3-24. The many reflections within any audio studio will alter the microphone's apparent polar response with respect to frequency. But there is no way to predict the net effect of these reflections, which will vary from one studio to another and at different locations within the same studio. In fact, the engineer will have to take into account the varying reflective conditions within the studio when determining the best locations for certain instruments, or the exact placement of a particular microphone in front of an instrument or ensemble.

In any case, the reflection free anechoic chamber serves as a repeatable standard measuring condition enabling the engineer to compare the ideal polar response patterns of many different microphones. The recording engineer can, and should, study these polar responses so as to be able to predict, with reasonable accuracy, the performance he or she may expect within the studio.

Although polar patterns are drawn only in two dimensions as an artistic and measuring convenience, it should be understood that the patterns are actually three dimensional, as shown in the five examples of Figure 3-25.

So far, our examples of polar responses have shown single line patterns, and as mentioned earlier, generally represent the best case response at around 1000 Hz. This would seem to imply that at off-axis positions, the microphone is equally sensitive or insensitive to all sounds, regardless of frequency. In practice, sadly to say, this is not the case. For a more accurate indication of the microphone's off-axis response, a polar pattern at several frequencies, equally representing high and low, should be drawn. A typical polar pattern response is shown in Figure 3-26A. From

Figure 3-24. A large anechoic chamber. The wedges on all surfaces eliminate virtually all reflections within the room.

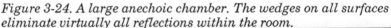

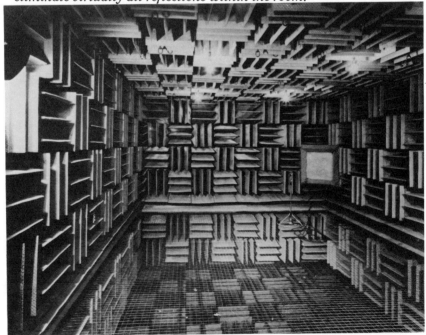

these response curves, we may draw graphs of the microphone's frequency response at various off-axis angles, as shown in Figure 3-26B.

These response curves indicate that although the microphone performs satisfactorily with respect to on-axis sound, its off-axis response is quite irregular. This condition is known as off-axis coloration, so called because of the distorted, or colored, frequency responses obtained. Off-axis coloration may take the form of an unpleasant and muddy sound, since the microphone's off-axis high frequency response usually falls off at a much greater rate than the lower frequencies. This condition particularly affects the sound of the surrounding ambient field. It is interesting to note the differences in polar responses between the patterns of a multi-pattern Braunmühl-Weber capsule microphone and the corresponding polar responses of a multi-pattern back-to-back cardioid type of design. Neither one is perfect, but the prudent engineer may wish to select one over the other depending on the situation at hand.

Proximity Effect

Another characteristic of pressure-gradient microphones is called the proximity effect. This is an increase in bass response, in proportion to the high frequencies, as the microphone is moved closer to the sound source. The condition is illustrated in Figure 3-27, where on-axis response at various microphone to source distance is shown. Notice that as the distance decreases, the bass response rises considerably. This rising bass response may be beneficial in some cases, helping to achieve a more robust sound for a voice. However, the slightest movement of the singer, or announcer, toward or away from the microphone, will change the overall frequency response noticeably. In hand-held applications, where the working distance is continually changing, a microphone without proximity effect, such as an omni-directional type, may be required. Even when the microphone is stand mounted close to, for instance, an acoustic guitar, the variations in bass response may be noticeable as the guitarist moves about while playing. On the other hand, when the microphone is placed in front of a stationary guitar amplifier, the working distance may be varied by the engineer to achieve the desired bass response.

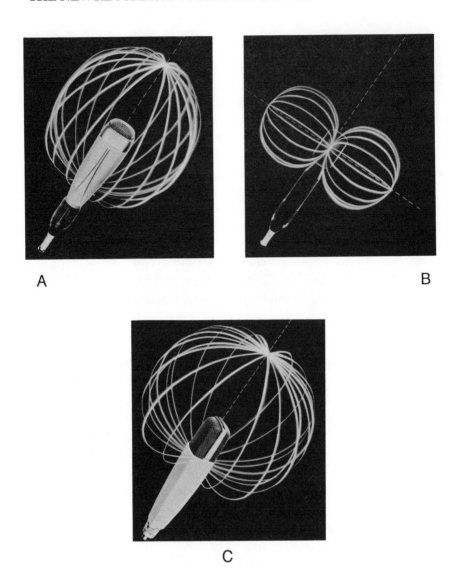

Figure 3-25 (A) the omni-directional polar pattern, (B) the bi-directional polar pattern, and (C) the uni-directional (cardioid) polar pattern.

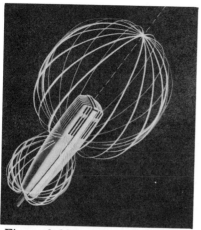

Figure 3-25D. The
uni-directional (super cardioid)
polar pattern.

Figure 3-25E. The
ultra-directional ("shotgun")
polar pattern (Sennheiser
photos).

Most large diaphragm cardioid microphones have a built in switchable high pass filter to counteract the proximity effect. The filter restores the low-end response to normal at some specified close working distance. At greater distances, the filter should be switched out, since its fixed low-end attenuation is now unnecessarily attenuating the microphone's normal low frequency response. Microphones with omni-directional polar patterns are free of this effect.

ELECTRICAL SPECIFICATIONS

Microphone Impedance

For professional studio applications, low impedance microphones are practically an industry standard. Although high impedance microphones are not necessarily inferior in themselves, the long cable lengths required in most studio installations prohibit their use.

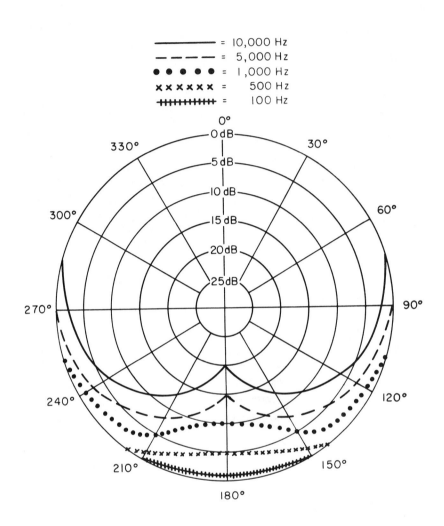

Figure 3-26A. Complete polar pattern for an inexpensive cardioid microphone.

To understand why, an equivalent circuit for a microphone that is connected by a length of cable to a console microphone pre-amplifier is drawn in Figure 3-28. Note that R_S and R_L are in series with the source voltage, E. Therefore, if R_S is much smaller then R_L, most of the generated voltage will appear across the console input, R_L. C represents the typical capacitance of any microphone

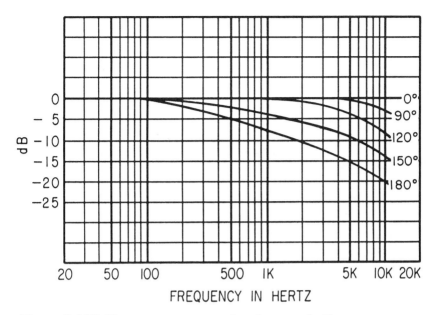

Figure 3-26B. Frequency response at various angles for an inexpensive cardioid microphone.

cable—the longer the cable, the greater the capacitance. Now, as frequency increases, this capacitance lowers the impedance of the cable/console combination. Since the microphone's impedance remains constant, the voltage across C (and consequently across R_L) falls off as the frequency rises, since more and more of the total voltage drop is across R_S. This phenomena can be expressed by the following equation.

$$F = \frac{1}{2\pi R_T C_T}$$

where:

F = the frequency at which the highs will begin to roll-off at a rate of 6 dB / 8va.

R_T = the total resistance in the circuit expressed as $R_T = \dfrac{1}{R_S + R_L}$

C_T = the total capacitance in the circuit expressed by the number of picofarads per foot multiplied by the total cable length.

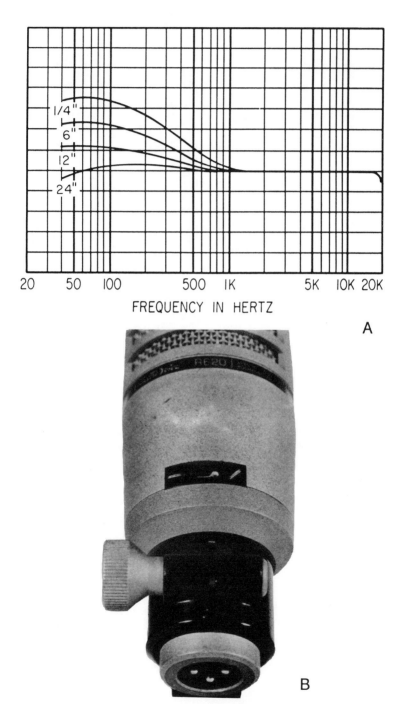

Figure 3-27. (A) typical proximity effects at various working distances, (B) a switchable bass roll-off filter to minimize the proximity effect.

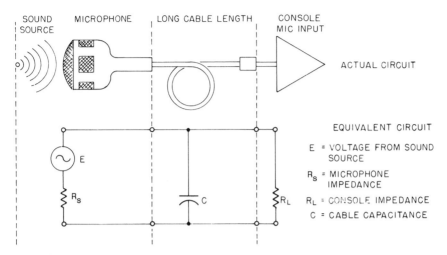

Figure 3-28. The equivalent circuit of a microphone connected to a console input.

It can be seen that with a high impedance microphone, this fall-off of high frequencies will be quite noticeable within the audio bandwidth, unless cable lengths, and therefore total capacitance, are kept to an absolute minimum. On the other hand, a low impedance microphone will allow the use of long cable runs up to several hundred feet with no adverse effect on the frequency response. Although the cable capacitance remains the same, the microphone's relatively low impedance keeps the high frequency attenuation well above the audible audio bandwidth.

Microphone Sensitivity

A microphone's sensitivity rating tells the user something about its relative efficiency in converting acoustic energy to electrical energy. Sensitivity is usually expressed in dB below a specified reference level. The two types of rating methods are:

1) the open circuit voltage rating, and

2) the maximum power rating.

The majority of microphone manufacturers today use the open circuit voltage rating method. The other method, maximum power rating, is leftover from the days of matching impedances for maximum power transfer. Most modern circuits are bridging and result in the more efficient maximum current transfer.

In the open circuit rating method, either the microphone is not connected to any input, or the input impedance to which it is connected is at least twenty times higher than the impedance of the microphone itself. The reference sound pressure level can be either 1 microbar (1 dyne/cm^2 or 74 dB) or 1 Pascal, abbreviated 1 Pa (10 dynes/cm^2 or 94 dB). The second level of 1 Pa is the most currently used reference. The zero reference is 1 volt. In other words, if a sound pressure level of 1 Pascal resulted in a 1 volt output, the microphone's sensitivity would be 0 dB referenced to 1 Pa. In practice, much lower output voltages are produced, and typical open circuit voltage ratings are on the order of –85 dB to –35 dB. To prevent confusion, the sensitivity specification should clearly state the reference used. For example, a –60 dB (re: 1V/microbar) is equivalent to –80 dB (re: 1V/Pa).

Microphone Lines: Balanced And Unbalanced

A balanced line is one which uses two conductors plus a shield or drain wire, while an unbalanced line contains only one conductor, with the shield or drain wire serving as the second conductor. Figure 3-29 shows both types of lines, as well as typical balanced and unbalanced circuits. An important advantage of the balanced line is that any unwanted noise signals induced in the microphone cable will be picked up by both conductors (one positive and one negative), and will cancel when the cable is terminated properly. In the unbalanced line, the noise voltage will travel down the single conductor, and be transmitted to the next stage of the circuit.

Providing that the audio signal is of sufficiently high level (such as a +4 dBm line level signal), the noise may not be heard as anything but a slight raising of the noise floor of the system, especially if the unbalanced line is reasonably short. But, as noted before, microphone lines tend to be quite long, and the signal levels very low. Consequently, the slightest noise or hum induced in the microphone line may become almost as loud as the microphone's output signal. For this reason, balanced lines are an absolute necessity between a microphone and its console pre-amplifier.

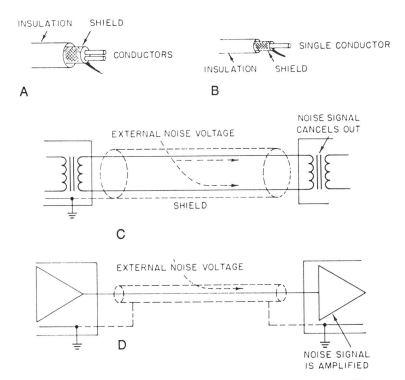

Figure 3-29. At (A) a balanced line, (B) is unbalanced. At (C) a balanced circuit, and at (D) unbalanced.

Microphone Polarity

Practically all professional microphones use a three pin output connector, commonly called a Cannon connector or an XLR, with pin 1 used as the shield and the output signal appearing across pins 2 and 3. A positive pressure on the diaphragm of the microphone will usually produce a positive voltage at pin 2 with respect to pin 3. Most major microphone manufacturers adhere to this convention, however, it is by no means completely standard.

Before putting a new microphone in service, the prudent engineer will verify the relative polarity of the output pins, so that phase reversals can be avoided. This can be done by checking the documentation that came with the microphone, or by comparing the questionable microphone with a known standard. The front of the two microphones should be pointed at the same sound source and their outputs mixed together and monitored. If the combined level is less than either single microphone level, phase cancellation is occurring. In the ideal situation, the output level of the combined microphones will be 6 dB greater on the VU meters than either of them separately. If an out-of-phase microphone is found, it should be immediately rewired. When this is not possible, a short adapter cable should be permanently attached to the non-standard microphone along with a label stating the condition.

DISTORTION IN MICROPHONES

For all practical purposes, it is almost impossible to produce a sound pressure level indoors that will overload a professional quality moving coil (dynamic) microphone. Some older ribbon microphones could be overloaded, and actually damaged by very high sound pressure levels, but more recent versions should be able to withstand most sound levels found in the studio. However, a very high microphone output level may overload the microphone pre-amplifier in the recording console. Most consoles contain a sensitivity control that allows the engineer to adjust the gain of the microphone pre-amplifier as well as a switchable pad that will insert a fixed amount of attenuation in the microphone line ahead of the pre-amplifier. In cases where such a facility is not built in, or in the case where the console adjustment is insufficient, an attenuation pad may be inserted in the microphone line. Figure 3-30 shows a commercially available attenuation pad and also gives resistance values and a diagram for 10 and 20 dB attenuation circuits.

In a condenser microphone, the voltage produced by the capacitor/diaphragm may be sufficient to overload the microphone's built-in pre-amplifier. Attenuation facilities at the console will be of no use, since the overload occurs within the microphone itself. To protect the pre-amplifier against this overload, many condenser microphones have a built-in pad that inserts 10 or 20 dB of attenuation between the diaphragm and the pre-amplifier. Figure 3-31A illustrates a microphone with a switchable pad, and Figure 3-31B shows another arrangement where a 10 or 20 dB pad may be physically inserted between the diaphragm capsule and the pre-amplifier when required.

Figure 3-30A. A commercially available in-line microphone attenuator.

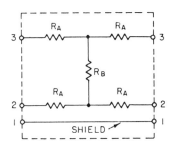

Figure 3-30B. Circuit values for a microphone line attenuator.

For 10 dB attenuation R_a=56 ohms, R_b=150 ohms

For 20 dB attenuation R_a=82 ohms, R_b=39 ohms

Caution—this type of attenuator should not be used with a phantom-powered condenser microphone since it will interfere with the voltage being supplied to the microphone.

Microphone Noises: Sibilance and Vibration

Although a microphone's diaphragm must vibrate in order for it to produce an output voltage, some care must be taken to prevent certain unwanted vibrations from distorting the signal output. For example, a stream of air blown across a microphone would certainly create an unpleasantly distracting noise as the diaphragm is set into vibration by the wind. Although this is highly unlikely within the recording studio, a close-up voice can often produce a shock wave that distorts the microphone's output. In particular, sibilant words containing "p," "t," and "b" may create an objectionable pop due to the movement of air across the diaphragm. Pressure gradient microphones (cardioid and figure-8 patterns) are particularly susceptible to this, since the pressure differential between the front and back of the diaphragm is considerable.

To minimize these noises, a wind screen or pop filter may be placed over the microphone. The wind screen is made from an open pore acoustical foam material that does not affect the microphone's sensitivity in the audible range. On the other hand, the screen does prevent puffs of wind from striking the diaphragm

A

B

*Figure 3-31. (A) a condenser microphone with a built-in switchable
attenuation pad, and a switchable high-pass filter (AKG C414EB
P48), (B) a condenser microphone with an insertable attenuation pad
(Schoeps DZC 10, Schoeps photo).*

B

A

Figure 3-32. (A) a dynamic microphone with a built-in wind screen (Beyer M500, Beyer photo), (B) an accessory wind screen placed over a condenser microphone (Neumann U-87, Gotham Audio photo).

Figure 3-32C. Accessory windscreens.

with full force. When a windscreen is used on a microphone with rear ports, it is important to shield these entrances as well, so that the pressure differential is reduced, rather than accentuated. Figure 3-32 illustrates several microphones protected by wind screens. In addition to its primary function, the wind screen also protects the diaphragm from moisture and dust particles. Especially in close-up vocal pickups, it is a good idea to use a wind screen as a matter of routine. The screen should be rinsed out frequently to remove accumulated dust and grime. Needless to say, it would be much more difficult and time consuming to periodically clean the diaphragm itself.

Most studio structures are susceptible to at least some building vibration, particularly in heavy traffic metropolitan areas. Even though the vibrations are inaudible to the listener in the studio, they may be transmitted via the microphone stand to the microphone, creating an audible rumble over the control room monitor speakers. Even in a rumble free studio, certain impact noises are accompanied by considerable vibration. For example, an over enthusiastic kick drum may set up vibrations in the floor which

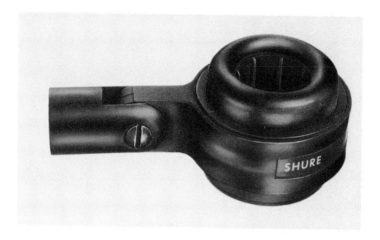

Figure 33A. A Shure A-55M shock mount (Shure photo).

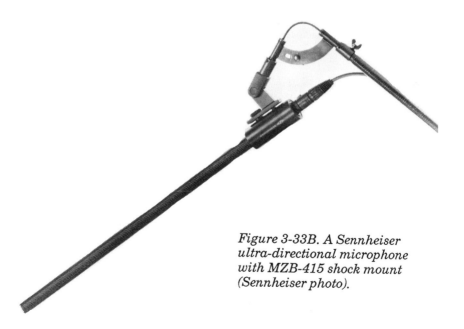

Figure 3-33B. A Sennheiser ultra-directional microphone with MZB-415 shock mount (Sennheiser photo).

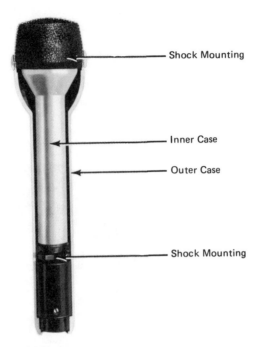

Figure 3-34. Cutaway view of a microphone in a double casing to minimize transmitted vibration (Electro-Voice RE-50, E-V photo).

may travel up the microphone stand and cause the microphone diaphragm to react. Most manufacturers produce shock mounts that are designed to mechanically isolate the microphone from its stand thereby cutting down on vibration induced noise. Representative examples of shock mounts are seen in Figure 3-33. Cardioid microphones tend to exaggerate mechanical shock and vibration, and in hand-held applications, the noises may be quite distracting. Some microphones which are designed to be hand held, such as shown in Figure 3-34, have the inner shell suspended from the outer casing to keep transmitted handling noise to a minimum.

Chapter 4

MICROPHONE TECHNIQUES

The knowledge and understanding of microphones and microphone technique is probably the single most important area of study for the recording engineer, and although the successful utilization of microphones is largely a subjective matter, there are certain "ground rules" that should be understood before preparing for any important recording session. The engineer needs to be aware of these different philosophies of microphone placement technique, so that he may intelligently choose the basic approach that will best serve his needs. It cannot be emphasized too strongly that the choice and positioning of microphones by the recording engineer is most often the difference between a good recording and a mediocre or bad one.

The first law of correct microphone usage has been successfully ignored almost from the day of its discovery.

It is: *Never use more than two microphones.*

Although most recording sessions would be impossible (and a great deal of this book unnecessary) if anyone took this law seriously, the engineer should understand its significance before setting up a third, fourth or twentieth microphone.

As discussed in Chapter 2, it is perhaps no accident that we have only two ears. Their positioning, and the interaction between them and the brain, allows us to form an incredibly accurate impression of the relative intensity and the location of any noise or sound within our hearing range. With the exception of those few sounds that originate quite close to one ear only (whispers, telephone conversations, and the like) we hear almost everything with both ears. Our impressions of direction usually derive from the phase shifts and time of arrival differences of a sound, as well as intensity gradients. In fact, our sense of localization for low frequencies tends to be phase dependent, while our perception of direction for high frequencies is usually determined by intensity differences.

As an example, consider the listener at a concert in a large theater or concert hall. The orchestra is spread across the full width and depth of the stage, with the strings nearest the front and the percussion instruments in the rear. The woodwind and brasses are arrayed in between. If there is a chorus, it may be standing behind the orchestra on risers. The larger the production, the more distance there is going to be between the front rows of violins and cellos and the last rows of the chorus. As can be seen in Figure 4-1, the sound from the chorus will reach the listener slightly later than that of the front strings. This time differential can be measured and is based on the speed of sound in air as discussed in Chapter 2. As we sit and listen with our eyes closed, this time lag is so slight that it escapes conscious notice, yet our ear/brain combination processes this information

Figure 4-1. Sounds from the more distant orchestral sections take a little longer to reach the listener.

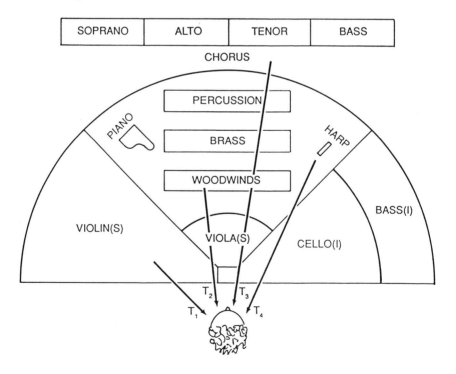

and correctly concludes that the chorus is placed behind the orchestra. Even when the chorus is louder than the strings, our brain is not fooled into thinking that they have moved in front of the orchestra.

Despite our excellent perception of width and depth, we really have no control over what we hear as we sit in a concert hall. But in the recording studio, or in recording that orchestra in the hall, a microphone or series of microphones may often be placed in front of each instrumental section as well as the chorus, allowing the engineer considerable control over what he hears and sends to tape. The working distance between the performers and the microphones will be arranged so that each microphone favors that particular section, as in Figure 4-2. To accomplish this, microphones must be placed reasonably close to each section, to better distinguish it from the rest of the ensemble. Note that the stage set up for recording is not necessarily the same as the or-

Figure 4-2. With a multiple microphone setup, time of arrival differences are minimized, depriving the listener of much of the spatial information for the sake of improved control over balances.

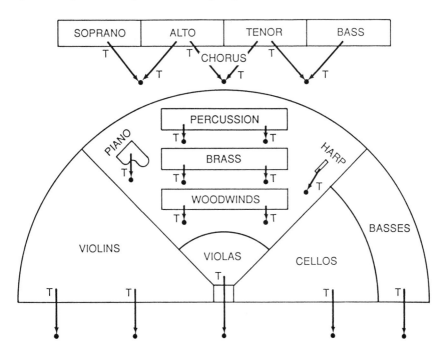

chestra's concert seating. But in arranging microphones in this manner, much valuable directional and spatial information can be lost for the sake of greater intensity control over the various sections of the orchestra. Unfortunately, this lost information is all but impossible to retrieve in even the most sophisticated recording systems. The engineer should clearly understand this characteristic problem with multiple microphones before concluding that it is the only way to record.

In a simple two microphone set up, the entire ensemble is heard by both microphones. Presumably, all the subtle differences in performer to microphone spacings, angle and time of arrival, etc. are retained. Ideally, it will sound as if the listener were seated at the location of the microphone pair. In the multi-microphone set up, these subtleties are lost, since each performer or group of performers is recorded from closely spaced separate microphones. The consequences of this are that time of arrival differences are minimized or completely eliminated since each microphone transmits its information simultaneously. In the control room, the various microphone outputs may be satisfactorily arranged in a left to right plane, but there is no completely successful way of creating the illusion of one instrument located behind another. In other words, we have created a two dimensional orchestra, one without a sense of depth. It is rarely satisfactory to place the rear instrument microphones at a lower level than the more forward located ones, especially if in the actual performance, the music calls for the rear groups (such as the chorus) to be louder. However, some relief to this situation can be achieved by electronically delaying the arrival of the rear located microphone outputs by a time factor approximately equal to their displacement from the front microphones. Of course, the practical day-to-day realities of the recording studio often take precedent over the ideal notions of the purist techniques, particularly in the area of popular music and multi-track recording. Nevertheless, the recording engineer must understand the trade-offs between multiple microphones and stereophonic microphone techniques.

Stereo Techniques: Binaural Systems

There are many methods in use for selecting and placing a single pair of microphones for a stereophonic pick up. Perhaps the most obvious technique would be to space two omni-directional microphones on either side of an acoustic baffle (Fig-

Figure 4-3. A binaural recording setup.

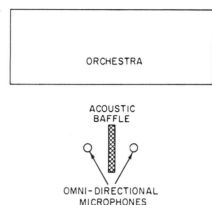

ure 4-3) in an attempt to simulate the condition of actually being seated at the location of the microphones. This technique, known as binaural recording, is most realistic on playback when wearing headphones, since the microphones seem to become an extension of the listener's ears, in effect transporting the subject to the site of the recording. However, it can be quite a disconcerting effect when, as you move your head from left to right, the stereophonic stage moves also.

A binaural recording played over loudspeakers is even less satisfactory. To understand why, consider a sound source off at some distance to the left of the binaural pair, as seen in Figure 4-4A. Both microphones will pick up about the same intensity of sound, along with the slight phase shift or time of arrival differences that would give the listener at the site, or the one wearing headphones, the necessary directional clues. However, over the spaced loudspeakers, these subtleties will be pretty much lost, and the approximately equal sound intensity at each speaker will produce a phantom image of the sound that appears to be somewhere near the center of the loudspeaker pair. On the other hand, a sound that is close and directly on the left will be primarily picked up by the left microphone and will be principally directed to the left speaker, giving the impression that the sound is off to the extreme left, rather than close up as is actually the case. These distortions of space and directional information rule out the effectiveness of binaural recording in professional applications.

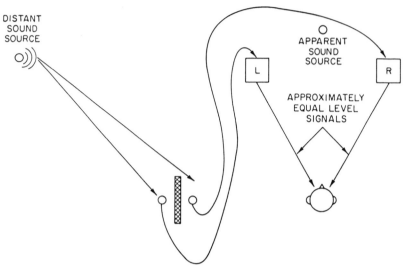

Figure 4-4A. When loudspeakers are used, the listener may think the sound source is somewhere in the center of the room, rather than on the extreme left.

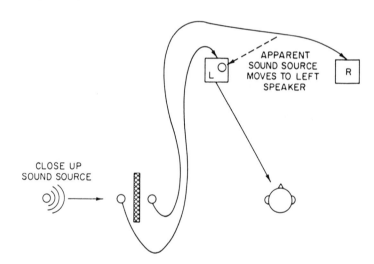

Figure 4-4B. As the sound source moves in closer, the listener hears the apparent source move from center to extreme left.

Stereo Techniques: Coincident Systems

Coincident recording systems are those in which the diaphragms of the two microphones are arrayed in the same vertical plane. This means that the cues that give us our perception of

THE STEREO MICROPHONE

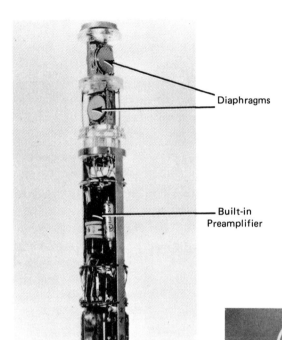

Diaphragms

Built-in
Preamplifier

*Figure 4-5A. A condenser stereo
microphone.
[Gotham Audio photo]*

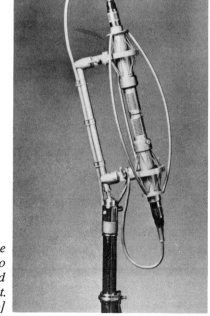

*Figure 4-5B. A stereo microphone
may also be made from two
separate microphones, held
together in a special bracket.
[Schoeps photo]*

direction and spacing are limited to intensity only. Since, as the capsules are coincident, there are no time-of-arrival differences. This can be accomplished by lining up two radially oriented microphones, one on top of the other as shown in Figure 4-5B, or by using a so-called stereo microphone. The latter is actually two separate microphone systems, housed in one case, as shown in Figure 4-5A. In a stereo microphone each system usually consists of a Braunmühl-Weber capsule and has continuously variable patterns that can be selected remotely. The upper microphone capsule can be rotated through an arc of 180° or more, and the two outputs are kept electronically separate.

Blumlein System

One of the more useful systems in the category of coincident stereo recording is the Blumlein system, named after the British experimenter Alvin Dower Blumlein. This simple but elegant system was first mentioned in a British patent by Blumlein in 1926. In operation, the stereo microphone pattern controls are both set to bi-directional or figure-8, and the capsules are oriented at a 90° angle to each other. This points one capsule toward the left side of the orchestra and the other toward the right. The null point or point of maximum attenuation of the left figure-8 is then facing the right side of the orchestra and the right null is facing left as shown in Figure 4-6. The patterns overlap in the center of the array at exactly the point where each figure-8 pattern has fallen 3 dB in sensitivity. If these microphone outputs were to be sent to a pair of spaced loudspeakers we would hear that sounds arriving from the left would be reproduced in the left speaker and the same relationship would occur on the right. Sounds from the center would enter both capsules equally but 3 dB lower in level and when reproduced by both loudspeakers would appear to be in the center and at the proper level as the signals combined. This system conveys a very accurate impression of both the width and depth of the orchestra. It is quite easy to determine which instruments are in the foreground and which are further back, although the engineer has no control over the internal balance of the ensemble. The rear lobes of the figure-8 patterns are pointing back into the hall or studio and present an equally accurate picture of the reverberation characteristics therein. The distance between the microphone(s) and the orchestra is usually equal to about half the width of the ensemble. This ratio of direct to re-

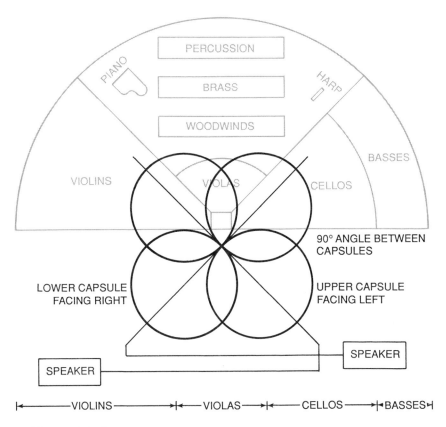

Figure 4-6. A stereo microphone set for recording using the Blumlein system.

verberant sound relationship conveys a sense of space and gives the listener an impression of the distance between audience and performer.

X-Y Systems

Sometimes, however, the ambient field in the recording location is less than perfect, or we simply wish to capture a more "present" sound. By switching the pattern selectors from figure-8 to cardioid we eliminate the back lobes and make the sound of the microphone array appear drier (less reverberant-to-direct ratio) and more present in nature. This X-Y technique is often used along with flanking microphones, a technique which will be discussed later in the Chapter. The problem with this X-Y approach

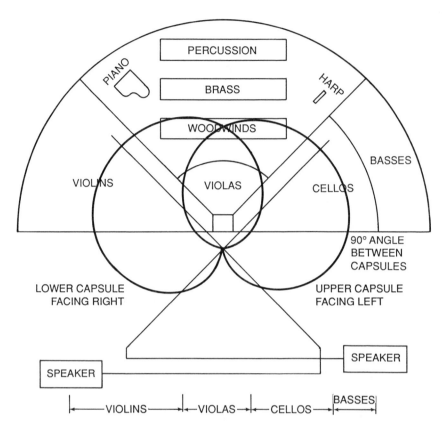

Figure 4-7. Two cardioids in an X-Y configuration showing pattern overlap.

is that the overlapping cardioid patterns cross very near their maximum sensitivity point (Figure 4-7). When listened to over a pair of loudspeakers, this technique narrows the stereo image of the ensemble due to the common information in each microphone output. This problem may be alleviated by widening the angle between the capsules or by narrowing the patterns and making them closer in polar response to a figure-8. A good compromise seems to be a pair of crossed hyper-cardioid patterns arrayed at an angle of 110°. This gives more of the ambient field than the overlapping cardioid patterns, yet does considerably widen the image of the ensemble.

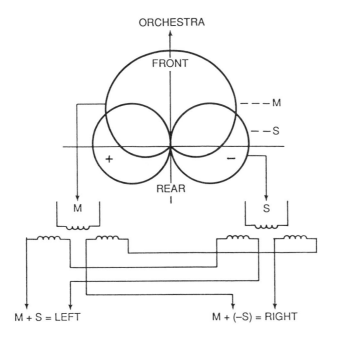

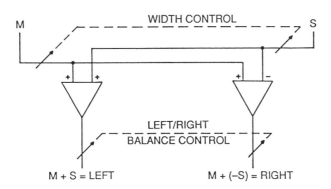

Figure 4-8. At the top, a stereo microphone with its patterns set for M-S recording. Transformers derive the eqivalent left and right signal. Below, an active M-S matrix system provides left and right signals and a width control.

M-S System

Another system that utilizes a stereo microphone or coincident pair is the M-S system. M-S, which stands for Middle-Side, uses a cardioid microphone pointed straight ahead at the middle of the orchestra, while a figure-8 microphone is pointed sideways so that one of its null points is facing the orchestra. This microphone setup is illustrated in Figure 4-8A, and it should be apparent that the cardioid microphone, which has a single output, picks up the entire ensemble, while the figure-8 microphone favors the extreme left and right sides. Center information reaches the null point of the figure-8 pattern and is pretty much canceled out. To form a suitable stereo image, the outputs of the two microphones are combined in a matrix system.

To understand how this matrix works, assume that the front of the figure-8 is pointing to the left. Therefore, signals originating left of center will be picked up by both the forward facing cardioid and the positive front of the figure-8 microphone. If their outputs are combined, these signals will add together. On the other hand, right of center signals will be picked up by the negative rear lobe of the figure-8 pattern, and when summed with the forward facing cardioid, the signals will tend to cancel. This arrangement of cardioid and figure-8 will favor left of center information only. However, if the output of the figure-8 microphone is reversed in phase electrically, the effect will be the same as if its left to right orientation had been physically reversed. Now a combination with the cardioid signal will yield a right-handed signal instead.

As shown in Figure 4-8B, a matrix system provides both types of combinations with separate outputs for each. By controlling the amount of the S-pattern sent to the matrix, we can effectively control the apparent width of the overall pick up, and by adjusting the left-right gains at the output of the matrix we can steer the array in the horizontal plane of the stereo image. In this M-S system, the forward facing microphone does not always have to be a cardioid. It can be an omni, or even another figure-8. Some combinations of different patterns and their X-Y equivalents are shown in Figure 4-9. Note that a matrixed M-S using two figure-8 patterns is equivalent to a non-matrixed Blumlein array. A major advantage of this system is its ability to provide a pure monophonic signal, and as such is highly favored by broadcasters.

Stereo Techniques: Near-coincident Systems

All of the preceding stereophonic microphone systems had one very important factor in common. They all relied solely on intensity differences in order to duplicate the left-right orientation of

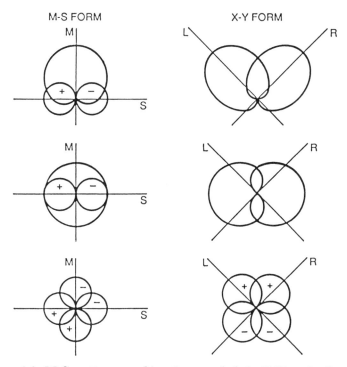

Figure 4-9. M-S pattern combinations and their X-Y equivalents.

the ensemble. We have seen that the instrumental placement is extremely accurate and that because of the rear-oriented part of the patterns, the entire stereo stage is bounded by a very even sense of ambience. In order to achieve this balance, the microphone-to-source distance has to be very precisely determined, and any inaccuracies in placement can cause a muddy shallow sound. Yet even when properly done, many engineers feel that these coincident arrays lack a sense of warmth and perspective that we normally perceive in a room. This may be due to the absence of time of arrival cues, that seem to be so important to our ear/brain combination. Because of this, several so-called near-coincident systems have evolved. They offer many of the same advantages that are found in coincident systems in terms of instrumental placement and mono compatibility, yet may exhibit a broader sense of space and warmth with the addition of lateral time difference cues.

ORTF System

A system that is very popular in Europe was originated by the French National Broadcasting System whose official name is "Office de Radiodiffusion-Television Francaise" or ORTF. The ORTF system is formed by spacing two cardioid microphones so that their diaphragms are 17 centimeters apart and with an angle of 110° between the forward facing patterns. This spacing and angle is similar to the way our ears are positioned on our head, yet does not resemble the earlier discussed binaural system because of the lack of a baffle between the microphones. It does, however, simulate our listening experience. At low frequencies its directional sense comes from intensity cues only (a long wavelength produces minimal phase differences between the two microphones since they are so close together), and at high frequencies time of incidence cues are included which add a greater sense of width and spaciousness to the sound. Where the patterns overlap (45°) each cardioid's output is attenuated by 3 dB. This, as in the Blumlein system gives a properly-balanced center signal. Many engineers feel that this system rivals the Blumlein array in instrumental placement accuracy, yet without being so dependent on the sonic characteristics of the recording space. The overall angle of pickup for the ORTF is 180°, and it seems to work very well relatively close to the ensemble, giving good presence without sacrificing width or depth.

NOS System

Another near-coincident system has been developed by the Dutch Broadcasting System (Nederlandsche Omroep Stichting). This system, which is called the NOS array, uses two cardioid microphones at an angle of 90° with a spacing of 30 centimeters between diaphragms. This is similar to the ORTF system, but shifts the range where low frequency phase differences become unimportant to a lower point in the frequency bandwidth. This adds even more of an apparent openness to the sound. The overall angle of coverage for the NOS system is 160°, and it therefore is very useful with smaller ensembles. Figure 4-10 illustrates these two near-coincident systems.

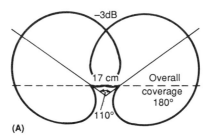

Figure 4-10. At (A) an ORTF array and at (B) an NOS array.

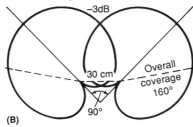

Stereo Techniques: Spaced Microphone Systems

Notice, from the differences between the ORTF and the NOS systems, that the further apart we move the microphones, the smaller the angle between them becomes in order to maintain the overlap at the minus 3 dB sensitivity point, and the narrower the overall angle of coverage becomes. As we reach a distance of 4 or 5 feet another problem occurs. Let us say that we have a pair of microphones spaced apart from each other at distance of 10 feet. When these outputs are transmitted through a pair of loud-speakers the left-originating signals will go exclusively to the left speaker, and the opposite will be true for the right. Because of level losses due to the inverse square law discussed in Chapter 2, no left component of any significance will appear in the right speaker. Only sounds that originate exactly in the center will appear in the center, and yet this material will be lower in level because of the aforementioned inverse square law. Any sound that is slightly off-center will have a tendency to "pull" to the extreme right or left. This creates a "hole in the middle" effect that can be very disconcerting. To solve this problem, a third microphone can be added with its output assigned to both left and right stereo channels. The level of this third microphone should be carefully monitored so that an even left to right distribution of sound is heard, with no microphone appearing louder than another.

With coincident or near-coincident systems, a directional polar pattern is essential for proper imaging. Obviously a pair of omni-directional microphones will create a monophonic reproduction since the outputs of both microphones will be indistinguishable from one another. However, a good choice for the spaced apart technique would be to use omni-directional microphones. This allows the microphones to be placed closer to the ensemble without sacrificing any of the room ambience, and also does away with most of the coloration created by the off-axis response of the cardioid patterns. This technique does not yield as accurate a monophonic sum as a coincident type system, but gives a large sense of space and good tonal accuracy which has been used successfully in many recordings.

Stereo Techniques: Additional Microphones

Since the practical limitations of the recording environment may not allow the engineer to achieve a satisfactory balance with just one coincident or near-coincident pair, additional microphones may be used to supplement the principle microphones or to accentuate one or more sections of the orchestra. However, they must be used very carefully so as not to detract from the stereo perspective produced by the main array. To get accurate coverage of a very wide stage where the engineer does not wish the microphone-to-source distance to be too great, a combination of coincident and spaced apart techniques is often useful. If a stereo microphone is giving good depth and placement but is losing the outside edges of the orchestra, a pair of flanking cardioids or omnis may solve the problem. Placing a microphone halfway between the center of the orchestra and both the extreme left and right edge effectively extends the width of the stereo microphone without overly affecting the imaging or placement.

Suppose that, even after adding these flanking microphones, the woodwind melodic lines are still being covered by other instruments. At this point, we have to begin adding accent microphones. Accent microphones are microphones or pairs of microphones that are placed on individuals or individual sections of the orchestra to make them more audible in the recording. It is important to note that they are used more to "point up" the sound of these instruments than for actual level. And since the extra microphones are somewhat closer to the instruments than the main stereo array, their output will reach the listener's ear some fraction of a second earlier, focusing his attention on it. To keep these accent microphones from thus deteriorating the overall pickup, their output will probably have to be kept quite low in level. Some electronic time delay may be added to these outputs to time their arrival with the central array. Figure 4-11 shows a symphonic orchestra set up for recording with a central array, a flanking pair and several types of accent microphones.

Figure 4-11. An orchestral recording setup with a central array, flanking and accent microphones.

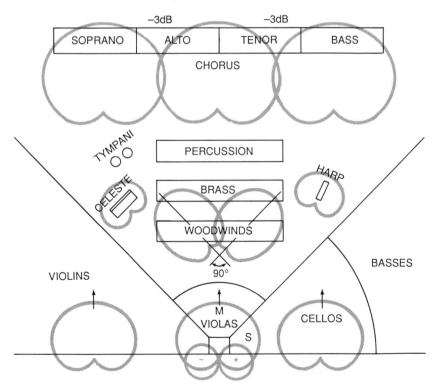

The advantage of the various stereo techniques just described is that the sound of the orchestra as an ensemble is well preserved. There is a good representation of depth, as well as left to right information. Within reason, low level instruments may be clearly heard and located within the ensemble, despite the presence of louder instruments in the same vicinity. The obvious limitation of this technique is that the engineer has only minimal control over the instrumental balance, and at a later date cannot effect major changes of individual parts without affecting the entire ensemble. In fact, with the advent of the digital recording process in the late 1970s, this essentially "direct-to-two channel" system for remote classical recordings, caused many recording engineers to have to relearn the stereo microphone techniques discussed above. Since, with the two channel digital system it was no longer possible to "fix it in the mix." It is, and has always been essential for the recording or balance engineer to fully understand the musical concepts of orchestral balance and timbre, so that he can fulfill his function to the satisfaction of the producer and ensemble conductor.

MULTI-MICROPHONE TECHNIQUES

Although the advantages of the various stereo microphone techniques should be clearly understood, the needs of the modern recording session may often preclude their successful applications. Due to budget considerations, it may be out of the question to hire an orchestra of sufficient size to be self-balancing, even with the help of a skillful conductor. Or, the musical arrangement may be such that an instrument, or instruments, will be heard out of proportion to its natural balance within the ensemble. Finally, as is found in the contemporary popular recording session, several musicians play many different parts a few at a time, and these parts may then need to be individually modified without affecting the sections recorded earlier. In many of these cases, stereo microphone techniques may not be able to do the job required, and the engineer must be prepared to mix and match these techniques with a multi-miking technique that may be more appropriate to the demands of the session.

The beginning engineer is always anxious to learn proper multi-microphone techniques, and it was not so long ago, that the student of recording could find little or nothing published concerning "correct" microphone placement. Many apprentice engineers have often insisted that the experienced engineer should be able to tell him or her which microphone is best for each instrument, and where that microphone should be placed. Today, many so-called microphone "cookbooks," which purport to give the beginner the perfect microphone placement for every instrument, have appeared. However, beyond a few simple rules, microphone technique is largely a matter of personal taste, and engineers rarely agree on anything that has to do with choice and placement of microphones. Microphone selection and placement is an art, and the engineer is the artist creating a sonic portrait with different texture techniques and color selections from the microphone palette. When asked, "How do you mic a piano," the experienced engineer will invariably ask, "What type of piano, what kind of space is it located in, who is playing it, and what are they playing." The range of choices are endless, yet to be commercially successful, there are certain parameters within which the engineer must work. Many of the rules and limitations of microphone placement and selection have been discussed earlier, and they are paraphrased here, along with a few new ones.

1. Always take off-axis coloration and proximity effect into consideration when selecting microphones.

2. Avoid overload, either with an attenuator in the microphone line, or in the case of a condenser microphone, by inserting a pad between the diaphragm and the microphone's own pre-amplifier, if this pre-amplifier is being overloaded.

3. Protect the microphone against wind and vibration noises.

4. Exercise caution when using acoustic baffles. Move the microphone when possible, rather than use a baffle.

5. Make sure all microphone lines are properly shielded, balanced and terminated correctly.

6. Be sure that there are no electrical phase reversals in the signal path.

7. Don't use two microphones when one microphone will do a better job.

8. Never use equalization as a substitute for poor microphone selection or placement.

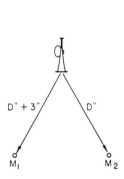

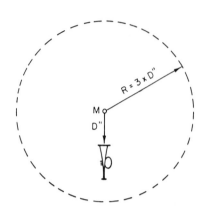

Figure 4-12A. When there is a slight path length difference, acoustic phase cancellations may be expected.

Figure 4-12B. To avoid phase cancellations, measure the distance between the instrument and the microphone. No other microphone should be within a radius of three times this distance.

Beyond these rather obvious precautions, microphone usage is largely a matter of personal choice, and the remainder of this chapter should in no way be considered as a "rule book" of microphone technique.

Multi-microphone Techniques: Avoiding Phase Cancellation

In Chapter 2, Figure 2-12 showed how two in-phase microphones could be positioned so that one was receiving a pressure maxima while the other received a pressure minima from the same musical instrument, and it was noted that when their outputs were combined these signals could cancel. Unless the instrument was perfectly centered and did not move, an unlikely event, some wavelengths would reach the microphones acoustically out of phase. And with each slight movement, a different set of

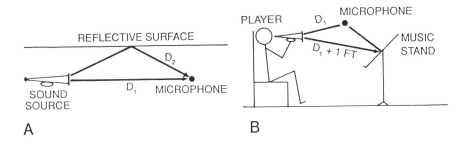

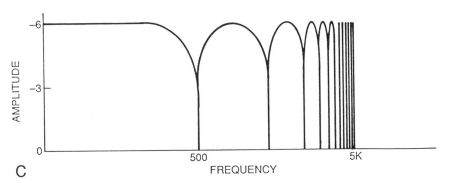

Figure 4-13. At (A) and (B) multiple sound pathways to a single microphone. At (C) frequency response caused by multiple path interference.

wavelengths, and therefore frequencies, would be affected as the relative path lengths between the instrument and each microphone fluctuated. Figure 4-12A illustrates the problem. A slightly off-center instrument creates a path length difference of three inches. The frequency with a half-wavelength of three inches (that is a wavelength, λ, of six inches) is:

$$F = \frac{V}{\lambda} = \frac{1130 \text{ ft/sec}}{0.5 \text{ ft/sec}} = 2260 \text{ cycles/sec (Hz)}$$

Therefore, this frequency would be prone to cancellation whenever the path length difference approached 3 inches. Although it is certainly impossible to completely eliminate all interaction between microphones, most phase cancellation problems can be

115

minimized by observing a 3 to 1 relationship. That is, if a microphone is 1 foot away from an instrument, no other microphone should be within three feet of this microphone, as shown in Figure 4-12B. Although small path length differences will still occur, the inverse square distance ratio is sufficiently large to minimize or eliminate any cancellations.

Another source of phase cancellation to be avoided is also caused by path length differences, but only to a single microphone. These differences occur between the direct signal reaching the microphone and a reflection of that signal from a nearby surface, a situation illustrated in Figure 4-13A. If this path difference is once again 3 inches, cancellation will occur at 2260 Hz as mentioned above. Reinforcements as well as cancellations occur, and continue to occur at multiples of the offending frequency. The amount of signal degradation will depend on the relative loudness of each signal, with the worst case being when the signals are nearly equal in level. This causes a phenomena called comb filtering—so called because the resultant reinforcements and cancellations create a frequency response curve that resembles a comb. A typical situation where this can be a problem would be an instrumentalist sitting above a highly reflective surface such as a hard wood floor, or a speaker giving an address in front of a podium. To illustrate, a trumpet player is sitting in a chair with a metal music stand in front of him as shown in Figure 4-13B. The microphone is placed in front of him and above the stand. If the path length difference between the direct sound of the trumpet and the reflected sound from the stand is 1 foot, there will be cancellation at 565 Hz, reinforcement at 1130 Hz, cancellation at 1685 Hz, etc., producing a frequency response curve similar to the one illustrated in Figure 4-13C, at the microphone output. This problem can be solved by always using a 2 to 1 relationship between the microphone and the reflecting surface. So that if a microphone is 1 foot away from an instrument, the microphone should also be at least 2 feet away from the nearest reflecting surface. If the reflecting surface, the instrumentalist, or the microphone cannot be moved, another possible solution is to cover the offending surface with a sound absorbent material.

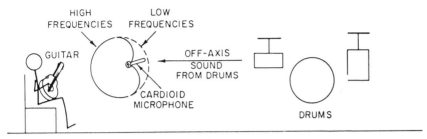

Figure 4-14. A cardioid microphone with poor off-axis response may pick up too much low-frequency off-axis sound.

Multi-Microphone Techniques: Minimizing Leakage

As mentioned earlier, leakage (unwanted sounds from other instruments in the room) may be minimized by close microphone positioning, or by interposing some acoustical barriers between the wanted and the unwanted sounds. However, these techniques must be applied with great care so that in the attempt for greater control, the overall sound quality does not deteriorate unnecessarily. Although the loss of some depth may be unavoidable when using a close placement technique, some of the other problems may be avoided through a better understanding of microphone usage and selection.

In an effort to provide greater electrical separation between instruments, the engineer's first impulse may be to use a cardioid microphone, reasoning that its comparative insensitivity to off-axis sounds may help keep leakage at a minimum. However, the off-axis response of the microphone itself must be taken into account. Cardioid microphones, it must be remembered, are not totally deaf to rear-oriented sounds. In fact, at 1000 Hz, most cardioid patterns are attenuated only 25 to 40 dB at 180°. A cardioid microphone with poor off-axis response may very well attenuate rear-originating high frequencies, yet that same microphone may function as an omni-directional microphone at low frequencies. As an obvious disadvantage of this off-axis microphone coloration, consider this. A cardioid microphone is aimed at an acoustic guitar, and pointed away from the drum set, as seen in Figure 4-14. The higher frequencies of the cymbals and snare drum may be significantly attenuated at the microphone, yet the lower frequencies of the toms and kick drums will still be heard. The resultant drum sound, as heard by all microphones, will con-

117

sequently be "bottom heavy," although the on-axis guitar itself may be entirely satisfactory. In fact, there may even be some multi-path phase distortion of the drum sound due to the leakage of the low frequencies into the guitar microphone. If there are many such microphones in use, each contributing some low frequency leakage, the cumulative effect may very well be an unpleasant muddy sound with a great sacrifice in overall clarity. In an effort to further minimize off-axis coloration, the microphone may be moved even closer to the guitar to keep the leakage to an absolute minimum. However, the poor off-axis response of some cardioid microphones is often accompanied by a pronounced proximity effect, which at very small working distances may cause an excessive bass rise in the sound of the instrument.

In many applications, these various restrictions may be effectively bypassed by using an omni-directional microphone. Free of proximity effects and most off-axis coloration, the microphone can be used very close to the sound source without excessive bass build up, and slight changes in working distances as the musician moves will not cause frequency response fluctuations. Here, it must be remembered, that the omni-directional pattern on many dual diaphragm microphones may retain the undesirable characteristics of the cardioid microphone if, as mentioned earlier, its omni characteristic is derived from two cardioid patterns. This does not rule out the use of cardioid patterns in the studio, however.

Many times the sound of a cardioid microphone is required to achieve the effect at hand, as well as the fact that many of today's high quality cardioid patterns are relatively free of excessive off-axis coloration and have a smooth proximity effect that may contribute substantially to the warmth of the sound. One of the benefits of the 3 to 1 rule for minimal phase cancellation between microphones is that when this rule is followed, there will usually be 9 dB of separation between the adjacent microphones. This may be enough to also minimize off-axis coloration from leakage in studio grade microphones.

It should also be kept in mind that the sides of a microphone with a figure-8 pattern are generally less sensitive than the rear of a cardioid pattern. Accordingly, it is often possible to obtain good separation by pointing the dead side of the figure-8 pattern towards the unwanted sound, as long as there are no undesirable sounds facing the rear lobe of the pattern.

Figure 4-15. An isolation booth at Alpha Audio, Richmond, Virginia (Alpha Audio photo).

It is important to remember that, when using single microphones to pick up an instrument, some of the depth and three-dimensional perspective of that instrument is often lost. This phenomena is most apparent when overdubbing a single instrument using only one microphone. It can be likened to listening to that instrument with one ear. Frequency, amplitude, timbre and all the other characteristics of the sound may be there, but the instrument may appear flat and two dimensional in character. It is often possible, and desirable to recall the coincident and near-coincident techniques discussed earlier. Using an X-Y pair of cardioid microphones on an acoustic guitar can produce a sense of depth and space for that instrument that no single microphone can match. Obviously, this is the case only when the two outputs are kept apart and stored on separate tracks of the multi-track recorder.

Acoustic Barriers

In a further attempt at minimizing leakage, various acoustic barriers are often set up between the microphone and the unwanted sounds. The most obvious and effective barrier is the isolation booth. This is usually a completely enclosed room (Figure 4-15) in which a musician, or small group of musicians, may

Figure 4-16A. A typical setup using gobos.

Figure 4-16B. The gobo may prevent off-axis sound from reaching the cardioid microphone's rear-entry ports.

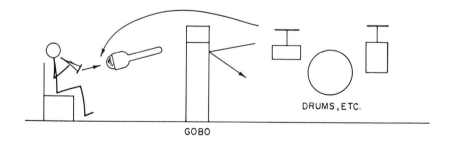

DRUMS, ETC.

GOBO

be placed. Although such a room may provide the required isolation from unwanted sounds, it may also be somewhat of an artistic compromise, since the musicians thus isolated will often find it difficult to perform in ensemble with the rest of the group, despite whatever sophisticated earphone monitoring system may be at hand.

Moveable acoustic barriers, popularly known as "gobos," a word of uncertain derivation, are frequently seen in use in modern recording studios. The idea is to establish greater acoustical isolation between instruments by arranging the gobos as required. The gobos may be easily moved to meet the needs of the particular recording session. However, they too should be used with discretion, since an improperly used gobo can do more harm than good. They are often used on the supposition that they will help keep unwanted sounds from reaching the microphone. The gobos are placed somewhere between a loud sound source and a microphone that is to be shielded from this sound, so that the microphone may better hear the specific instrument placed in front of it. A typical set up is shown in Figure 4-16A.

There are several reasons why this gobo may create more problems than it solves. First, if the microphone is a cardioid, its side and rear entry ports must not be obstructed if the microphone is to function as intended. Assuming that the gobo is a perfect sound absorber (which it isn't), it has effectively absorbed all the off-axis sounds which would have otherwise reached the ports, as illustrated in Figure 4-16B. Therefore, all sounds (including the unwanted ones) reach the microphone diaphragm by the front entrance only, thereby effectively creating an omni-directional pattern (and not a very good one at that). Secondly, the gobo is not a total absorber of all frequencies. Since it is often placed quite close to the microphone, its surfaces—although absorptive—will nonetheless reflect some frequencies back towards the microphone, while absorbing others. This cause of multi-path phase cancellation (similar to that mentioned earlier) can cause a deterioration of the overall sound that far out weighs whatever partial isolation has been accomplished. And lastly, the diffraction phenomenon discussed in Chapter 2 must be taken into account. As sound travels toward the gobo, low frequencies are diffracted around it, while high frequencies are either absorbed or reflected. Therefore, the microphone hears the diffracted low frequencies all

Figure 4-17. A contact microphone attached to a guitar (C-ducer photo).

too well, while the absence of high frequency components results in an unpleasantly muddy sound pickup.

Multi-Microphone Techniques: Special Purpose Microphones

The contact microphone responds to the mechanical vibrations of the musical instrument to which it is attached. Therefore, it hears little or nothing of the sounds of other instruments within the studio. Specific operating principles vary from one manufacturer to another. Some actually contain a very small electret microphone, while others work like an electric guitar pickup. A representative example is shown in Figure 4-17. This type of microphone is of course the ultimate extreme in close microphone placement, as it only hears the direct sound of one instrument. Although it offers the engineer maximum control, the sound may not be as "musical" as would be desired. We are accustomed to hearing at least some indirect sound along with any instrument that we hear, and the contact microphone's ultra-close perspective completely eliminates this component of the total sound. On the other hand, when isolation booths are either unavailable or undesired, the contact microphone may allow the engineer to pick up a quiet instrument in the midst of a loud ensemble.

A specialized microphone that has received considerable attention of late is the PZM or Pressure Zone Microphone. A small electret condenser element is located extremely close to (usually only a few hundredths of an inch) and facing a small (4 inch by 6 inch) boundary plate. The operational principal is that since the microphone is so close to a fixed and rigid plane, it can only sense changes in air pressure, as air particle velocity is zero next to a stiff boundary. Since all sound entering the microphone diaphragm is reflected from this closely spaced plate, there are no multiple path length differences to create phase cancellation or random incidence effects, and therefore off-axis coloration is nonexistent since all sound enters the diaphragm from similar angles. The microphone has a polar response that is hemispherical with respect to the boundary plate. The microphone itself is high impedance and must be used with its own power/impedance converter. A popular version of a PZM is pictured in Figure 4-18. One of the major problems with this system is that the low frequency response is limited by the size of the boundary plate, and in order for the PZM to cover the full audio spectrum, the plate must be relatively large. Mounting the PZM on a rigid wall or studio window has produced some good results, and engineers who use these microphones often construct elaborate plexi-glass arrays to record in symphonic concert halls or large studios.

Lavalier microphones are principally designed to be worn around the neck or attached to the clothing, and their frequency response is designed to be flat when the microphone is resting on the chest. They are used chiefly for sound reinforcement applications, but have occasionally been used to record an acoustic bass. The older type of microphone pictured in Figure 4-19A is usually wrapped in foam rubber and inserted in the "f hole" of an upright bass, while the newer style of clip-on lavalier (pictured in Figure 4-19B and seen on your nightly news program) is fastened

Figure 4-18. A PZM microphone (Crown photo).

to the bridge of the instrument. The rising frequency response of these microphones, which is designed to bring out the consonants in the human voice, can help bring out the articulation of the bass. However, most professional bass players who record on a regular basis have a contact microphone installed on their instrument. On the other hand, neither of these techniques will produce a sound that can equal a well-placed professional studio microphone.

MULTI-MICROPHONE TECHNIQUES: MIKING VARIOUS MUSICAL INSTRUMENTS

As previously mentioned, there is no one correct microphone or placement spot for recording any instrument. The reason one engineer's recording sounds different from another is that they each subscribe to a slightly different concept of microphone usage, and it is always open to discussion as to which is the better recording. However, there are certain problem instruments that should be mentioned.

The Electric Guitar

The electric guitar is by now such an integral part of the recording session that its use is almost taken for granted. The guitar amplifier is a fixture in most, if not all, modern studios. If we were to place a microphone on the guitar itself, as with an acoustic guitar, the results would not be very satisfactory since the sound of the electric guitar is produced by the combination of the

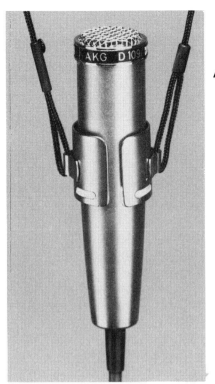

A

B

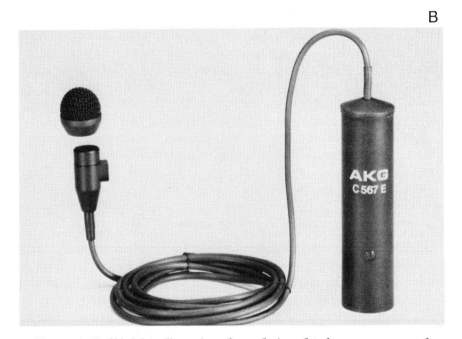

Figure 4-19. (A) A lavalier microphone designed to be worn on a cord around the neck (AKG photo), (B) a clip-on lavalier or lapel microphone.

strings, the pickup, and also the amplifier. A typical method for recording this instrument would be to place a microphone in front of the guitar amplifier loudspeaker. It is also possible to take the sound of the guitar "direct." This take-off point can be after the guitar but before the effects pedals, or after the pedals and before the amplifier, or even as a direct out from the pre-amplifier of the guitar amplifier itself. As always, there are advantages and disadvantages to this type of direct pickup. Since many guitar amplifiers are electronically noisy, the direct pickup gives the engineer a much cleaner signal with which to work. On the other hand, the guitar amplifier is usually considered an integral part of the electric guitar sound, and when it is bypassed it eliminates the characteristic sound of that particular guitar amplifier's loudspeaker. Figure 4-20 show the signal path from an electric guitar to a console and the possible direct points.

The output from the guitar itself is usually high impedance and can vary considerably in level between different types of pickups, and so a transformer or "direct box" is required to match the output to microphone level and impedance. For reasons cited earlier in Chapter 3, the guitar's high impedance output cannot be fed directly through a long cable to the console microphone preamplifier. If the guitarist wishes to hear himself in the studio from the amplifier, rather than from the headphone cue system, a split feed or "Y" connector can be used. Most direct boxes contain a loop-through to feed the guitar amplifier while providing a balanced low-impedance isolated output to the recording console. Direct boxes can be passive devices, and as such do cause some insertion loss, or active devices that can actually improve the signal to noise ratio of the guitar/amplifier interface. The active direct boxes usually require phantom power or batteries. Two typical direct boxes are pictured in Figure 4-21.

Electronic Keyboard Instruments

Many of today's bands use multiple electronic keyboards, and the transformers and direct boxes just described can be used with them as well. Many of these instruments have multiple, or stereo, outputs, so several boxes may be required. Some of the more sophisticated synthesizers also furnish balanced isolated microphone level or line level low impedance outputs that do not require transformers or direct boxes. Many of these electronic instruments may be connected together with MIDI (Musical

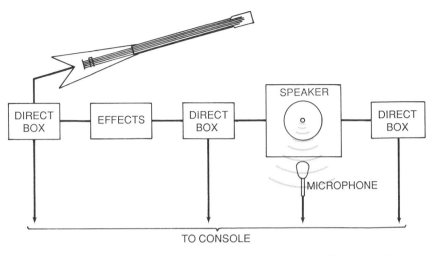

Figure 4-20. The signal path from guitar to recording console showing possible access or direct take-off points.

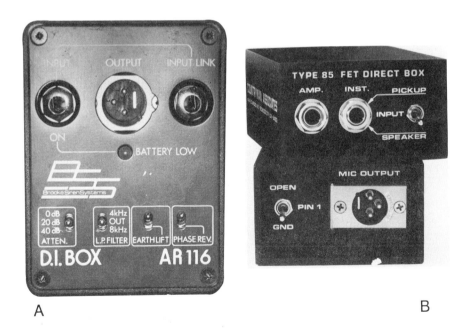

A

B

Figure 4-21. An active (A) Brooke Siren AR116) and a passive (B) direct box (Countryman DI, Countryman photo).

Instrument Digital Interface—a system that will be discussed in Chapter 19), and to prevent interference it is important to keep the MIDI control lines away from the low-level high-impedance signal outputs prior to converting them at the direct box.

The Acoustic Guitar

When an acoustic guitar is used as part of a rhythm section, a single microphone is usually placed fairly close, to keep the leakage at a minimum. Here, proper technique is mostly a matter of choosing the microphone that produces the most pleasing sound. Perhaps the greatest advantage is in the guitar player who understands enough of the nature of multi-track recording to make sure that he remains at a reasonable constant distance from the microphone.

However, when the guitarist is also the vocalist, correct microphone placement is not quite so straightforward. Of course, one way would be to record the guitar and the vocal on two separate passes of the multi-track tape recorder, but it is surprising how difficult this can be for a musician who usually performs both parts simultaneously. If the vocal and the guitar are miked separately, as is often done, some question arises as to how to satisfactorily balance the two microphone outputs. If one microphone is routed to the left and the other to the right, we have the unlikely situation of the musician singing and playing from opposite sides of the room. Yet if both microphones are center-placed, the monaural combination conveys little or no stereo perspective.

In many cases, a better recording could be made with a stereo microphone placed somewhere in front of the musician. Assuming the performer is capable of balancing his vocal and guitar performance, the stereo microphone will pick up a blend of the two, and at the same time convey the feeling that the recording is in fact in stereo. If balance is a problem, an accent microphone may be added to the guitar and panned to the center for the extra required amount of sound. Another possible solution is to use an X-Y or near- coincident pair of microphones for the guitar and a single microphone, sent to both channels, for the vocal.

The Drum Set

There is probably more discussion about how to mike "a drum kit," than for any other instrument except the piano. In fact, the drum set used for today's music can vary from the standard 5 piece kit with 3 cymbals to a giant 12-piece set with dual kick drums and many cymbals. A standard set includes a bass drum (commonly called the kick drum), a snare drum, 3 tom-toms with two mounted on the bass drum and one floor standing, a hi-hat cymbal set, which is two cymbals controlled by a foot pedal, and two other cymbals, usually a "crash" and a "ride."

The engineer will often use a number of microphones for the drum setup. Since each part of the drum set has its own distinctive "sound," the engineer may balance the overall sound to suit the needs of the session. A typical setup is shown in Figure 4-22. Two overhead microphones are used as an overall pickup, and there are additional microphones used on the kick drum, the snare drum, for the two top toms, for the floor tom, and for the hi-hat. And it is not at all uncommon to find additional microphones in use for the bottom of the snare drum, for roto-toms, extra cymbals, etc.

Transient percussive peaks, especially from the snare drum and cymbals, will surely be way above the apparent levels seen on the VU meters. If possible these instruments should be measured using meters that have PPM ballistic characteristics. This type of metering was discussed in Chapter 2. If this metering is not available, and until the engineer has some practical experience relating the VU levels to the peaks sent to the tape recorder, particular caution should be exercised to prevent overloading any component in the signal path. It is particularly likely that a condenser microphone placed close to the snare drum will require an attenuation pad between the microphone capsule diaphragm and the microphone's preamplifier.

Although the choice, and specific placement, of individual microphones will depend—as always—on personal taste, the engineer should keep in mind the consequences of the multi-microphone setup. To keep the individual drum sounds better isolated for maximum control, cardioid microphones are often used. These cardioid microphones should be chosen carefully, though, since the disadvantage of proximity effect and off-axis coloration may outweigh the directional sensitivity advantage of the microphone.

129

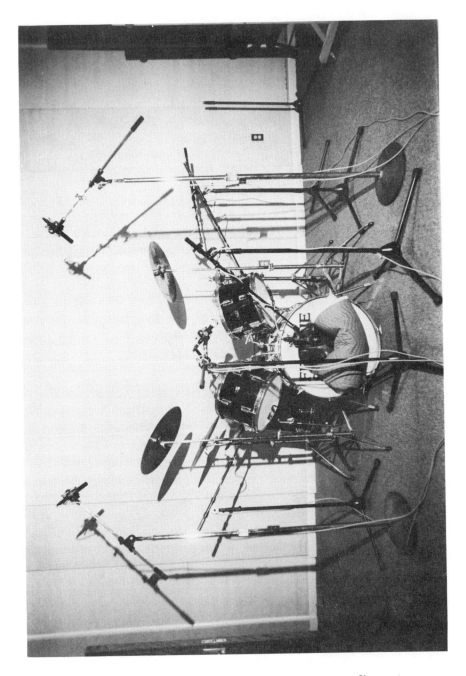

Figure 4-22. A typical multi-microphone drum recording setup.

When multi-microphones are used, there is often little physical clearance between the microphones and the various parts of the drum set. And of course, the microphones must be carefully placed where they will not accidentally be struck by the drummer as he moves from one part of the set to another. Several condenser microphone systems offer a series of extension tubes and swivels which can allow considerable flexibility in microphone placement when physical clearances are a problem. As the drummer moves around the set, there may be a lot of generated air noise, and in some cases it is advisable to place wind screens on some of the microphones—particularly the overheads.

The overall pickup can be a source of potential phase cancellation, particularly in the case of the cymbals, which move considerably each time they are struck. The movement creates continually changing path lengths to the two overhead microphones, and it may be a good idea to spend a little time listening to the mono mix over the monitor system, to make sure there are no serious cancellation problems. Often moving one microphone slightly will usually clear up the problem.

On many sessions, the front facing head of the bass drum is removed, and a blanket put inside the drum, sometimes touching the batter head. Although this certainly affects the tonality of the drum, it also produces a more percussive attack that many producers like. (A method of restoring the bass drum's tonality is discussed in Chapter 8.) The kick drum microphone may be placed inside the drum, and here the proximity effect may be used to advantage.

Electronic Drums

Many recordings today are made with synthesized or sampled drums. The sounds are produced by either striking tap keys or pseudo drums that contain a trigger which causes a pre-recorded or synthesized sound to be sent to the output of the drum machine. Some may be programmed to play a specific rhythm by themselves for a specified period of time, and most can be MIDI controlled. The drum synthesizer or sampler may have an output for each drum or a stereo mix of the entire kit or a combination of the two. Some give discrete outputs for each instrument with the exception of just a stereo output for the toms. These outputs may be high or low impedance and balanced or unbalanced depending on the manufacturer, and the engineer is reminded that transformers and direct boxes may be required. Most drummers who use synthesized or sampled drums still prefer the sound of acoustic cymbals, so the drum kit setup often contains a combination of electronic and acoustic instruments. It is sometimes problematic when the overhead microphones, so placed for the cymbals, also pick up the sound of the drum sticks hitting the trigger pads. Judicious use of the null point on a figure-8 microphone can get rid of these annoying sounds.

The Piano

To achieve adequate overall coverage of a grand piano, a coincident or near-coincident array would have to be placed several feet away, due to the instrument's size. Since this may present problems with leakage from other instruments, the engineer will often use two or more closely placed microphones instead in order to gain good coverage with maximum isolation. In such cases, there is inevitably some acoustic phase interaction between the microphones. As before, it is important to monitor the microphone outputs in mono prior to recording to make sure that there are no problems later on.

The open lid of the grand piano acts as a reflector for the sound produced inside the instrument and is an integral part of the piano sound, and yet it also reflects the sounds of other instruments in the nearby area. A microphone placed somewhere between the strings and the lid will pick up both wanted and

Figure 4-23. A microphone placed as shown may pick up the reflections of other instruments from the piano lid.

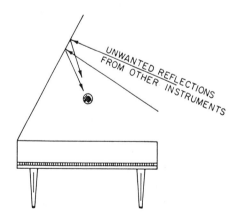

unwanted reflections from the lid, as seen in Figure 4-23, and care must be taken to prevent these other reflections from interfering with the overall sound.

The engineer should bear in mind that most of the piano sound comes from the sounding board, and that there is little point in aiming the microphone(s) at the hammers, as is so often seen. In fact, one of the most resonance areas of the piano is more toward the foot where the treble strings cross the bass strings.

Solo piano recordings are best made using the coincident techniques described in Chapter 3.

Strings, Brass and Woodwinds

The close-up perspective that so often works well on rhythm instruments (guitars, keyboards, drums, percussion and bass) is much less effective on strings, brass and woodwinds. In most cases, these instruments should sound as if they were spread over a reasonably large area. Pin-point localization of individual instruments is usually undesirable, unless required in a strictly solo sense. Keeping the microphones at some distance will create a much better illusion of listening to an ensemble, rather than to a collection of isolated point source sounds. Normally, these types of instruments are recorded as a group, but at a different time than the rhythm instruments, so leakage is not a problem.

CHAPTER 5

LOUDSPEAKERS

In evaluating a microphone, the environment in which it is placed may often be ignored, as ultra-close miking reduces the contribution of the room's acoustics to a negligible factor. On the other hand, the effect of the listening room on the loudspeaker must never be ignored, since it has a great influence on what the listener hears. But before describing the room/speaker interface, some background information on loudspeaker theory and application is required.

Schematically, the microphone and the loudspeaker bear a striking resemblance in operating principle if not in outward appearance. In both, the diaphragm is the center of the transducing system. In the microphone, its motion converts acoustic energy into electrical energy. The loudspeaker diaphragm reverses the process; electrical energy is converted back into acoustic energy.

A typical moving-coil loudspeaker is shown in Figure 5-1. When an alternating current signal is applied to the voice coil,

Figure 5-1. Cutaway view of a moving-coil loudspeaker (JBL LE ST, JBL photo).

the diaphragm moves back and forth, displacing the surrounding air molecules and creating a sound wave which eventually reaches the listener. Due to its structural reliability, the moving-coil system is the basis of practically all studio monitor systems.

SOME LOUDSPEAKER TERMINOLOGY

Later in the chapter, terms such as compliance, resonance, efficiency, etc. are introduced. These terms—as they apply to the loudspeaker—are briefly described below.

Resonance

The fundamental frequency at which a tuning fork or taut string vibrates may be called its resonant frequency. Although the device may actually be vibrating at many frequencies, at the frequency of resonance the opposition of the surrounding air is at a minimum. This frequency is a function of the device's mass and stiffness. All vibrating devices have a resonant frequency, and the loudspeaker is no exception. Depending on the mass and stiffness of the speaker cone and diaphragm/voice coil assembly, this frequency will vary. Generally, the larger the speaker diameter, the lower will be the resonant frequency.

Transient Response and Damping

Just as a tuning fork continues to vibrate long after it is struck, a speaker diaphragm does not instantly cease its motion the moment the applied signal is withdrawn. Accordingly, its transient response, which is its ability to follow precisely the more percussive waveforms, may suffer. This occurs especially at or near the speaker's resonant frequency. To improve transient response, some form of acoustical, mechanical, or electrical resistance may be applied to the moving system. This opposition, or damping, helps to keep the speaker movement directly related to the applied signal, and in the absence of that signal, the speaker diaphragm is brought to an almost instantaneous halt.

Compliance

Compliance, expressed in Newtons per meter (abbreviated N/m), is the ease with which a speaker diaphragm moves. It is measured by dividing the diaphragm displacement by the applied magnetic force. A highly damped speaker will have little compliance, since the diaphragm movement per unit of applied force will be quite small. Without damping, compliance will reach a maximum at the speaker's resonant frequency. As damping is increased, compliance is reduced, and as a result, the resonant frequency of the speaker is likewise raised.

Efficiency

As in other physical systems, speaker efficiency is a ratio of power output to power input. In this case, the input power is electrical, while the output power is acoustical. A speaker's efficiency is usually defined as a specific output (in dB), measured at a distance of one meter and derived from an input of one watt.

THE IDEAL SOUND SOURCE

In the study of acoustics, reference is often made to an ideal sound source. This is usually considered to be a point source of sound, suspended in free space. It is described as a pulsating sphere of infinitely small dimension. As the sphere releases energy, sound waves radiate away from it in all directions. This is often referred to as radiation into full space (or free space), described in mathematical terms as a radiation angle of 4π steradians. If the point source is considered to be at the center of another larger sphere, the measured sound level will be the same at all points on the sphere's circumference, as illustrated in Figure 5-2.

The Effect of Room Surfaces on the Ideal Sound Source

If our ideal sound source is now moved against a wall, as shown in Figure 5-2B, the radiation sphere will be bisected by the wall. Assuming this to be a solid, the total sound energy from the point source will now be forced to radiate into half-space only, or 2π steradians. Therefore, at any point on the hemisphere, the measured sound level will be 6 dB greater than if the measurement was made in full space. (Intensity is analogous to voltage, and therefore its decibel value increases by 6 dB when it is doubled). If the point source is now moved into a corner, the intersection of the two walls will cut the radiation angle in half again, and the intensity rises another 6 dB, as shown in Figure 5-2C. Finally, if the point source is placed at floor or ceiling-level,

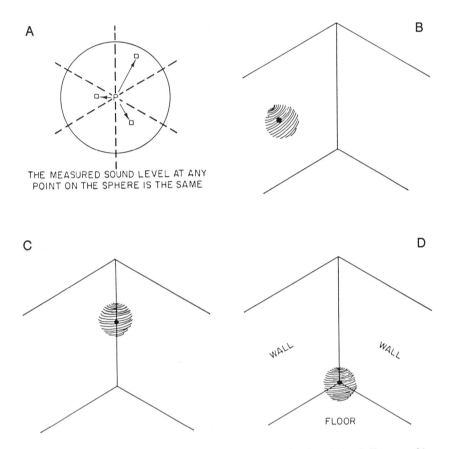

Figure 5-2. At (A) An ideal sound source, radiating into full space (4π steradians), at (B) when the point source is placed against a wall, the total energy radiates into half space (2π steradians), at (C) the point source is at the intersection of two surfaces, the total energy radiates into quarter space (π steradians), and at (D) the point source is placed against the intersection of three surfaces, so the total energy radiates into ⅛ space (π/2 steradians).

the intersection of the three surfaces will again halve the radiation angle, and the intensity will rise once more by 6 dB, as in Figure 5-2D.

Loudspeaker Radiation, or Polar Patterns

Polar patterns may be drawn for each of the theoretically ideal conditions just described. Although similar in principle to the microphone polar pattern, the loudspeaker pattern is an indication of the intensity radiated from the sound source into the surrounding space. The patterns are shown in Figure 5-3, and the room surfaces that have influenced the radiation are indicated in the illustration. Since both vertical (walls) and horizontal (ceiling or floor) surfaces may affect the radiation angle, patterns are often given in both the horizontal and vertical planes, as seen in the figure.

PRACTICAL LOUDSPEAKERS

As with other theoretically ideal systems, the point source of sound does not exist in reality. Practical loudspeakers may be considered to be spherical radiators. For example, if we draw a speaker diaphragm schematically, as in Figure 5-4, we can anticipate that it may radiate into the angle shown, rather than into full space. For one thing, the speaker housing gets in its own way, just as the body of a flashlight prevents its light from radiating backwards.

Diffraction

It will be found that a speaker's radiation angle varies considerably with frequency, for once again the diffraction phenomenon described in Chapter 2 must be considered. The size of the speaker itself becomes an obstacle to small wavelengths (high frequencies), tending to focus them into an narrow radiation angle. On the other hand, long wavelengths (low frequencies) are readily diffracted around the speaker assembly. Therefore, the radiation pattern of a practical loudspeaker suspended in free space may be as shown in Figure 5-5. Note that low frequencies are radiated over a wide angle, while higher frequencies are focused into a progressively narrower beam of sound. Provided the listener is directly in front of the speaker, the frequency response is flat, as seen in the illustration. But, as with many microphones, off-axis response may be quite distorted, or colored.

The Effect of Room Surfaces on the Practical Loudspeaker

From our brief study of the ideal sound source, it will be realized that speaker placement within the room will severely affect performance. For example, if the loudspeaker represented in Figure 5-5 is placed against a wall, this surface will reflect whatever

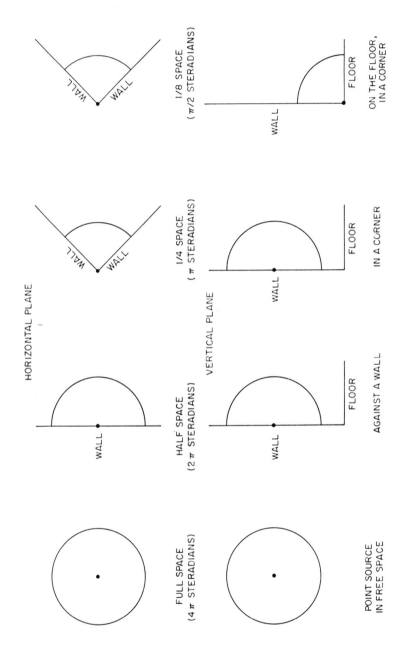

Figure 5-3. Polar patterns for speaker placements in differing positions.

Figure 5-4. The radiation angle of a practical loudspeaker.

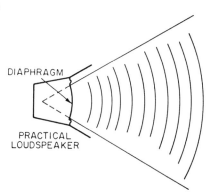

DIAPHRAGM

PRACTICAL
LOUDSPEAKER

rear energy there is back toward the front. Since this rear energy is predominantly longer wavelengths (due to diffraction), the apparent on-axis low-frequency response will rise, while the high-frequency response remains unaffected. And if the speaker is moved into a corner, or to the floor or ceiling, the low-frequency response will rise even more. When the speaker is placed at the intersection of three room surfaces, the low-frequency response will be boosted to a maximum. Figure 5-6 illustrates the effect that the room exerts on the speaker for each of these conditions.

THE DIRECT RADIATOR
Speaker Enclosure Systems

Just as the walls, ceiling and floor influence the loudspeaker's performance, so does the cabinet in which it may be enclosed. Speaker enclosures may be classified as direct or indirect radia-

Figure 5-5. Radiation pattern of a practical loudspeaker showing the effects of diffraction.

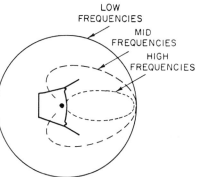

LOW
FREQUENCIES

MID
FREQUENCIES

HIGH
FREQUENCIES

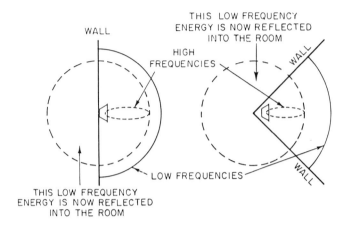

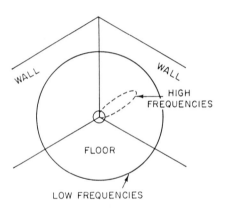

Figure 5-6. Each additional room surface reflects more of the refracted low frequency energy into the room. The more directional high frequencies may not be affected by the room surfaces.

tors, and examples of both types are described here. As its name implies, the direct radiator system is designed so that the speaker radiates directly into the listening room.

The Infinite Baffle

As shown in Figure 5-7, the infinite baffle is the simplest form of direct radiator, consisting simply of a hole cut in a wall. Assuming that the other room surfaces are sufficiently distant, the speaker's full space radiation pattern is minimally affected, since the speaker is free to radiate pretty much as it would in free space. Of course, the energy that is dissipated in the rear is

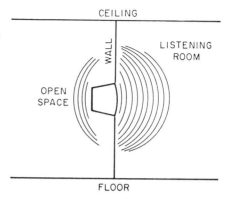

Figure 5-7. The infinite baffle. The speaker's full space radiation pattern is minimally affected by the wall.

wasted, from the point of view of the listening room, and the infinite baffle also makes the impractical assumption that a large space behind the speaker wall is readily available.

The Open Baffle

The open baffle system is likewise impractical, but should be discussed at some length since it forms the beginning of the practical speaker enclosure. To understand its purpose, consider an unmounted loudspeaker, as shown in Figure 5-8. As the diaphragm moves forward, the air molecules directly in front of it are compressed, while at the same time there is a rarefaction immediately behind the diaphragm. As the diaphragm moves back and forth, sound waves should be radiated away from the speaker, as indeed is the case with high-frequency sounds. However, when the diaphragm is moving relatively slowly (low

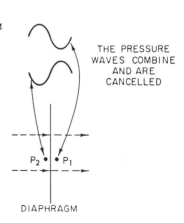

Figure 5-8. An unmounted speaker. As the diaphragm moves forward, a long wavelength forward pressure wave P_1, may be cancelled by a combining with the rear wave P_2.

143

frequencies), the sound pressure wave on one side of the diaphragm may simply cancel with that on the other, as seen in the figure.

To prevent this type of low-frequency cancellation, the speaker may be mounted in an open baffle, as shown in Figure 5-9A. Now, sound waves from the rear must travel around the baffle before they are combined with those from the front. It has been found that the longer the baffle length, the lower will be the frequency at which cancellations begin. The baffle length should equal one quarter the wavelength of the lowest frequency that is desired to reproduce without cancellation. As seen in Figure 5-9A, a frequency whose wavelength equals four times the baffle length

Figure 5-9. Frequency response of an open baffle system.

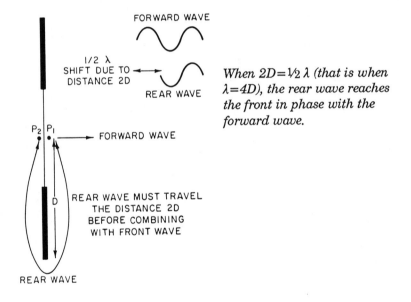

FORWARD WAVE

1/2 λ
SHIFT DUE TO
DISTANCE 2D

REAR WAVE

When 2D=½ λ (that is when λ=4D), the rear wave reaches the front in phase with the forward wave.

P₂ P₁

FORWARD WAVE

D

REAR WAVE MUST TRAVEL
THE DISTANCE 2D
BEFORE COMBINING
WITH FRONT WAVE

REAR WAVE

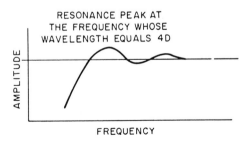

RESONANCE PEAK AT
THE FREQUENCY WHOSE
WAVELENGTH EQUALS 4D

AMPLITUDE

FREQUENCY

(λ = 4D) will now arrive at the front of the speaker in phase with the forward wave, producing a maximum reinforcement.

Longer wavelength signals will be progressively attenuated, due to both phase cancellations and the speaker's own inherent low-frequency limit. Frequencies whose wavelengths are somewhat shorter than 4D will also tend to be attenuated somewhat, although as the wavelength decreases, the rear wave has less and less of an effect due to the diminishing radiation angle described earlier.

The frequency response (or rather, wavelength response) of the open baffle system will appear as shown in Figure 5-9B. Note that there is a peak at the frequency where λ = 4D, for it is at this point that the rear and front waves add to produce a maximum sound pressure level, or resonance peak. Another disadvantage of the open baffle is the dimension required for good low-frequency response. A little arithmetic will reveal that the quarter wavelength of 50 Hz is about 5.5 feet. Therefore, an open baffle tuned to this resonant frequency must be 11 feet in diameter, that is, 5.5 feet in radius from the speaker cut-out—hardly a practical dimension!

The Folded Baffle

The folded baffle seen in Figure 5-10 offers some relief in size over the open baffle system. By folding the baffle as shown, it is possible to achieve a smaller enclosure without raising the resonant frequency described earlier. However, when the sides take on any appreciable dimension, the speaker cabinet acquires the acoustic properties of an open column of air. That is, it produces

Figure 5-10. The folded baffle. Acoustically, the enclosure resembles an open pipe and may resonate at $\lambda=4L$.

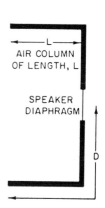

Figure 5-11. The sealed enclosure, or acoustic-suspension system.

THE ENCLOSED VOLUME OF AIR DAMPS THE SPEAKER MOVEMENT

SPEAKER DIAPHRAGM

a resonance at the frequency whose wavelength equals four times the length of the column created by the baffle sides. Therefore, if the baffle sides are 1 foot long, the enclosed air column will resonate at 275 Hz, while the baffle itself will continue to resonate at $\lambda = 4D$, as described earlier.

Figure 5-12. An acoustic-suspension system. The woofer's free space resonance is 18 Hz, while the system resonance frequency is 42 Hz.

The Sealed Enclosure, or Acoustic Suspension System

The sealed enclosure, shown in Figure 5-11, eliminates the acoustic resonance peaks of the open and folded baffle systems. This elimination occurs since it is impossible for rear waves to reach the front of the speaker. In addition, the enclosed volume of air acts as an acoustic resistance (damping) against the rear of the speaker cone, thus lowering the system's compliance. As the compliance is reduced, the speaker's resonant frequency is raised as was noted earlier. Depending on the design parameters, the resonant frequency of the speaker/enclosure system may be an octave or more above the resonant frequency of the speaker itself in free space.

Since in the sealed enclosure the speaker is, in effect, resting on the enclosed air column, it is often referred to as an acoustic suspension system. A representative example is shown in Figure 5-12. The sealed enclosure may also be called an infinite baffle, since, like the true infinite baffle described earlier, the system prevents rear waves from reaching the front of the speaker. However, the true infinite baffle has an unlimited air space behind it, while the sealed enclosure does not.

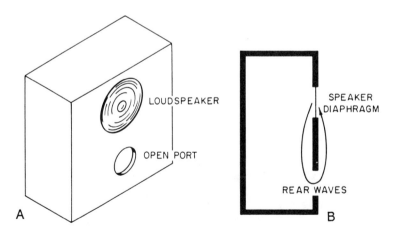

Figure 5-13. (A) the open port allows rear waves to reach the front of the system, (B) rear waves reach the front.

The Vented, or Bass Reflex, Enclosure

One limitation of the acoustic suspension system is that the rear waves are trapped within the enclosure. Consequently, the speaker's efficiency rating is reduced since this portion of the total output power is lost. The vented enclosure, shown in Figure 5-13A, allows the rear waves to reach the front, thus improving the system's efficiency.

The Tuned Port

The volume of air within an enclosure has a certain compliance. That is, it acts as an acoustic capacitance, affecting the system's resonant frequency as was discussed earlier. If a port is cut into the enclosure, the opening allows sound waves to escape. However, the port has a certain acoustic inductance, analogous to inductance in an electrical circuit. The system becomes, in effect, a capacitance (the enclosure) in parallel with an inductance (the port). The dimensions of both may be designed to create an acoustic resonance at a specified frequency. It has been found that if this frequency is the same as the speaker's own resonant frequency, the system resonance will drop in amplitude. In fact, it will exhibit two resonance points. One above and the other below the original speaker resonant frequency. As a result, the usable low-frequency response of the system is extended downward. However, due to open baffle-type cancellation effects, the low-frequency attenuation below resonance will probably fall off at a sharper rate than in the sealed enclosure system.

Figure 5-14. A vented enclosure system. (JBL 4412, JBL photo).

In the open baffle systems described earlier, baffle dimensions had to be quite large to keep phase cancellations at as low a frequency as possible. In the vented system, the acoustic phase shift of the enclosure and port accomplishes the same thing, and low frequencies (above resonance) emerge from the port in phase with the front of the speaker, as is illustrated in Figure 5-13B. An example of a vented enclosure system is seen in Figure 5-14. This type of enclosure is also often referred to as a Phase-Inversion Enclosure.

Vented Enclosure with Passive Radiator

As sound waves travel through the open port just described, a certain amount of acoustic friction acts against the air particles. The friction is greatest at the edge of the opening, diminishing toward the center. To make the movement of the air particles more uniform across the entire opening, a passive radiator may be placed in the port. Sometimes called a slave or drone cone, the passive radiator may be nothing more than a non-powered speaker assembly. The air pressure against the back of the passive radiator forces it to move in and out. In the front, a sound wave is radiated that is more uniform than one from a simple open port. Figure 5-15 shows a vented enclosure system using a passive radiator.

Summary Of Direct Radiators

A direct radiator is a speaker that is coupled directly to the air in front of it. Although at each stage in the development from infinite baffle to vented enclosure with passive radiator, the efficiency of the acoustic coupling of diaphragm-to-air increased, the direct radiator still remains a relatively inefficient system. The poor efficiency is a function of the high mechanical impedance of the speaker diaphragm attempting to transfer energy to the low acoustic impedance of the surrounding air.

In an electrical circuit, when maximum power transfer is required, an impedance-matching transformer may be used between any two stages where there is a significant impedance mismatch. For example, without such a transformer, a high-impedance microphone will function with minimum efficiency when connected to a low-impedance microphone pre-amplifier.

Speakers

Figure 5—15. A vented enclosure with a passive radiator (Electro-Voice photo).

Passive Radiator

In a direct radiator speaker system, the diaphragm-to-air coupling is pretty much a "brute force" method. A high electrical input power applied to the speaker terminals produces a low acoustical output power in front of the diaphragm. Even a so-called high efficiency direct radiator system may have an efficiency of not much more than 5 percent.

HORN-LOADED SYSTEMS

In an indirect radiator, the speaker diaphragm is coupled to the surrounding air by a device that functions as an acoustic transformer. The horn system shown in Figure 5-16 is a well-known example of this type of indirect radiator. Note that the speaker diaphragm with a horn in front of it is no longer able to radiate into a large air mass. The throat of the horn is considerably smaller than the diaphragm diameter, and like the action of water

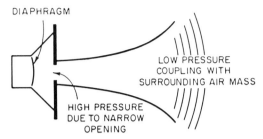

Figure 5-16A. The horn acts as an acoustic impedance-matching transformer.

Figure 5-16B. A representative horn design (JBL photo).

being forced into a narrower diameter pipe, there is a resultant high pressure area developed at the beginning of the throat. This high acoustic impedance is closer to the mechanical impedance of the speaker, resulting in a more efficient transfer of power.

As the sound wave travels the length of the horn, its gradually flaring shape disperses the sound pressure over a progressively larger cross-sectional area. Eventually, the sound wave reaches the open air, by which time its pressure has been reduced substantially. The original high pressure/high impedance sound wave has become a low pressure/low impedance wave front. The transformer action of the horn results in a more efficient coupling with the surrounding air. As a result, the sound level will be considerably higher than with a direct radiator system. This type of indirect radiator is often referred to as a horn-loaded system.

Radiation Characteristics of Horn-Loaded Systems

Although the horn-loaded indirect radiator system has a higher efficiency than a direct radiator, its radiation pattern tends to narrow appreciably at high frequencies, as the neck and inner surfaces of the horn focus the high frequencies into a narrow beam, as shown in Figure 5-17.

In an effort to widen the radiation pattern, multi-cellular horns of the type seen in Figure 5-18 have been developed. The multi-

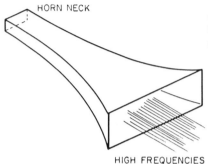

Figure 5-17. The tapered horn tends to narrow the radiation angle of high frequencies.

cell construction distributes the sound wave among two or more horn sections, resulting in a wider radiation pattern in both the horizontal and vertical planes. The horizontal radiation angle is usually wider than the vertical angle, but this is usually not a significant drawback since a wide vertical angle is probably not required in the majority of applications. Typical radiation angles for a multi-cellular horn are on the order of 90 to 120 degrees in the horizontal plane and 30 to 40 degrees in the vertical one.

The acoustic lens was designed to provide a wider radiation angle for high frequencies, especially in the horizontal plane. Based on optical principles, the lens bends the sound "rays" pass-

Figure 5-18. A multi-cellular horn (Community Light & Sound photo).

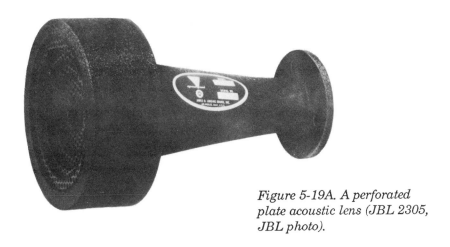

Figure 5-19A. A perforated plate acoustic lens (JBL 2305, JBL photo).

Figure 5-19B. A slanted plate acoustic lens (JBL HL 91, JBL photo).

ing through it, dispersing them over a greater area. Figure 5-19 shows examples of the acoustic lens.

Recent developments in horn-loaded indirect radiators have produced a new horn design called the Bi-Radial horn. This horn provides constant coverage with respect to frequency from a crossover point of about 1000 Hz to beyond 16 kHz. The horn provides a 100 degree by 100 degree vertical/horizontal coverage pattern. This radiation pattern is more closely related to that of a direct radiator mounted in a proper enclosure, and as such can provide a two-way, horn-loaded system with relatively wide coverage angles in all planes.

Folded Horns

A straight horn designed for low-frequency operation would be quite long, and physically impractical. However, the horn may be folded as shown in Figure 5-20 to fit within a physically manageable area. The long wavelength efficiency of such a design is excellent, since the diffraction phenomenon allows low frequencies to readily pass through this acoustic labyrinth. However, high-frequency output will be very inefficient, and a separate high-frequency system will be required. The speaker system shown in Figure 5-21 is a combination of a low-frequency folded horn and straight horns for mid-and high frequencies.

The Compression Driver

The compression driver is a special-purpose transducer designed to be used in mid- and high-frequency horn systems. The

Figure 5-20. Cutaway view of a folded-horn system.

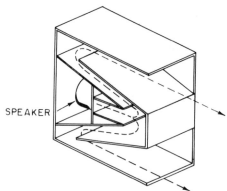

SPEAKER

Figure 5-21. A speaker using the folded-horn principle (Electro-Voice Sentry IV, E-V photo).

Middle and high frequency straight horns

Low frequency folded horn system

unit shown in Figure 5-22 has a 4-inch diameter aluminum voice coil/diaphragm and a 2-inch diameter throat. The relatively small diaphragm has a high resonant frequency and is generally more efficient in horn-loaded applications than a massive speaker cone assembly. The comparatively narrow throat diameter is designed for maximum efficiency coupling with the horn assembly.

MULTI-SPEAKER SYSTEMS

Like most musical instruments, a given loudspeaker may be most efficient over a portion of the audio bandwidth. For example, a family of stringed instruments ranging in size from the physically small violin to the oversized double bass is required to cover the entire musical spectrum. Likewise, a small high-frequency speaker may be incapable of reproducing low frequen-

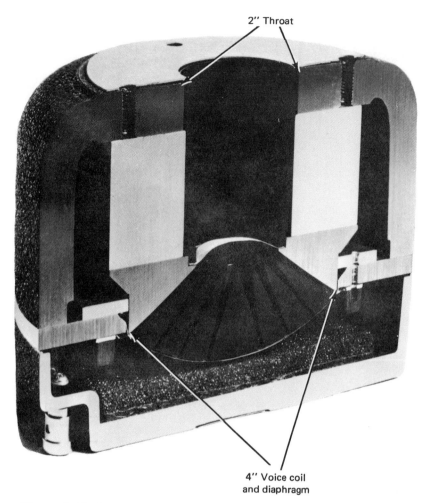

2″ Throat

4″ Voice coil
and diaphragm

Figure 5-22. Cutaway view of a compression driver (JBL 2440, JBL photo).

cies, and vice versa. Accordingly, many studio speaker systems employ two or more speakers, each optimized for a specific segment of the audio bandwidth. In its simplest form, a wide-range system may comprise a high-frequency tweeter and a low-frequency woofer. (The terms describe accurately, if irreverently, the sound output of the two speakers.) These systems may or may not combine direct and indirect radiators.

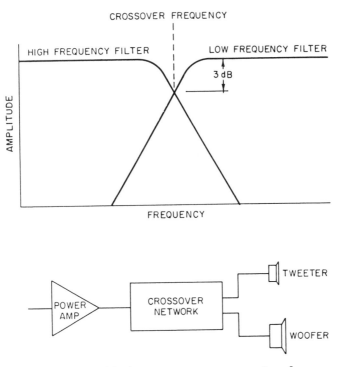

Figure 5-23. A two-way crossover network.

Crossover Networks

In most cases, a crossover network is used with a multi-speaker system. In a two-way system, as shown in Figure 5-23, the crossover uses high-pass and low-pass filters to route the signal to the proper radiator, where in a three-way system, a band-pass filter is added for the mid-range. The network passes only the appropriate frequency band to each speaker, while suppressing frequencies outside the band. Thus, no speaker receives unusable power from a signal outside its own pass-band. In addition, the tweeter, and mid-range if applicable, is protected against overload from high-level, low-frequency signal components.

Crossover Phase Distortion

In Figure 5-23, note that there is some overlap in the frequency pass-bands, and that the output from both speakers is down 3 dB at the crossover frequency. Therefore, both speakers deliver the same amount of power at the crossover frequency flattening out the response over the crossover ranges. This assumes, however, that the speakers are in phase at the crossover frequency when in fact this is most often not the case. Each filter introduces a phase shift as it attenuates frequencies outside its bandwidth. In one typical situation, each filter shifts the output signal by 90 degrees at the crossover frequency. However, the phase shifts are in opposite directions, giving a net phase shift of 180 degrees between speakers at the crossover frequency. Therefore, there will be a severe acoustic phase cancellation in this region unless one of the speakers is electrically reversed in phase. This reversal puts the speakers back in phase at the crossover frequency, and out-of-phase within their pass bands. However, since the speakers are only reproducing the same signal in the vicinity of crossover, there will be little cancellation over the rest of the audio bandwidth. Of course, if the phase shift at the crossover frequency is not exactly ±90° degrees, the wiring reversal will be ineffective.

Acoustic Phase Shift in Multi-Speaker Systems

The acoustic center of a loudspeaker is the point at which sound waves appear to originate. Especially in horn-loaded systems, the acoustic center may be somewhat removed from the actual center line of the diaphragm at rest. When more than one speaker is to be used in an enclosure, it is important that their acoustic centers all lie in the same vertical plane, to prevent acoustic phase cancellations in the vicinity of the crossover frequency. These cancellations cause poor imaging and increase listener fatigue, and is often called "time smear." If the electrical phase shift at the crossover frequency cannot be corrected by the wiring reversal described above, one of the speakers may be moved slightly so that its acoustical center is shifted by the distance required to cancel out the crossover network's electrical phase shift. Another method called Time-Align™ electrically adjusts the crossover to compensate for phase cancellations caused by speaker displacement. Studies by Blauert and Laws have determined the minimum amount of acceptable time delay discrepancies, and most manufacturers today strive to keep their systems below these limits.

The Coaxial Speaker

Many loudspeaker systems are of the two- or three-way variety and, by eliminating time smear, excellent results are achieved. However, as mentioned earlier in this chapter, the ideal sound source is a single point in space radiating equally in all directions. Obviously, no loudspeaker system can truly be a single point radiator, but by mounting two radiators together on the same speaker frame, this ideal is approached. This loudspeaker, called a coaxial loudspeaker, uses two concentric radiators—one mounted inside the other—to cover the audio spectrum. The system may use two direct radiators—one for the treble range and one for the bass, or may contain a direct radiator for the low frequencies and an indirect radiator or horn-loaded system for the highs. The system can be mounted in any of the previously described enclosures, and may or may not use a passive radiator depending on the in-

Figure 5-24. A coaxial loudspeaker with an indirect radiator for the highs (UREI 811C, JBL photo).

dividual manufacturer's design. A typical coaxial loudspeaker is shown in Figure 5-24.

Multi-Speaker and Coaxial System Characteristics

Excellent results can be obtained from both multi-driver speaker systems and from coaxial speaker systems. However, both systems have advantages and drawbacks. In coaxial systems the high frequencies and the low frequencies radiate from the same physical area and they have a tendency to interfere with each other. This is called IM or intermodulation distortion. On the other hand, the coaxial system maintains the best imaging since the entire audio spectrum is radiating from the same point. Even though a multi-driver system is phase aligned, the distance-to-listener relationship between the speakers shifts with the vertical movement of the listener. Another consideration is the overall dispersion angle of the system. Because most coaxial speakers use a small compression driver and horn for the upper frequencies, the overall coverage angle of the system is relatively narrow. This is particularly true in the vertical angle, so placement of most coaxial systems must be very precise.

It can be said that while coaxial speakers exhibit higher intermodulation distortion and the lowest dispersion angles, these systems have the best imaging. And although imaging in multi-speaker systems may leave something to be desired, intermodulation distortion and placement latitude are substantially better.

Figure 5-25. A bi-amplification system. The crossover network is placed ahead of the amplification.

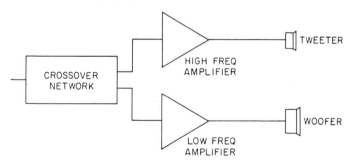

Bi-Amplification

In a bi-amplification system, the tweeter and the woofer are driven by separate amplifiers, with the crossover network placed before the amplification, as shown in Figure 5-25. When a single amplifier drives a passive crossover network, the network itself must be capable of sustaining the full power output of the amplifier. In addition, harmonic distortion components of the low-frequency output may be delivered to, and reproduced in, the high-frequency output section.

On the other hand, an active crossover network placed ahead of the amplification completely isolates low- and high-frequency components. Distortion in one range will not be transmitted to the other. And, since woofers characteristically require more power than tweeters, a lower power amplifier may be used in the high-frequency leg of the system. In fact, a well designed bi-amplified system will require less total power than the same speaker system driven by a single amplifier.

Just as bi-amplification has increased the efficiency and accuracy of two-way systems, tri-amplification is beneficial to three-way monitor systems. Bi- and tri-amplification are not usually possible with coaxial radiators, but additional amplification could be used to drive a supplementary woofer.

THE ROOM/SPEAKER INTERFACE

As we have already seen, room surfaces are a considerable influence on loudspeaker performance. However, this influence extends far beyond the effects on bass response that have already been discussed. Earlier, it was seen (Figure 5-6) that nearby surfaces reflect low-frequency energy back into the room. And, as the

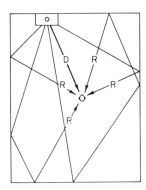

Figure 5-26. The listener hears mostly reflected signals, although the direct sound does arrive first.

D=direct signal

R=reflected signal

sound energy radiates away from the speaker, it eventually reaches the more distant surfaces. These in turn reflect some portion of the sound wave back into the room. The listener hears not only the direct sound coming from the speaker, but also the multiplicity of reflections from all the room surfaces. In fact, in most cases, the amplitude of the reflections near the listener's ear is greater than that of the direct sound, as may be seen in Figure 5-26. Therefore, the character of these reflections will play a very important part in the listener's impression of what he hears.

Room surfaces are neither perfect reflectors nor perfect absorbers. The frequencies that are efficiently reflected—or absorbed—depend on surface textures and density, the air space behind the surfaces, the rigidity of the surfaces, and so on. In fact, a change in any one of the these parameters may very well exert an influence on the overall sound that is greater than would be heard if the speaker system itself was replaced with a different type. Depending on the complex interaction between the speaker and the room, the overall sound quality may be described as bright, dull, live, dead, boomy, shrill, or by any of a seemingly endless number of similar adjectives. In other words, the room becomes part of the monitor system, and its effect must be taken into consideration when evaluating any speaker.

Standing Waves

When a sound wave strikes a wall and reflects back into the room, there may be areas in the room where the direct and reflected waves interact to form a standing wave. The phenomenon may be quite apparent when listening to a single frequency tone from an audio signal generator. To explain the standing wave, consider a sound wave reflected back on itself, as seen in Figure 5-27. The sound source, S, eventually strikes the wall, W. The listener, L, standing somewhere on the line, S-W, may hear either a strong signal or none at all, depending on the wavelength of the signal and listener's distance from the wall. When the round trip distance from L to W is a whole number multiple of the wavelength, the reflected sound wave reinforces the direct wave, and the listener hears a strong signal. But when the distance brings the wave back shifted by a half wavelength, the waves cancel and the listener hears nothing.

The first dead spot will be a ¼ wavelength from the wall, and there will be others at half wavelength intervals (¾ λ, 1-¼ λ,

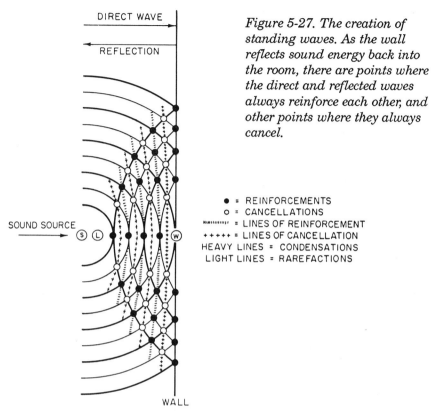

Figure 5-27. The creation of standing waves. As the wall reflects sound energy back into the room, there are points where the direct and reflected waves always reinforce each other, and other points where they always cancel.

● = REINFORCEMENTS
○ = CANCELLATIONS
ᴡᴜᴜᴜᴜ = LINES OF REINFORCEMENT
+ + + + + = LINES OF CANCELLATION
HEAVY LINES = CONDENSATIONS
LIGHT LINES = RAREFACTIONS

1-¾ λ, etc.) as the listener moves away from the wall. In between these dead spots will be points at which the waves always reinforce each other. Since these live and dead areas remain stationary, the condition is known as a stationary, or standing wave.

Figure 5-28. Non-parallel surfaces help to minimize standing waves.

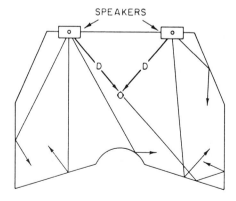

Standing waves make it difficult to impossible to evaluate intelligently what one hears over the monitor system. For example, the producer, although sitting next to the engineer, may hear an entirely different balance due to the different cancellation and reinforcement patterns at each location.

An effective means of minimizing standing waves is to construct non-parallel wall surfaces in the listening room, as shown in Figure 5-28. In the illustration, sound waves striking the walls are reflected back into the room at an angle, thus helping to minimize the build-up of any standing waves.

Wall Treatment

As noted earlier, the major portion of the sound energy within the room is made up of reflected signals. If there is an excessive amount of reflections, clarity will be sacrificed, and it may be difficult to pinpoint the actual location of each sound source. On the other hand, when wall treatment reduces the reflections to a minimum, the room becomes acoustically lifeless. Many well-designed control rooms have adjacent wall surfaces that are alternately reflective and absorptive. The reflective walls give the room a reasonable amount of liveness, while the absorptive surfaces prevent multiple reflections from interfering with clarity.

Room Resonance Modes

Just as each speaker system enclosure has its characteristic resonance point, the listening room itself will have certain resonances, or room modes. These occurs at frequencies whose wavelengths are twice one of the room's dimensions. Thus, a room that is 15 feet in length will have a main resonance frequency of $F=V/\lambda = V/2L = 1130/30 = 37.67$ Hz. If the room is 10 feet wide, it will have a secondary resonance at $1130/20 = 56.5$ Hz.

Not unlike the other speaker enclosures discussed earlier, the room enclosure will attenuate frequencies whose wavelengths exceed 2L. In other words, an extended low-frequency response is a function of both the design of the loudspeaker and the dimensions of the room. Regardless of the speaker system in use, it is unlikely that a small room will have a satisfactory bass response.

Room Dimension Ratios

The length, width, and height of a listening room should be unequal so that the same resonance frequency is not created in two dimensions, thereby accentuating it even more. In addition to the fundamental resonance frequencies of the room's dimensions, there may also be resonances at the harmonics of these frequencies. Therefore, ratios of length-to-width-to-height should be chosen so as to avoid common harmonic resonances in two or more dimensions. Over the years, several "ideal" ratios have been proposed by acoustical engineers. An often-quoted formula is the "golden section," (1 : 1.62 : 2.62) first recommended by the ancient Greeks, but still much favored today. Needless to say, there is very much more to room acoustics than choosing the right ratio. But the point is to try to avoid those dimension ratios that will obviously cause room mode problems.

System Power Requirements

It is a relatively easy task to determine the amount of power required to reach a specified monitoring level in a given room. As mentioned earlier, most loudspeaker systems state an efficiency rating based on an input of one electrical watt. From this information, using the inverse square law and the power formula from Chapter 1, the amount of amplification power for a given system can be calculated.

For example, a loudspeaker system is rated at a sensitivity of 99 dB for an input of 1 watt at a distance of 1 meter. The loudspeaker specifications may abbreviate this as 99 dB/1w/1m. If we desire to listen, say, at a distance of 4 meters at a maximum sound level of 107 dB, we can calculate the required amplifier power required as follows.

Original specification	99 dB	1 watt	1 meter
Double the Distance	93 dB	1 watt	2 meters
(Inverse Square Law)			
Double the Distance	87 dB	1 watt	4 meters
10 times the power	97 dB	10 watts	4 meters
(10 log 10/1 = 10 dB)			
10 times the power	107 dB	100 watts	4 meters

Of course, this does not take into consideration the fact that peak levels may be as much as 9 dB above the required listening level, in which case additional power will be needed. Actually, an additional 3 dB of level is usually obtained since most monitor loudspeaker systems are used in stereo pairs.

2 times the power	(107 dB)	110 dB	100 watts 4 meters
(10 log 2/1 = 3 dB)	(each system)		

Even so, for our system to accurately reproduce peak levels of 116 dB, 400 watts (two more doublings) of power per loudspeaker system should be available.

If a system containing a compression driver and horn for the high frequencies and a large woofer for the low frequencies is bi-amped, two smaller power amplifiers may be used. As mentioned earlier, a bi-amplified system with an active crossover may require less total power than the same system with a passive crossover driven by a single amplifier. Let us say that we are using a woofer with a sensitivity of 102 dB/1w/1m and a compression driver/horn combination rated at 112 dB/1w/1m. For the same listening level as above (116 dB at 4 meters with both speakers driven), the power requirement for the lows is 200 watts per channel, while only 20 watts per channel is required for the highs.

Although the described systems are capable of these extremely high levels, it is not advisable to listen this loudly under normal conditions. The above examples show the maximum output possible for the listed systems including a headroom factor. Monitor levels in the 90 dB range are closer to the norm, and this allows a headroom of at least 15 dB above the average level, making these systems capable of handling any peak information that may come along.

Room Equalization

Room equalization is the practice of tailoring the frequency response of the signal delivered to the speaker to correct for certain frequency anomalies created by the room. For example, if the room modes create a substantial resonance peak at 100 Hz, a filter in the speaker line may be tuned to attenuate the power output at this frequency, thus flattening out the system response. Peaks throughout the audio spectrum may likewise be attenuated, and to a less extent, slight dips in response may sometimes be brought up. Most room equalizers are of the graphic

A

B

Figure 5-29. Several typical monitor loudspeaker systems. At (A) a JBL 4430 two-way system and 4435 two-way with dual woofers, and (B) UREI 811C coaxial system and 813C and 815C coaxial systems with supplementary woofers.

type and have frequency centers spaced one-third octave apart. This type of equalizer will be explored in greater depth in Chapter 7 on Equalizers and Filters.

As may be expected, the room equalization process is ineffective against standing wave cancellations, and in general should not be used in an attempt to cover up serious deficiencies in room design.

Summary

Loudspeaker performance is a complex function of speaker design, enclosure style, and the room in which the system is placed. In effect, the room becomes part of the speaker system, and has a profound effect on what the listener hears.

While microphones may be (and are) moved or replaced with ease, the speaker and its location tend to become somewhat of a permanent fixture in the control room. The engineer who insists that only his favorite speaker tells what's "really on the tape" is no doubt blissfully unaware of all the variables at work in his control room, helping him to form his impression of the perfect system. One need only hear the same program over the same speaker in another room to realize that the speaker itself is but a small part of the total monitoring system. Figure 5-29 shows several typical studio monitors.

SECTION III

SIGNAL PROCESSING DEVICES

The path between the microphone and the loudspeaker is rarely an electronically straight line. Along the way, the signal may pass through one or more processing devices designed to make the sound more, or perhaps less, realistic.

Time domain processing such as artificial echo and reverberation may be applied to simulate the concert hall, or to create a new and otherwise unobtainable effect. Frequency domain manipulation may allow subtle correction, or can deliberately distort the natural sound and response of an instrument or group of instruments. Amplitude domain processing includes compression, limiting, and expansion which not only allow us to shape the dynamic range of a signal, but give us the basis for most noise reduction systems.

The beginning of Chapter 6 deals with time relationships and the creation of reverberation systems, while the last section discusses time related effects such as phasing, flanging, chorusing and harmonizing. Chapter 7 addresses frequency processing and looks at equalizers and filters. Chapter 8 explains how we can change the dynamic range of a signal, either to fit the storage medium or as a corrective measure, while Chapter 9 takes this dynamic processing into the realm of noise reduction.

In addition to the more traditional signal-processing equipment found in the modern recording studio, many multi-use signal-processing devices have appeared. They may combine amplitude- and frequency-domain processing or time- and frequency-domain processing, or even allow signal manipulation in time, as well as frequency and amplitude domains singly or in combination. Since they do not fall into any one particular category, but have operating parameters similar to the more traditional devices, a special section discussing this type of equipment is included at the end of Chapter 8.

Chapter 6

TIME DOMAIN PROCESSING: ECHO AND REVERBERATION

With the exception of the anechoic chamber, all monitoring environments have some effect on what the listener hears. The perceived sound of a musical instrument will vary from one room to another, and an acoustically dead studio will never be confused for a concert hall with superb natural acoustics.

When the listener is at a reasonable distance from a musical instrument, he hears something quite different than the direct output of the instrument. Although some sound certainly reaches the ear by way of a direct path from the instrument, other signals are also present as the sound radiates from its source to the various room surfaces of walls, ceiling and floor. Each of these surfaces absorbs some portion of the sound and reflects other portions back into the room. Consequently, the listener hears an incredibly complex mixture of direct and reflected information with properties that vary according to where he or she is seated. If very close to the sound source, the listener will hear mostly the direct signal. On the other hand, the listener at the rear of a large concert hall may hear a signal that is made up of almost totally reflected sounds.

The character of the reflected sound is influenced by the construction of the room surfaces and the room's volume. Some materials are more reflective than others, and all have some influence on the frequency response and dynamic range of the reflected signal. Carpeting, for example, tends to absorb higher frequencies, while glass may efficiently reflect these same frequencies. In the older concert halls one often finds paneling, thick plaster surfaces and parquet wood floors, all of which reflect sound and contribute to that elusive concert hall realism. On the other hand, the surfaces of a well-designed popular music studio may reflect very little sound back into the room. And, since so much recording is done with close microphone placement, the

Figure 6-1A. The Mormon Tabernacle – Salt Lake City, Utah. The hard plaster ceiling, wood surfaces and large volume make the room quite reverberant. Dimensions: 250 ft. long, 150 ft. wide, 80 ft. high. [LDS photo]

Figure 6-1B. RCA Studio A – New York City. A large studio, designed for "concert hall" acoustics. 95 ft. long, 56 ft. wide, 19-29 ft. high (variable).

Figure 6-1C. RCA Studio E – New York City. A small rock studio, designed for a minimum amount of reverberation. [RCA photos]

microphone "hears" a signal that is, for all practical purposes, only the direct sound of the instrument. Whether the primarily direct pickup is due to close miking, a dead room, or a combination of both, the resultant sound is usually described as "dry," or "dead," or by some other subjective term that suggests the absence of reflected information. As a corrective measure, some sort of signal processing is often required to simulate a more natural sound. Or, for a special effect, an apparently greater than normal amount of reflected information may be required. The engineer of today has many tools at his disposal to either simulate the ambience of a concert hall, or to create a unique effect that would otherwise be unattainable naturally.

Before describing these methods, a few definitions and a brief discussion of room acoustics is required.

Echo: One, or at most a few, repetitions of a sound.

Reverberation: Many repetitions of a sound, becoming more closely spaced (denser) and diminishing in amplitude with time.

Delay: The initial time interval between a direct sound and its first echoes.

Decay: The time it takes for the sound and its echoes and reverberation to die away.

Room Acoustics

The total energy present within any listening environment is a mixture of three components: 1) the original or direct sound, 2) the early reflections (echoes), and 3) the later, more diffuse reflections or "reverberation." These three components are illustrated in Figure 6-2. Although there is of course only one direct path from the sound source to the listener, there will be several paths for the early reflections, and many more for the later reflections within the typical music listening room. A pictorial representation showing the distribution of a typical sound field, related to time with respect to amplitude, is shown in Figure 6-3.

First, the direct sound (1), is heard. After a very short interval (T_1), a repetition is heard as the direct sound is reflected from a nearby surface and reaches the listener's ear. Still later (T_2), another repetition is heard (probably from a different direction), and then (T_3), perhaps another, as the sound reflects from other nearby surfaces. As time passes, more and more echoes and repetitions of echoes occur, as the sound waves spread through the

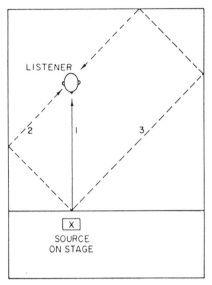

Figure 6-2. Echo and reverberation within a room. The listener hears a combination of:

1. Direct sound

2. Early reflections (echoes)

3. Later reflections (reverberation)

listening environment, striking and being reflected from the myriad surfaces within the room. Now, at (T_4, T_5, T_6...), the reflections have become so closely spaced that they fall almost on top of one another and the listener is no longer aware of their individual identities. These multiple repetitions of echoes are the

Figure 6-3. Pictorial representation of a sound field, showing direct sound, echoes, and reverberation.

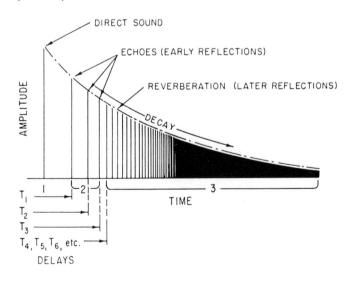

late sound field or reverberant field. Reverberation time is defined as the period of time it takes for the original sound pressure level to drop to one-millionth of its original intensity. If we were to convert that figure to a decibel amount using the formula for acoustic power (Chapter 1),

$$NdB = 10 \log \frac{P}{P_{ref}} = 10 \log \frac{1}{0.000001} = 10 \log 1{,}000{,}000 = 10(6) = 60 \text{ dB}$$

the equivalent drop in level would be 60 dB. Therefore, it can be said that reverberation time is the time it takes the sound and all its components to diminish 60 dB from its original level, hence the popular representation T_{60}.

As a matter of fact, even the very earliest reflections (T_1, T_2, T_3) that make up the early sound field are seldom consciously noted as such. Instead, their presence is sensed rather than distinctly heard. Our ear/brain combination takes all these factors into consideration and tells us the kind of space we appear to be in. Actually, if a listener were blindfolded and led into an unknown room, by hearing an impulse sound such as a snare drum rim shot, he or she could very closely determine the size of the room, the distance from the snare drum, and the probable composition of the surfaces in the room. Our brain interprets the time between the direct sound and the first perceived reflections to tell us the size of the room. The proportion of direct sound to the reverberant sound defines the apparent distance we are from the sound source, and finally, the length of the reverberant field gives us an idea of the apparent reflectivity of the surfaces. Needless to say, that all these factors are interrelated, but we can summarize by saying that:

The time interval between the direct sound and the early reflections give us the apparent size of the room.

The apparent distance from the source of the sound is determined by the proportion of the direct sound to the reverberant sound.

The length of the decay tells us how reflective or absorbent the surfaces of the room tend to be, and in conjunction with the audio bandwidth of the late sound field implies the composition of those surfaces.

In order to simulate this natural condition, the engineer will be called upon to artificially produce one or more of these variables.

Simulating Reverberation: Electro-Mechanical Systems

The engineer of today is extremely fortunate to have at his or her disposal many sophisticated reverberation computers that, using complicated pre-programmed algorithms, can simulate almost any natural space and quite a few that cannot be found naturally. However, in order to have a complete understanding of all the variable parameters found in these units, the beginning engineer should be aware of the precursors of these highly-developed systems. And, in many cases, these devices that simulate a part of the total reverberant field may be put to good use to create other effects.

Simulating Early Reflections

To produce a discrete echo, some sort of signal duplicating and delaying process is required. Formerly, this delay was accomplished with an auxiliary tape recorder. In addition to the normal recording process, the signal to be treated would also be sent to this extra machine. Depending on the tape speed and the distance between the record and playback heads, the output of tape would be delayed by some fraction of a second. Figure 6-4 illustrates the tape delay process, and lists the delays available when the heads are 2 inches apart, which is typical of many professional analog

Figure 6-4. Artificial echo, produced by a tape-delay system.

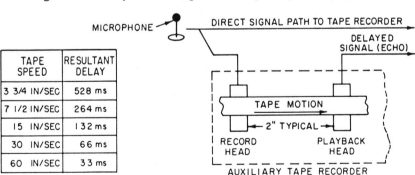

TAPE SPEED	RESULTANT DELAY
3 3/4 IN/SEC	528 ms
7 1/2 IN/SEC	264 ms
15 IN/SEC	132 ms
30 IN/SEC	66 ms
60 IN/SEC	33 ms

ms = MILLISECONDS (THOUSANDTHS OF A SECOND)

tape recorders. If it is possible to continuously vary the speed of the machine, additional delays become available. This system is certainly usable, but could be rather inconvenient since the "echo tape" needs to be rewound frequently, and not everyone has an "extra" tape recorder to dedicate to this task.

With the introduction of digital technology to audio, the digital delay line has taken over the task of the tape delay system. The obvious advantage of the digital delay line is that the delay is provided electronically, with no moving parts in the system. The input signal is filtered and then sampled similarly to the process used for digital recording, which will be discussed in Chapter 16. This digitized signal is then delayed by putting it in through a shift registrar containing over a thousand sections. The signal is shifted through these sections by clock pulses, and the signal may be retrieved at any point in time resulting in a delay of that amount. Many of the newer types of digital delay lines have substituted RAM (Random Access Memory) for the shift register technique, and this along with VLSI (Very Large Scale Integrated) circuits have considerably lowered the cost of longer delays. As in a digital audio tape recorder, the frequency response of the system is limited by the sampling rate, and the dynamic range or signal-to-noise ratio is fixed by the number of bits in the system (approximately 6 dB per bit). The maximum delay time is limited by the number of shift registers or the amount of RAM available.

Delays are continuously variable over a very wide range, and can be found from as low as 1 or 2 milliseconds to over a full second. Many units have additional memory available as an option that can extend the delay to as much as 2 or 3 seconds. Also, many delay lines have two or more outputs, so that the input signal may produce two or more echoes, each one delayed for a different amount of time. Figure 6-5 shows a typical digital-delay system.

There were some analog delay lines in use at one time, but the higher quality and lowered cost of the digital delay line has caused them to vanish from the professional studio.

Simulating Later Reflections

Later reflections, or what we know as reverberation, was described earlier as a series of closely spaced reflections diminishing in amplitude with time. In fact, so closely spaced that it is im-

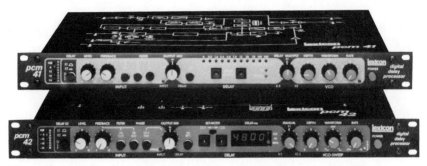

Figure 6-5. Two versatile digital delay lines. These units offer controlled feedback for multiple echoes as well as continuously variable delay up to 4.8 seconds (Lexicon PCM41 and PCM42, Lexicon photo.)

possible to perceive them as discrete echoes. Rather, their cumulative effect creates an impression of room ambience. The time intervals between the multiple reflections are entirely random, and to create such an irregular pattern using multiple taps on a delay line is not a very satisfactory solution since the delay outputs are all derived from the same regularly paced clock. Early experiments, using a feedback loop to provide delays of delays, did not achieve the random patterns that are necessary for convincing reverberation.

A more practical solution would be to set some kind of elastic medium in motion with an applied audio signal. This simulates the random multiple echo pattern of natural reverberation without actually producing discrete echoes. We can then pick up the back-and-forth vibrations of the medium by a special type of microphone attached to the vibrating medium. When the applied signal is removed, the vibrations gradually diminish, simulating the natural decay of room reverberation.

Several types of vibrating mediums have been used and are still being used with excellent results. Some of these devices have been so successful that we identify their sound with certain types of music. Perhaps the most widely used device of this type is the artificial reverberation plate. This unit consists of a steel plate, protectively suspended within a wooden cabinet, as seen in Figure 6-6. The element is driven by an audio signal, and sets the plate in motion. As the plate flexes back and forth, the motion is sensed by two contact pickups also attached to the plate. The audio signal produced by these two pickups thus simulates the reverberant field of a large space. When the applied signal ceases,

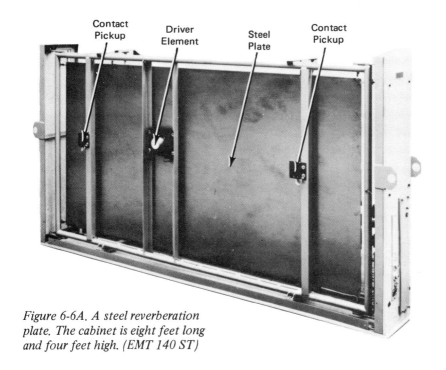

Figure 6-6A. A steel reverberation plate. The cabinet is eight feet long and four feet high. (EMT 140 ST)

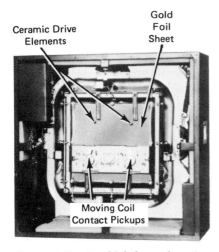

Figure 6-6B. A gold foil reverberation plate – front view. A thin gold foil sheet replaces the original steel plate. (EMT 240)

Figure 6-6C. A gold foil reverberation plate – rear view. The vertical "venetian blinds" are a mechanical damper used to vary the reverberation time. (EMT 240) [Gotham Audio photos]

179

inertia keeps the plate in motion for several seconds. Reverberation time of the suspended plate is approximately 7 seconds, and by using a mechanical damping system, this decay time can be reduced as desired. It is important to locate the plate in an acoustically quiet environment, as any vibration induced in the plate by an unwanted source will end up in the reverberation outputs. Reverberation plates come in various sizes, and some have successfully used materials other than steel for the plate. However, the density of the reverberation is directly dependent on the size and material of the plate itself, and reducing this size can degrade the character of the reverberation. Although the plate reverberator produces a remarkably good simulation of the late sound field, it is a rather large and relatively expensive device.

Another type of mechanical vibration system uses one or a series of coiled springs. Although specific construction details vary from one manufacturer to another, this type of system uses a long coiled spring suspended between a driver and a pickup element. The applied signal sets the spring in motion, and this mechanical motion is sensed and converted to an electrical signal. The simplest spring units are easily recognized by a characteristic metallic sound quality which is unconvincing as a simulation of natural reverberation. However, as a special effect on, for instance, an electric guitar, the "springy" sound may create a special sound texture not otherwise attainable. These inexpensive spring units are found built into a wide variety of guitar amplifiers and analog electric keyboard instruments. To capture this sound, the engineer must remember to insert the direct box or transformer at the output of the amplifier rather than at the output of the guitar as previously mentioned in Chapter 4.

The most elegant reverberation device is the acoustic reverberation chamber, actually a highly reverberant room in which all surfaces have been treated for maximum reflectivity. A loudspeaker placed within the room transmits the signal to be processed, and two microphones placed some distance away pick up the multiplicity of echoes produced as the signal is reflected again and again within the room. Such a room is shown in Figure 6-7. Although the room is unsatisfactory for normal listening, the overly reverberant sound, combined with the direct unprocessed or "dry" signal, creates an illusion that the recording was made in a very large room with normal reverberant characteristics. The acoustic chamber may well be the very best way to simulate a

Figure 6-7A. Although the room is not large, its highly reflective surfaces simulate the natural reverberation characteristics of a concert hall.

Figure 6-7B. The convex surfaces help create a more diffuse sound.

natural ambience, but it is quickly disappearing from use in professional recording studios. As digital reverberators become better and less expensive, it is hard to justify the luxury of a room dedicated exclusively to creating reverberation.

The Complete Electro-Mechanical Stereo Reverberation System

By its nature, natural reverberation is diffuse, and the listener is scarcely conscious of a recognizable location from which the reverberation is coming. Rather, the reverberation surrounds the listener from all sides. Therefore, any reverberation device with only one output is limited in its effectiveness to simulate the natural condition. A single output will be just that—a point source of sound, reverberant in quality but not diffuse. Consequently, the definitive reverberation system should have at least two outputs, both derived from the same mono or stereo input. Note that the steel-plate system described earlier had two pickup devices located at different distances from the driver element. If the two outputs were compared, one at a time, they would sound practically identical since they are products of the same input. But if one output is routed to the right and the other to the left, the subtle variations in phase will create an overall ambient field that closely resembles the natural condition. It must be clearly understood that any single source of sound panned to the center is not the same as a stereo signal, in which left and right may be practically identical, yet different because of random phase shifts. Although the center panned mono signal comes out of both speakers, it still lacks the stereo "dimension."

A totally flexible echo-reverberation system will provide separate control of delay time, echoes, reverberation, and decay. Figure 6-8 illustrates the basic routing paths of a well-designed system that uses a delay system to create a discrete early reflection, with its second output being used to drive the reverberation unit. This system creates the effect of a center-placed direct sound, followed by a left discrete reflection followed by a dense stereo reverberant field. The figure is a simplified drawing of a fairly involved system. In practice, the various signal paths feeding the loudspeakers would first be combined so that there would be only

Figure 6-8. A complete stereo echo/reverberation system.

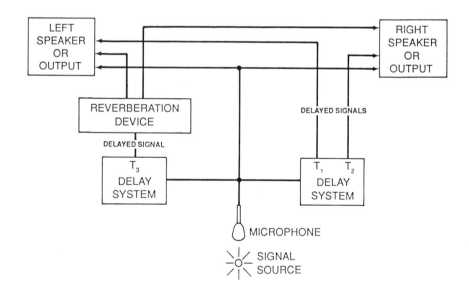

one feed to each side of the system. And once the desired mixture of direct sound, echo, and reverberation was established, this complex program would of course be fed to a two-track tape recorder to produce a master tape.

Simulating Reverberation: Reverberation Computers

With the advent of modern digital circuits and microprocessors, it has become possible to integrate a complete stereo reverberation system into one package. These systems combine digital signal delay technology with sophisticated computer algorithms to simulate the reaction of a sound in a defined architectural space. They give the user control over the early reflections, the reverberant or late sound field as well as the ability to control the perspective of the listener to the source of the sound. The output of these systems is remarkably smooth and natural, and they have developed to a point where many people cannot discern the differences between the product of one of these devices and a natural concert environment when the created reverberation is properly mixed back in with the direct sound.

The software programs are located on VLSI (Very Large Scale Integrated) circuits, and most offer the flexibility of changing or updating the ROMs (Read Only Memories) as new and better programs are introduced. A typical reverberation computer may contain several concert hall programs with varying sizes and simulations of early reflections and air absorption, several "plate" programs which mimic the response and sound of the more popular steel and gold foil plate reverberation devices, acoustic chamber programs to simulate the sound of a highly reflective diffuse room, room programs to simulate a vocal overdub or announcer's booth, and special effects programs such as chorusing, infinite echo, gated reverberation, reverse reverberation, sound on sound effects and many more. All of these predetermined programs can then be manipulated locally from either the control panel or a small easily-positioned remote control device. The possible changes within the program usually include the decay time of high- and low-frequency bands, time between early reflections and the onset of reverberation, high-frequency roll-off to simulate damping, depth perspective, density of the reverberant field, and the frequency envelope of the overall output. After each of these

183

Figure 6-9. A reverberation computer and its remote-control head. The system is capable of many effects in addition to multiple types of reverberation (Lexicon 480L, Lexicon photo).

parameters has been changed to the engineer's liking, the modified programs can then be stored in non-volatile memories for later retrieval.

Many of the available computer reverberation systems are discrete stereo devices with two inputs and as many as four outputs, while others contain monophonic inputs and stereo outputs similar to the more familiar plates and springs. Figure 6-9 shows a current reverberation computer and its associated control head.

Time Domain Processing: Special Effects—Doubling

Previously, digital delay lines were discussed regarding their use as a producer of echoes to simulate the early sound field in a reverberation system. And as mentioned, it is of course possible to produce a delay so short that the ear cannot recognize it as such, even if its level equals that of the direct sound. Generally, as the time interval between the two signals is increased from 20 to 40 milliseconds, there comes a point within that range at which the echo separates from the direct signal and becomes clearly audible. The actual time value at which this happens depends on the nature of the signal in question. The echo of a drum figure might be clearly heard at 20 milliseconds, while a legato string line may require twice that delay or more before the echo is heard.

These very short delays may often be used to simulate the effects of, say, a larger violin section. In a string ensemble, the playing is never precisely synchronized. If it were, the group would sound like one very loud violin, and it is the very imprecision of attack and release within the ensemble that gives the listener an aural cue as to the size of the section. (Of course, if this effect is overdone, the listener will object to the sloppy playing.) Now, by selecting a delay that is too short to create an audible echo, the engineer can apparently increase the size of the violin section. The almost instantaneous repetition of the signal simulates that very slight impression which is characteristic of a large group. The result may be particularly effective if the delayed signal is placed somewhat away from the direct signal, to create the illusion that the ensemble is spread out over a wider area. A judicious amount of reverberation added to the phantom violins will also help, especially if the reverberation is generated from the real violins.

Another popular use for doubling is to thicken or broaden a solo vocal line. The engineer can generate a duplicate of the original vocal line using a delay shorter than the integration time of the human ear. That is to say, shorter than 20 to 30 milliseconds. Adding this delayed signal in equal proportion with the original voice creates a thicker, denser vocal sound. Delays as short as 5 milliseconds can be effective, and as the delay is increased, the vocal sound becomes broader and broader. Of course, once the delay is recognized as a discrete echo, the effect becomes quite different, changing from a broadening effect to a doubling effect.

These techniques can be successfully used on any one track or combination of tracks during the mixdown process, and with multiple devices available, it is not uncommon to hear one effect on the solo vocal and another panned across the stereo image for the background singers or instrumentalists.

Time Domain Processing: Special Effects—Phasing and Flanging

Many attempts have been made to describe in print the unique effect known as phasing, or flanging. The effect is created by canceling some frequencies within the audio bandwidth while others are reinforced. Moreover, the frequencies at which cancellation and reinforcement take place are continuously shifting up and down the audio range. For the person who has not heard the effect first hand, descriptive phrases may not contribute much to the understanding of just what phasing and flanging really sound like.

In the studio, the effect was first produced when a signal was fed to two tape recorders simultaneously, and whose outputs were then combined. The speed of one of the recorders was varied just a little bit by applying a slight pressure to the flange of the supply reel (hence the term "flanging"). As the machine's speed varied, so did the tape's transit time between the record and playback heads. Compared to the other tape recorder, the very slight time delay differential produced a series of phase shift cancellations and reinforcements when the outputs of the two machines were mixed together. As the time delay varied, the cancellations and reinforcements moved up and down the audio bandwidth, producing the effect that is now known as flanging.

In an effort to produce a suitable flanging effect without the use of an auxiliary tape recorder, electronic phasing systems were developed. In these systems, the cancellations were produced by combining the outputs of a series of phase shift networks (analog) with the direct signal. The nulls could be moved up and down the audio bandwidth by varying the resistance value in each phase shift network, and the number of cancellations and reinforcements was dependent on the number of phase shift networks built into the circuit. However, there were no constant harmonic relationships between the nulls as in flanging, and although electronic phasing units produce an interesting effect, they do not have the depth of sound of the flanging effect.

Digital technology has made possible a variable delay line that more closely resembles tape recorder flanging. Here, the tape recorder's time delay differential is simulated by a delay system that is continuously variable between about 200 microseconds and 15 milliseconds. The speed of the time delay variable is controlled by a VCO (voltage-controlled oscillator), and when combined with the direct signal produces a series of nulls at regular harmonic intervals over the entire audio bandwidth. As the delay time increases to maximum, the spacing between adjacent nulls decreases. Figure 6-10 is a series of frequency response curves, showing the effects of phasing and flanging.

Time Domain Processing: Special Effects—Chorusing

Chorusing is an outgrowth of the techniques used for doubling and phasing. Instead of creating just a single delay and adding it to the direct sound, a number of delayed signals are derived from the input signal and then electronically phased. This creates a random series of small tonal and rhythmic errors that are reminiscent of a large ensemble. Many electronic organs make good use of this effect to simulate a pipe organ by chorusing a single oscillator to simulate a number of different ranks playing together. Chorusing is not particularly effective on singles or duos, but can add a very interesting texture to larger groups. Many digital processing systems offer chorusing as one of their programs, often allowing the engineer to vary the timing and amplitude of the individual chorus voices.

Time Domain Processing: Special Effects—Harmonizers

A harmonizer is a digital device that generates one or two signals that are variable in pitch above and/or below the input signal. In a normal analog tape playback process, raising or lowering the speed of the tape machine will not only affect the pitch of the music, but will also raise or lower the tempo accordingly. However, if we manually edit out some of the duration of each and every note over a given period of time, and play that tape back at the original speed, the tempo will appear to increase without affecting pitch. Conversely, if we use this laborious process to edit in extra note values, this will lengthen the duration of each note. Then, if the tape speed is increased, the pitch will have raised without changing the tempo. Obviously, this razor blade editing and speed manipulation process can be accomplished much more efficiently. In the harmonizer, this is accomplished by converting the input signal to a series of digital samples and by varying the

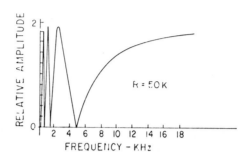

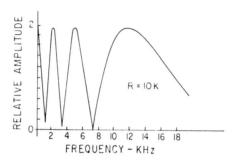

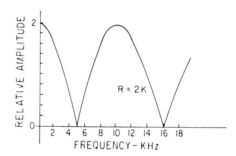

Figure 6-10A. Phasing. The output of an 8 section phase network is combined with the direct signal. Varying a resistance produces the phasing effect as the cancellations move up and down the audio bandwidth.

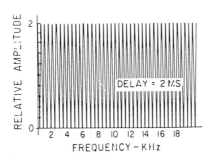

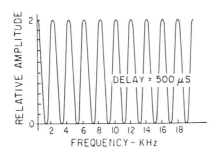

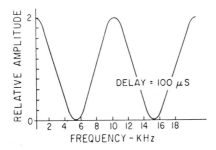

Figure 6-10B. Flanging. The output of a delay line is combined with the direct signal. Varying the delay time produces the flanging effect. (Graphs courtesy of Eventide Clock Works).

clock speed while duplicating or deleting parts of notes as needed while in the digital domain. A harmonizer is shown in Figure 6-11 and will typically provide an output that has a range of two octaves above or below the original input signal. It is also possible to delay the output by a varying amount so that the harmonized signal can be phased or flanging effect used as well.

A sophisticated extension of this process also allows tempo and pace compression/expansion of the spoken word. For instance, keeping the voice pitch the same and varying the delivery speed will allow the engineer to fit that 32 second commercial into that 30 second time slot. However, as of this writing, this technology will not operate over the full audio bandwidth, and therefore is not practical for music at this time.

These "time compression" machines may be stand-alone units or part of a sophisticated digital special-effects processor. The length of storage time, the amount of time compression, and the frequency bandwidth available are all a function of how much RAM (Random Access Memory) is available in the processor. As additional memory for various digital effects devices becomes less expensive and more available, more sophisticated and longer effects become possible.

Time-Domain Processing: Special Effects—Sampling

A further extension of digital-delay technology allows the engineer to record a sample of a sound and store it in RAM for later retrieval at the tap of a key. Since the stored sound is in the digital domain, it can be reproduced at any speed or pitch combination desired. Many digital keyboards use samples of real acous-

Figure 6-11. A sophisticated modern Harmonizer (Eventide H969, Eventide photo).

tic instruments as the basis for many of their sounds. The original sound is stored in an EPROM (Erasable Programmable Read Only Memory) or ROM and called upon as desired. Once again, the length and quality of the stored sample is directly related to the amount of RAM available. Samples of various sounds are also commonly available on 3.5-inch floppy disks, and can therefore be transferred from one machine to another.

Often, the recording engineer will be called on to record samples for use with a specific project. The prudent engineer will use all of the proper techniques for microphone placement and selection when recording these samples even though they will later be digitally manipulated and processed. It should not need to be stated that *the better the source material, the better the final product will be.*

Coincident and near-coincident microphone techniques work extremely well for collecting samples, and the reader is referred to Chapter 4 for a review of these procedures.

Chapter 7

FREQUENCY DOMAIN PROCESSING: EQUALIZERS AND FILTERS

The term Equalization may be somewhat misleading since—like alignment—it seems to imply some sort of necessary adjustment process to bring an audio signal within published specifications. Some equalization is of course done for this reason. For example, frequency adjustments are made to overcome the limitations of the recording medium. However, these adjustments, when correctly made, should have no apparent effect on the program as heard by the listener. On the other hand, equalization may be a form of signal processing, and the adjustments are made to noticeably modify the frequency response of the signal being treated. When this is done, there is no intention to conform to a standard. Changes are made according to the taste of the engineer or producer, and the signal is equalized to suit the standards of the moment. These standards may again change at the very next moment, according to the taste of the listener.

The well-equipped studio will have a variety of program equalizers on hand. Some are built into the recording console and permanently assigned to specific signal paths. Others may be installed in an auxiliary equipment rack, to be used when and where required. Both types are shown in Figure 7-1. The equalizer may provide one or more variable controls with which the engineer can modify various portions of the audio bandwidth. Typically, these controls are distributed among low, middle, and high frequencies.

Low-Frequency Equalization

Figure 7-2 shows the effect of two types of low-frequency equalization. The solid lines sloping downward illustrate typical high pass filter curves, while the solid lines sloping upward are shelving curves showing low-frequency boost. The dashed line

Figure 7-1A. An equalizer designed for in-console installation but that can also be mounted in a special frame for outboard use (Neve Prism Series, Neve photo).

Figure 7-1B. A self contained equalizer designed to be mounted in a standard equipment rack. This model offers filtering as well as four bands of equalization per channel (UREI 546, JBL photo).

also illustrates a shelving curve, but with low-frequency attenuation.

The high pass filter is usually identified by its cut-off frequency —that is, the frequency at which the output level has fallen by 3 dB. Beyond this point, the level falls off at a steady rate, or slope, expressed in decibels per octave (dB/8va). Generally, a high pass filter offers a choice of several cut-off frequencies. The slope or rate of fall is usually given in the published specifications, and is not adjustable by the user.

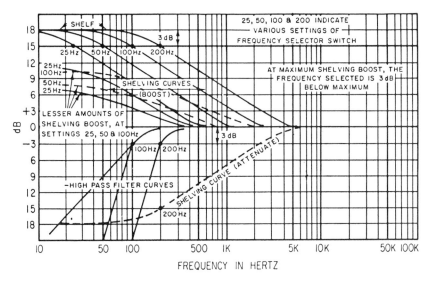

Figure 7-2. Typical low-frequency equalization curves.

Note that the shelving curves in Figure 7-2 show a response that rises (or falls), and that the slope eventually flattens out, or shelves, at some low frequency. This equalizer is identified by its turnover frequency. That is, the frequency at which the slope begins to turn over or flatten out to a shelf. This frequency is generally 3 dB below the maximum amount of boost (or attenuation). Thus, if the shelving equalizer has been set for a maximum boost of +18 dB, and the turnover frequency selected is 100 Hz, then the level at 100 Hz will be +15 dB (3 dB below +18 dB.)

Mid-Frequency Equalization

Figure 7-3A shows some typical mid-frequency equalization settings. Note that the response reaches a maximum boost or attenuation at the frequency selected, and then returns to zero as the frequency is raised or lowered beyond this point. This type of equalization is often referred to as a "haystack" due to the characteristic shape of the response curve, however, its correct name is peaking equalization.

In Figure 7-3B the three boost settings at a 1,000 Hz center frequency illustrate narrow, medium and wide bandwidths. Note that when the same narrow bandwidth curve is drawn at 10,000 Hz, the bandwidth is arithmetically much greater. At 100 Hz, it is, of course, much smaller. Therefore, a bandwidth expressed in

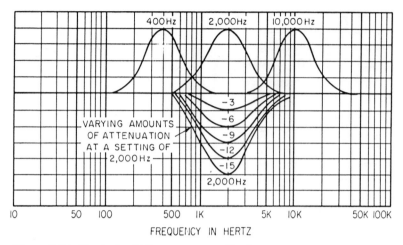

Figure 7-3A. Typical mid frequency equalization curves.

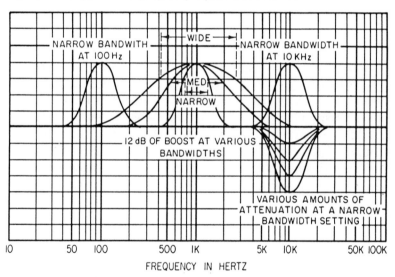

Figure 7-3B. Typical mid frequency equalization bandwidth curves.

hertz is only meaningful when the center frequency is also known. To eliminate this ambiguity, the bandwidth is often expressed in terms of Q, a ratio that is equal to the center frequency, f_c, (in hertz) divided by the bandwidth, (in hertz), or Q = f_c/bw. From the graph, it should be seen that the Q of all three narrow bandwidths remains the same, regardless of the center frequency chosen. Some equalizers have a variable Q control, allowing the engineer to vary the bandwidth as required. Typical values of "Q" are 0.5 to 3, with 3 representing a very narrow bandwidth and 0.5 designating a wide bandwidth.

High-Frequency Equalization

As with low frequencies, the equalization at high frequencies may be either shelving or low pass, such as a high-frequency filter. Typical curves for both are drawn in Figure 7-4. As before, the shelving curve is identified by the turnover frequency, or the frequency at which the response is 3 dB from maximum. And, the cut-off frequency of the low pass filter is the point at which the response has dropped by 3 dB, beyond which it falls off at a fixed dB/8 Va slope.

Inboard console equalizers may have some overlap in the available settings of the low-, middle-, and high-frequency equalization. Figure 7-5 is a response curve for an equalizer with a combination of low-frequency cut-off, low-frequency shelving boost, some mid-frequency attenuation, and a high-frequency shelving boost. The individual effect of each equalizer section is shown, together with a dashed line curve representing the resultant composite response of the four adjustments. Built-in console equalizers are often found with four bands: high, upper middle, lower middle, and low. Many of them allow the engineer to switch the high and low sections to either peaking or shelving charac-

Figure 7-4. Typical high-frequency equalization curves.

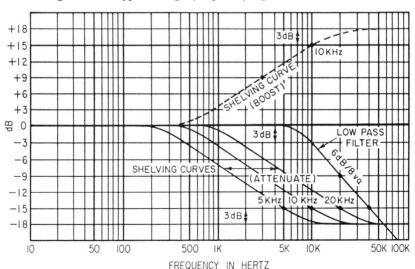

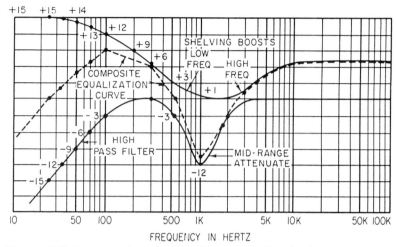

Figure 7-5. A composite equalization curve. The dashed line illustrates the overall eqalization that results from the addition of the low-, mid-, and high-frequency curves shown on the graph.

teristics. In addition to the four-band equalizer, a set of high-pass and low-pass filters with adjustable cut-off frequency selections is often found. The frequency selector control on most recording console equalizers is in the form of a rotary stepped position switch or may be a detented vertical or horizontal sliding switch. Each position selects a different turnover or cut-off frequency, and depending on the equalizer's versatility, there may be between two and six or more frequencies available per section. Some console equalizers also have a continuously variable frequency select, with each band of equalization covering a specific but overlapping range. This allows the engineer to tune the equalizer to any frequency within the equalizer's range. Or, while recording, the frequency selector may be swept back and forth as a special effect.

Parametric Equalizers

On a parametric equalizer, the frequency selection control is always continuously variable over a wide band of frequencies. In addition to having selectable frequencies and variable amplitude, the parametric equalizer offers the flexibility of variable "Q" or bandwidth. This allows the engineer to select the width of the bell-shaped curve for boosting or attenuating. For convenience, this width is usually defined in terms of octaves, but may be defined by some manufacturers as "Q." Common ranges are from a wide range of 4 octaves down to a narrow band of a ½ octave. These may be continuously variable or switch selectable in between the two bandwidth extremes.

Therefore, a parametric equalizer allows the engineer to select the amount of boost or cut, the center frequency of the equalization curve, and the "Q" or bandwidth of the curve. A typical outboard parametric equalizer is shown in Figure 7-1B. Note, that as well as having two channels of four-band full-parametric equalization, each band can be switched on and off individually and in addition to this, a band pass filter (discussed later in this chapter) is furnished for each channel.

Graphic Equalizers

The graphic equalizer is so-called because the physical positioning of the controls gives a graphic display of the resulting frequency response, as shown in Figure 7-6A. Here, each slide control boosts or attenuates the response around the frequency assigned to it. The shape of the response for each band is peaking like the mid-frequency boost/attenuate settings shown in Figure 7-3A. Individual bandwidths are not adjustable, but should be sufficiently small to limit the effect of each control to a narrow bandwidth centered around its frequency. Frequencies on professional graphic equalizers are based on the ISO (International Standards Organization) standard frequencies. The distance between the frequency bands can be from as small as a ⅙ octave to as wide as one octave, with octave and third-octave spacing being the most common. Some graphic equalizers combine ⅓-octave spacing in the lower range with ⅙-octave spacing in the higher frequencies for maximum control.

A full range graphic equalizer is usually found as an auxiliary piece of equipment, since its size and cost preclude it from being included in each channel or monitor signal path within a recording console. However, smaller graphic equalizers are now available in a format that makes them physically compatible with other inboard equalizers, and they can therefore be built into the recording console input channel. Figure 7-6B shows a typical example.

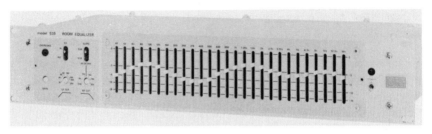

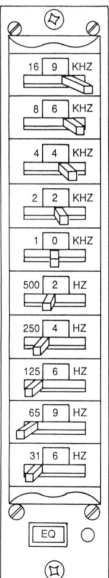

Figure 7-6A. An attenuate only graphic equalizer with 1/3 octave intervals. This unit also contains high- and low-pass filtering (Urei 539, JBL photo).

Figure 7-6B. A drawing of an inboard graphic equalizer. The unit illustrated has 10 bands with octave spacings (Sony Figure).

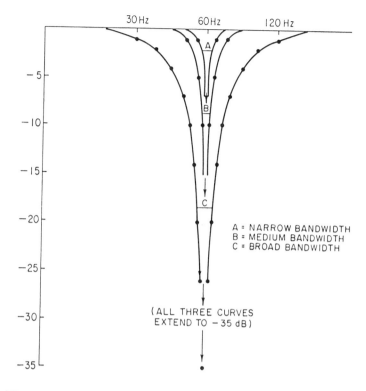

Figure 7-7A. A notch filter, set for 35 dB attenuation at 60 Hz.

Figure 7-7B. A combination notch and band pass filter (UREI 565, UREI photo).

Notch Filters

The notch filter is a specialized form of frequency attenuator, generally used to tune out a very narrow band of frequencies. A typical application is shown in Figure 7-7A, where a notch filter has been set at 60 Hz, to remove a.c. hum from a program. The very narrow bandwidth prevents the severe attenuation at 60 Hz from unduly affecting the rest of the audio bandwidth. The notch filter usually has two bands available so that the octave harmonic above the troublesome frequency can also be attenuated if necessary.

Band Pass Filters

A band pass filter is an equalizer with both low and high-frequency attenuation. The band of frequencies between the two cut-off points is "passed," that is, it is not affected by the equalizer. Although any such arrangement of low and high-frequency filtering constitutes a band pass filter, the term is usually reserved for applications where the "pass band" is fairly narrow. Figure 7-7B shows the face plate of a filter set that combines the functions of notch and band pass filtering.

The band pass filter is a frequency attenuating device, while the mid-frequency equalizer boosts the frequencies in its pass band. For comparison, the two are drawn in Figure 7-8. Note that the mid-frequency equalization rises to a maximum at its center frequency and then quickly falls off again to a flat response. By contrast, the band pass filter remains flat over its pass band, and falls off at either end. Therefore, the mid-frequency equalizer passes all frequencies, while the band pass filter does not.

Figure 7-8. Comparison of a band-pass filter and a mid-range boost equalizer.

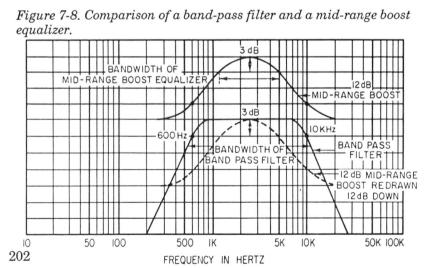

Effect of Equalization on Dynamic Range

In applying any sort of equalization to a high level signal, it is important to bear in mind that since a frequency boost raises the level of certain parts of the audio band, it places these frequencies just that much closer to the maximum permissible level. If the overall signal is already at a maximum, the equalization could cause noticeable distortion of amplifiers or tape. Consequently, the overall level may have to be brought down to keep the equalized band of frequencies within safe limits. Although the overall dynamic range remains the same, the maximum permissible level is now enjoyed only by those frequencies that were equalized (that is, boosted). Consequently, the dynamic range may seem to be somewhat less than before the equalization was applied. On the other hand, some attenuation of a troublesome band of frequencies may permit the overall level to be brought up, resulting in an apparently (and actual) louder program.

Equalizer Phase Shift

Since the equalizer achieves its frequency boost or attenuation through the use of reactive components (inductors and capacitors), a certain amount of phase shift accompanies any equalization added to a signal path. Figure 7-9A shows typical phase shift

Figure 7-9A. Typical phase shift characteristics for mid-range boost equalization.

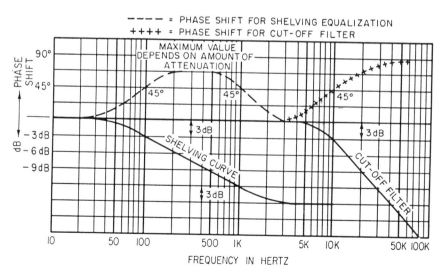

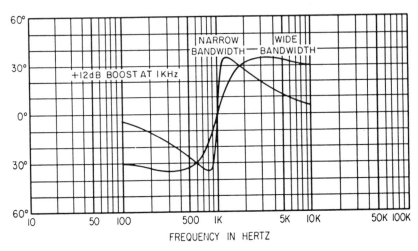

Figure 7-9B. Typical phase-shift characteristics for mid-range boost equalization.

characteristics for shelving and cut-off filters. Figure 7-9B illustrates the effect of a mid-frequency boost equalizer. It is for this very reason that minimal equalization should be used whenever possible. And as mentioned in Chapter 4, on Microphone Technique, "equalization is not a substitute for poor microphone selection or placement."

Active and Passive Equalizers

An active equalizer is actually an amplifier, so designed that certain frequencies are amplified while others are not, according to the equalizer settings chosen. The basic active equalizer may be a unity gain amplifier, with additional gain supplied only to those frequencies that are to be boosted.

On the other hand, a passive equalizer does not amplify any frequencies, since it contains no active elements. In a passive equalizer, a boost at, say, 1,000 Hz is actually accomplished by attenuating the rest of the audio band, using passive elements only, that is—resistors, capacitors and inductors. This is usually followed by a fixed gain amplifier that raises the level of the entire bandwidth, effectively raising the selected frequency above the others.

Chapter 8

AMPLITUDE DOMAIN PROCESSING: COMPRESSORS, LIMITERS AND EXPANDERS

At the present state-of-the-art of recording, there are still some practical restrictions on the dynamic range available to the engineer using analog magnetic tape as a storage medium. Digital storage methods also have their limitations. The sound level of a symphony orchestra with a chorus can reach 110 dB, and enthusiastic rock or metal groups may be even louder. By comparison, the dynamic range available on the analog magnetic medium may be about 72 dB, or less if a safety margin for peaks is allowed. Even with the 98 dB signal-to-noise ratio of professional digital recording, an exuberant performance can exceed the dynamic boundaries of the storage medium. The restrictions placed on the recording by both the analog and digital storage mediums will be discussed at great length in Chapters 10 and 13 respectively. But, whatever the system used, the dynamic range of the recorded program must often be compressed so that it does not exceed the limitations of the recording storage medium.

While recording, the engineer may raise the recorded level of a low-level program, and decrease that level during louder passages. This gain riding is an important part of many successful recordings, yet it will not solve all dynamic range problems. In many cases, the engineer cannot anticipate and control every high-level peak that comes his way. Occasional high-level signals from a few instruments may not be troublesome in themselves, but when from time to time they occur simultaneously, the cumulative signal will exceed the maximum permissible level. In many cases in the popular field, it is unlikely that the engineer can anticipate these conditions in time to take corrective steps before they occur, as sometimes no two consecutive versions of a song are the same. During the classical recording session, the engineer's familiarity with the music and the ability to read the score (a musical road map) can assist in the anticipation of these loud sections. This along with pre-recording rehearsal can often alleviate the troublesome levels.

As a complement to the method just discussed, the engineer may need to use signal processing devices known as compressors and limiters to meet the restriction of the recording medium. The terms compression and limiting have been in the audio vocabulary for years, yet there is often some confusion over their definitions. This arises from the fact that both the compressor and the limiter are devices that restrict the dynamic range of a signal, and the difference between them is one of degree, with the limiter having the most effect. To simply define:

Compressor: An amplifier, whose gain decreases as its input level is increased.

Limiter: A compressor, whose output level remains constant, regardless of its input level.

Both definitions are valid only after the signal being processed reaches a certain level. Therefore, we have one more definition:

Threshold: The level above which the compressor or limiter begins functioning.

These terms are further defined in Figure 8-1, which is a graph of input versus output for an idealized combination compressor/limiter. Notice that as the output level increases from –10 dB

Figure 8-1. A graph of compressor and limiter functions.
T_C = *compression threshold.* T_L= *limiting function.*

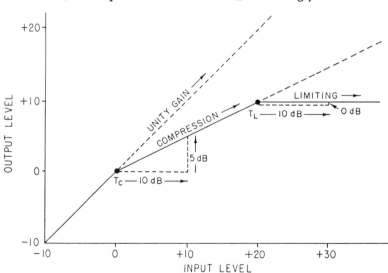

to 0 dB, the output level likewise increases from –10 dB to 0 dB. Here, the device is functioning as a simple unity gain amplifier, with no effect on the signal level. However, once the signal level exceeds the compression threshold of 0 dB, the output level is found by following the compression curve, and it may be seen that a further increase of 10 dB in input will yield only 5 dB more output level. In other words, the device now has a compression ratio of 10 to 5, or 2:1. Since this 2:1 compression ratio took effect only after the signal level exceeded 0 dB, we call 0 dB the compression threshold, and that is the point at which the compressor begins functioning.

Once the input level reaches +20 dB, there is no further increase in output level. Hence, the device is now operating as a limiter, with a limiting threshold of +20 dB. As drawn in Figure 8-1, the limiter's compression ratio is (∞):1. In actual practice, compression ratios of 10:1, 12:1 or greater are usually considered as limiting. Notice that once the +20 dB limiting threshold has been reached, the output level remains at +10 dB, despite further increases in input level. Therefore, it should be understood that the limiter threshold does not necessarily indicate the maximum allowable output level of the device. Rather, it indicates the input level at which the limiter begins working.

In Figure 8-2, note that the same compression ratio of 2:1 will have different effects on the overall dynamic range depending on the point at which the compression begins. Also, the position of the compression threshold will influence the point at which limiting must begin, if a certain maximum output level is not to be exceeded. For example, note that when the output levels are to be kept below +10 dB, then the lower the compression threshold, the higher the limiting threshold may be.

In Figure 8-3, the faceplate of a combination compressor/limiter is shown. Note that the compression threshold may be varied from –20 dB to +10 dB, allowing considerable control over the point at which compression begins. However, in the case of a compressor that does not have such a control, the same effect may be realized by inserting an amplifier/attenuator combination before the compressor, and a complementary attenuator/amplifier, if necessary, after it. For example, consider a compressor with a fixed threshold of –10 dB. In Figure 8-4, input signal (A), with a dynamic range of 30 dB is compressed to an output signal, (a), with a dynamic range of 20 dB, and a maximum level of 0 dB.

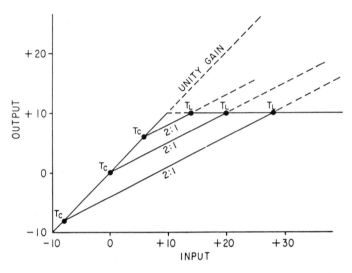

Figure 8-2. To prevent output levels in excess of +10 dB, the limiter threshold setting will vary, depending on where the compression threshold was set.

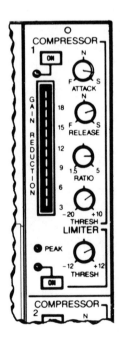

Figure 8-3. A compressor/limiter designed for in-console mounting with separate threshold adjustments for compression and limiting (Sony MXP-2000 Dynamics module, Sony figure).

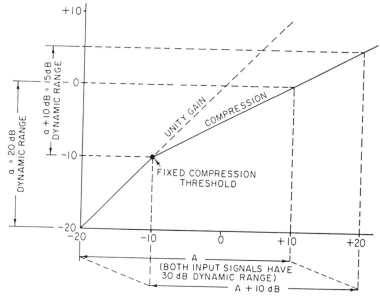

Figure 8-4. In a compressor/limiter with a fixed threshold, the output dynamic range may be varied by boosting (or attenuating) the input signal level before compression.

However, if the input signal is amplified 10 dB before reaching the compressor, as shown in the figure by (A + 10 dB), the output signal will have a dynamic range of only 15 dB, and its maximum output level will be +5 dB. This increased output level may now be attenuated by 5 dB, if it is necessary to keep the maximum output level at 0 dB as before.

When there is some amount of gain before compression, Figure 8-4 can be redrawn as shown in Figure 8-5. Here, the dB gain before threshold raises the transfer characteristic above the unity gain line, as shown. Beyond the threshold, the system gain steadily decreases as the compression curve approaches the unity gain line. The point at which they intersect is known as the rotation point. At this point, the gain of the compressor is 1:1, or unity. Beyond the rotation point, the gain continues to decrease. It should be noted that, as a consequence of the gain before threshold, the compressor raises low-level (below the rotation point) signals, and lowers high-level (above the rotation point) signals. Thus, low-level signals may be brought up above the residual noise level while at the same time, high-level signals are prevented from saturating the recording medium.

209

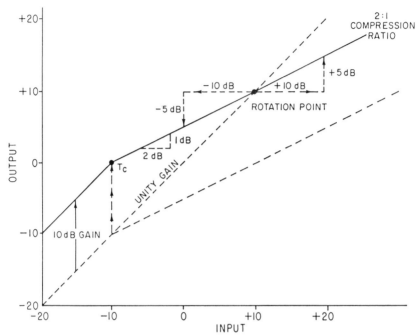

Figure 8-5. Graph of a compressor, with gain before threshold. Input levels below the rotation point are raised. Input levels above the rotation are lowered.

Many compressors offer the engineer a variety of compression ratios from which to choose. Figure 8-6A illustrates four different compression ratios, all beginning at the same threshold point. Assuming that the output level must be kept below +10 dB, it will be seen that the greater the compression ratio, the wider may be the dynamic range of the input signal. On the other hand, the four ratios of 8-6A might each begin at a different threshold, as seen in Figure 8-6B. In this illustration, each threshold/ratio combination passes through the same rotation point, and each has a different effect on the total program. The relatively gradual 1.5:1 ratio affects the program from –20 dB, while the more severe 4:1 ratio does not begin until the input signal level reaches –3 dB.

It is an easy matter to graphically determine the compression ratio and threshold required to prevent a wide dynamic range program from exceeding a specified output dynamic range. However, it should be realized that the action of the compressor may become audibly obtrusive, especially at higher compression ratios. To understand why, remember that the compressor is a variable

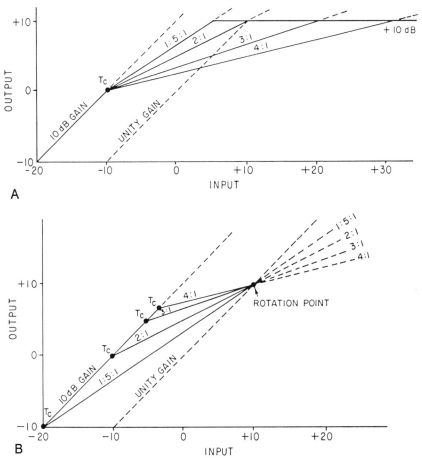

Figure 8-6. At (A)four compression ratios, all beginning at the same threshold. At (B) four compression ratios, each passing through the same rotation point. Note that each ratio begins at a different threshold.

gain device. As defined earlier, the compressor is an amplifier whose gain decreases as the input level increases, and the higher the compression ratio, the greater is this gain change.

Pumping or Breathing

The gain (or attenuation) of an amplifier may be expressed either as a positive number (0.25, 1, 3.5, etc.) or as a dB value (–10 dB, 0 dB, +10 dB, etc.). The positive number value is a ratio of output to input voltage. Thus, if the input voltage is 0.5 volts, and the output is 0.2 volts, the gain is 0.2 divided by 0.5, or

211

simply 0.4. If the input and output are equal, the gain is of course 1, or unity. However, it is usually more convenient to express the output in terms of dB above or below the input level. Thus, a unity gain amplifier has a gain of 1, which would be expressed as a decibel gain of 0 dB. A compressor will have a negative dB gain, usually called a gain reduction. Figure 8-7 graphs the gain reduction from several compression ratios. It will be seen that as the compression ratio is increased, a constant high-level signal of say,

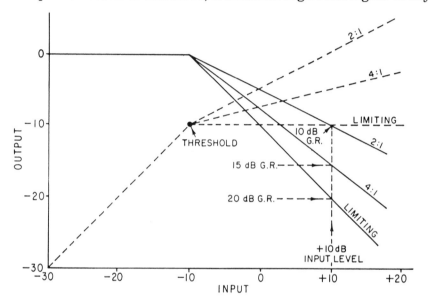

INPUT	2:1 RATIO		4:1 RATIO		LIMITING	
	OUTPUT	GAIN REDUCTION	OUTPUT	GAIN REDUCTION	OUTPUT	GAIN REDUCTION
-30	-30	0	-30	0	-30	0
-25	-25	0	-25	0	-25	0
-20	-20	0	-20	0	-20	0
-15	-15	0	-15	0	-15	0
-10	-10	0	-10	0	-10	0
-5	-7.5	2.5	-8.75	3.75	-10	5
0	-5	5	-7.5	7.5	-10	10
+5	-2.5	7.5	-6.25	11.75	-10	15
+10	0	10	-5	15	-10	20
+15	+2.5	12.5	-3.75	18.75	-10	25
+20	+5	15	-2.5	22.5	-10	30

Figure 8-7. The solid lines show the amount of gain reduction at various compression ratios. The corresponding compression ratios are drawn as dashed lines.

212

+10 dB, will cause more gain reduction. When the high level is removed, the amount of gain reduction decreases as the compressor returns to unity gain. If the gain reduction fluctuates rapidly, it may be quite audible as the background noise goes up and down in time with the compressor action, causing a breathing-like sound. On the other hand, if the compressor takes a relatively long time to restore itself after a high-level signal has caused gain reduction, then other low-level signals following the high-level signal will also be reduced in gain.

Compressor Release Time

The amount of time it takes for a compressor to return to its normal gain-before-threshold is known as its release, or recovery time. Some compressors have an operator-adjustable release time. Figure 8-8 shows the effect of various release times on a series of beats. In the illustration, the first beat is above the compressor's threshold, while the next four beats are all below the threshold and will not cause the compressor to react. However, if the release time is relatively long, these beats may be affected by the initial gain reduction caused by the first beat, as shown in Figure 8-8B. Here the compressor gradually returns to unity gain. At the time of the second beat, there is still 6 dB of gain reduction—at the third beat, 4 dB, and so on. As a result of this gradual release time, the dynamic range of the series is considerably changed. In Figure 8-8C, the release time has been considerably shortened, and only the second beat is affected by the gain reduction. In this case, the rapid return to unity gain may cause an audible breathing sound, as the system gain rapidly increases. There is no inherently correct release time setting as it really depends on the type of signal being processed. More often than not, the release time is varied by the engineer to produce the least objectionable effect.

Compressor Attack Time

The attack time of a compressor is the time it takes for it to react to a signal above the threshold level. On some compressors, it too may be adjustable. In many cases, a long attack time will allow the first part of a sustained note to pass through the compressor unaffected. If the note persists in duration, the compressor will attenuate it after a fraction of a second. Subjectively, the

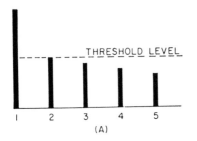

Figure 8-8A. A series of beats, only the first of which is above the compressor's threshold.

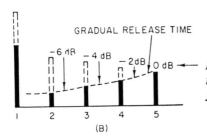

Figure 8-8B. Progressively less gain reduction, as compressor recovers from the initial beat.

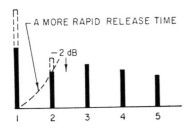

Figure 8-8C. A relatively fast release time prevents the initial gain reduction from having a long-time effect.

note may sound more percussive due to this type of compression. For example, a longer attack time may help to accentuate a compressed bass line that is otherwise difficult to distinguish, especially in a busy instrumental arrangement.

Often compression may be applied to the overall program rather than to a particular instrument. Known as program compression, this practice will prevent the cumulative levels of the various instruments from getting too high or too low. This type of gain reduction must be approached with care, since the adverse effects of the compression action are heard on the entire program, and excessive compression will probably be audibly distracting.

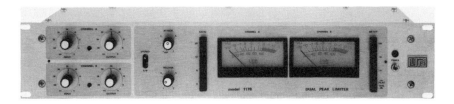

Figure 8-9. A stereo peak limiter/compressor with variable attack and release times (UREI 1178, JBL photo).

Program compression is often used to raise the apparent loudness of a signal, and the type of detection circuitry used in a compressor or limiter can also vary.

Detection Circuitry

Many compressors use a detection circuit that responds when the RMS (Root Mean Square) value of the signal is above the threshold point, while others respond to the peak value of the signal. The RMS detector reacts in a manner similar to the way our ear responds to changes in air pressure (as discussed in Chapter 2), and has a reaction or attack time of about 0.3 (three-tenths) of a second. On the other hand, a compressor/limiter that is designed to respond to peak amplitudes has a detector with a response time of around 0.000025 seconds (25 microseconds) and will cause gain reduction to occur immediately for nearly any signal. This can accentuate the modulation effect called breathing that was mentioned earlier. Figure 8-9 shows a peak compressor/limiter.

Many broadcast facilities use these two types of compressor/limiters in tandem. The RMS section is used to compress the signal and raise the gain to as close to 100 percent modulation of the transmitter as possible. This is followed by a peak detection device that prevents any sudden highly transient signal from exceeding the legal power limit licensed to the station. Thus, an average (but boosted) level program with no peaks will seem louder than a low-level program with occasional high peaks. Figure 8-10 illustrates this. Program B will sound much louder than Program A, despite A's higher peaks, since its average level is obviously much higher. In the race for louder sounding Compact Cassettes, Compact Discs and FM Broadcasts, this type of loud-

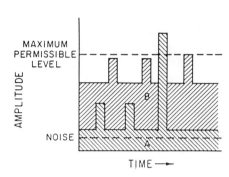

Figure 8-10. Program B will sound a lot louder than program A despite the latter's peaks, since its average level is higher.

ness boosting is often overdone, much to the detriment of the finished product.

When a stereo tape, disc or broadcast is program compressed, the gain regulating sections of the left and right compressors must be electronically interlocked, so that compression in one side causes an equal amount of gain reduction in the other. This keeps the overall left-to-right stereo program in balance.

Consider a stereo program in which the right channel occasionally needs some compression. During that compression, a center-placed soloist would appear to drift to the left whenever the gain of the right channel is reduced by the compressor. To prevent this center-channel drift, the stereo interlock function reduces the gain of both channels whenever either one goes into compression. This stabilizes the information that is common to both channels and keeps the soloist from shifting right or left during processing.

Amplitude Domain Processing: Compressors and Limiters—Special Effects

As mentioned earlier (Chapter 2), the energy distribution of the human voice is such that sibilants are apt to be significantly louder than other voice sounds. The high frequency/high energy content of many "s" sounds may overload an amplifier even when the apparent listening level does not appear to be unduly loud. A special compressor called a de-esser provides a function that helps to keep these sibilants under control. These de-essers incorporate a high-frequency equalization boost in the compressor's gain reduction control circuitry so that frequencies in the sibilant range will cause more compression action than do other frequencies. Therefore, during those fractions of a second when a distortion prone sibilant passes through the compressor, the gain is reduced by a more than usual amount. On most compressors, the gain reduction lowers the level of the entire signal. However, on more sophisticated devices, the audio bandwidth may be split into several sections with each section being treated independently. The signals are then re-combined after processing. In this way, the sibilant band may be isolated, and compressed more than the rest of the audio program, and when the signals are re-combined, the sibilant sounds are reduced in level without affecting the rest of the program.

Duckers

Some compressors have a second input which accesses the detector input only. This "side-chain" or "key" input allows the engineer to use a separate signal to trigger the gain reduction of the program material passing through the compressor. This type of device is often used as a voice-over compressor or "ducker" and will permit an announcer's voice to take precedence over a musical background. The musical program is routed through the compressor, and the voice signal (or a multiple of it) is routed to the key input. The voice signal is what actuates the compressor, causing gain reduction in the musical background, but not in the voice path itself. The voice and music are then combined into a mono or stereo program as the case may warrant. Now, as the announcer speaks, the background level of the music is automatically lowered. As a further refinement, the threshold of the compressor can be adjusted separately from the key input threshold. This provides voice-actuated gain reduction only when the musical program is above a certain level. Therefore, if the music is already sufficiently low in level so as not to obscure the announcer's voice, no further gain reduction is provided.

Amplitude Domain Processors: Expanders

Like the compressor, the expander affects the dynamic range of a program. But, as its name suggests, the expander widens or expands the dynamic range, rather than restricting it. Two definitions describe its operation:

Expander: An amplifier whose gain decreases as its input level is decreased.

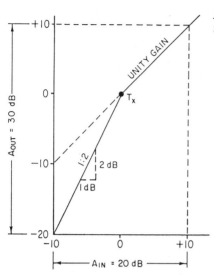

Figure 8-11. Graph of an expander with a 1:2 ratio.

Threshold: The level below which the expanding action takes place. (Note that the expander functions below the threshold—just the opposite of a compressor.)

Figure 8-11 is an input/output graph for an expander with a 1:2 expansion ratio. Note that when the input level lies below the expander threshold, the output level changes 2 dB for every 1 dB change in input level. As drawn, an input signal with a 20 dB dynamic range produces an output with a 30 dB range. Although the maximum output level equals the maximum input level, the dynamic range has been expanded since the minimum output level is now 10 dB less than the minimum input level. In other words, the dynamic range has been expanded downward.

Expansion, when used prior to recording to increase the dynamic range of a program, must be approached with caution since the low-level components of the signal are now even closer to the residual noise floor or minimum level of the recording medium. On the other hand, if the overall level is raised after expansion, the high-level components of the signal are brought closer to the medium's maximum permissible level. Since it is so often necessary to compress the dynamic range of a program to meet the restrictions of the recording storage medium, this application of expansion is rarely used.

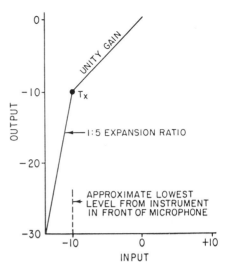

Figure 8-12. The expander as a noise gate. Noise signals at a level below the expander threshold are significantly attenuated.

Amplitude Domain Processing: Expanders as Noise Gates

In many typical recording situations, there is often a certain amount of undesirable low-level sound present in the studio. Air-conditioning noise, chair squeaks, and the sounds of nearby instruments are some of the many noises that a microphone may hear. These sounds may be adequately masked when the sound level from the instrument in front of the microphone is playing. However, when the instrument is silent, this background noise can become audible. An expander may be used to reduce this noise by selecting a large expansion ratio, with a threshold level at a point above the noise level, but just below the lowest output level of the instrument in front of the microphone. As seen in Figure 8-12, the low-level noise signals are practically eliminated, as they are expanded below audibility. This function of the expander is often called a noise gate since the effect is to cut off the noise without affecting the musical program. In fact, many expanders that are being manufactured today are simply called noise gates, and have as many as 6 independent gates on one mainframe. The effect is often referred to simply as gating. Of course, the line between the noise and the music is not often clearly defined, and it is all too easy to mis-adjust the noise gate and cut off the very quietist musical passages along with the

219

noise. As before, this type of expansion must be approached with care.

Amplitude Domain Processors: Expanders—Special Effects

As just mentioned, an expansion threshold that is set too highly will cut off the low-level end of a program along with the noise. Although this certainly is not desirable in most cases, it may be effective on some percussive sounds (drums, hand claps, etc.). As an example, a snare drum produces a series of high-level transients, each of which should quickly fade away. If each drum attack sustains too long, the overall sound may lack the subjective tightness that is usually sought in many popular music recording sessions. An expander threshold that is set at a relatively high level, well into the drum sound itself, will bring the level down quickly after each attack. This effect is shown in Figure 8-13. The same technique may be applied to most percussive instruments. It is not uncommon when using electronic drums to hear extraneous sounds at the end of a note, particularly when that sound was created by sampling. In a live performance, this objectionable sound may be lost in the noise floor of the sound system or in the audience noise. But in the recording studio,

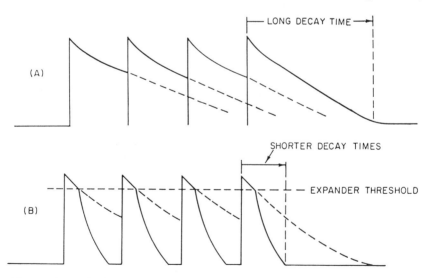

Figure 8-13. At (A) a series of transient attacks, with long decay times and at (B) a high-level expansion threshold shortens the apparent decay time of each transient.

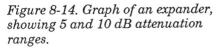

Figure 8-14. Graph of an expander, showing 5 and 10 dB attenuation ranges.

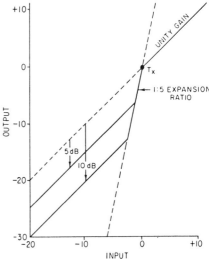

when using a direct box to access the sound of the electronic drums, the extraneous noise at the end of the sample will be clearly heard. An expander or noise gate can be used to attenuate or remove these low-level sounds between each attack.

During the attack itself, the expander cannot remove noise since it reacts to the overall program level and has no way of distinguishing wanted from unwanted sounds. For this reason, the noise gate function of an expander may only be marginally effective on sustained instruments such as organ and strings. When either instrument is not playing, the expander may attenuate the noise, but as before, the noise will reappear whenever the instrument begins playing. And, due to the sustained nature of the instrument, the noise may be heard through the music. Consequently, its sudden disappearance and reappearance in time with the music may be more of a distraction than a help. No matter how effective the noise gate can be, it is not a substitute for good musicianship, and should not be expected to transform mediocre players into skilled artists.

A popular effect called a "gated reverb" is often used on percussion instruments. The gate is used to cause the reverb (such as from a plate) to decay at an unnaturally fast rate. The gate is usually set so that the reverberation from the preceding note is fully decayed prior to the attack of the next one.

Most expanders have controls that govern ratio, threshold, attack time, release time and range. Ratio and threshold have been discussed, and the attack- and release-time adjustments react the same as the similar controls on the compressor, controlling how fast the expander reacts to changes in level, and how fast the gain returns to unity. As with the compressor, very short release times are more noticeable than longer values. Since it may be desirable to restrict the amount of low-level attenuation provided by the expander, a variable range control may be provided. Its effect is shown is Figure 8-14, where it will be observed that low-level signals are attenuated by only 5 or 10 dB. The range control may be continuously variable from 0 to about –80 dB. It may also be desirable to control the length of time attenuation lasts between attack and release, and some units provide a variable sustain control for this purpose.

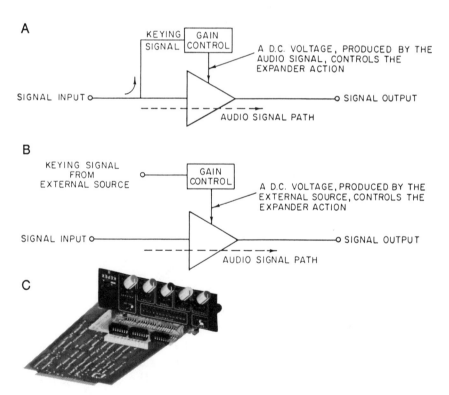

Figure 8-15. At (A) normal expander operation and at (B) externally keyed operation while at (C) a "KEPEX" noise gate. A popular KEyable Program EXpander (Valley People Kepex II, Valley People photo).

Amplitude Domain Processors: Noise Gates—Special Effects

So far, the expander has been described as a self-keying device— meaning that the expanding action is controlled by the program passing through the expander, as shown in Figure 8-15A. However, some expanders may instead be controlled, or keyed, by an external signal, as in Figure 8-15B (and similar to the ducking application mentioned in the discussion on compressors). Here, it is the level of the external keying signal, rather than the signal being expanded, that regulates the amount of expansion. If the keying signal is at a constant level above the threshold, the expander will simply stay on, functioning as a unity gain amplifier, regardless of the dynamic range of the signal passing through it. It should be clearly understood that the keying signal is not heard at the expander's output. It simply provides a control voltage to regulate the gain of the expander and thereby the level of the signal passing through it. When the keying signal is removed, the audio signal passing through the expander will fade out. The length of the fade will depend on the sustain and release time of the expander. An automatic fade-out may be accomplished by setting the release time between 3 and 6 seconds. When the keying signal is suddenly removed, the program through the expander will gradually fade away over that period of time.

Unique effects can be achieved with an expander by keying a sustained musical instrument with a control voltage derived from a percussive instrument. With a maximum range setting and a relatively short release time, the sustained instrument, say an

Figure 8-16. An expander used to modify the sound of one instrument with the envelope of another.

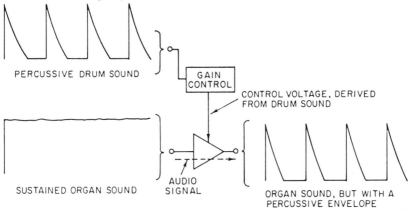

PERCUSSIVE DRUM SOUND

GAIN CONTROL

CONTROL VOLTAGE, DERIVED FROM DRUM SOUND

SUSTAINED ORGAN SOUND

AUDIO SIGNAL

ORGAN SOUND, BUT WITH A PERCUSSIVE ENVELOPE

organ setting on a synthesizer, is routed through the expander. The expander is then keyed on and off, perhaps by a drum track. The expander switches on and off with every drum transient attack, and imposes this percussive envelope on the sound of the organ, as shown in Figure 8-16.

In another application, a bass drum or tom-tom (and some other percussion instruments) may be "tuned" by feeding a low frequency audio signal through the expander. The intention is to hear the low-frequency tone each time the expander is keyed on. The expander is keyed by the signal of say, the bass drum, thus passing the low- frequency tone each time the drum is struck. The signal generator may be tuned as desired, and the output of the expander is mixed with the regular drum sound to impart a definite tonality to the sound.

Signal-Processing Devices: Multi-function Processors.

As mentioned in Chapter 6, some digital time-domain signal processors have been developed that combine many functions in one machine. It is not uncommon to find processors capable of multiple types of reverberation, gated reverberation, chorusing, harmonizing, time compression and pitch shift in one package. Other multi-use amplitude-domain or so-called "dynamics" processors may include compressors, limiters, de-essers, auto-pan and auto-fade functions, along with expanders and noise gates. Many of these multi-function signal processors also include variable filtering (high-pass, low-pass and band-pass) along with their other functions. Now, instead of a stack of compressors, a rack of gates, and several groups of delay and reverberation equipment, a small number of multi-function processors can meet most signal processing needs.

The newer generation processors also often allow the engineer to combine several functions in any logical order. For instance, an engineer may choose to gate and then de-ess an overly sibilant vocal prior to compressing it. It is certainly more productive to accomplish all of these functions within one unit rather than chaining together three separate units, each with their own additive noise level. Dynamics processors of this type usually also have the traditional side-chain or key inputs as well, and these inputs can be filtered, gated or compressed as necessary.

Figure 8-17. Several digital multi-effects processors. At (A) a Yamaha SPX9011, (B) Drawmer M500, and at (C) Eventide Ultra-Harmonizer.

Some units are discrete two-channel devices, while others may be of the one-in, two-out variety. The largest versions of these systems may well combine two complete processors on one frame, thereby providing two separate types of signal processing that can then be assigned to any of four or more outputs. It is even possible for one engineer to be using one half of the machine while another uses the other half for a different purpose.

Metering for input and output levels as well as readouts for delay time, thresholds, ratios, etc. are usually found on the front panel or on a conveniently-sized remote control unit. The processors usually have a series of factory pre-set programs or "patches" that can be accessed from the panel or remote. The engineer may then modify or change the various parameters within the program and store his or her personalized version in another memory location, often with an alpha-numeric label or description. Figures 6-10 and 8-17 show several of these processors.

As complicated and comprehensive as these multi-function processors can be, their use is still governed by the same operating parameters as the simpler single-use equipment. A thorough understanding of each component device discussed in Chapters 6, 7, and 8 is still essential for the proper use of the more sophisticated combination multi-use systems.

Chapter 9

ANALOG NOISE-REDUCTION PRINCIPLES

Noise, like music, is sound. However, unlike music, it is un-wanted sound. For our purposes, we will ignore the fact that one man's music may be another man's noise, and concentrate on those noises that all agree do not belong in the recording studio.

With care, some of these noises may be eliminated or min-imized completely. Coughs, chair squeaks, and dropped mutes may be removed by editing or doing a retake. However, there are not yet available any devices that will remove the sound of a chair squeak from a violin solo, or a falling music stand from a trombone solo. And, if the percussionist strikes the microphone instead of the instrument in front of him, the noise will be pain-fully obvious. Other noises are a function of the recording me-dium itself. For example, it is all too well known that every com-ponent in the signal path, from microphone to amplifier, introduces a little noise into the system. This noise may be in the form of a hum resulting from faulty shielding, or a hiss from an amplifier output. However, in a well designed and functioning studio, the cumulative effect of noise in the signal path should remain negligible, and the greatest noise source will probably be the magnetic tape medium itself. For even if a totally noiseless program could be recorded, on playback the analog tape will con-tain modulation noise and asperity noises that were not there before.

These noises are a function of the magnetic recording process, and even digital recording systems have some by-products that may be found to be objectionable. Major advances in analog tape formulation and manufacture have lowered this noise to an im-pressive minimum, yet it is still there, and probably will never be totally removed. But just as a loud thunderclap will momentarily block out the sound of falling rain, loud programs will effectively mask low-level noise, and the listener will be entirely unaware of its presence. However, at lower levels, the program material may not be loud enough to mask the noise and the listener will hear it along with the music. Although asperity noise is often masked by the signal causing it, the increase in modulation noise may be apparent over the rest of the audio bandwidth. In fact, even during a rather loud passage of low-frequency music, the program may not completely mask the noise present in the higher frequencies.

The advent of digital tape recording in professional recording studios has not negated the need for analog noise-reduction systems. Many Compact Discs are produced without going through an analog storage medium, and thus do not require noise reduction. However, many mediums such as film and television, as well as the smaller recording studios, still rely heavily on analog noise-reduction principles. Recent advances in noise-reduction technology have nearly equaled the digital medium in performance.

ANALOG NOISE

Since noise is sound, perhaps it might seem that it should have some frequency or frequencies associated with it. And indeed certain kinds of noise are identified with frequency. For example, a hum induced in a poorly shielded cable is readily recognized as a 60 Hz tone, and rumble, either in a studio building or on an analog turntable, will also have measurable frequency.

But what of the ever present tape hiss? The term "hiss" itself suggests that this particular noise is high pitched. There are other quite similar sounds, or rather noises such as that made by an amplifier or found between stations on the FM radio dial. All three, however, are a form of white noise. The term is analogous

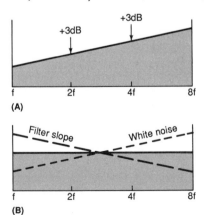

Figure 9-1. At (A) white noise. Equal sound energy at each frequency. At (B) pink noise. This is equal sound energy within each octave.

to white light, which is light that contains energy at all wave lengths, such as sunlight. When passed through a prism, white light is dispersed into hundreds of equal intensity hues, each representing the light energy of a particular wavelength. Likewise, white noise contains equal sound energy at every frequency within the audio bandwidth. But despite the equal energy present at each and every audio frequency, white noise is thought of as being mainly hiss, or high pitched in sound. This is because each successively higher octave contains twice as many discrete frequencies as the octave just below it. For example, the octave that begins at 1000 Hz (1 kHz to 2 kHz) contains 1,000 discrete frequencies, which is twice the number of frequencies for the octave that ends at 1,000 Hz (500 Hz to 1 kHz) which has 500 discrete frequencies. Therefore, any octave contains twice the energy of the octave immediately below it, and so seems louder. The higher octaves mask the sound energy of the lower ones, and the ear perceives a sound aptly described as hiss. However, there is definitely low-frequency energy or noise, present with tape hiss.

With white noise, the doubling of energy per octave signifies a power gain of 3 dB/8 Va, or if monitored on a spectrum analyzer, a voltage gain of 6 dB/8 Va. (A spectrum analyzer is a device that meters the energy level of a number of frequency bands simultaneously.) Although generated white noise is often used in acoustical measurements, it is often more meaningful to make use of a wide band noise source that maintains a constant energy level per octave. This may be realized by inserting 6 dB/8 Va filter at the output of the white noise generator, thus cancelling its inherent energy rise. This filtered white noise is known as pink noise, also named for its relationship to light of the same color. White and pink noise energy spectra are illustrated in Figure 9-1.

Analog Noise-Reduction Principles: Signal-to- Noise Ratios

The residual noise level of a device is its output level in the absence of an applied signal at the input. With a sensitive meter, a very small voltage may be read, which represents the amount of white noise present in the system. Recording consoles, processing equipment, and tape recorders will usually include within their specifications some reference to residual noise level. For example, a tape recorder may have a noise level of –90 dB. Obviously, this means that the noise voltage is 90 dB below some reference level. When comparing specifications, it is important to make sure that the reference level being used is the same for both devices, as different references can produce vastly different readings. It should be understood that the noise level of a tape recorder represents the output voltage level when the machine is on, but not running. If a roll of new unused tape is now played, the measured noise level will be somewhat higher, and when the machine is placed in the record mode, still with no input signal applied, the noise level will increase again.

Noise measurements are often discussed in terms of a signal-to-noise ratio (abbreviated s/n). Since a ratio is either a fraction or a comparison of two quantities, it might seem that a signal-to-noise ratio should include two values, one for the signal and another for the noise. For example, if the level of our reference signal is +4 dB, and the noise level is measured at –65 dB, we might expect to find the signal-to-noise ratio written as +4 dB/ –65 dB. This fractional format suggests that some form of division is possible, but since decibel values cannot be directly divided, they must first be converted into voltages (or powers, if more convenient). The equivalent voltages are: +4 dB = 1.226 volts; –65 dB = 0.435 millivolts. Therefore:

$$\text{s/n} = \frac{+4 \text{ dB}}{-65 \text{ dB}} = \frac{1.226 \text{ volts}}{0.435 \times 10^{-3} \text{ volts}} = 2.818 \times 10^3$$

Now, although 2.818×10^3 is a mathematically correct signal-to-noise ratio, it is not of much practical use to the recording engineer who is concerned with the decibel difference between signal and noise. The decibel quantity equal to 20 log 2.818×10^3 is a more useful figure.

$$N_{dB} = 20 \log \text{s/n} = 20 \log(2.818 \times 10^3) = 69 \text{ dB}$$

Because of the nature of the logarithm, it will be noted that 69 dB is the simple arithmetic difference between +4 dB and –65 dB, and it tells us exactly what we wish to know. That is, how much below the reference signal is the noise level. So, although this decibel value is really twenty times the logarithm of the signal-to-noise ratio, in practice it has come to be popularly known simply as the signal-to-noise ratio. As in other popular misuses of terminology, little harm is done, provided that the engineer is not confused by the practice.

NOISE-REDUCTION SYSTEMS

Good engineering practice demands that noise levels be kept as low as possible. Particularly in multi-track recording, the engineer must be concerned with the build-up in noise level as the number of tracks increase. It is a common procedure to record each individual track at a high level, regardless of the eventual track-to-track balance so that as great a signal-to-noise ratio as possible is achieved on each track. When, during mixdown, the track is mixed at a lower level, the noise level is also reduced. This helps to keep the total noise within reason Even so, the noise level of the total program (when mixed down to the stereo master tape) will increase by 6 dB for every doubling of tracks similar to the rising energy level of white noise discussed earlier.

Although signal-processing devices are usually thought of as a means of altering the signal to produce a desired effect, there are several devices whose sole purpose is to reduce the noise level without audibly affecting the quality of the signal itself. Basically, these noise-reduction devices can be classified as static or dynamic, and as complementary or non-complementary.

The terms, static and dynamic, refer to the way in which a noise-reduction device (or any other device, for that matter) reacts to the signal passing through it. An equalizer is a static device. Its settings do not change once they have been set by the engineer. On the other hand, a compressor reacts to the program material, and is therefore considered to be a dynamic device.

In a complementary system, some type of processing is done before recording, with equal and opposite (complementary) processing done on playback. In a tape recorder, pre- and post-emphasis might be considered as a complementary equalization process. In a non-complementary system, processing is done only once, either before or after recording. The signal processing devices discussed in Chapters 6, 7 and 8 are all non-complementary devices.

Noise-Reduction Systems: Static Systems

In its simplest form, noise reduction may consist of a filter adjusted to attenuate the frequency band in which the noise is found. This filter would be considered a static non-complementary system. Such filters may be marginally effective, with the exception of a few noise sources such as 60 cycle hum, most noise is wide band, that is, it exists over all or most of the audio spectrum. Filtering also affects the signal frequencies as well as the noise. In the case of a very low-frequency cut-off filter, such as to minimize structurally transmitted rumble, the effect on the program may be negligible. But, in most other cases, the filter becomes musically objectionable long before the noise is removed.

In a static complementary noise-reduction system, high-frequency boost is applied before recording in an effort to keep these frequencies well above the noise floor. Then during playback, a complementary roll-off restores the high frequencies to normal, while lowering the tape noise level. This form of noise reduction may also be minimally effective. The high-frequency pre-emphasis puts these signals just that much closer to the saturation point of the tape. Therefore, if the program has a significant amount of high-frequency energy to start with, the overall record level will probably have to be lowered, negating any noise-reduction advantage. For most typical music programs, the pre- and post-emphasis built into the tape recorder itself furnishes as much of this type of noise reduction as is practical. This will be discussed further in Chapter 10 on Magnetic Tape.

Both of the above examples of noise reduction are called static, since their noise-reduction properties are fixed, and the nature of the program material in no way affects the action of the filter or of the pre/post-emphasis.

Noise Reduction Systems: Dynamic Systems

The expander may be considered as a dynamic non-complementary noise-reduction device. The expansion threshold may be set just above the residual noise level. Therefore, as the signal falls below threshold, the system gain is reduced, sharply attenuating both signal and noise. Another way of looking at the same effect is when a gradually increasing low-level input signal is quickly boosted above the noise floor. Higher-level inputs (above threshold) follow the unity gain slope, and use the masking effect to cover the residual noise. Expanders are also frequently used as noise gates, to attenuate a microphone or tape recorder output in the absence of a program signal. However, since the device is reacting to overall program level, there is always the risk that the very low-level signals will be lost if they fall below the threshold of the device. Therefore, as a noise-reduction device, the expander must be used with caution. Its effectiveness varies greatly according to the nature of the program being treated. The preceding chapter deals in detail with the expander's operating characteristics.

A compressor may also be considered in the same category of noise-reduction devices. By compressing the dynamic range of the program, the overall gain can then be brought up, thereby raising the lower level segments above the noise, while preventing peaks from saturating the tape.

Both expansion and compression generally leave something to be desired in the area of noise reduction. The signal processing effects of either device alone become noticeably audible long before any significant noise reduction has been accomplished. Therefore, while compressors and expanders are valuable studio tools, they are rarely considered for noise reduction.

Noise-Reduction Systems: Studio Systems

As just described, neither the compressor nor the expander is an effective noise reducer. However, a complementary combination of the two devices can achieve a degree of noise reduction not anticipated by observing the characteristics of either unit used alone. The compressor/expander combination is termed a compander, and it is the basic principle behind the operation of most commercially available studio noise-reduction systems. Analog noise-reduction techniques have not become standardized, and the various systems currently in use are not compatible. That is, a tape that has been recorded using one system cannot be played back properly on another. Even systems that are manufactured by the same company, but that are designed for different applications, are not compatible and may not be intermixed.

In theory, the compressor/expander (compander) noise-reduction system is reasonably straightforward, though in practice some highly sophisticated circuitry is required. To help understand the basic principles, consider a music program with a dynamic range of 100 dB, and a recording medium whose maximum dynamic range is 75 dB. A simple compressor with a 100:75 (4:3) compression ratio will keep the high-level program peaks at or below 75 dB. However, as pointed out in Chapter 8, such compression will also attenuate low-level signals, placing them even further below the residual noise floor. As a noise reducer, this system does not look too promising. After recording, we may recover our 100 dB dynamic range with a complementary expander set to a 3:4 ratio. But the expansion will also bring up the noise level along with the program material. A more likely approach would be to select a convenient compressor rotation point so that input levels above this point would be reduced in level, while levels below the rotation point would be raised, thereby bringing them up above the noise floor.

Whenever a dynamic complementary noise-reduction system (compander) is used, it is particularly important that the tape recorder's electronics are properly aligned. In the playback mode, the noise-reduction system's expander restores the recorded signal to its proper level and frequency response, while the noise level is brought down. For optimum operation, the tape recorder itself must be well aligned so that the expansion does not react to errors of gain or frequency response within the tape recorder. If the noise-reduction system's output does not match the original input, the deviation is know as tracking error.

Due to the necessity of noise reduction within the multi-track recording system, and the different design concepts and incompatibility of the devices, the various systems will be described in some detail.

THE DBX NOISE-REDUCTION SYSTEM

The dbx Noise-Reduction System uses a compander similar to the one just described. However, certain refinements have been made in order to minimize the audible effects of compression and expansion. In the basic compander system, the noise level continually varies according to the degree of expansion in the playback circuit. Now, although the human ear may eventually disregard a steady level of noise, a fluctuating one—even at low level—becomes a distraction. And, as mentioned earlier in the chapter, hiss may be quite audible when the program is primarily in the lower frequency range. Therefore, although the basic compander may allow us a greater dynamic range, its noise-reduction capabilities require improvement.

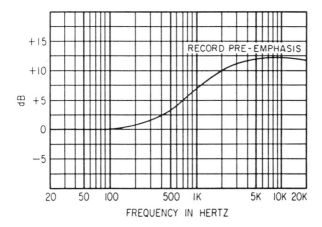

Figure 9-2. The 12 dB high frequency pre-emphasis in the dbx system's record circuit.

In the dbx Type I Noise-Reduction System, that improvement is realized by a 12 dB high-frequency pre- and post-emphasis network. High frequencies are boosted prior to recording (Figure 9-2) and then attenuated on playback. Since tape noise occurs after the pre-emphasis, the post-emphasis reduces the noise while restoring the original frequency balance. If the tape's saturation and self-erasing characteristics (discussed in Chapter 10) could be ignored, this high-frequency pre- and post-emphasis might be the extent of the noise-reduction system. High frequencies would be boosted above the hiss before recording, and then returned to normal on playback, with the resultant post-emphasis dropping the hiss level below audibility. However, as mentioned earlier concerning static complementary systems, the dbx's considerable high end boost will certainly drive the tape into saturation in the presence of any sort of high-frequency program material. To prevent this, the level sensing circuitry in the compressor (record side) contains an additional high-frequency boost. Consequently, when the program contains high-frequency components, the compressor over-reacts and in effect works against the program pre-emphasis by bringing the entire level down, thereby keeping the boosted high frequencies from overloading the tape.

Figure 9-3 is a block diagram of the dbx Type I record/playback system, and Figure 9-4 is a graph of the compressor/expander functions. On the graph, a program with a 100 dB dynamic range is applied to the dbx systems input. In the record mode, the sys-

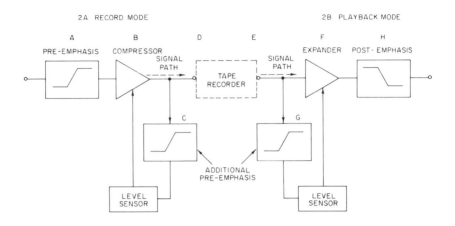

Figure 9-3. Block Diagram of the dbx Noise Reduction System.
A. High-frequency equalization boost is applied to input signals.
B. Input signal is compressed.
C. Significant high frequency components cause greater amounts of
compression due to additional pre-emphasis of the level sensing circuit.
D. Input signal is recorded.
E. Output signal is reproduced.
F. Output signal is expanded.
G. Significant frequency components cause greater amount of
expansion.
H. High-frequency equalization attenuation restores original flat
frequency response of program.

tem functions as a compressor with a 2:1 compression ratio. The program's –80 dB to +20 dB range is compressed to –40 dB to +10 dB. As a result, low-level program material is raised above the noise level of the tape, while high-level peaks are kept below the saturation point. When the compressed program is played back, the dbx system functions as an expander, as shown in Figure 9-4B. The dynamic range of the signal is restored to 100 dB, and the –60 dB noise floor is reproduced at –120 dB which is well below the threshold of audibility.

Another benefit of the dbx Type I Noise-Reduction System is in the area of headroom improvement. Note that the compressor reduces the input levels that lie above the rotation point. Therefore, higher level output signals from the console may be handled by the tape recorder. Although the magnetic capacity of the tape is not improved, the dbx expander restores the compressed high-level signals to their original value, thus improving the tape's apparent headroom capabilities.

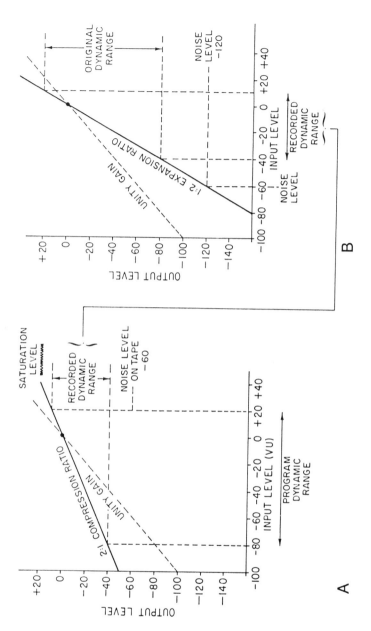

Figure 9-4A. In the record mode, the input signal is compressed by a 2:1 ratio. The adjustable rotation point has been set for a 0 VU (= |+4 dBm).

Figure 9-4B. In the playback mode, the signal recorded on the tape is expanded at a 1:2 ratio. The rotation point remains at 0 VU.

Reduction of noise added to the signal by the tape recorder	At +4 dBm signal level, hiss and high frequency modulation noise are reduced by 10 dB on signals with dominant energy below 500 Hz.
	At -16 dBm signal level there is an additional 10 dBm of noise reduction.
	At -36 dBm signal level there is an addition 20 dB of noise reduction.
	At -56 dBm input level there is an additional 30 dB of noise reduction.
	At -76 dBm input level there is a total of about 40 dB noise reduction.

Figure 9-5. dbx Noise Reduction System specifications.

Figure 9-5 is a partial listing of the dbx Type I Noise-Reduction System's specifications. Note that the specifications claim 10 dB of noise reduction on signals with dominant energy below 500 Hz. This type of signal takes full advantage of the system's pre- and post-emphasis circuit, since most of the musical energy lies below the high-frequency equalization boost that was shown in Figure 9-2. The specifications also claim varying amounts of additional noise reduction depending on the level of the input signal. This may be seen from Figure 9-6 which shows that the dbx's compressor raises the input levels cited in the specifications by 10, 20, and 30 dB respectively. Therefore, the complementary playback expander will lower these levels the same amount, simultaneously reducing the noise level by 10, 20 and 30 dB.

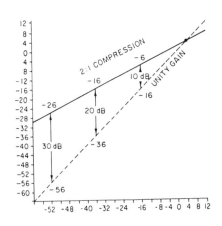

Figure 9-6. The dbx compressor raises the low-level signals. The further they are below the rotation point, the greater the increase in level.

Another type of dbx Noise-Reduction System is in use in the consumer marketplace on Compact Cassette recorders, dbx encoded FM radio broadcasts and dbx encoded phonograph records. This dbx Type II system was developed as a lower-cost alternative to the Type I professional system, and relies on similar noise-reduction principles. The main difference is the absence of the additional pre-emphasis circuit that affects the level sensor in the presence of significant high-frequency components. Instead of this circuit, the dbx Type II system uses a different set of initial pre- and post-emphasis curves. These differences make the two systems incompatible, and a tape encoded with Type II should not be decoded with Type I, and vice versa since in the expander section tracking errors will occur. Type II phonograph records and FM radio broadcasts have become quite rare, but a version of the dbx Type II system has been adopted by the Television Industry as the NAB (National Association of Broadcasters) standard for MTS (Multi-channel Television Sound) broadcasts. Figure 9-7 shows a comparison of the dbx Type I and the dbx Type II pre- and post-emphasis curves.

It is extremely important that the tape recorder(s) in use be aligned properly for input/output characteristics as well as record and playback equalization to prevent tracking errors as discussed earlier. Since the dbx Noise-Reduction Systems affects the entire frequency bandwidth and dynamic range simultaneously, gain loss errors can be corrected by adjusting the playback level after decoding the signal. However this will raise the noise floor by the

Figure 9-7. Pre- and post-emphasis curves for the dbx Type I and Type II noise-reduction systems.

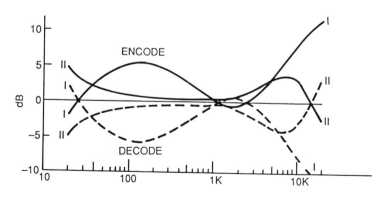

same number of dB. However, if the error was one of equalization rather than overall level, the equalization error would be doubled while the rest of the bandwidth would be properly reproduced. This type of tracking error would be quite noticeable, and extremely difficult to correct later on.

THE DOLBY TYPE A NOISE-REDUCTION SYSTEM

Unlike the dbx noise-reduction system, the Dolby Type A system does not react to high-level program material. In the former system, high as well as low levels are compressed prior to recording with corresponding expansion on playback. The Dolby A system takes into account the fact that compression and expansion actions are most likely to be audible in high-level program material, and that noise reduction is unnecessary once the level if sufficient to mask the background noise. Accordingly, the noise-reduction system operates on low-level signals only. Figure 9-8A is a simplified description of the basic principle of the Dolby 'A' system in the record mode. To explain how the system works, consider a very low-level input signal, with a value of about 2.5 millivolts (about –50 dB). This input signal is routed, a) by way of a compressor in the side chain, and b) directly to a combining amplifier. The effective compression ratio is 2:1 and its gain-before-threshold is 2.16. Therefore, low-level signal voltages through the compressor are multiplied by a factor of 2.16. The signal that travels the direct path is multiplied by 1 (unity gain). At the summing amplifier, the two signals add to produce an output voltage that is 3.16 (2.16 + 1) times the voltage input. Therefore, the gain of the system is:

$$N_{dB} = 20 \log \frac{\text{Output}}{\text{Input}} = 20 \log \frac{3.16 \times 2.5 \text{ millivolts}}{2.5 \text{ millivolts}} =$$

$$20 \log 3.16 = 20 \times 0.49968 = 10 \text{ dB}$$

In other words, the low-level signal has been amplified by 10 dB.

As the input level is increased beyond the compressor's threshold, its gain is reduced, and the compressor's output contributes less and less to the summing amplifier. By the time the input signal has increased to –10 dB, the system has become a simple unity gain amplifier since the compressor's contribution to

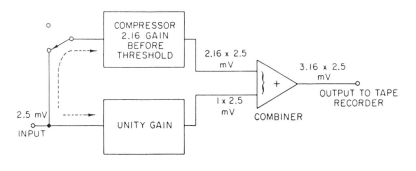

RECORD MODE

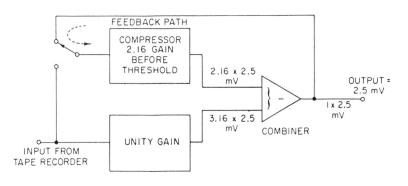

PLAYBACK MODE

Figure 9-8. Block diagram of the Dolby Type A Noise Reduction System. Low-level signals are raised before recording and then restored to normal before playback.

the summing amplifier is now negligible compared to the direct path.

In the playback mode, the compressor is placed in a feedback path as seen in Figure 9-8B, and its output is combined subtractively with the direct signal—that is, combined with the boosted low-level signal that was recorded on the tape. If the feedback path were not there, the systems's output would equal the input, since the combining amplifier itself is simply a unity gain device. However, the feedback loop reduces the overall system gain, in this case, by the amount of gain through the compressor. The principles of feedback require a textbook of their own, but we may get a fair idea of the nature of this type of circuit if we can

241

assume, for the moment, that the output of the combing amplifier is 2.5 millivolts. The compressor's gain-before-threshold remains at 2.16; consequently, its output is 2.16 x 2.5 millivolts. This output, combined subtractively with the direct input signal that was boosted earlier to 3.16 x 2.5 millivolts, gives us a system output of (3.16 - 2.16) x 2.5 millivolts = 1 x 2.5 millivolts = 2.5 millivolts. The playback mode system has thus attenuated the recorded signal back to 2.5 millivolts, that is, to its original value.

Figure 9-9 is a graph of the Dolby system transfer characteristics in both the record and playback modes. The graph summarizes the noise-reduction action. In the record mode, low-level signals are boosted by 10 dB, while higher level signals are passed at unity gain. In the playback mode, the boosted low-level signals are attenuated to the original level, while once again, the higher signal levels are passed at unity gain. Note that even though the side chain remains a compressor, its subtractive combination with the direct signal produces an expansion characteristic. From a study of the graph, it can be seen that the compressor/expansion action takes place over a relatively small segment of the entire dynamic range. Therefore, much of the signal is unaffected by the companding action.

To further enhance the system and reduce the audible effects of companding, the audio bandwidth is split into four sections. Each section has its own compression/expansion chain and is thus unaffected by the other. Above 5 kHz, the companding action increases gradually, until at 15 kHz and above, there is 15 dB

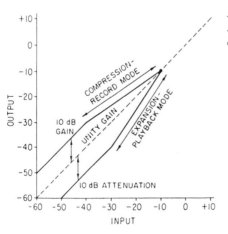

Figure 9-9. Dolby Noise Reduction System transfer characteristics.

of noise reduction. The four frequency bands are derived by routing the full bandwidth signal through a set of passive filters. These filters are:

1. 80 Hz low-pass filter.
2. 80 Hz to 3 kHz band-pass filter.
3. 3 kHz high-pass filter.
4. 9 kHz high-pass filter.

The output of these filters is then sent to the individual compander inputs. It is the overlap of the top two bands that creates the extra 5 dB of noise reduction. The selection of these bands takes into account that fact that at low to moderate program levels, most of the music may lie within the 80 Hz to 3 kHz band, with much less energy found at higher and lower frequencies. Therefore, the full noise-reduction capabilities may continue in operation in the high-frequency (above 3 kHz) ranges, keeping tape hiss at a minimum, while the music is unaffected by companding.

Since the Dolby system's companding action affects only a small portion of the program's dynamic range, tracking errors will be confined only to levels below –10 dB, and since the program material may be above or below that level, these errors cannot be corrected later on. The Dolby system is more tolerant of equalization errors since the tracking error is confined to a small portion of the total dynamic range, but gain errors must be eliminated before playing back the tape through a Dolby expander. To remove these gain-related problems, and since there are several magnetic tape operating levels in use, it is important that all Dolby encoded tapes contain a Dolby level tone at the beginning for Dolby alignment purposes. This tone may be at any convenient magnetic reference level, as long as it matches the level at which the recording was made. When the tape is played back at a later date, the tone is used to verify the input level to the Dolby expander. If the tone does not line up with the Dolby level marker on the Dolby meter panel, the tape recorder output level (or the Dolby input level control) must be adjusted before playing the tape. It is extremely important for this tone to be placed at the head of the tape and that the equalization standard (NAB or IEC) be set properly, since many studios and broadcast facilities use different standards and various elevated operating levels. The Dolby alignment tone is a warble tone that is unique, and is difficult to mistake for anything else.

Dolby B and C Noise Reduction Systems

Two simplified versions of the Dolby Noise-Reduction System are used for the Compact Cassette and some small format reel-to-reel machines. These systems, known as Dolby B (using a 1.5 kHz high-pass filter) and Dolby C (using a 375 Hz high-pass filter), are single band devices. Their intention is to reduce the most audible (high-frequency) portion of tape noise. Commonly found as built-in circuits in Compact Cassette recorder/players, Dolby C is also found as an outboard system for small format multi-channel tape recorders. Dolby B gives 10 dB of noise reduction and Dolby C, which uses two series connected sliding band companders and spectral skewing, provides 20 dB of noise reduction.

THE TELCOM c4 NOISE-REDUCTION SYSTEM

The Telcom c4 Noise-Reduction system combines some of the noise-reduction methods found in both the dbx and Dolby systems. The system uses a compression and expansion ratio of 1.5:1 and 1:1.5 respectively as opposed to the 2 to 1 relationship found in the previously discussed systems. The companding action is constant over the entire dynamic range and therefore extends the dynamic range by a factor of 1.5. A tape recorder system with a possible dynamic range of 70 dB, will have its signal-to-noise ratio improved to 105 dB with the addition of the Telcom system. In addition to this full range companding, the Telcom system separates the audio bandwidth into four frequency bands. The system uses a rapid attack time coupled with a slow release time for minimum audibility. The attack and release times vary, and are optimized for each band in the system. The filters used to divide the frequency bands are:

1. 215 Hz low-pass filter.
2. 215 Hz—1450 Hz band-pass filter.
3. 1450 Hz—4800 Hz band-pass filter.
4. 4.8 kHz high-pass filter.

One of the advantages of this system is its lack of tracking error problems. Gain errors can be corrected on playback, like in the dbx system, while equalization errors are restricted to their particular audio band as in the Dolby system. A reference identification tone allows the engineer to calibrate the system and the tape together for proper playback. Telcom c4 is also used for other transmission lines such as cable, radio links, and satellite systems. A special version of the c4 system is available for these applications. This modified system uses a higher 1:2.5 compression ratio, along with a corresponding 2.5:1 expansion rate.

THE DOLBY SPECTRAL RECORDING NOISE-REDUCTION SYSTEM

The most recent addition to the list of noise-reduction systems is the Dolby Spectral Recording Noise-Reduction System, commonly called Dolby SR. It differs from the traditional Dolby A system in many ways, however it still utilizes a main signal pathway along with a side chain path. The main signal path is without dynamic signal processing while the side chain includes a complex series of multiple compressors. At the output of the system, the main signal path and the side chain signal path are summed additively or subtractively depending on whether the encode or decode function is selected. Prior to compression, the high- and low-frequency components of the side chain signal are boosted in a manner called "spectral skewing." This effectively raises the overall levels further above the noise floor and adds gain prior to compression.

The side chain signal is divided into three multi-level dynamic stages with the high- and middle-level stages subdivided into high-frequency and low-frequency bands. The low-level stage is not divided, but operates in the high-frequency range only. The crossover frequency between the high and low frequencies of the high and middle dynamic stages is 800 Hz, with the low-level stage using an 800 Hz high pass filter. The filters have gradual slopes and this results in an overlap in the 200 Hz to 3 kHz region. Therefore, this four octave intelligibility range is processed by both the high-frequency and the low-frequency compressor in the high-level and mid-level stage, while only the high-frequency component of the low-level stage is affected. This gives a total of five compressors in simultaneous action for each encoding or decoding channel of the system. Each compressor uses a combination of fixed and sliding threshold bands and a 2:1 compression ratio. The thresholds for the multi-level dynamic stages are –30 dB, –48 dB, and –62 dB respectively. This creates dynamic processing for the low frequencies from –48 dB to –5 dB and from –62 dB to –5 dB for the high frequencies. No dynamic processing occurs outside these limits, but full signal boosting or "spectral skewing" is still in effect.

The intention of the Dolby SR system is to only reduce the noise that can be heard by the human ear, and therefore subsonic and supersonic sounds are unaffected. This results in a decrease in modulation noise and intermodulation distortion. Reductions in harmonic distortion in the recording system are also achieved as well as the elimination of virtually all audible tape hiss. The overall decode and encode curves bear a resemblance to the Robinson and Dadson Equal Loudness Contours discussed and pictured in Chapter 2. Figure 9-10 shows a simplified block diagram of the Dolby SR system.

The dual path multi-level staggered Dolby SR System is much less susceptible to tracking errors than the Type A system, but Dolby calibration is still required. A pink noise generator is included in the unit and is used to calibrate not only level, but equalization of the recording system as well. The operating level, full bandwidth calibration eliminates tracking errors of both gain and equalization and insures that the Dolby SR Noise-Reduction System is inaudible in use under all conditions.

Noise-Reduction Systems Summary

All the noise-reduction systems previously discussed are based on the compander principle. Compression on recording is followed by expansion on playback. The gain of low-level signals is raised so that they are recorded as high above the noise floor as possible. On playback, the low-level signals are restored to their normal levels, while the gain reduction reduces the noise level by the same amount. Representative production models of each of the noise-reduction systems described in this chapter are pictured in Figures 9-11 through 9-14.

Due to the significant differences between the various systems, a tape encoded in one system, may not be decoded with another system's playback unit. If an encoded tape is played back with no complementary noise-reduction system, or with the wrong system, its dynamic range and frequency response will be distorted. It must also be remembered that compander noise-reduction systems are for use with transmission systems only, and that signal inputs and outputs must be related. Therefore a system such as the Dolby 'A' system could not be used to quiet down, say, a noisy reverberation chamber. Such a chamber would be creating new

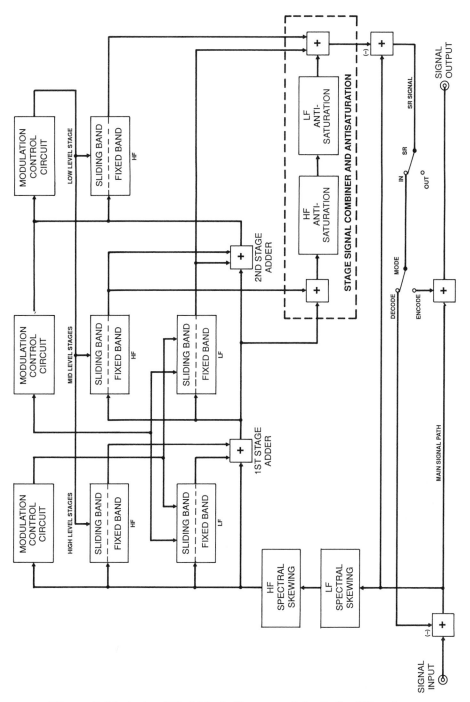

Figure 9-10. A simplified block diagram of the Dolby SR noise reduction system (Dolby Figure)

Figure 9-11. A dbx Type I two-channel noise reduction unit (dbx 150x, dbx photo).

Figure 9-12. A Dolby Type A and Type SR two channel noise reduction unit (Dolby 363, Dolby photo).

Figure 9-13. A Telcom c4 two-channel noise reduction unit (Telcom 300, ANT photo).

sounds that would be inserted between the encoder and the decoder and would cause severe tracking errors.

Noise-reduction systems are often designed with an automatic switching function that inserts the system in the input line to the tape recorder during recording and into the playback or output

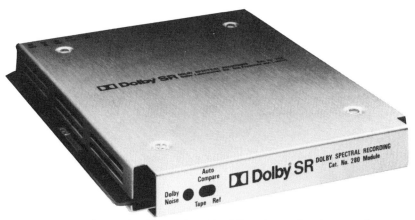

Figure 9-14. A single channel Dolby SR noise-reduction card designed for mounting in a multi-channel frame (Dolby 280, Dolby photo).

line at all other times. Thus, the same noise-reduction device serves a dual function, and can be used for encode and decode though not at the same time. This is an economic advantage, but this arrangement prevents the engineer from properly monitoring the tape while recording.

Several companies now offer what are called "TTM" noise-reduction frames. These are rack frames that contain a power supply and switching facilities along with a number of open slots. The slots are designed to accept noise-reduction circuit cards from all the major manufacturers of noise-reduction systems. A typical TTM frame will accept dbx Type I and Type II system cards as well as Dolby A, Dolby SR and Telcom c4 circuits. This allows the engineer to select which ever system he prefers, as well as to accommodate the various tapes that may be brought into the studio. By simply switching to the appropriate card, the proper noise-reduction system is inserted into the designated signal path.

SECTION IV

ANALOG AUDIO RECORDING SYSTEMS

The tape recorder is rarely thought of as a signal processing device or a transducer, for at all times its output is expected to be a faithful replica of its input. Yet it does indeed process the signal, first from electrical energy to magnetic energy, and later back to electrical energy.

Chapter 10 begins with a brief discussion of the basic principles of magnetic recording, in which tape and tape recorder are viewed as component parts of a total system. The chapter continues with an examination into the makeup and characteristics of modern magnetic tape. Included is a discussion of elementary magnetic principles.

Chapter 11 examines the tape recorder transport, electronic systems, and the entire record/playback process, while Chapter 12 describes the all-important alignment procedures that allow the tape and tape recorder to work together as an integrated system.

Chapter 10

MAGNETIC TAPE

Regardless of the amount of technical sophistication built into modern tape recorder systems, they consist basically of a few essential parts. Primary among a list of such parts would be magnetic tape. However, before looking in detail at the tape itself, it is important to understand the basic theory of operation of a magnetic system.

SYSTEM FUNDAMENTALS

As illustrated in Figure 10-1, the transport system moves the magnetic tape past the recording head where the program to be recorded is magnetically stored on the tape. When the stored program passes the playback head, the playback amplifier produces a signal that corresponds to the input signal, as originally applied to the record amplifier. In practice, the record/playback process is of course considerably more involved, and to better understand it we need to review some of the basic principles of magnetism.

Basic Magnetism

The ancient philosophers knew that a certain type of rock, known as lodestone, would mysteriously draw to it particles of iron. This power came to be known as magnetic attraction, and in

Figure 10-1. The basic tape recorder system.

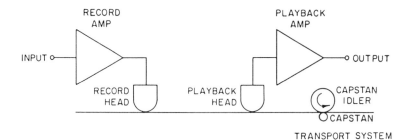

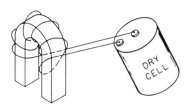

Figure 10-2. An artificial magnet.

time it was recognized to be a physical, not spiritual quality. Materials possessing this power are now called magnets.

An artificial magnet can be created by winding a coil of wire around a bar of metal, as shown in Figure 10-2. When a direct current is applied to the coil, a magnetic field is set up, and the bar becomes a magnet. Depending on the particular material, the bar may or may not remain magnetized after the current is withdrawn. Hardened steel will retain its magnetic properties long after the applied current ceases, whereas soft iron is considered a temporary magnet. Although it can be readily magnetized, it does not retain the magnetization in the absence of an applied current.

If a hard ferrous material—that is, a material with the capacity to acquire permanent magnetic characteristics—is temporarily subjected to a magnetic field and then removed from the vicinity of the field, the residual magnetism now stored in the magnet can be measured. This measurement will enable us to determine the strength of the force that magnetized the material. The measurement may be made whenever it is convenient to do so, since the material was permanently magnetized at the instant it was withdrawn from the applied magnetic field. It follows then that a series of ferrous particles may be magnetized, each by a different magnetic field strength, and later, measurements of each particle will tell us, as before, the strength of the applied magnetic field at the instant that the particle was magnetized. Simply, this is the principle of magnetic recording.

The Magnetic System

Magnetic tape consists of a polyester-type base material coated with a solution containing gamma ferric oxide particles. The particles become magnetized when they pass through the magnetic field that has been created at the record head. Later, the magnetic tape may be played back, and the stored magnetism retrieved by way of the playback head. The pattern of magnetism that is

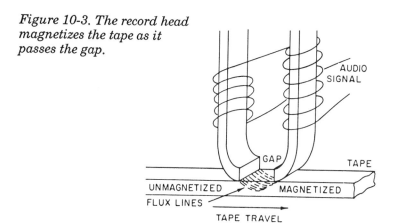

Figure 10-3. The record head magnetizes the tape as it passes the gap.

spread longitudinally along the length of the magnetic tape is analogous to the signal that created the magnetism, and it is the record amplifier that converts the applied signal voltage from the console or other device into the current that flows through the record head.

The record head itself is, in effect, a temporary magnet. An alternating current, proportional to the audio signal to be recorded, is fed through the coil in the head. The coil is wrapped around a soft iron ferrite core, in which the applied current creates an intense magnetic field (Figure 10-3). A gap has been cut in the core, and this gap is bridged by magnetic lines of force, known as flux. Flux is the magnetic equivalent of current flow. As the magnetic tape passes the gap, some of the flux passes through the tape, magnetizing it. The flux lines readily penetrate the tape, since this path offers less reluctance to the flux than the air gap itself. Reluctance is the term for opposition to a magnetic force, and is analogous to resistance in an electrical circuit.

The playback head is similar to the record head in construction and operation. A coil of wire is wrapped around a soft iron ferrite core. The tape, previously magnetized by the record head, passes by the gap in the playback head. The tape flux penetrates this gap, inducing a current, proportional to the flux, within the coil winding. The playback amplifier converts this induced current into a voltage which then appears at the tape recorder's outputs.

Figure 10-4 shows the essential components of the tape transport system. The tape to be recorded (or played back) is placed on the supply reel side of the transport. The tape is threaded past

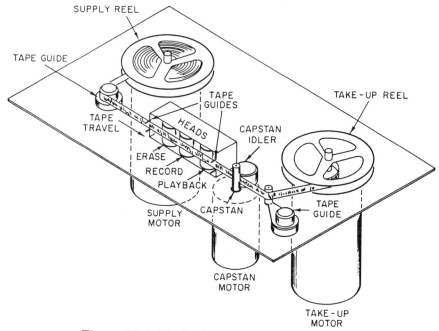

Figure 10-4. The basic tape transport system.

the tape guides and head assembly to the empty take-up reel. The capstan idler or "pinch roller" presses the tape against the capstan, pulling it past the heads at the required speed, while the take-up motor winds the tape onto the empty reel.

Magnetic Tape

It was previously noted that magnetic tape consists of a base material upon which has been placed a magnetic coating. This coating consists of a solution in which gamma ferric oxide (Fe_2O_3) particles are suspended. Depending on the particular application for which the tape is intended, each particle is from 7 to 20 micro-inches in length. The particles are generally one-third to one-sixth as wide as they are long. The particles are mixed in a ball mill with other materials such as a plasticizer, conductants, dispersants and lubricants. The mixture is composed of 30 percent solvents, 10 percent solids (other than the oxide), and 60 percent oxide particles. When properly mixed, the solution has the look and consistency of chocolate syrup and the smell of nail polish.

In a continuous process, the oxide formulation is then spread on the moving base film. Many methods can be used to spread the mixture, with reverse roll coating, gravure coating and knife edge coating the preferred methods.

Before the formulation has set, the tape is passed through a strong direct current magnetic field which physically arranges the particles in a lengthwise orientation with respect to the tape. For video applications, the particles are oriented in a vertical direction. For the system to work efficiently, the particles should be oriented perpendicular to the head gaps of the recording/playback system.

The tape is then dried, which drives off the solvents, and then calendered. The tape is passed between two high pressure heated rollers, and this calendering process smooths the surface of the tape. This is a critical step since the tape's smoothness greatly affects the tape to head contact. Bumps in the tape cause the tape to lift away from the head for a brief instant, and it is these small surface imperfections in the tape that cause dropouts.

After calendering, the tape is stored and "cured" for a brief period of time. This allows the tape to stabilize and the last of the solvents to evaporate. At the end of the storage time the tape is slit into the proper widths and packed for shipment.

Each magnetic particle consists of one or more domains. A domain is defined as 10^{18} molecules of gamma ferric oxide, and is the smallest physical unit that can be considered a magnet. The domains are considered to be totally magnetized at all times, but since their magnetic orientation within the oxide particles is random, the net total magnetism of the tape is zero. When an applied magnetic force, as in the record head, applies a weak magnetic field, only those domains whose existing magnetic orientation approximates the direction of the applied field will be forced from their natural "unstressed" state into magnetic alignment with the field. When the field is withdrawn, most—if not all—of the domains will return to their original unstressed random orientation. In other words, the tape remains non-magnetized.

If a stronger magnetic force field is applied, many more domains will be forced into alignment with it. When the field is withdrawn, some domains will return to their original random or unstressed orientation, while other domains will remain in the orientation forced upon them by the applied magnetic field. Consequently, the tape will remain magnetized. This residual magnetism is not quite as strong as the applied magnetic force (since some of the domains returned to their unstressed orientation when the force was withdrawn), yet the tape definitely remains in a measurable state of magnetization.

If an even stronger magnetic force is applied, all the domains will be forced into alignment with it. When this happens, the tape is said to be saturated, that is, no further magnetic action can take place. Now, when the magnetic force is withdrawn, very few domains will return to their original unstressed orientation, and the tape is now in its maximum possible magnetized state. Once the applied magnetic field forces the tape into saturation, any further increase in the field strength will have no further effect on the tape. When all the domains have been forced into alignment with the applied magnetic field, the tape is incapable of further responding to even greater field strengths.

Magnetic Characteristics

In order to be of practical use as a program storage medium, a magnetic tape has to possess a linear transfer characteristic. That is, its playback output must be a non-distorted (or linear) replica of the original recorded input signal. Low- and high-level signals must retain their proper relative amplitudes if a usable recording is to be made. But, when we apply the basic properties of magnetism to recording tape, we may find that the weakest audio signals do not get recorded at all. While moderate-level signals are recorded satisfactorily, very high-level signals are distorted if the signal strength is sufficient to drive the tape into saturation. In other words, magnetic tape recording seems at the moment to be a non-linear process, as in fact it is if corrective steps are not taken. Before describing these corrective measures, we can illustrate the magnetic properties of recording tape by drawing the so-called hysteresis loop, as shown in Figure 10-5.

The Hysteresis Loop

Magnetic force, measured in units called oersteds, is symbolized by the letter H. When a tape passes through a magnetic field, the magnetization that remains on the tape after the magnetic field is withdrawn is called remanent magnetism. This remanent magnetism is measured in gauss, and is symbolized by the letter B. A

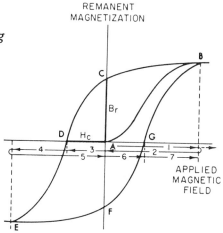

Figure 10-5. The hysteresis
loop. A graph of the
magnetism left on a recording
tape by an applied magnetic
field.

B_r = retentivity,

H_c = coercivity.

tape's ability to store magnetic energy is referred to as its retentivity, B_r. To illustrate the magnetic tape's storage capabilities, we shall apply a direct current to the record head. Starting at zero, the current will be gradually increased in the positive direction. In Figure 10-5, the applied current creates a gradually increasing positive magnetic force (arrow 1). The positive magnetization of the tape increases, non-linearly, from zero (A) to positive saturation (B). Once the saturation point has been reached, any additional increase in magnetic force (the dashed line extension of arrow 1) has no further effect on the tape.

When the applied force is gradually decreased to zero by decreasing the applied current (arrow 2), the magnetism left on the tape decreases, not to the zero value at (A), but to (C). The heavy vertical line, B_r, represents the retentivity of the tape, that is, the residual magnetism left on the tape after the applied magnetic force has been reduced to zero. If we cease our experiment at this point, the tape would remain magnetized. But, if a gradually increasing negative force is now applied (arrow 3), the tape's magnetism will be reduced to zero (D) when that force reaches the magnitude represented by the solid horizontal line Hc. Hc is the coercivity of the tape. This is the force required to completely demagnetize it, and return all the domains to their unstressed state. As the negative force continues to increase (arrow 4), the tape will be negatively magnetized. The magnetism will increase from zero (D), to negative saturation (E). In either condition of saturation, all domains are magnetically aligned with the applied

259

magnetic field. The terms negative and positive simply refer to the opposite direction that the lines of force, and consequently the orientation of the domains, may take. When the negative force is diminished to zero (arrow 5), the residual magnetism falls off to (F). Once more, the tape is left in a magnetized state, but the polarity is opposite that shown earlier as B_r. To restore the tape to a non-magnetized state (G), a gradually increasing positive force must be re-applied (arrow 6), and a further increase in the positive direction (arrow 7) will once again drive the tape to positive saturation (B).

In this rather tedious step-by-step explanation of the properties of the magnetic-tape medium, direct current was used so that we could observe the effect of a force of gradually changing magnitude and polarity. In practice, of course, we will apply an alternating current, such as a sine wave, to the record head and thus to the tape. However, in terms of the properties of magnetic tape, frequencies within the audio range may be considered as fluctuating direct current voltages.

The Transfer Characteristic

To study the effect of recording an alternating current signal on to tape, we may draw a transfer characteristic, such as the one shown in Figure 10-6. This transfer characteristic is simply a graph of retentivity versus applied magnetic force. Although the curve superficially resembles the line between (A) and (B) in Figure 10-5, it is actually derived mathematically from a series of hysteresis loops. The hysteresis loop shown in Figure 10-5 il-

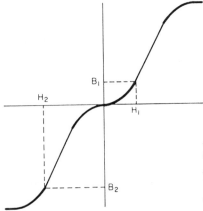

Figure 10-6. A typical transfer characteristic for magnetic tape. An applied magnetic force of H_1 will store a magnetic field of B_1 on the tape.

lustrates the retentivity of a tape that was driven to the saturation point. However, if the applied force had been somewhat less, the hysteresis loop would have been smaller and somewhat differently shaped, thereby giving a different value of retentivity. For any value of applied force, there is a corresponding value of retentivity once that force is withdrawn. For example, if a positive force of H_1 is applied, as shown in Figure 10-6, the tape will be left with a retentivity of B_1. If a negative force, H_2, is applied, the retentivity will be B_2, and so on. Therefore, the curve of Figure 10-6 should be understood to be a plot of retentivity for any value of magnetic force applied, between negative and positive saturation.

In Figure 10-7, the transfer characteristic is redrawn in an exaggerated form for clarity of explanation. Five waveforms, (A-E), are shown, representing various magnitudes of alternating current supplied to the record head. In waveform (A), the progressively longer arrows indicate an increasing magnetic force, first positive, and then negative. The smallest arrows indicate forces that do not permanently affect the tape. The next two sets of arrows indicate forces that do affect the tape slightly, and the largest arrows indicate an applied force operating for the moment within the linear portion of the transfer characteristic. The resulting magnetism left on the tape as a result of waveform (A) may be plotted as shown on the output side of the transfer characteristic. Obviously, the output is quite distorted, both in wave shape and amplitude. The output is redrawn at (A'), and the outputs from the other wave forms (B-E), are shown as (B'-E'). Note that waveform (C) does not produce at all, and that waveform (E') is flat-topped, since the magnitude of the input signal has driven the tape into saturation.

These output waveforms illustrate the non-linear properties of magnetic tape as a storage medium. However, it should be noted that there are two segments of the transfer characteristic that are linear. These segments are identified in Figure 10-7 as well, and any portion of an input waveform that falls within these segments will be linearly reproduced. This may be noted in output waveforms (A') and (D'), where the sections measured by the vertical arrows are seen to be non-distorted reproductions of the equivalent section of the input.

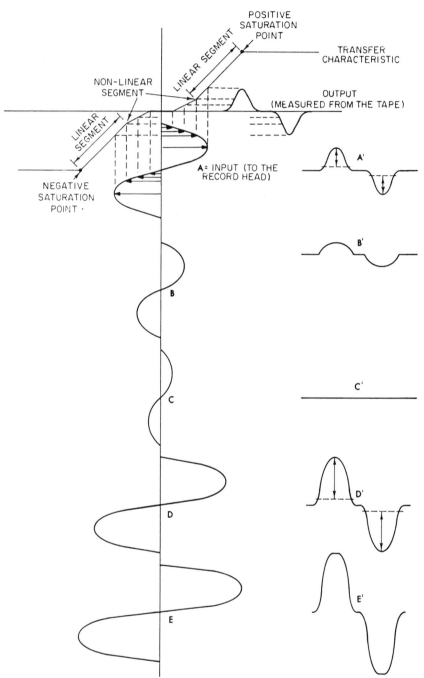

Figure 10-7. The effects of a non-linear transfer characteristic. Various levels of input signals (A through E) produce distorted (non-linear) output waveshapes (A^1-E^1).

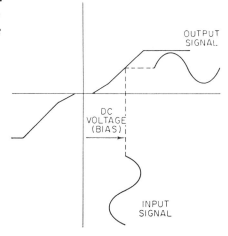

Figure 10-8. Achieving a linear transfer characteristic by using DC bias. The DC bias shifts the applied signal into one of the linear portions of the transfer characteristic.

Bias

In Figure 10-7, the applied signal is an alternating current varying between zero and some positive, and then negative, maximum amplitude. As noted earlier, only when the amplitude forces the tape's magnetization into the linear portion of the transfer characteristic will the output be a faithful reproduction of the input. If an additional direct current were also applied, the audio signal would now alternate above and below that direct current value instead of about the zero point as before. In Figure 10-8, a positive direct current, called a bias current, is applied to the record head. The magnitude of this bias current places it, as shown, midway in the positive linear portion of the transfer characteristic. Now, when the audio signal is also applied, the resultant magnetization will vary about this bias level, and the output will fall within this linear segment.

Despite the obvious improvement in linearity, direct current biasing does not allow the tape to be used to its full potential. By observation, it may be seen that only a small part of the entire transfer characteristic is being used. Consequently, the full magnetic capabilities of the tape are not being utilized. Furthermore, input levels must be considerably restricted so that signal values do not fall outside the positive linear segment of the transfer curve. As a further disadvantage, this type of biasing tends to saturate the record head core and magnetize it permanently, introducing noise onto the tape and perhaps partially erasing it. Yet

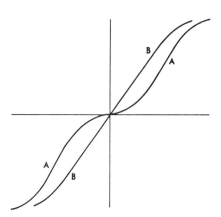

Figure 10-9. The apparent linearizing properties of high-frequency AC bias.

A = typical non-linear transfer characteristics of magnetic tape (no bias signal applied.)

B = apparent transfer characteristics in the presence of an applied high-frequency bias voltage.

despite these limitations, direct current biasing is a marked improvement over recording without any bias.

Many precursors of the modern magnetic tape recorder used direct current bias, but it was found that using a very high-frequency alternating current as a source of bias provided a more satisfactory method of overcoming the non-linearity of magnetic tape. Alternating current bias, typically a frequency of 5 to 10 times the highest frequency to be recorded, is well beyond our hearing limits. In fact, it may indeed be too high to be reproduced by some playback heads. However, the bias is actually recorded on the tape, and may be heard as a high-pitched sound if a segment of recorded tape is very slowly rocked back and forth, as in editing, across the playback head. From the shape of the transfer curve, it might be expected that the bias frequency would be recorded in a distorted form, much like any of the other frequencies illustrated in Figure 10-7. However, it has been found that at very high frequencies, the transfer characteristic becomes nearly linear over most of the range between positive and negative saturation. The degree of linearity increases with the amplitude of the bias, as shown by the curves in Figure 10-9. In simple terms, it would seem that the rapid alternations of the bias frequency overcome the magnetic medium's inertia to change in applied force. Remember that the non-linear transfer characteristic, first seen in Figure 10-6, was mathematically derived from a series of hysteresis loops, and as such it represents the effects of gradually changing values of applied magnetic force. In magnetic terms, any audio frequency may be considered to be a gradually changing force. By contrast, the bias frequency is a rapidly changing force. The tape is in a constant state of continuous magnetic agitation, and its resistance to change has been overcome.

Of course, the transfer to tape of a bias frequency, while no doubt academically intriguing, is of questionable artistic interest. We are, after all, concerned with recording music and speech, and not with the behavior of some frequency many times beyond the range of human hearing. However, AC bias allows us to store on tape a faithful reproduction of the applied audio signal, at an amplitude that takes full advantage of the full storage capabilities of the tape. Rather than simply applying the audio signal directly to the record head, it is first combined with the bias current, which is supplied by a bias oscillator built into the electronics of the tape recorder. The bias frequency may be as low as 150 kHz or as high as 450 kHz. The mixture of the two will appear as shown in Figure 10-10. The figure shows that the audio signal has become an envelope on the larger amplitude bias signal. This simple addition of bias plus audio is fed to the record head. The bias frequency is linearly recorded on the tape, along with the relatively slight amplitude changes caused by the audio envelope.

Bias Requirements and Effects

When an audio signal is recorded without bias, the output contains a large segment of third harmonic distortion. That is, the output waveform will contain a component that is three times the frequency of the applied audio signal. As bias is added, this distortion is reduced as the bias linearizes the transfer charac-

Figure 10-10. Combining bias and audio signals at the record head.

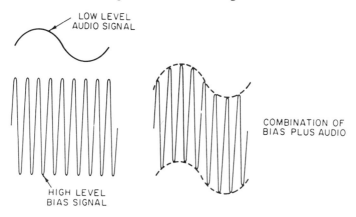

LOW LEVEL
AUDIO SIGNAL

HIGH LEVEL
BIAS SIGNAL

COMBINATION OF
BIAS PLUS AUDIO

teristic. This linearizing effect is a function of not only frequency, but of amplitude as well. As the bias amplitude is increased from zero, the transfer curve becomes more and more linear, resulting in less and less third harmonic distortion. Conversely, as bias is decreased below optimum, distortion increases.

This may lead us to think that the optimum bias level is the level required to reduce third harmonic distortion to a minimum. Unfortunately, it is not that simple. In a typical situation, it may be found that at some point before minimum distortion is reached, the high-frequency response of the audio signal begins to fall off significantly. Part of this loss is frequency dependent and occurs as the wavelength on tape of the applied audio signal becomes equal to the record head gap space. This loss, called scanning loss, is supplemented by the fact that as the tape leaves the record head, a secondary half-gap is created and causes some self-erasure of higher frequencies. Both of these phenomena are affected by tape speed since this varies the physical length of a wave on a given amount of tape (discussed in Chapter 2). The remainder of this loss is a function of the fact that the sensitivity of the tape changes with the amount of applied bias. However, the tape sensitivity varies over the audio frequency band so that when the proper amount of bias for maximum low frequencies output is found, that level does not coincide with the amount of bias required for maximum high-frequency output. For example, if the bias level is gradually increased from zero, while recording a 15 kHz tone, that frequency will be recorded on tape at a gradually increasing amplitude until the optimum bias for that 15 kHz tone is reached. Further increase in the bias level will result in a decrease in the amplitude of the recorded 15 kHz signal. If we now record a low-frequency signal, we will discover that the bias level must be increased several dB beyond what was required for maximum output at 15 kHz in order to achieve the maximum possible output for the low frequency.

Different tapes from various manufacturers have slightly different oxide thickness and formulations, and these different coercivity values affect the overall transfer characteristic of the magnetic domains. These effects are most noticeable in the high-frequency response of the tape as well as its overall sensitivity. Tape recorder alignment will be discussed in detail in Chapter 12, but it must be remembered that a compromise setting must be sought that balances all of these factors.

A Bias Summary

Without bias, magnetic recording is a non-linear process. That is, the audio program stored on the tape will be a distorted replica of the original input signal.

Bias is a high-frequency (typically 10 times the highest audio frequency to be recorded), high-amplitude signal that is mixed with the applied audio signal and then sent to the record head.

It is applied to the tape to overcome its non-linear transfer characteristic.

Bias affects overall output level, high- and low-frequency relative sensitivity, and third harmonic distortion.

The amount of bias required is affected by record head gap space, tape coercivity and oxide formulation, and tape speed.

PROPERTIES OF MAGNETIC TAPE

The engineer should be aware that the operating parameters of magnetic recording tape will differ appreciably from one manufacturer to another, as well as between different types of tape from the same manufacturer. Although tape recorder alignment will be covered later (Chapter 12), here it should be understood that if a tape recorder is aligned using a certain kind of tape, it will not necessarily give optimum performance when a different type of tape is substituted. There should certainly be consistency between one reel and another of the same type of tape, but in all other cases, the engineer should be prepared to realign his tape recorders when changing types of tape. Even the so-called bias compatible tapes will benefit from optimizing the tape recorder/tape interface for each type of tape used.

Manufacturers specify the magnetic, physical, and electroacoustic characteristics of their product, each of which will be discussed separately.

Magnetic Properties

Coercivity: The coercivity (abbr. H_c) of a tape, measured in oersteds, is an indication of its sensitivity to an applied magnetic field. The published specifications usually list the strength of the magnetic field needed to bring a saturated tape to full erasure. The coercivity of representative studio tapes generally ranges between 280 and 380 oersteds.

Retentivity: As discussed earlier, retentivity is a measure of a magnetic tape's flux density after a magnetic field producing full saturation has been withdrawn. Retentivity is expressed in gauss.

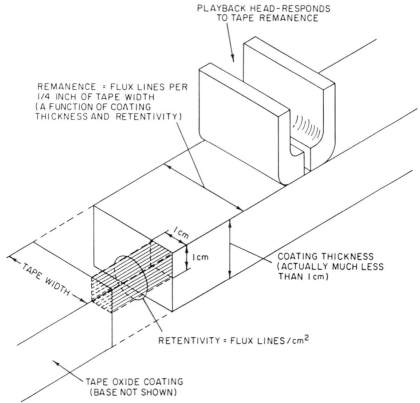

Figure 10-11. A comparison of remanence and retentivity.

Gauss is the magnetic flux lines per cross sectional square centimeter of tape.

Remanence: Remanence describes the same condition as retentivity, but is expressed in lines of flux per linear quarter-inch of tape width. This specification is particularly significant, since the playback head's output level is a direct function of the tape's remanence. Figure 10-11 illustrates the measurement of both retentivity and remanence.

Sensitivity: Sensitivity is an indication of a tape's relative output level as compared to some specified reference tape. Thus, given the same input level, a tape with a sensitivity of +2 will produce an output level 2 dB higher than the standard reference tape.

Harmonic Distortion: Recorded third harmonic distortion, in addition to being a function of bias level, will also be found to increase as the recorded level of the tape approaches saturation.

Maximum allowable recorded level is usually defined as that level at which the third harmonic distortion reaches 3 percent.

Headroom: A tapes headroom is defined as the difference between standard operating level (to be explained shortly) and the 3 percent third harmonic distortion point. Thus, if a tape reaches 3 percent third harmonic distortion when the applied input level is 9 dB above 0 VU (when 0 VU = standard operating level), it is said to have a 9 dB headroom.

High Output Tapes

It would be very difficult and expensive to design a meter that could read magnetic flux level directly from tape. Most professional tape recorders use a level of +4 dBm to equal 0 VU. When magnetic tape was first put into professional use, a magnetic level that equaled the 0 VU on the tape recorder meters was needed as a reference. Many percussive type sounds may exhibit peak values of 9 or 10 dB above the average level read as 0 VU on a loudness related volume indicator. (This was discussed in Chapter 2.) To compensate for this, the standard operating magnetic level on tape was set so that a reading of zero on the tape recorder VU meters would be 9 dB below the 3 percent third harmonic distortion point. This translated to a magnetic fluxivity level of 185 nanowebers per meter (abbr. nw/m). Today, standard operating level on tape is still defined as 185 nw/m, and for many years this defined the +4 dBm = 0 VU point.

As a result of advances in oxide formulation techniques, tapes with higher sensitivity and greater headroom are now in use. The sensitivity improvement is a function of the greater retentivity of these high output tapes. For a given oxide coating thickness, this greater flux density results in a higher remanence value and therefore, a higher output level. Also, along with greater retentivity came higher coercivity which is expressed as greater available headroom. Because of this, the signal may be applied to the tape at a higher level. This takes advantage of the headroom improvement by raising the program material above the residual noise floor by the amount of the increase. Or, the tape may be recorded at standard operating level, with the increased headroom allowing occasional high peaks to be recorded with less distortion. These elevated operating levels have become standardized, and this as well as the record equalization changes afforded by the increased sensitivity will be discussed in Chapter 12 on Alignment.

Physical Properties

In addition to the oxide coating described earlier, magnetic tape consists of a base material upon which the oxide formulation is coated, and a back coating, both of which are described here.

Early tape made use of a paper base, and it was on this which the gamma ferric oxide was distributed. Later developments produced both acetate and mylar base films with the thickness of the base ranging from 0.5 mils to 1.55 mils. So-called "extended play" tapes used the thinner base film so that more tape could be wound on a given reel size. However, professional mastering tapes today use a base film thickness of either 1.0 or 1.5 mils with the latter being preferred for greatest stability. A compound polyester base film with a very high tensile strength that resists breaking as well as providing low stretch is currently used for professional audio tape.

Similar to the oxide coating, the back coating of a tape is a thin layer of carbon pigment (rather than oxide particles) suspended in a binder. The resultant surface texture reduces the possibility of slippage as the tape is pulled by the capstan and capstan idler. The back coating also provides a more even tape wind, particularly at high speeds. This is critical as an uneven wind can cause edge damage with a resultant loss of some signal. The coating is generally more abrasion resistant than uncoated polyester and in addition, its low resistivity minimizes the build-up of static charges. Typical back coating thicknesses range between 0.05 and 0.15 mils.

A typical studio grade professional mastering tape that relies on a base film thickness of 1.5 mils may total 2.03 mils in thickness when the oxide formulation and back coating mixture are added. This so-called 1.5 mil tape will normally have a total length of 2500 feet when wound on a 10-½ inch NAB (National Association of Broadcasters) reel. Occasionally a reel of 1.0 mil tape will be required and will normally be found to have a total length of 3600 feet. The record/playback times of these tape length at a speed of 15 inches per second is 33 minutes and 45 minutes respectively.

The Print-Through Phenomena

Since magnetic tape is stored on reels, each segment is wound between two other segments. The tape's magnetic field may be sufficient to partially magnetize these adjacent segments, resulting in print-through. Print-through can be defined as the unintentional transfer of a magnetic signal to adjacent layers of tape. It is usually 55 to 65 dB in level below the printing signal, and appears as pre- and post-echoes of the recorded signal. On many recordings, the program itself will mask the print-through, especially the post-echoes. However, print-through may be noticeable at the beginning and end of a recording, and during sudden changes in dynamic level, where a quite passage is not loud enough to mask the echo of a loud passage directly preceding or following it.

Pre-print is much worse than post-print, and it is therefore advisable to store tape tails out—that is, without rewinding after playing. This way, the worst case print-through comes as a post-echo and stands the greatest likelihood of being masked by the program itself.

Print-through occurs as soon as the tape is wound on the reel just after passing the record/playback head. Temperature and humidity play a small but insignificant role in the amount of print-through found on a master tape. Modern back coatings assist in reducing print-through, but the elevated operating levels used on high coercivity tapes increase the problem.

Print-through may be reduced by fast forwarding and rewinding the tape prior to playback. This "exercising" of the tape ever so slightly rearranges the alignment of adjacent layers and seems to partially erase the print-through without affecting the original signal. Any of the noise-reduction systems discussed in Chapter 9 will alleviate the problem by lowering the print-through along with the tape hiss to below an audible level. Print-through is not a problem in digital systems as will be explained in later chapters.

Chapter 11

THE TAPE RECORDER

The magnetic tape recorder, as we know it today, has been in use in its present basic form since the early 1950s. The basic transport design shown earlier in Figure 10-4 is as applicable today as it was then. However, early tape recorders were monophonic devices, and the audio signal took up almost the entire tape width.

TRACK FORMAT STANDARDS

These elementary machines utilized a tape that was ¼-inch in width. The record and playback heads placed a magnetic stripe along the length of the tape that was approximately the full width of the tape. This full-track format was recorded in one direction only. Therefore, if the supply reel and take-up reel were switched at the end of one pass so that the tape could be played in the opposite direction, the program material would be heard backwards.

Soon thereafter, the tape heads were divided into two parts so that the magnetic stripe of recorded energy would take up half as much space as before. Using one set of record electronics, this allowed the engineer to put twice as much information on the tape for a given length. Track 1, the upper track, would be recorded from left to right as before. At the end of the reel, the tape would be placed back on the supply side, effectively inverting the tape and reversing the positions of track 1 and 2. This top track (track 2) was then recorded. This became known as recording on "both sides" of the tape, even though it is known that both signals are on the same oxide surface, just separate and going in opposite directions. It is not uncommon today to hear someone say, "When you get to the end of the tape, turn it over and play the other side."

The next logical progression was to add a second set of record and play electronics so that both tracks could be recorded or played together. Since the two channels of material were recorded on the same tape at the same time, they were always synchronized together on playback. This half-track stereo format remains the professional standard in use for two-channel recording today. Note that it is the record/playback head configuration that determines the track format. The blank tape is no particular format until a recording is made on it.

The consumer high-fidelity manufacturers then divided the tape once again so that a stereo program could be recorded on "each side" of the tape. This is known as a quarter-track format. Quarter-track stereo displaces the tracks to try to keep crosstalk (interference between adjacent channels) to a minimum. Tracks 1 and 3 carry the stereo program in one direction, while tracks 2 and 4 carry it in the other. It would seem that any number of tracks can be thus obtained by continually deriving more and more tracks from ¼-inch tape. However, each time the size of the magnetic stripe is reduced, less flux density passes the head for a given signal. This results in a lower remanence value for each track, moving the signal closer to the residual noise level of the tape. This lowers the signal-to-noise ratio of the track by 3 dB acoustically, effectively lowering the possible musical dynamic range that can be put on the tape.

Wider tapes were developed so that more tracks could be put on a single tape without reducing the track width. Four tracks on half-inch tape retains the half-track format. In fact, some professional studios have returned to the full-track format by using two channels of information going the same direction on half-inch tape. Figure 11-1 shows most of the available analog magnetic tape formats in use today. The corresponding record/playback head configuration is also shown. Note that there are guard bands between each track to prevent crosstalk, and that even the full-track format on ¼-inch tape is slightly smaller than the full width of the tape. Notice also, that professional 4-track, 8-track, and 16-track are all half-track format.

Developments in tape sensitivity and lower noise, due to better oxides, led to the 2-inch tape 24-track format. This format is a hybrid that utilizes quarter-track format track widths but with greater spacing between tracks. Attempts were made to establish a 3-inch tape 32-track format, but problems with tape guidance and the advent of multiple machine synchronization caused it to be discontinued.

Many so-called semi-professional tape recorders use the smaller quarter-track format for home multi-track recording. These smaller formats are usually coupled with machines that operate at a reduced input/output signal level, such as 0 VU = –10 dBm, along with unbalanced signal lines. Many of these machines are quite good when equipped with noise reduction, and the lowered cost has made it possible for many musicians to experiment with multi-tracking at home prior to making a recording in a professional studio.

Tape Speed

Most reel-to-reel tape recorders found in the professional studio offer several tape speeds. Rates of 15 inches per second, that is, when 15 linear inches of tape pass the head every second, and 30 inches per second (abbr. in./sec.) are the primary speeds. This is equivalent to 38 cm./sec. and 76 cm./sec. in countries using the metric standard. Speeds of 7-½ or 3-¾ in./sec. are seldom used as they tend to accentuate dropouts on the tape. The lower speeds also will not allow the engineer to record high-frequency signals at full saturation levels on the tape. This will be discussed later in the chapter.

The Record Process

The record head is the transducer that converts the applied audio signal (the record current) into magnetic lines of force (flux) which in turn penetrate and magnetize the tape. In an effort to achieve a flat frequency response, it might seem that the record current should be kept constant regardless of the frequency of the applied audio signal. However, as we shall see, there are several good reasons why this is not the case.

If we were to analyze any piece of music from an acoustical power point of view, we might find that much of the energy lies within the middle-frequency range. For example, if a series of sound level meters were tuned to respond to various segments of the audio bandwidth, we might find the situation illustrated in Figure 11-2. The meters assigned to the frequency limits, such as the extreme lows and highs, would show readings considerably less than the meters tuned to the mid-range frequencies. This is because there is often less going on at very high or very low frequencies. Accordingly, if we were to record the music as is, the

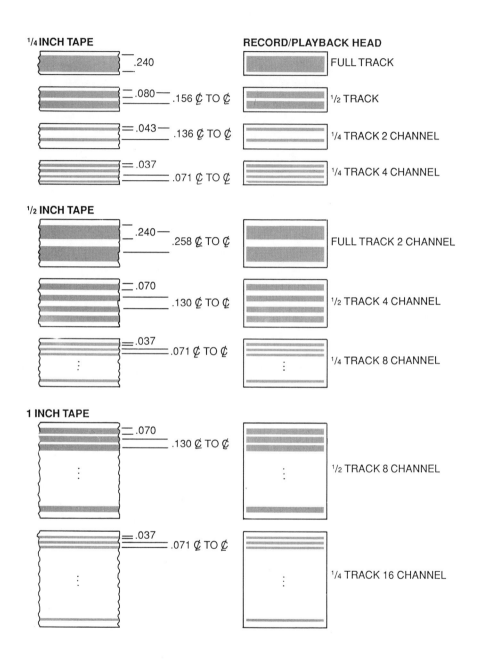

Figure 11-1. Above and at the top of the facing page, analog tape track formats commonly in use.

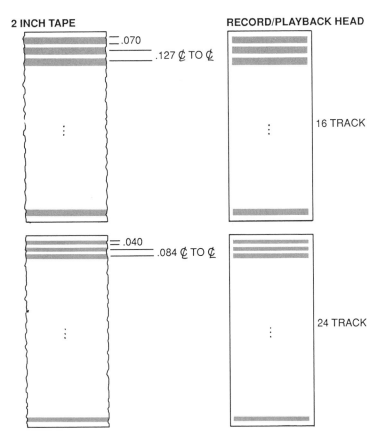

2 INCH TAPE   RECORD/PLAYBACK HEAD

.070

.127 ¢ TO ¢

16 TRACK

.040

.084 ¢ TO ¢

24 TRACK

mid-range frequencies would be the first to near the saturation level of the tape. Note, once again in Figure 11-2, that the saturation line slopes downward at the high-frequency end of the spectrum. This represents the tape's tendency towards earlier saturation at higher frequencies. From the illustration, we can see that if the level is kept down so that the mid-range is just below saturation, the low and high frequencies are well below saturation. And of course, this places these frequencies that much closer to the residual noise level, or noise floor of the tape.

Record Equalization

If these low and high frequencies were boosted somewhat, just before the record head, they would be recorded at a higher than normal amplitude, well above the residual noise level. The resultant recording would now have an unnatural amount of bass and treble, but complementary circuitry just after the playback head

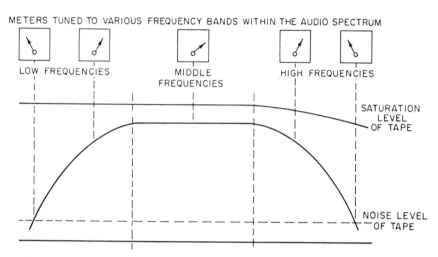

Figure 11-2. Energy distribution curve of a musical program. The exact shape of the curve will vary according to the nature of the program.

could restore the signal to its normal balance, and in so doing, lower the apparent noise level. For, as the playback circuit restored the frequencies to normal balance by lowering the lows and highs, the recorded noise would likewise be lowered. This is in effect complementary static noise reduction, as discussed in Chapter 9.

It should be clearly understood that tape recorder equalization has nothing to do with changing the apparent frequency balance of the program as heard by the listener. All equalization described within this chapter is intended solely as a compensation for the various limitations of the analog recording medium and to improve the faithfulness of the recording to the original program. When a properly adjusted tape recorder is in use, the listener should be unaware of the tape recorder equalization. This is in marked contrast to "program equalization" done at the recording console or on outboard equalizers to audibly change the frequency balance according to the tastes of the engineer or producer. The boosting of low and high frequencies, just before the applied audio signal reaches the record head is known as record pre-emphasis, and is often simply referred to as record equalization.

Due to the properties of magnetic recording tape, high frequencies will cause saturation sooner, that is, at a lower level than mid-range or low frequencies. Accordingly, high frequencies may not be boosted quite as much as low frequencies. There is also some tendency toward self-erasure at high frequencies. These facts, along with the differences in available oxide formulations (whose differences affect high frequencies more than lows), are the reason that record equalization adjustments on a tape recorder adjust high frequencies only. Low frequencies are more affected by the bias settings, and because of this fact, low-frequency boost is not user-adjustable.

The Playback Process

The playback circuit must compensate for the record pre-emphasis and restore the signal to its normal balance. In addition, equalization must be included to compensate for the output characteristics of the playback head itself. The playback head is the transducer that responds to the magnetic flux stored on the tape. It produces an output voltage that is directly proportional to the rate of change of the magnetic flux. Since this rate of change doubles every time the frequency doubles, we find that as the frequency increases, the output voltage rises according to the following formula:

$$e = N \, (d\tau/dT)$$

> where:
>
> e = output voltage
>
> N = number of coil turns of wire in the playback head
>
> $d\tau/dT$ = rate of change of flux (analogous to frequency)

Now, since a doubling of voltage equals a 6 dB increase, we may say that, for a constant-level recorded signal, the playback output will increase at the rate of 6 dB per octave. This rise will continue until the wavelength of the recorded signal is equal to twice the length of the playback head's gap. It is at this point that the rate of change of flux within the gap is greatest, and so the output voltage is at its maximum. It is the gap itself that measures the flux level. As the word implies, the gap is a physical air space across which the tape passes. The distance across the gap has been called gap width by some, and gap length by others,

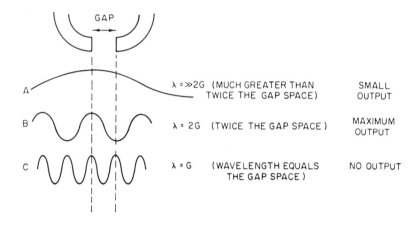

Figure 11-3. Various wavelengths within the playback head-gap space.

resulting in some mild confusion. For our purposes, the dimension will be called simply gap space, and will be labelled, G.

To understand the effect of the gap on the output level, wavelengths for several frequencies are shown in Figure 11-3. It should be understood that these wavelengths are passing across the gap at a constant velocity—for example, 15 in./sec. Although it is convenient to think of these wavelengths in terms of some frequencies, it should be kept in mind that each wavelength represents a certain length of tape, and depending on the tape speed, the frequency reproduced by this wavelength will vary. For example, at 15 in./sec., a 1 mil wavelength will produce a 15 kHz tone. If we play the tape at half speed (7.5 in./sec.), the same 1 mil wavelength now produces a tone of 7.5 kHz. In Figure 11-3, a wavelength A corresponds to a relatively low frequency. The flux level is changing slowly, that is, the rate of change within the gap is relatively slow, and the output voltage is therefore small. As the frequency rises, so does the rate of change within the gap, until the frequency corresponding to wavelength B is reached. At this wavelength ($\lambda = 2$ G), the rate of change is at its greatest since, as a positive peak crosses one side of the gap, a negative peak crosses the other, and vice versa.

Beyond this wavelength, the output level falls off sharply, and at half this wavelength (λ= G), the output is zero, because as one positive peak crosses one side of the gap, another crosses the other, for a net change of zero. Across the gap there is no rate of change, and therefore no output voltage. This is illustrated by wavelength C in Figure 11-3. At each successive halving of the wavelength, the output will again be zero, while in between these points the output will sharply rise and fall, as shown in Figure 11-4. On a professional-quality playback head, the gap space is typically around 0.25 mils. Therefore, a frequency whose wavelength is 0.25 mils would give zero output as just described.

Remember that on tape, the wavelength is the physical distance taken up by one cycle of the frequency in question. Every time the tape speed is doubled (for example from 7.5 in./sec. to 15 in./sec.), twice as much tape is used, and the wavelength for any frequency is therefore twice as long. Consequently, the frequency at which maximum output occurs is likewise doubled. This is why high-frequency response is extended with each doubling of tape speed. At 15 in./sec., 0.25 mils corresponds to a frequency of 75,000 Hz, certainly well past the audio range, so zero at this frequency would be of no concern. Maximum output would occur at a frequency with a 0.1 mil wavelength, that is to say, 37,500 Hz. At 7.5 in./sec., this same wavelength would yield 18,750 Hz, still sufficiently high for most purposes, but now within the audible range. If this gap loss was the only limitation on upper frequency response, we might safely ignore it when operating at speeds of 7.5 in./sec. or greater. At 7.5 in./sec., the rapid fall-off in output level, from maximum to zero, occurs within the octave

Figure 11-4. Output characteristics of a playback head when reproducing a constant flux tape. The output rises at 6 dB/8va until the wavelength equals twice the space. The output falls off rapidly to zero at λ = G.

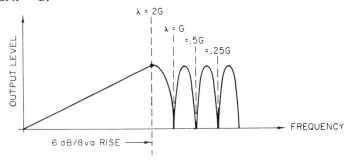

that begins at $\lambda = 2G$ (18,750 Hz at 7.5 in.\sec.) and poses no real practical problem.

However, there are other limitations within the playback head, and in the tape itself, which will account for losses that affect the upper audio frequencies even at 15 or 30 in./sec. The cumulative effect of these losses, added to the gap loss effect, may noticeably restrict the upper audio frequency response. These losses are due to a variety of causes.

On the tape, higher frequencies have a tendency towards self-erasure, and bias current may also reduce high-frequency response somewhat. Within the heads, eddy currents are a further contribution to high-frequency roll-off. And the slightest separation between head and tape will cause noticeable high-frequency dropout. Further losses will occur if the record head and the playback head are not in correct mechanical alignment with respect to each other, and to the tape path. Some of these losses will be discussed in detail in the chapter on tape recorder alignment. These losses combine to prevent the tape from recording a full level high-frequency signal at speeds below 15 in./sec.

Playback Equalization

To compensate for the 6 dB/8 Va rise in the output voltage which occurs over most of the audio range, a playback equalization circuit with a 6 dB/8 Va cut is employed. But, at the highest audio frequencies this 6 dB/8 Va cut must be replaced with a high-frequency boost to help overcome the losses just described. Of course, once $\lambda = G$, there is zero output from the playback head and no amount of equalization will help. However, proper playback equalization should keep the frequency response flat within the entire practical range.

The NAB (National Association of Broadcasters) Standard Reproducing Characteristic is shown in Figure 11-5. It should be understood that this post-emphasis equalization is in addition to the 6 dB/8 Va cut just mentioned. The combination of the NAB characteristic and the 6 dB/8 Va cut is shown in Figure 11-6. The low end roll-off within the NAB standard is to compensate for the low-frequency boost in the record circuit, and it restores these frequencies to their normal balance. Since the high frequencies were also boosted in the record circuit, it might seem that a complementary roll-off would be required in the playback circuit, as indeed would be the case if the record and playback losses de-

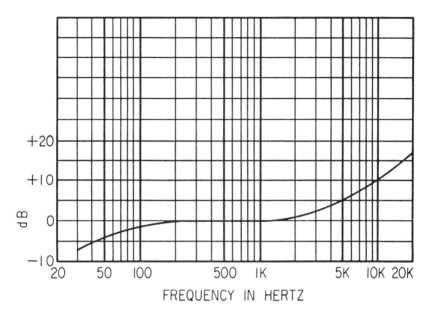

Figure 11-5. The NAB Standard Reproducing Characteristic. (7.5, 15in./sec.).

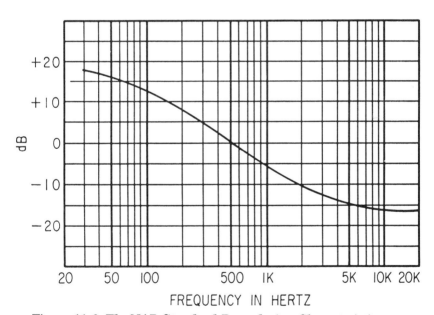

Figure 11-6. The NAB Standard Reproducing Characteristic combined with a 6 dB/8va roll-off. Transition frequencies are 50 Hz and 3180 Hz. (7.5 and 15 in./sec.).

scribed earlier were not a factor. However, the high end pre-emphasis (in the record circuit) only partially overcomes these losses, and so, additional boost, rather than a roll-off, is required in the playback circuit.

As a consequence of the record/playback losses, there is no published record equalization standard. At the lower frequencies, the boost is nearly the opposite of the NAB Reproducing Characteristic. However, the cumulative effect of the various high-frequency losses occurring within the record/playback chain cannot be predicted, since they are dependent on the bias level setting, the recorded level, the type of tape, etc. Therefore, the proper record equalization is simply that which will yield a flat frequency response when the playback circuit has been aligned according to the NAB standard.

Playback Equalization Standards

As just mentioned, an equalization standard based on the NAB Reproducing Standard is used to compensate for the anomalies found in the magnetic recording/playback process. However, tapes and recording equipment used and produced in Europe will often conform to the CCIR Standard (Consultative Committee for International Radio). This is also referred to as the IEC Standard (International Electrotechnical Commission). In the United States, the NAB reproducing curves are used for tape speeds of 7.5 in./sec. and 15 in./sec., while in Europe the IEC or CCIR reproducing curves are used for these same speeds. The 7.5 in./sec. and 15 in./sec. CCIR curves differ slightly. In both Europe and the United States, another reproducing curve, known as the AES Reproducing Curve (Audio Engineering Society) is used for 30 in./sec. These standards differ in relation to the point at which high-frequency boost and low-frequency roll-off occur. These transition points (the point where the Reproducing Curve flattens out) are defined as time constants. The actual frequencies can be determined from the time constants based on the following formula:

$$f = \frac{1}{2 \pi \tau}$$

where:

f = the transition frequency

π = 3.14

τ = the time constant

The IEC curves have a somewhat greater high-frequency post-emphasis than that prescribed by the NAB characteristic, yet there is no low-frequency roll-off since no low-frequency record pre-emphasis is used. The AES curve uses less high-frequency post-emphasis than either the NAB or CCIR Reproducing Standards at the high end, and no low-frequency roll-off. Figure 11-7 illustrates the IEC curves, while Figure 11-8 shows the 30 in./sec. AES curve. The following chart gives the time constants and transition frequencies for the various standards.

Speed	Standard	Time Constant	High Transition	Low Transition
7.5 in./sec.	NAB	3180&50 μsecs	3180 Hz	50 Hz
15 in./sec.	NAB	3180&50 μsecs	3180 Hz	50 Hz
7.5 in./sec.	IEC	70 μsecs	2275 Hz	—
15 in./sec.	IEC	35 μsecs	4550 Hz	—
30 in./sec.	AES	17.5 μsecs	9100 Hz	—

Figure 11-9 summarizes the frequency characteristics and corrective equalization found within the modern tape recorder.

Figure 11-7. The IEC standard reproducing characteristic combined with a 6 dB/8va roll-off. Transition frequencies are 2275 Hz (7.5 in./sec.) and 4550 Hz (15 in./sec.).

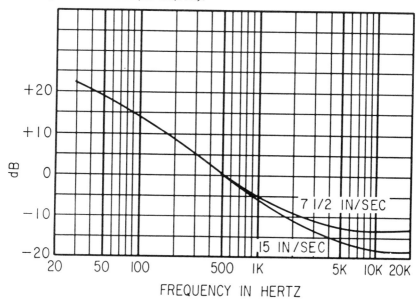

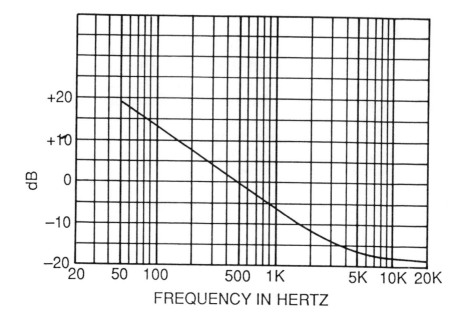

Figure 11-8. The AES standard reproducing characteristic combined with a 6 dB/8va roll-off and a transition frequency of 9100 Hz.

The Erase Head

The function of the erase head is to remove any remanent magnetization from previous use of the tape. The need for an efficient erase mechanism is not unique to magnetic recording. Notebook pages, blackboards, and magnetic tape are alike in that they have to be erased after each use if they are to be re-used. To simply record over an already recorded tape would be just as confusing, aurally, as the visual confusion that would result from writing over a previously used page of notes.

In the tape path, the erase head immediately precedes the record head. Generally, the tape recorder's high-frequency bias oscillator also supplies a very strong alternating current to the erase head. This "erase current" completely saturates the tape, and of course, there is no audio signal mixed with it, as in the record head circuit. This heavy erase current forces the tape's magnetic particles out of their previous magnetic orientation, and into saturation. The high frequency of the erase current alternately drives the tape from positive to negative saturation, and as each segment of the tape moves out of the magnetic field around

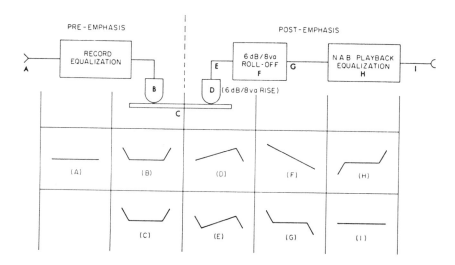

Figure 11-9. Summary of the frequency characteristics and corrective equalization within a tape recorder.

A. *A flat frequency response is applied to the input.*

B. *Record equalization boosts low and high frequencies.*

C. *Tape is recorded with boosted low and high frequencies.*

D. *Playback head exhibits 6dB/8va rise in output level, with rapid fall-off beyond λ = 2G.*

E. *Recorded response,* c, *as reproduced by playback head with 6dB/8va rise. High end boost of response c may partially counteract rapid fall-off beyond λ= 2G.*

F. *6 dB/8va. roll-off to compensate for playback head characteristic.*

G. *Resultant response after 6dB/8va roll-off.*

H. *N.A.B. equalization to restore flat response.*

I. *Resultant flat frequency response corresponds to input response* a.

the erase head, the effect of the field on the segment becomes less and less. The hysteresis loop for the segment grows smaller and smaller, consequently the remanent flux diminishes eventually to zero, and the tape segment leaves the vicinity of the erase head completely demagnetized.

Of course, all of this happens very quickly, as the tape travels past the erase head on its way to the record head. By the time the tape arrives at the record head, all traces of previously recorded information have been removed, and the tape is ready to accept the new signal.

The Tape Transport System

For optimum performance of the recorder's electronics system, it is essential that the magnetic tape maintain constant contact with the head over which it passes. The slightest up-and-down movement, or variation in tape-to-head pressure will seriously degrade the tape recorder's performance. Even a slight speed error will become a serious problem if the tape thus recorded is played back on a different machine.

In addition to the supply, take-up, and capstan motors briefly mentioned earlier, the complete tape transport system includes a series of tape path guides, located on either side, as well as within, the head assembly. What follows is a description of the

Figure 11-10. The capstan/capstan idler system. The capstan idler is often called a pinch roller (Ampex photo).

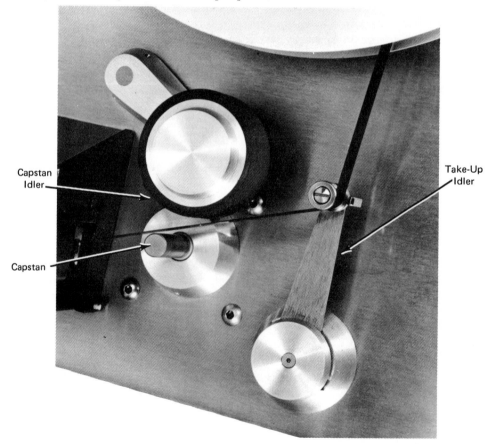

Capstan Idler

Take-Up Idler

Capstan

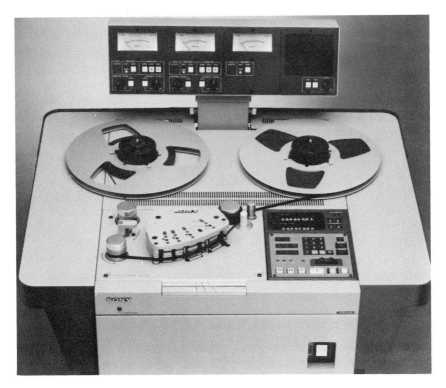

Figure 11-11. Top view of a two-channel quarter-inch analog tape recorder. The third meter is for time code (Sony APR-5000, Sony photo).

various components within the complete transport system. Although construction details may vary from one tape recorder model to another, most of the components mentioned may be found on every studio grade reel-to-reel tape recorder, be it analog or digital.

Figure 11-10 is a close-up of the capstan/pressure roller assembly. As shown, the machine is stopped, and the pressure roller has swung away from the spinning capstan. When the play button is depressed, the roller swings down against the capstan, pinching the tape between them, and pulling it past the heads at a constant speed.

In Figure 11-11, the tops of the supply and take-up reel motors are seen. When the machine is in the play or record mode, both motors attempt to wind the tape onto their respective reels. But, since the capstan motor is pulling the tape in the direction of the take-up motor, the tape winds off the supply reel and onto the take-up reel as intended. However, the reverse torque applied to the supply reel prevents the tape from exiting the supply reel too quickly, and the constant back tension promotes good tape to head contact. If this torque were excessive, the tape might be stretched as the capstan and supply motors attempted to pull the tape in opposite directions.

Reel Tensions

The reels are kept under tension by a current applied to both the take-up and supply reel motors. The greater that current, the greater the tape tension. With a constant applied current, the actual mechanical tension on the tape will vary with the amount of tape left on the reel. As less tape remains on the supply reel, the hold-back tension on the tape becomes greater and greater. Similarly, the take-up tension on the take-up reel decreases as it fills up with tape. Overall, the tension must be sufficient to maintain good tape-to-head contact, yet not so great as to cause tape stretching or to affect the speed of the tape past the heads. Although a full roll of tape on either reel requires more tension than an almost empty reel, the tension is usually adjusted for some mid-point value between the optimum tension for full and empty reels. Many of the current microprocessor-based tape machines actually sample the tension at specific intervals, and by varying the current applied to the respective reels, can optimize the tension continuously as the tape pack moves from one reel to another.

Most studio recording is done with reels of tape wound on NAB hubs, similar to the ones shown in Figure 11-12. The inner diameter of these hubs is 4-½ inches. Nevertheless, it is often necessary to use smaller plastic reels, also shown in Figure 11-12. These may have an inner diameter of only 2-¼ inches, and the normal tension adjustment, made with the NAB hub, would place an undue amount of tension on tape being wound on such a reel. Many older tape recorders have a reel size switch (or switches) which change the tension to a lesser amount when smaller hub diameter reels are to be used.

Multi-track tape recorders, all designed for NAB hubs, are notorious for being extremely critical in response to reel tension. The inertia of a large reel of 2-inch tape can put great demands on the supply and take-up reel motors. Older multi-track ma-

*Figure 11-12. Tape reels of various sizes. Note the relatively large
diameter on the metal reels. The plastic reels have a much smaller
inner diameter, with the exception of the test-tape reel (upper right.)
Its extra large inner diameter protects the tape against excessive reel
tension.*

chines often need to be re-tensioned (a time-consuming process)
when changing from 10 1/2 inch NAB reels to ¼-inch NAB reels.
These larger reels, which hold twice as much tape as the 10-½
inch reel, are sometimes used when more recording time per reel
is necessary. However, the modern microprocessor-controlled
transport successfully copes with these changes in tension requirements with a minimum of operator adjustment.

Idler(s)

These idler(s) provide guidance for tape height, and help to
also reduce wow and flutter (discussed later). The idlers turn
with the tape motion and help keep the tape moving smoothly.
These rollers may also contain the mechanically-driven tape
counter mechanism. This mechanism may provide a readout in an
hour/minute/second format. Even though the counter may be an
electronic device, the physical tape motion is what is measured.
Therefore, absolute tape positions are not possible since any tape

slippage on the idler can create minor timing errors. Absolute tape addressing can only be carried out when a timing code is placed on the tape itself. This type of system will be discussed in great detail in Chapter 15 on SMPTE time code. A tape-motion sensor may be placed between these supply side idlers as well.

Located just beyond the capstan/pinch roller assembly, the take-up idler serves as a guide for proper tape height, and in some machines contains a microswitch that senses tape presence and functions as a transport on/off switch. When no tape is threaded, or the tension is not proper, the machine will not enter any mode that would cause the tape to move. This prevents tape spillage or breakage, and in the event of tape breakage while in any moving mode will cause the transport to stop. Similarly, when either reel runs out of tape, the switch stops both reels from spinning.

Braking Systems

Some tape recorders employ a mechanical braking system on both reel motors. In the stop mode, a clutch system may allow the reels to spin freely in one direction only, allowing tape to be wound up on either reel, yet preventing it from accidentally spilling off. In the play, fast forward, and rewind modes, the brakes may be applied only to the reel motor from which the tape is being unwound, as a precaution against tape spillage. Once the machine stops, the brakes are applied to both reel motors.

In some recorders, mechanical brakes have been completely eliminated, with all braking being done electronically. In the stop mode, the reels are kept under tension by a current applied to both motors. Since both reels are attempting to take up tape, the tape may slowly creep across the heads while the machine is stopped, if the braking currents are not properly balanced.

However, most tape recorders today apply a combination of mechanical brakes along with electronic reel tensioning. This allows for electronic braking during wind and rewind (which is more gentle to the tape) and total stoppage with no creeping when in the stop mode.

Edit Switch

On some machines, when the edit button is pressed, the capstan/pinch roller pulls tape across the heads in the usual manner, however, the take-up reel motor is disabled so that the tape spills off the machine, rather than winding onto the take-up reel. This is called the dump mode and allows the unwanted part of the tape (when editing) to spill to the floor. On other transports the edit switch may just release the mechanical brakes while keeping a minimal amount of tension on the reel motors. This allows the engineer to easily move the tape across the heads by hand, and in combination with the play switch may cause the transport to enter the dump mode.

Fast Forward and Rewind Switches

When either the fast forward or the rewind switch is pressed, the pressure roller releases the tape, and the appropriate reel motor begins spinning very quickly, winding or rewinding the tape at high speed. In either mode, tape lifters hold the tape away from the heads. This prevents excessive head wear, and prevents the sudden increase in flux change across the playback head gap from reaching the playback electronics. Many tape recorders have a "library wind" or "shuttle speed" that restricts the maximum wind or rewind speed to a fixed inches per second rate. This allows a better tape pack for storage and prevents edge damage. Typical rates are between 150 in./sec. and 180 in./sec. The edit button may defeat the tape lifters in the shuttle mode so that pauses between recorded material can be found by ear. However, care should be taken to make sure that the playback monitor volume is lowered first, so as to avoid loudspeaker and ear damage.

Wow and Flutter

Proper uniform tape speed is a function of the capstan motor, pressure roller (capstan idler) tension, and the torque applied to the reel motors. Two common irregularities in tape speed are termed wow and flutter. The terms closely describe the type of sound that may be heard if the irregularity becomes excessive.

Wow is a slowly varying pitch change, which may be caused by a variety of factors. Chief among them may be transport misalignment, particularly tension discrepancies between the take-up

Figure 11-13. Detailed view of the head assembly showing wide-profile heads, tape guides, and scrape-flutter idler.

and supply reels, an out-of-round capstan or pressure roller, or a worn bearing that may cause a low-frequency fluctuation in the tape speed that results in an audible wow noticeable especially on sustained tones.

Flutter, as the word implies, is a very rapid speed fluctuation, producing a fluttering kind of sound. It is usually traced to some sort of tape vibration, not unlike that of a string on a violin which has been set into motion by pulling the bow across it. For example, as the tape moves across the transport system, at various locations it passes over, and is supported by, tape guides. The unsupported tape between these guides may be forced into mechanical vibration, and if a record or playback head detects this vibration, or flutter, the listener hears a high-frequency modulation of the music program.

Scrape Flutter Idlers

To keep the flutter frequency as high as possible—well beyond the audio range—so-called scrape flutter idlers may be installed between the heads as shown in Figure 11-13. The scrape flutter idler reduces the length of unsupported tape, thus raising the resultant vibration, or flutter, frequency. The supply side idler also acts as a flutter idler, isolating the supply reel from the head assembly, and reducing the length of unsupported tape on that side of the transport.

Variable Speed Operation

The capstan on most tape recorders is driven by a direct current servo motor. Here, a tachometer registers the motor speed (and hence the tape speed) and compares it to a reference signal

Figure 11-14. A typical remote controller for a multi-track tape recorder.

supplied from either a built-in oscillator or a crystal frequency. An error signal equivalent to any difference between the two signals continuously corrects the capstan motor, keeping it precisely on speed.

For variable speed operation, the built-in reference frequency is changed by the operator by way of a variable potentiometer. As the reference is changed, the tape speed varies continuously over a wide range, as the error signal brings the capstan motor into synchronization with the applied reference signal. Many tape recorders today have this as a standard feature, and either the positive or negative percentage of change, or the change in plus or minus semi-tones is noted electronically on the front panel.

Tape Transport Remote Control

Most multi-track tape recorders are equipped for remote control operation, so that the engineer may control the transport from his position at the console. This allows the multi-track tape recorder, with its attendant cooling fans and transport mechanics to be located away from critical listening areas. Most remote controllers will provide access to input/output switching, safe/ready status (to be discussed in Section VI), as well as the play, rewind, etc. transport functions. Many also include an auto-locater function which can store a number of tape locations. A read out will often give the engineer the current location while a keyboard will allow him to call a new location in an hour, minute, and second format. This data is then stored in a memory and assigned a number. To call that location, the engineer simply enters that number followed by a search command. When the auto-locater is engaged, the transport will enter the appropriate wind or rewind mode and move to the new location. Once there, the transport will either stop or begin playing the tape depending on the status required and pre-programmed by the engineer.

Analog Tape Recorder Alignment Procedures

PRELIMINARIES

In order to completely evaluate a tape recorder's level and frequency response performance, a test recording must be made and played back. Since the recording is evaluated by observing the machine's own playback meter, or by externally measuring the machine's playback output, the playback circuit must be properly aligned first. Only after proper playback calibration should adjustments be made to the record circuit.

Before beginning the alignment procedure, all tape guides and heads should be thoroughly cleaned. Head-cleaning fluid is readily available, and should be applied with a cotton swab to all surfaces with which the tape comes in contact. It is possible that some head cleaners may damage the rubber capstan pressure roller, and it therefore should be cleaned with denatured alcohol.

Heads and tape guides should be routinely demagnetized at regular intervals, since after a few hours of use it is possible for these surfaces to become slightly magnetized. This small amount of magnetization may cause erasure of some higher frequencies. In severe cases, a tape passing over a magnetized head or tape guide will be partially erased throughout the frequency band. With the tape recorder turned off, a head demagnetizer should be brought slowly toward the heads and slowly moved away again. The demagnetizer must be well clear of the heads when it is turned on and off.

Test Tapes

To properly align the tape recorder's playback electronics, precision test tapes must be used. These tapes, made under controlled laboratory conditions, contain a series of test tones at levels corresponding to the selected reproduction curve (NAB, IEC, etc., see Chapter 11) at a standard reference fluxivity measured in nanowebers per meter. A nanoweber (abbreviated nw) is 1×10^{-9} weber. The specification refers to the number of flux lines per unit of tape width. It is these flux lines that will be detected by the playback head and converted into an output signal voltage. Fluxivity should not be confused with remanence, which was described earlier as the magnetism left on a tape after a saturation producing force has been withdrawn. Fluxivity, on the other hand, is an indication of the magnetic field strength of the test signal recorded on the tape. Consequently, for a given playback head, a greater fluxivity on the tape will produce a higher playback output level.

Operating Levels

There are three basic operating levels in use today, and in order to understand how they were derived, a look at the advances in the dynamic range of magnetic tape is in order.

The tape that was developed shortly after World War II had an approximate dynamic range of 68 dB. This was the level in decibels between the noise floor of the tape (the point at which the signal would be masked by the tape's residual noise), and the point of maximum permissible amplitude (the point near saturation where the tape reached 3 percent third harmonic distortion). A point 9 dB below saturation was arbitrarily chosen to equal 0 VU (= +4 dBm). This point below saturation was chosen so that there would be a safety margin above 0 VU before distortion made the tape unusable. This point corresponds to a level of 185 nw/m at a frequency of 700 Hz and has become known as standard operating level. Later developments in the magnetic oxide itself, along with the manufacturer's ability to put thicker oxide coatings on the tape, both lowered the noise floor and raised the saturation point. When the headroom above 0 VU reached 12 dB due to oxide improvements, a choice could be made concerning the trade-off between headroom, print-through and low noise.

By keeping the 0 VU point at 185 nw/m, 12 dB of headroom could be maintained while keeping the same noise level. But, by raising the zero point 3 dB, the noise floor could effectively be lowered by 3 dB while maintaining 9 dB of headroom. This elevated operating level has a fluxivity of 260 nw/m, and has become known as a +3 EOL (Elevated Operating Level). Further developments in magnetic tape created a +6 EOL at 370 nw/m. This lowered the noise floor an additional 3 dB yet retained 9 dB of headroom for peaks and sudden transients. Note that magnetic fluxivity corresponds to the 20 log formula used for voltage doubling (2 x 185 nw/m = 370 nw/m = +6 EOL).

However, print-through increases in proportion to the rise in operating level. The greater the level on tape, the more audible print-through becomes. 260 nw/m or +3 EOL has become the most used standard at this point in time. However, many multitrack studios prefer the lower noise of +6 EOL (370 nw/m), and in many archival situations standard operating level of 185 nw/m is still used. Some confusion may arise when the engineer finds himself with an alignment tape labeled "Standard Operating Level of 200 nw/m." This will usually refer to a test tone of 1,000 Hz rather than 700 Hz. In actuality, since fluxivity changes with frequency, these levels are the same and only the frequency of measurement is different.

TAPE RECORDER ALIGNMENT

For purposes of explanation, adjustments to the electronic and mechanical systems are discussed separately. However, there is a certain amount of interaction between these systems. As each is adjusted, the performance of the other should be verified.

Playback Electronics Alignment

On most tape recorders, the electronics system parameters are screwdriver adjustable, however, on many of the newer machines electronic alignment takes place by changing values that are stored in a microprocessor memory. These values, when selected, are often changed with a thumb wheel or other rotary control. In other systems, values may also be changed by holding down a push button until the correct reading is attained on the VU meter. Several types of calibration panels and systems are shown in Figure 12-1.

There is also, usually on the front of the machine near the VU meter, a switch or series of switches that will allow the engineer to select the origin of the signal that is delivered to the output jacks of the tape recorder as well as what is read on the associated channel's meter. These switches select input, reproduce, or sync. When input is selected, the signal being sent to the recorder is sent through the input level controls, metered on the VU meters and delivered to the output jacks at the rear of the

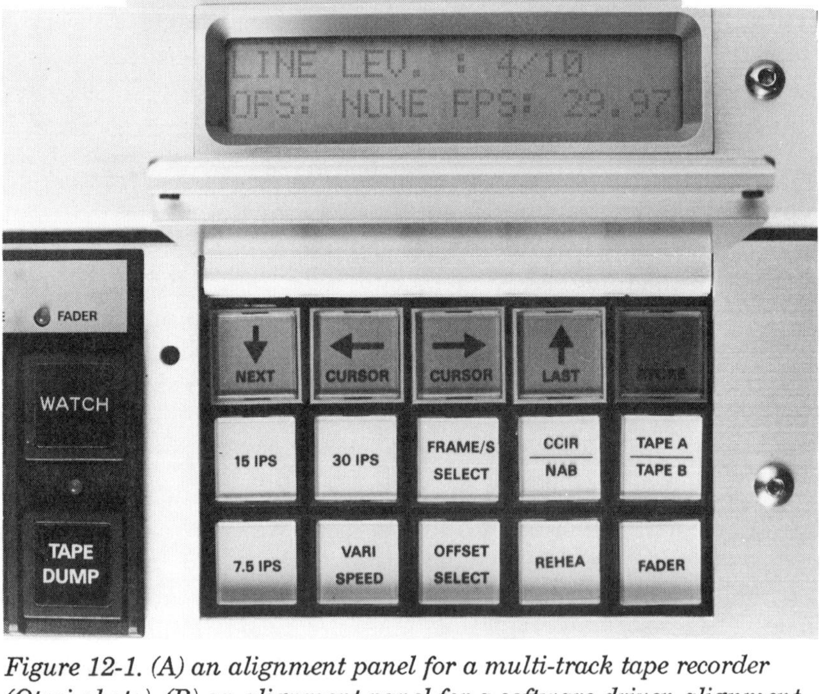

Figure 12-1. (A) an alignment panel for a multi-track tape recorder (Otari photo), (B) an alignment panel for a software-driven alignment system for a two-channel three-speed tape recorder (Studer A820, Studer photo).

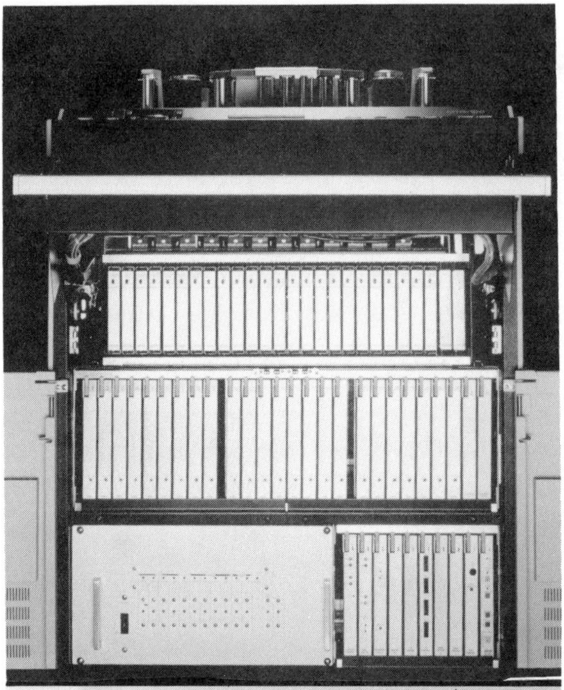

machine. When reproduce is selected, the output of the playback head is sent through the reproduce level controls, metered, and sent to the output jacks. Sync, which stands for synchronization, will be discussed in detail in Section VIII "The Recording Process." These input/repro/sync switches are independent of the record function of the tape recorder, and allow the engineer to monitor either the input of the machine or the playback signal from the tape.

Another set of switches located in the same area select the record or the safe mode. When safe is selected no recording is possible. Safe locks out the record and erase functions of the machine, and pushing the play and record button will only cause the machine to play. This lock out prevents any accidental erasure of a master tape. When ready or record is selected the tape recorder is ready to go into the record mode, and pushing the record and play buttons simultaneously will energize the bias and erase circuits and send the applied signal to the record head. When adjusting the tape recorder's playback electronics, the machine should be placed in reproduce and safe. Reproduce is selected so that the applied test tape can be monitored both visually and aurally, and the safe mode prevents accidental erasure of a valuable and expensive test and alignment tape. It is assumed that the following procedures will be performed for each channel of playback electronics, and that alignment is being performed per the NAB standard reproducing characteristics. All noise reduction should be switched off or removed from the tape recorder's circuit.

Generally, the first tone on the test tape is 700 Hz or 1,000 Hz, and is used for setting the proper playback output level. If using a standard operating level alignment tape to set a machine for standard level, the tone should read 0 VU. However, if the machine is to be aligned, using the standard tape, to an elevated level such as +3 EOL or +6 EOL, the VU meter should read –3 VU or –6 VU respectively. (If 185 nw/m = –6 VU, 0 VU = 370 nw/m.) 0 VU will usually produce a level of +4 dBm at the balanced (three conductor) output of the tape recorder, but could, in the case of some small format machines, produce a level of –10 dBm. If the engineer elects to use an elevated level test tape, the metered reading should be adjusted accordingly.

Just after the level set tone, the test tape will usually provide a series of high-frequency tones. The first one is usually specified for azimuth adjustment which will be discussed later in the chapter. However, it is at this point that the playback head azimuth should be adjusted. If the azimuth is not correct at this point, all further adjustments will be incorrect by the amount of the azimuth error. The remaining high-frequency tones are monitored while adjusting the machine's high-frequency playback equalization control. The tones have been recorded in accordance with the NAB standard reproduce characteristic (see Figures 11-5, and 6) so that when the machine is properly aligned, the tones will read the same as the first reference tone (0 VU, –3 VU, or –6 VU depending on the operating level) on the playback meters.

Most tape recorders contain an additional equalization control to adjust the low-frequency response of the playback circuit. However, the fringing phenomenon—an apparent low-frequency boost—must be taken into account when evaluating the machine's low-frequency performance. To explain, many test tapes are made in a full-track format. That is, as discussed in Chapter 10, the reference tones are recorded across the entire width of the tape. In this way, the tape can be used with any head format available for that tape width. However, at long wavelengths (low frequencies), a playback head tends to respond to flux recorded over an area greater than its normal track width. Accordingly, the machine's low-frequency response appears to be higher than normal. If the test tape had been recorded over just the width of the track being measured, this fringing effect would not occur. The amount of fringing varies from one playback head to another, and so no attempt has been made to compensate for it in the preparation of the test tape. Most manufacturers indicate in the machine's documentation how much fringing is to be expected with that particular machine's head configuration, and at the various tape speeds available on that transport. However, when the actual amount of fringing is unknown, low-frequency playback equalization adjustments may be deferred until after the record circuit adjustments are complete. Low-frequency tones at a standard reference level are then recorded and the low-frequency equalization is then adjusted for flat response. Since the tones are being recorded at the proper width for the playback head in use, there will be no fringing, and the low-frequency response may be adjusted to read the same as the beginning reference tone. (This procedure makes the assumption that the non-adjustable low-frequency record equalization is correct.)

After the playback response has been set, no further adjustment should be made to the playback circuit or level controls. This is, however, only an adjustment for the first or primary tape speed to be used. For machines with multiple speeds, the manufacturer usually includes a set of adjustments for each speed. For instance, if the primary speed of 15 in./sec. had been adjusted to the NAB reproducing characteristic, the engineer would now proceed to equalize the playback of the other available speeds but without adjusting the overall playback output levels. Typically, an AES Standard Reproducing Characteristic test tape would now be used to adjust the 30 in./sec. high and low-frequency response. On some machines, both speeds would have to be set up for the same operating level, while on others independent playback level controls would allow the engineer to select different operating levels for different speeds. For instance, a tape recorder could be set to play at an elevated operating level of +3 EOL at 15 in./sec. using some form of noise reduction, and also be adjusted for an operating level of 370 nw/m (+6 EOL) without noise reduction at 30 in./sec. for lowest noise since, as discussed in Chapter 9, all noise-reduction systems can cause problems on some types of program material.

Since the NAB playback characteristic is standard in the United States for speeds of 7-½ and 15 in./sec., few studios are likely to have an IEC (or CCIR) test tape available. Nevertheless, many U.S. facilities regularly receive tapes from abroad that may have been recorded using the IEC characteristic. Assuming a tape recorder's playback response has been properly aligned for IEC playback, an NAB test tape played on such a machine should display the response shown in Figure 12-2. Therefore, when it is necessary to adjust a machine for IEC playback, an NAB test tape

Figure 12-2. Tape recorder frequency response when an NAB test tape is played on a machine properly aligned to the IEC (CCIR) reproducing characteristic.

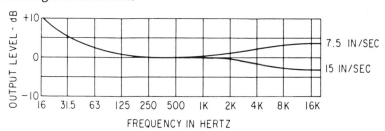

may be used, and the playback adjusted to match the response shown in the figure. Many modern machines now offer both NAB and IEC equalization circuits, and the engineer can select between them at the touch of a switch. However, this means that at some point the machine's circuits will have to be adjusted for all these standards. A 3-speed dual-equalization tape recorder will require 12 different equalization adjustments and the studio or technician must own the corresponding test tapes (3 speeds times 2 equalization standards times high- and low-frequency response adjustments)!

Record Electronics Alignment

Now that the playback electronics of the tape recorder have been adjusted to the prevailing standard the record electronics need to be adjusted to match. It will be assumed for the purpose of this discussion that the machine has been calibrated to the NAB standard reproduction characteristics. By calibrating the record electronics to match the playback characteristics just set, we are assured that all recordings made on this tape recorder correspond to the NAB standard. Once again, it is assumed that the alignment procedures will be performed for each channel of the tape recorder.

To begin aligning the record function of the machine, the tape recorder is threaded with a fresh reel of tape of the type that will be used for later recording, and the machine is switched to the ready mode. An externally supplied oscillator is used to first calibrate the input/output characteristics of the tape recorder to the selected operating level. While monitoring input, a 1,000 Hz sine wave with a level of +4 dBm (–10 dBm for some machines) is fed to the channel to be aligned and the input level control is adjusted so that a reading of 0 VU is obtained on the meter. The machine is then set in motion in record and the channel is then switched to the reproduce mode. The record gain control (not the input level control) is adjusted so that the meter reads 0 VU. This raises or lowers the gain of the record circuit to match the operating level selected during playback alignment. If the machine's playback level has been raised to a +6 EOL, then the record circuit gain must be raised to match. Some older tape recorders will not have enough gain in the record circuit to be used at elevated operating levels. If this is the case, lower operating levels will have to be used with the corresponding rise in noise level. This

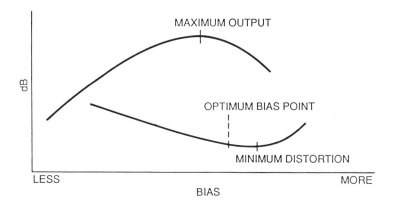

Figure 12-3. Tape output versus distortion. Note that the maximum output level (MOL) does not line up with the minimum distortion point.

would necessitate the realignment of the playback side before further record adjustments could be made.

The record head azimuth would now be adjusted, and as mentioned earlier, this will be discussed fully under mechanical alignments.

Once the initial record level and azimuth adjustments have been made, the bias is adjusted. Bias is set using a short wavelength signal to find the bias peak. This peak is the point where an additional amount of bias would cause a fall in high-frequency response of the tape. Recommended alignment frequencies are 20 kHz at 30 in./sec., 10 kHz at 15 in./sec., and 5 kHz at 7-½ in./sec. As mentioned in Chapter 10, proper bias is a trade off between maximum output level and lowest distortion, and the two points do not usually coincide. Figure 12-3 shows the relationship between output and distortion. Note that minimum distortion is obtained when additional bias current is applied beyond the bias peak. Bias is set by applying the proper frequency signal to the recorder's inputs, and while monitoring reproduce, adding bias until the bias peak is found. Then, continuing to add more bias current, causing the recorded output level to drop, based the size of the record head gap space. At this point, the tape's sensitivity is fairly uniform across the audio bandwidth, and the third harmonic distortion is quite low. The exact amount of overbias is usually specified in the tape recorder's operation manual, however, the following chart summarizes these figures for a tape speed of 15 in./sec.

Record Head Gap Space	Amount of Overbias
1 mil	1.5 dB
0.5 mil	2.5 dB
0.25 mil	3.0 dB

These figures change with tape speed, head configuration and tape type. Therefore, the prudent engineer will not fail to consult the respective manufacturer's specifications. Figure 12-4 shows the electrical performance characteristics of two types of magnetic recording tape. In Figure 12-4B, it will be noted that a further increase in bias level will lower the distortion even more, however, the tape's sensitivity also falls off and modulation noise begins to increase again.

After the bias has been properly set, the record level should be adjusted again using a frequency of 1,000 Hz. A change in bias level will cause a change in the input/output calibration of the

Figure 12-4. Electrical performance characteristics of two types of magnetic recording tape.

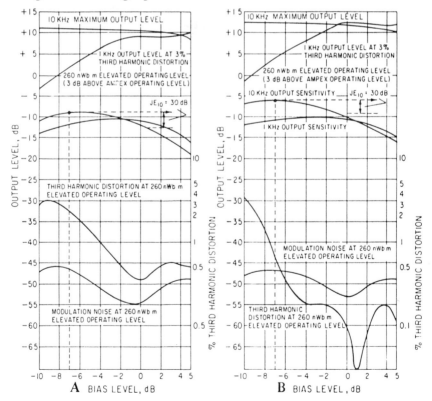

tape recorder, and this must be corrected before proceeding with the record equalization adjustments.

The record equalization control is used to adjust the record circuit response at high frequencies. The setting will vary depending on the characteristics of the tape being used, the bias level, and the design of the record head itself. A high-frequency tone (typically 15 kHz to 20 kHz) is recorded, and the equalization adjusted, as before, until the machine's output level matches the input level at this frequency. Once the high-frequency response has been adjusted, the signal generator or oscillator output frequency should be varied over the entire audio bandwidth to verify that the system response is within the required specifications. It is important to have available a signal oscillator with a continuously variable frequency adjustment rather than one with just a few fixed frequencies. Although the latter is adequate for routine signal tracing and spot checks of performance, it may not reveal response errors lying between the switch-selected frequencies. It is also possible to verify the machine's frequency alignment by applying pink noise to the input and metering the output with a real-time frequency analyzer.

MECHANICAL ALIGNMENT

In order for the tape recorder system to function properly, the tape must remain in good physical contact with all three heads. The slightest misalignment may cause errors in level and response that may be incorrectly attributed to the electronics systems. Figure 12-5 illustrates the five mechanical adjustments that may be required in the alignment or realignment of a head.

A. Tape-to-head contact or Rack. The tape must, of course, remain in firm contact with the head at all times. Since the head is convex, a slight wrap around this surface will help maintain good contact. However, excessive rack on one head may cause the tape to be lifted from a neighboring one.

B. Tilt or Zenith. The pressure of the head against the tape must be evenly distributed across the entire tape width. If the head (or the tape) is not truly vertical, the contact pressure may be greater at one edge than at the other, resulting in a skewing of the tape away from the centerline of the head.

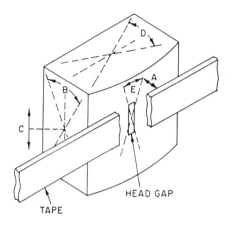

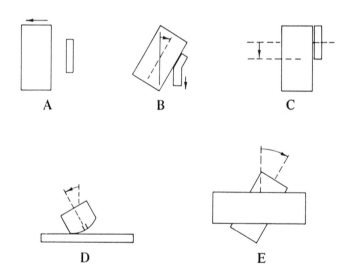

Figure 12-5. Exaggerated misalignment of the tape head.
A. Contact—Tape does not make good contact with the head.
B. Tilt—Tape makes uneven contact with head.
C. Height—Head height is misadjusted.
D. Tangency—Tape does not make good contact with head gap.
E. Azimuth—Tape head is not perpendicular to tape path.

C. Height. Head height must be properly adjusted so that each track is properly aligned with its corresponding head gap. A slight discrepancy between head heights in the same head block may result in loss of full erasure prior to recording, inter-channel crosstalk, and increased noise level. Height inaccuracies between tape recorders create non-standard playback characteristics that can cause a tape that sounded fine in one studio to seriously mis-track in another.

D. Wrap or Tangency. As a part of the tape-to-head criteria, the tape must remain tangent to the head gap for optimum performance. An error in Wrap angle adjustment may cause the tape to enter or leave the gap area prematurely. It is also important that the tape trail off the head as smoothly as possible to minimize the formation of a secondary head gap that can cause self erasure at high frequencies.

E. Azimuth. Azimuth adjustments are particularly critical, especially in the case of short wavelength signals. If the head gap is not exactly perpendicular to the direction of the tape travel, segments of the same recorded wavelength will enter and leave the gap at different increments of time, as shown in Figure 12-6. In the drawing, lines A and B represent an identical signal recorded on two tracks (or for that matter, A and B may be the edges of any one track). The sine waves represent the instantaneous amplitude of the signal(s). As shown, the head azimuth is misaligned and as a positive maxima passes over a line in the gap, a negative maxima passes over the same line.

Figure 12-6. An out-of-azimuth head gap. Different segments of the recorded wavelength cross the gap at the same time. (A) and (B) represent an identical signal recorded on two tracks.

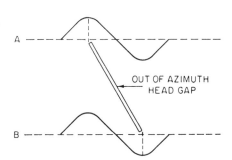

309

AZIMUTH ALIGNMENT

Whether the previously-mentioned illustration represents a single track width, or two tracks that may be eventually combined, the total output will be zero. In practice, a single track will rarely, if ever, cancel out completely, although two adjacent tracks that are out of azimuth will be severely attenuated when they are combined. In the case of some multi-track tape recorders, all head alignment adjustments have been made by the manufacturer and are permanently fixed. However, the heads of most machines with four or less tracks are user adjustable. Generally, the head is held in place, and adjusted with a series of screws. A properly installed head should not require repeated mechanical adjustments, with the exception of azimuth, which should be checked periodically as a matter of routine.

Use of the oscilloscope, described in Chapter 2, is the preferred method of verifying azimuth alignment. In Figure 2-15, various oscilloscope displays were shown, to illustrate the phase and coherency relationships between two signals. Here, Figure 12-7 shows the display when a test tape is monitored on the oscilloscope. If the head azimuth is correctly aligned, an in-phase display will be seen, since there is zero phase shift between the two oscilloscope inputs. However, if the head is slightly off-azimuth, there will be a phase shift displayed on the test instrument. Figure 12-7A indicates a properly aligned head, while the other oscilloscope displays indicate various amounts of phase shift, and therefore azimuth error. The error in degrees refers to the polar coordinates of the phase shift, and not the angle of the head!

If an oscilloscope is not available, it is possible to set the azimuth relatively closely by combining the output of the two outermost tracks out of phase. If one of the tracks is put electrically out of phase (reversing the positive and negative in a balanced line), and the combined outputs are monitored at a high level, the azimuth adjustment screw can be adjusted until the monitor output is at a minimum.

When checking the alignment of an adjustable multi-track head, the azimuth of two adjacent tracks may be checked first, and then, successively, more distant tracks, until the two outside tracks are compared. Ideally, a single setting will bring all tracks into perfect alignment, but in practice this is often not the case.

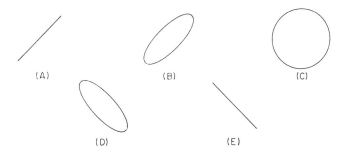

Figure 12-7. Oscilloscope displays for various amounts of azimuth error.
   A.—Properly aligned head, no azimuth error.
   B.—Azimuth error of about 45 degrees.
   C.—Azimuth error of 90 degrees
   D.—Azimuth error of about 135 degrees.
   E.—Azimuth error of 180 degrees.

Within the head itself, the gaps may be slightly misaligned, making complete azimuth alignment of all tracks impossible.

As already mentioned, azimuth alignment becomes more critical as the frequency increases. Therefore, it is often a good idea to make coarse azimuth adjustments at 1,000 Hz to 5,000 Hz, and to then play the successively higher tones on the test tape while making fine adjustments. When the azimuth is properly set, it should remain aligned over the entire audio bandwidth. If the scope display goes in and out of phase as the frequency is varied, the azimuth is improperly set.

Once the playback head is set, the record head azimuth may be adjusted by observing the playback head output on the oscilloscope while recording a tone and adjusting the azimuth screw on the record head. On machines with sync (record head) output capabilities, the test tape may be played while direct readings are made from the record head output.

SECTION V

DIGITAL AUDIO SYSTEMS

Despite many impressive advances in recording technology over the past century, at least one basic principle has remained unchanged. Ever since the first recording was etched onto a wax cylinder, the recorded format, if not the quality, has closely resembled the waveform of the original sound source.

In air, the sound source creates a series of pressure variations from which a recognizable waveform may be drawn. In the record groove, the stylus traces the same waveform, now permanently etched into the vinyl surface. Even on tape, the alternating magnetic field is a faithful reproduction of the acoustical sound wave. In each case, we may say that the stored information is directly analogous to the original source of the sound. It is an analog recording.

This has all changed, and now it is difficult to discuss audio without the word digital appearing in the conversation. The Compact Disc is inexorably replacing the vinyl phonograph record, and the DAT (rotary head Digital Audio Tape recorder) will undoubtedly have the same effect on the Compact Cassette.

This quantum leap forward in sound storage technology has placed an extra burden of care on the recording engineer. Small flaws in the recording are no longer covered by the surface noise of the vinyl or the hiss of the tape, but stand out for all to hear on the finished product.

How does this system work? What are its advantages? Chapter 13 takes a comprehensive look at the process we call digital recording and examines these questions. Then, Chapter 14 discusses the available hardware for storage, editing and playback of the digital information.

Digital Audio

No matter how simple or complex a waveform, any instant at which we examine its amplitude, we will find that the amplitude is different from any other adjacent instant in time. Of course, as the intervals between examinations become smaller and smaller, the change in amplitude becomes less and less. Nevertheless, the change is always continuous, and an infinite number of examinations will simply reveal an infinite number of amplitude variations. Ideally, the recorded waveform will be a faithful replica of the original, and for our purposes here, we may consider this to be so—until the signal is recorded on tape. At this point, a variety of distortion factors may be added, as shown in Figure 13-1. In effect, the distortion is an analog noise combined with the analog music as the tape is recorded. Later on, the playback head faithfully reproduces the signal, which is now a somewhat distorted version of the original source. Of course, the distortion may come from a variety of sources, as previously discussed in Chapter 10, such as improper bias, tape saturation, and so forth.

The problem, though certainly not the solution, is obvious. The playback head is incapable of making a distinction between the wanted and the unwanted components of the analog signal. In order for us to get around this difficulty, we must devise a method of recording in which the playback system will simply not recog-

Figure 13-1. The analog recording process combines the signal (A) and the noise (B), to create a distorted version (C) of the original sound source.

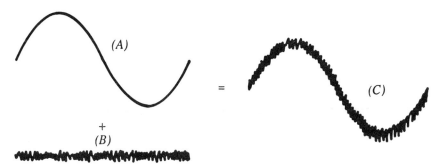

nize (and therefore, will not produce) the unwanted noise components of the recorded signal.

A useful analogy may be made by considering the early broadcast medium, and a spoken message which must be sent over a noisy transmission system. The analog receiver picks up the transmitted message along with enough noise to make the message difficult to understand. To get around the problem, we may encode the analog message into a series of dots and dashes (A = . – , B = – ... , etc.), and transmit these. At the receiving end, the listener (who has previously studied up on Morse code) mentally decodes the data stream of dots and dashes penetrating the transmission noise, then types out the message. Although our human decoder may get a serious headache, anyone else who reads the message will be unaware of the noise problem, which was simply not reproduced. Of course, the utility of the Morse code goes no further than the transmission of the printed word. It is of no use in the recording or reproducing of an actual sound source, since the small handful of dot/dash combinations falls far short of meeting the requirements for reproducing even the simplest sound wave.

Instead, we need an encoding system that is not only more versatile than Morse code, but also one that will not require operator assistance during the encode/decode process. Ideally such a system will faithfully decode and reproduce the recorded musical signal, while remaining insensitive to any (analog) noise components that are a function of the storage medium. Obviously, analog noise components that are a function of the recording session itself will also be faithfully reproduced. In fact, if our new system is really more effective in eliminating analog tape noise, we may find that some studio noises are much easier to hear since they are no longer masked by tape hiss.

DIGITAL DESIGN BASICS

We can begin our design of such a system by examining a familiar analog waveform, such as the one seen in Figure 13-2A. When viewed continuously, even this very simple waveform may be seen to possess an infinite number of discrete amplitudes as discussed earlier in this chapter. But now, let's view the waveform through a series of equally spaced "windows," and assume that we have no idea of what is happening between the windows. This is illustrated in Figure 13-2B and C, where we note that the more

Figure 13-2. A simple waveform may be thought of as an infinite series of discrete amplitudes. We may sample the waveform periodically, through a series of equally spaced "windows" (B,C). In the time intervals between samples (shaded areas) we have no information about the waveform.

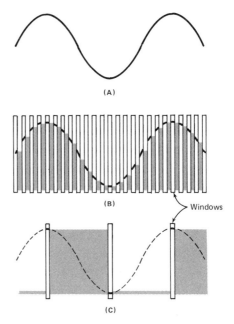

(A)

(B)

Windows

(C)

windows there are within a given distance, the more often we are able to see—that is, to sample—the waveform. Since we are really dealing in terms of time, we may say that the closer the spacings of the windows, the higher the sampling rate, and thus the more accurate our view of the waveform.

Assuming that the waveform in Figure 13-2C represents the highest audio frequency of interest, we may be surprised to discover that a sampling rate that is merely twice that frequency will be sufficient to give us all the information we need in order to recover (that is, decode) the original waveform. As long as we know the rate at which we are sampling, we can always determine the frequency of the sampled waveform.

Sampling Frequency

To illustrate this important point, simply sample-and-hold the value seen through the first window until we reach the second window. Then, sample-and-hold that value until the third window is reached, and so on. The resultant waveform is a square wave of the same frequency as the original sine wave. Since a square wave may be defined as a sine wave plus an infinite number of odd harmonics, we need only pass the square wave through a suitably designed low-pass filter to remove the harmonics, and to recover the original sine wave.

This may be quickly demonstrated with a square-wave generator, a low-pass filter, and an oscilloscope. Select any convenient generator frequency, f, and set the filter's cut-off frequency to 2f. With the filter in the circuit, the square wave output of the generator will be displayed as a sine wave of the same frequency on the oscilloscope.

The highest audio frequency that can be accurately sampled and the requisite sampling rate are often referred to as the Nyquist frequency and the Nyquist rate respectively, after H. Nyquist of Bell Laboratories, who first noted this 2:1 relationship. Nyquist determined that in order to accurately represent any waveform, we must have at least two samples from that waveform. In other words, when sampling a broadband signal, the sampling rate must be twice the highest frequency we let pass through the system. Thus, a Nyquist rate of say, 50 kHz will allow us to accurately sample any audio signal below a Nyquist frequency of 25 kHz.

Aliasing

If we attempt to sample a frequency that is higher than the Nyquist frequency, we generate an unharmonic pitch called an "alias" frequency. The alias frequency is equal to the sampling frequency minus the input signal that is above the Nyquist frequency. Therefore, if we attempt to sample a 32 kHz signal with a 50 kHz sampling rate, an 18 kHz alias frequency will be produced. This 18 kHz signal bears no musical relationship whatsoever to the 32 kHz signal. In fact, the 32 kHz signal is probably an overtone of a 16 kHz signal. It is unlikely that we could perceive this overtone in any event. However, after we send the squared-off waveform through the low-pass filter to remove the odd harmonics, the 32 kHz signal will be removed, but the aliased 18 kHz signal will still be there. Another way of visualizing this phenomenon is to picture the signal above the Nyquist frequency folding down into the audible bandwidth by the same amount that it is above. To prevent this unrelated frequency (which is quite audible) from occurring, the signal to be sampled is first fed through a low-pass filter to remove any high-frequency components that might produce these aliasing effects. This input filter is often called the anti-aliasing filter.

Because of the practical design limitations of filters and the possibility that the sampling point may occur at the same time as the zero crossing for high frequencies, a sampling rate is chosen that is somewhat higher than twice the highest frequency that needs to be represented. This assures that no information is distorted, and that a flat frequency response is maintained across the entire audio bandwidth.

Quantization

In Figure 13-2, we saw that the sample-and-hold process replaced the continuously variable sine wave with a square wave. In other words, a relatively simple waveform (Figure 13-2C) with only two levels has been substituted for the infinite number of levels that were previously seen (Figure 13-2A). This process of representing an analog waveform with a series of discrete levels (two, in this case) is known as quantization. The square wave is said to be a quantized waveform with two quantization levels. It should be noted here that no analog information gets lost due to the sample-and-hold/quantization processes. Because of the anti-aliasing (low-pass) filtering previously described, there is no information present above the Nyquist frequency, and so, quantization cannot lose what was not there in the first place.

Our next step is to devise a method of encoding the quantized amplitude information found at each sampling window. Although it is easy enough to define the maximum amplitude peaks as say, +100 and –100 with intermediate levels falling between these two extremes, recording these levels on tape is merely a needlessly complex variation of the traditional analog recording process. Instead we must seek out a method of recording this data in such a manner as to make it immune to tape-induced analog noise.

DIGITAL ENCODING: THE BINARY SYSTEM

To accomplish this, we must first convert our quantized analog amplitudes into a binary-coded digital system. Even without further elaboration, we may intuitively realize that a coded signal of any form is no longer an analog of the original audio signal. Therefore, if we can successfully devise a system that will encode, record, playback, and decode our signal, we can free ourselves

from the storage medium's noise which is neither encoded or decoded. What could be more elegant than using a series of on and
off pulses to represent our audio signal waveform.

A binary numbering system is simply one with a base of 2,
rather than our familiar base-10 decimal system. By the time
most of us have passed through high school, our familiar decimal
system of counting has become an almost intuitive process, and it
takes some concentration to "un-learn" the decimal system,
where ten symbols (0-9) are used to express any quantity. One
might suspect that if our ancestors had evolved with eight fingers
instead of ten, we would be using an octal system (0-7) instead.
Or, if those eight fingers were on each hand, we may have been
saddled with a hexa-decimal (6 + 10) system, which would require six more symbols beyond the familiar 0—9. The Table
shown in Figure 13-3 tabulates several of these alternative numbering systems, including the apparently quite primitive binary
system, in which only two symbols (0 and 1) are used. In each
case, we note that once we run out of symbols, we simply begin a
new column and start all over.

At first glance, the binary system may appear to be the least
promising of the lot. For example, an easily read decimal number
such as 217 becomes a rather awkward 110111001. We may well
ask ourselves, just what is the point of requiring eight bits (BI-
nary digiTS) to express a quantity that is certainly a lot easier to
read and understand in the decimal system? While the binary system is indeed somewhat a chore for most decimal-trained readers,
it is quite another matter for an electronic system. Here, the disadvantage of a long succession of bits is far out-weighed by the
fact that the status of each bit may be unambiguously conveyed
by a simple two-position switch. When the switch is closed, the
bit is 1, and when it is open the bit is 0. Alternatively, the presence of a voltage signifies 1, while the absence indicates 0.

Coding Systems

Taking this a step further, the simple pulse code shown in Figure 13-4A may be used to express any binary number. Even if the
waveform is severely distorted in transmission, the information is
still retrievable, provided the waveform manages to cross a defined threshold, as shown in Figure 13-4B. A binary 1 is indicated
whenever the signal is above the threshold, and a binary 0 is sig-
nified when it isn't. All other characteristics (actual recorded

Quantity	NUMBERING SYSTEMS			
	Binary (base 2)	**Octal** (8)	**Decimal** (10)	**Hexidecimal** (16)
	0	0	0	0
I	1	1	1	1
II	1 0	2	2	2
III	1 1	3	3	3
IIII	1 0 0	4	4	4
⧗	1 0 1	5	5	5
I ⧗	1 1 0	6	6	6
II ⧗	1 1 1	7	7	7
III ⧗	1 0 0 0	1 0	8	8
IIII ⧗	1 0 0 1	1 1	9	9
⧗ ⧗	1 0 1 0	1 2	1 0	A
I ⧗ ⧗	1 0 1 1	1 3	1 1	B
II ⧗ ⧗	1 1 0 0	1 4	1 2	C
III ⧗ ⧗	1 1 0 1	1 5	1 3	D
IIII ⧗ ⧗	1 1 1 0	1 6	1 4	E
⧗ ⧗ ⧗	1 1 1 1	1 7	1 5	F
I ⧗ ⧗ ⧗	1 0 0 0 0	2 0	1 6	1 0
II ⧗ ⧗ ⧗	1 0 0 0 1	2 1	1 7	1 1

example: $16 + 0 + 0 + 0 + 1 = 2 \times 8 + 1 =$ $10 + 7 =$ $16 + 1 = 17$ (decimal)

Figure 13-3. A comparison of various numbering systems, using binary, octal, decimal, and hexidecimal bases. The binary system is the foundation of digital recording technology, while the octal and hexidecimal systems are regularly found in contemporary electronic systems design.

level, distortion, etc.) are irrelevant, and have no effect on the transmitted or recorded information.

The waveform may be recorded as a series of positive and negative polarity voltages which alternatively saturate the tape in opposite magnetic directions. This ability of magnetic tape was discussed in Chapter 10. However, in such a brute-force recording system, "waveform fidelity" does not have the significance it had in the analog system, and consequently there is no need for a bias signal. This form of encoding is known as Pulse Code Modulation, or PCM encoding. Other methods such as Pulse Width Modulation (PWM), Pulse Number Modulation (PNM), and Pulse

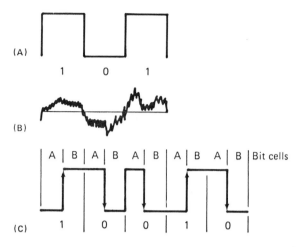

Figure 13-4. A simple square wave-like series of pulses (A) may be used to transmit binary-coded data. Even when the waveform is severely distorted (B) the binary-coded data is preserved. The data code may be modified (C) so that 1s and 0s are defined by positive and negative-going transitions instead.

Position Modulation (PPM) have been tried, but PCM is more easily coded to reduce the number of individual pulses necessary to represent a series of binary numbers. These coding, or modulation, schemes allow much greater amounts of data to be stored over a given tape area. Because of this, PCM has become the method of choice for representing the binary ones and zeroes.

As a practical matter, the waveform just described needs some modification to make it a useful recording system. For example, a long series of ones or zeroes will simply create a DC (direct current) component which will give no indication of when one bit stops and the next begins. Therefore, as a refinement in the recording of binary information, the waveform shown in Figure 13-4C may be used. In this particular modulation scheme, a 1 is indicated by a positive-going transition in the waveform, while a 0 is defined by a negative-going transition. When two or more identical bits appear in succession, there is a level change at the beginning of each successive identical bit. When a 1 is followed by a 0, or vice versa, there is no level change. This coding scheme allows the appropriate level-transitions to take place for all possible combinations of ones and zeroes. For study purposes, in Figure 13-4C, each bit may be divided into two bit cells, A and B, with the transition which defines the bit as a 1 or 0 occurring between the cells.

In the practical digital tape recorder, an even more sophisticated coding scheme may be employed. Without some form of modulation scheme, the time information that is derived from the spacings of the individual bit cells would be lost, unless some external source of timing was employed. A modulation scheme called the Non-return to Zero, or NRZ code is used by the video based digital recording systems. This code is very simple to use, but requires some external source of synchronization to determine the timing between successive ones or zeroes. This is provided by the control track pulses on the video recorder itself. Other codes such as the HDM-1 (High Density Modulation) code, the EFM (Eight to Fourteen Modulation) code, and the Miller code are used with various different storage mediums. These will be discussed in greater detail in Chapter 14, Digital Data Storage Systems.

THE DIGITAL WORD

Returning now to our analog source, at each sampling window we must convert the signal's amplitude into a binary number. In Figure 13-5, we may see that the more bits we have at our disposal, the better we may approximate (or quantize) the actual analog level.

A quantity expressed as a binary number is referred to as a digital word. Thus, 101 is a three-bit word, and 11010 is a five-bit word. A one-bit word permits us to use only two discrete levels (0,1), where a two-bit word yields four (00, 01, 10, 11) levels, and so on. In other words, a N-bit binary word will give us 2^N discrete levels.

Barring an infinite number of bits, the quantized waveform that we will encode is only an approximation of the analog input waveform, as was just shown in Figure 13-5. In the more detailed drawing shown in Figure 13-6, note that all analog levels within any sampling interval (that is, between any A-B pair) are represented by the quantization level, Q, that appears within this interval. Thus, a single quantization level now represents all the analog levels that occurred within the sampling interval. Obviously, the more bits that are available, the higher will be the resolution of the system. Yet, there will always be an analog amplitude that will fall between the available levels. This error is

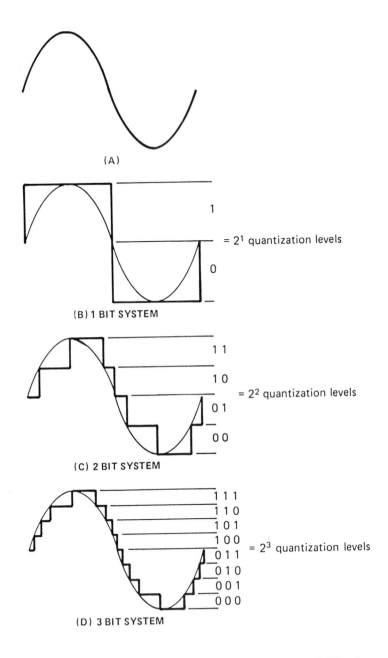

Figure 13-5. The more quantization levels that are available, the more accurate will be the quantized waveform. In each example given here, the sine wave represents the analog waveform, and the stepped waveform is its quantized equivalent.

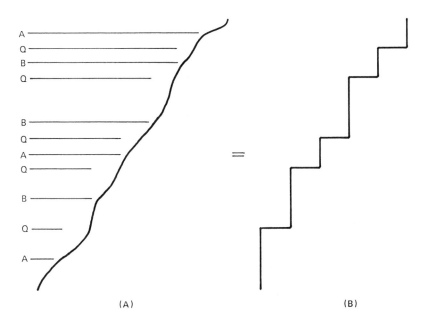

Figure 13-6. Detailed drawing of the quantization process. The analog waveform (A) becomes the quantized waveform (B). The resultant waveform error may produce quantization noise.

called quantization error and is limited to one-half the distance between two available levels. Most systems use 16-bit quantization that generates 2^{16} or 65,535 discrete levels. This number of bits generally lowers the noise caused by quantization error to an almost indistinguishable level.

The maximum signal level that can be encoded in the digital word is determined by the number of bits used and the maximum quantization error. This signal-to-error ratio is roughly equivalent to the more familiar signal-to-noise ratio of an analog system. Generally, the dynamic range of the system in dB, is given by the formula:

$$6.02 \, (N) + 1.76 = \text{System Dynamic Range in dB}$$

where N = the number of bits in the system

Therefore, the signal-to-noise ratio or dynamic range of a 16-bit system is:

$$6.02 \times 16 + 1.76 \text{ or } 97.98 \text{ dB}.$$

This approximately 98 dB range is considerably more than the maximum possible 76 dB signal-to-noise ratio of most analog tape systems as discussed in Chapter 10. Even a 14-bit digital system with 86 dB of dynamic range exceeds most analog systems by 10 dB.

THE RECORD PROCESS

Now that we have a basic understanding of how an analog waveform can be represented with a series of digital bits, we can look at the actual process of converting and storing a continuous analog audio signal. Figure 13-7 shows a block diagram of a typical PCM digital encoding system, and the following discussions will describe each of these sections.

The first item that the signal passes through is usually an amplifier of some sort. This amplifier raises (or lowers) the input signal to a level that is usable by the digital encoder. Digital processors are available with a wide range of input capabilities, ranging from unbalanced high impedance –10 dBm inputs to balanced low impedance +4 dBm inputs.

Dither

Following this amplifier in many systems is a dither generator. As mentioned earlier, there will always be an analog amplitude that will be exactly halfway between two possible levels. This last or least significant bit cannot decide whether to be a 1 or a 0, and as a result continually toggles between the two. This is the quan-

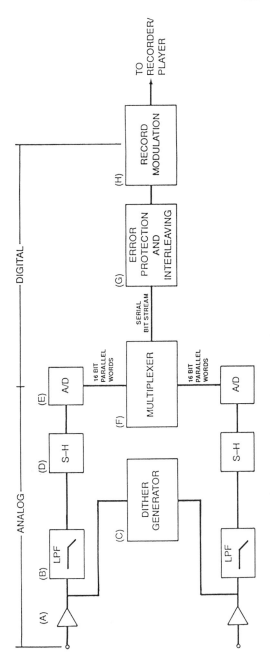

Figure 13-7. A simplified diagram of a two-channel analog to digital encoder. (A) Input Amplifier, (B) Low-Pass Filter, (C) Dither Generator, (D) Sample and Hold Circuit, (E) Analog to Digital Converter, (F) Multiplexer for parallel to serial data conversion, (G) Error Processing, and (H) Recording Modulation.

tization noise mentioned earlier, and even though it is 98 dB below the maximum signal, it can be audible since it is not being masked by tape noise. It can be especially evident during the fade-out at the end of a song or selection, and can be heard as a graininess in the signal at the very softest levels. This is often called granulation noise. To remove this noise, an analog noise signal called dither is added to the signal prior to quantization. The dither signal is usually a type of band-limited white noise, and the amount of dither that is added is usually between one-quarter to one-third the value of the least significant bit. This amounts to about 1 to 2 dB of actual level. Dither was first developed by Bell Labs during the 1960s when they were experimenting with digital video. Dither actually lowers the noise of the digital system. It pushes a toggling bit, that is causing quantizing error, to the next available level thereby reducing the noise.

The Anti-Aliasing Filter

The analog input signal with dither is then sent through a low-pass filter to remove any frequency components that are above the Nyquist frequency. If these audio frequencies are not removed at this point, they will cause the aliasing effects that were described earlier in this chapter. The design of this filter is critical, and various types of filters have been designed to give as flat a frequency response as possible with minimum phase distortion. Ideally an infinitely steep cut-off would be preferred, but this brick wall filter usually creates more problems than it solves. The typical anti-aliasing filter found in most professional digital recorders uses a steep 24 dB/8 Va slope that actually begins just below the Nyquist frequency. With a sampling rate of 48 kHz, the filter slope gives a flat response with little phase distortion up to 20 kHz. This allows a safety area of 4 kHz prior to the Nyquist frequency.

The Sample-and-Hold Circuit

The filtered signal next passes to a sample-and-hold circuit. At regular intervals, as defined by the sampling rate, the analog signal is sampled, and this value is held until the next sample is taken. The sampling rates currently found in use are 48 kHz and 44.1 kHz. The former is used by reel-to-reel digital recorders, while the latter is used by the rotary head video based systems.

The Compact Disc plays back at a sampling rate of 44.1 kHz, and the R-DAT or simply DAT, will playback at 44.1 kHz and 48 kHz, but will only record at the 48 kHz sampling rate when operating in the normal mode. A few video-based systems sample at a 44.056 kHz rate, and this difference will be discussed in the next chapter. It is important in PCM systems that the pulse spacing remain constant, and that the sampled value be held fully until the next sample occurs. If the sample were not held, the analog voltages would change between samples, and the following A to D converter would create false digital words.

The Analog-to-Digital Converter

Each sampled analog signal is now converted into a 16-bit digital word based on its voltage level, and this appears at the 16 outputs of the A/D converter. This circuit must decide which of the available quantization levels most closely approximates the analog input voltage for each sample, and derive a binary number from that chosen level. If the sampling rate is 48 kHz, this occurs 48,000 times per second or once every 20.416 microseconds. The circuit must be extremely fast and accurate since any under- or over- level assigning will create errors in the digital word.

The Multiplexer

Tape recorders (analog or digital) may be thought of as serial devices. That is, each recorded channel is only capable of processing a single data sequence. Depending on the type of recorder, this may be a continuously varying analog signal, or a serial bit stream of ones and zeroes. However, the A/D converter has a parallel output. All 16 bits appear simultaneously at the 16 output pins of the converter. Therefore, in order to record the 16-bit word on tape, the bits must be sent to the recorder one at a time (serially). The multiplexer accomplishes this by converting the 16 parallel bits into a serial output, usually utilizing a shift register. This bit stream is then sent to the next stage of the digital encoder.

At the multiplexer stage any necessary data coding is also done. Many systems require the use of an address bit to identify the locations of the data on the storage medium. A synchronization bit is also needed in some systems so that the beginning of

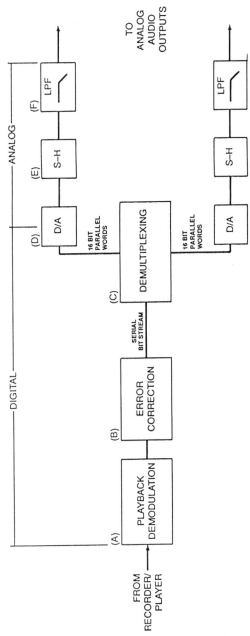

Figure 13-8, a simplified diagram of a two-channel digital to analog decoder. (A) Playback Demodulation, (B) Error Processing (detection and correction), (C) Demultiplexer for serial to parallel data conversion, (D) Digital to Analog Converter, (E) Sample and Hold Circuit for wave reconstruction, (F) Low-Pass or "Smoothing" Filter.

each digital word can be identified. Other identification bits or "flags" can signify the presence of pre-emphasis, represent index numbers, or even be used for absolute timing such as time-code numbers or reel numbers. These bits are often called "preambles" and are similar in nature to the "P" and "Q" codes added to the Compact Disc's data stream to identify the track and index numbers.

Error Protection and Interleaving

Digital tape is subject to the same coating imperfections found in analog tape formulations, and of course is just as susceptible to air-borne dust particles and dirt build-ups along the tape path. Consequently, there are the inevitable drop-outs in the serial data stream. However, although a reasonable number of drop-outs can be tolerated and may even go unnoticed on an analog tape, a digital tape drop-out may be impossible to ignore. Furthermore, there may even be drop-ins. This occurs when tiny magnetic particles become dislodged from the oxide surface at one location and become re-located elsewhere on the tape.

In the digital domain with the digital signal recorded as a series of ones and zeroes, a drop-out or -in creates an error in the code and the decoded signal is likely to contain an annoying noise or even an interval of silence.

Fortunately, the digital format permits various error detection and correction codes to be recorded along with the audio signal. Typically, the recorded data stream for each audio channel consists of four components: a preamble (sync bit and identification code), the audio data itself, a cyclic redundancy check (CRC) code and a parity check code. In some digital recording formats, the parity check code may be recorded at a separate location or on a different area of the tape. In fact, the entire data stream may be recorded several times and at different locations on the tape. Some systems may have as many as six data streams for each channel of audio information.

Error Detection: The Cyclic Redundancy Check Code

The CRC (Cyclic Redundancy Check) code is used as an error detection system. To understand the general theory of operation, consider an encoding system in which the audio data stream is examined at regular intervals, called data blocks. Each data block is mathematically divided by a fixed number. Although the division is of course a binary operation, we will use the more comfortable decimal system equivalent for ease of explanation.

We need to create a column of decimal numbers which represent our digital audio data stream. Each number is then to be divided by a fixed number which we have arbitrarily defined as 37.852. The quotient is ignored, and the remainder is noted and recorded (in binary form) at the end of the data block. This is the cyclic redundancy check code for this segment of the data stream. Later on, when the audio data stream is reproduced, it is again divided by that same number, and the remainder is compared to the reproduced CRC code. If the two numbers are not the same, it is an indication of an error. Either the data block, or the CRC itself, contains the error.

Of course, the CRC code is not capable of correcting the error. It is merely an error-detection system. To make the necessary correction, an additional code is required.

The Parity Block

Returning to the actual binary format to be recorded, let's examine a series of three simplified 5-bit data blocks shown here:

01100	Data Block 1
10111	Data Block 2
10101	Data Block 3
———	
01110	Parity Block

The parity block code is found by adding the data blocks and ignoring all arithmetic carries. Thus, although binary $1 + 1 = 10$, we discard the carried 1, and so we have $1 + 1 = 0$. In decimal notation, we might similarly discover that now $9 + 8 = 7$, rather than 17. Note that in our parity system, an odd number of ones in any column yields a parity bit of one, and an even number of ones makes the parity bit zero. As mentioned earlier, the parity check code is added to the serial bit stream and becomes part of the digital word for that particular sample. We will see how this parity block is used to correct errors detected by the CRC in the discussion on digital playback.

Interleaving

As a further safeguard against data errors, most systems use an interleaving format in which successive digital words are scattered so that no two successive words follow each other. Often, the data stream is first divided into odd and even word sequences.

Thus, a 12-bit word sequence is generated as 1, 3, 5, 7, 9, 11, 2, 4, 6, 8, 10, 12. This sequence may be further cross-interleaved to produce 1, 5, 9, 3, 7, 11, 2, 6, 10, 4, 8, 12. One of the more popular coding schemes is the Reed-Solomon code, and the Cross-Interleave Reed-Solomon Code (CIRC) is the standard for data recorded for the Compact Disc.

This interleaving means that a drop-out or other physical defect that could cause a data error in more than one word is dispersed across a larger area. When the data stream is restored to its proper sequence, it will be easier to restore the missing erroneous data since the error detection/correction parity scheme makes the assumption that only one block of data is wrong. CIRC prevents burst errors (large blocks of lost data) from creating non-correctable areas of digital data in the serial bit stream.

The Record Circuit

The digital bit stream is now almost ready to be recorded on magnetic tape or other storage medium, and it is at this point that the record modulation mentioned earlier (Non-return-to-Zero, Eight-to-Fourteen, HDM-1) takes place. The derived modulating voltages are sent to the record circuit where they are converted to magnetic reversals and recorded on the magnetic tape or other medium as positive and negative saturations. The reversals represent the binary ones and zeroes of the digital signal.

The Playback Process

Now that we have successfully digitized and stored the analog signal on some form of storage medium, be it magnetic or optical, we must now retrieve the digital information and reconstruct our original continuous analog waveform. The conversion, in most ways, is simply a reversal of the record process. Figure 13-8 shows a block diagram of a PCM decoding system.

The Playback Circuit (Demodulation)

The first step in the process is to convert the magnetic saturation reversals back to recognizable binary ones and zeroes. The output of the playback head is usually very low in level and some processing is needed to retrieve all the data. In actuality, the waveform has become rounded and the sharp transitions that were produced at the output of the encoder have been lost. A wave-shaping circuit restores the signal to more square wave-like transitions, thereby allowing the ones and zeroes to be recreated exactly. And, since we have completely recovered all the binary digits in the same order in which they were recorded, no data has been lost or distorted. The digital data has been retrieved without tape hiss, print-through, tape distortion, wow and flutter, or any of the other ills that plague analog magnetic tape.

Error Correction

The serial bit stream that we have just produced is now de-interleaved using a reversal of the original interleaving scheme. Drop-outs that occurred on the tape itself may have affected a number of words, but after de-interleaving these errors are most likely not successive in nature. This fact makes it easier for the digital decoder to detect and correct any data errors.

Earlier we created a series of three simplified 5-bit data blocks, and from them we generated a parity block which was recorded along with the digital data word. Now, let's assume that during playback, the CRC code has determined that there is a data error in Block 2. The three data blocks are now combined with the recorded parity block to produce a new parity block. The new parity block is combined with the incorrect data block, and this operation corrects the data that was in error.

01100	Data Block 1
01001	Data Block 2 (Incorrect)
10101	Data Block 3
01110	Recorded Parity Block

11110	New Parity Block
01001	Incorrect Data Block 2

10111	Corrected Data Block 2

Note that if an error occurs within the CRC code, indicating an error where none actually exists, the new parity block will not change the value of the data block. For example,

01100	Data Block 1
10111	Data Block 2
10101	Data Block 3 (Falsely assumed to be incorrect)
01110	Recorded Parity Block

00000	New Parity Block
10101	"Incorrect" Data Block 3

10101	"Corrected" Data Block 3 (No change)

As shown in the above example, block errors can be easily corrected when determined by the CRC code. Block code error correction systems are very effective. A further refinement of this technique uses a "Hamming" code to locate the error within the block. In effect, a parity bit is generated for each section of the 16-bit word, and the above process occurs in miniature.

Other types of error-correcting schemes are used by various manufacturers. Some use the mathematical approach as above, while others use convolutional or predictive type methods. Many of these methods can apply to the individual bit or to the whole word, or both. As digital continues to develop, we will see more and more sophisticated error detection and correction schemes in use.

Error Replacement and Concealment

Now, what if for some reason or other, an error is detected but cannot be corrected by the available parity blocks, Hamming codes, etc.? The decoder's first response will be to look elsewhere for redundant data. In the preamble of the digital word, there is an address code that will tell the D/A converter where to look for the redundant data. If this is not possible, other methods must be employed.

One of these methods is Interpolation. Since audio is a continuous and related signal, it is relatively easy in many cases to logically determine the missing data. If, for instance, I was counting from 1 to 10 and there were a silence where the word "five" would normally have been, it wouldn't take you long to figure out which word was missing. Similarly, if a string of voltages was being measured as 1.0 V, 1.1 V, 1.2 V, 1.3 V, 0 V, 1.5 V, it would seem logical that instead of the fifth reading being zero volts, it should be 1.4 volts. This is called linear interpolation, and it is when the digital converter makes up data that would logically fit in a sequence between two known values.

If, even after de-interleaving, there are two or more successive values missing, the decoder will usually hold the previous value to conceal the missing or erroneous data. A combination of linear and lateral interpolation may be used depending on the number of successive errors that are found to be non-correctable.

In the event that the above methods of correcting, replacing or concealing have not been able to produce a suitable data word to correct an error, the digital decoder will usually then mute. At this point the data word in error is changed to all zeroes, and the output of the decoder is muted. Even in this most severe case, our ear may not perceive the data as missing. An absence of sound is much less noticeable than a click or sputter from invalid data. It would take one thousand successive muted digital words to create a mute of about 20 milliseconds in the analog output. And, 20 milliseconds is recognized as the shortest noticeable integration time for the human ear. We may hear some distortion or roughness in the sound before that, but it is doubtful that a space in the music will be heard.

De-Multiplexing

After the serial data has been restored to its original form, it is now de-multiplexed. That is, it is restored to its parallel state before it is sent to the actual digital-to-analog converter. This restores the original sample timing by clocking out a parallel digital word at the same rate as the original waveform was sampled.

The Digital-to-Analog Converter

The digital to analog converter takes the parallel bit stream from the de-multiplexer and converts the 16-bit binary word back to an analog voltage value. These voltage values are equivalent to the levels of the originally sampled pulses derived from the input analog waveform.

The Sample-and-Hold Circuit

This series of voltage pulses is then put into another sample-and-hold circuit to reproduce the staircase waveform. The correct voltage value is held until the next sample is decoded. This effectively filters out any false readings between samples since the initial value is held until the D/A converter outputs another.

One artifact of the sample-and-hold function is a small high-frequency roll-off. A perfect D/A converter would output a series of pure pulses with nothing in between and exactly timed to the original samples. In this imperfect world, however, switching pulses, miscellaneous transients, etc., can occur between the samples. As just mentioned, the sample-and-hold function filters these but we create a phenomena called "aperture loss." This creates a high-frequency roll-off that is infinite at the sampling frequency, but that has only fallen by about 4 dB at the Nyquist frequency. Two methods are commonly applied to return the frequency response to a flat state. The first is to add some high-frequency pre-emphasis to the original input signal similar to that used in some analog noise-reduction units. This is sometimes switchable, and an identification flag is usually added to the preamble to indicate this to the decoder. Another method is to tailor the output filter to compensate for the fall-off of the highs. In either case, the response of the overall system remains flat.

The Output Filter

The reconstructed quantized signal is now passed through a low-pass filter to remove all unwanted high-frequency components which are a function of the square wave-like quantization waveform. This filter is sometimes called the reconstruction filter or smoothing filter, and usually has a very sharp roll-off (24 dB/8va) similar to the anti-aliasing filter found at the beginning of the system. This filter actually performs a superposition of the sin x/x function at each sample point, and as a result no data is lost. The resultant output signal is a faithful reproduction of the original input source.

THE DIGITAL ADVANTAGE

In the following section, various specifications of the digital tape recording process are reviewed, and comparisons are made with analog recording systems.

Tape Noise

An immediate advantage of the digital recording process is its immunity to tape hiss. Although analog noise may indeed distort the waveform of the digitally-encoded signal, the decoding process is insensitive to this form of distortion. At any instant, the D/A output is either a "1" or a "0." There is no such thing as a "1.003" or a "0.0025." In fact, the ones and zeroes may be thought of simply as HI and LOW logic states, whose actual voltage levels are irrelevant. Therefore, even a severe deviation from the defined level is of no practical consequence. The decoder looks for positive- and negative-going transitions, and is not concerned with the levels at either end of the transition. Thus, the analog noise component introduced by the tape medium is incapable of affecting the decoded signal output.

Dynamic Range

Dynamic range is no longer a function of the tape medium. Since the digital tape is always fully magnetized in one direction or another, saturation distortion is meaningless. The dynamic range is only limited by the number of bits that are available for each digital word. As already noted, most systems make use of 16 bits, which gives a dynamic range of almost 98 dB. Higher bit values may be used in the future.

Cross Talk

In analog tape recorders, the cross-talk specification is usually a function of head design limitations, and is typically in the –50 to –55 dB range. Cross talk within a record or playback head is an analog phenomena, and so has no significance to digital recording. It suffers the same fate as analog tape hiss, and it simply does not survive the decoding process.

However, in the absence of tape-head cross talk, the electronic cross talk within the analog sections of the tape recorder is now measurable, with typical specifications in the –80 to –95 dB range.

Print-through

Print-through from adjacent layers of tape manifests itself as an analog distortion of the signal waveform. The printed signal is below the switching threshold of the HI/LOW logic states and as such, is not recognized by the decoder. And, as before, the waveform distortion has no effect on the decoded output, and therefore the print-through signal is not present in the analog audio output.

Harmonic Distortion

The distortion characteristics of the digital format are significantly different from those associated with an analog system. In analog recording, distortion rises gradually as the tape's saturation level is approached. Generally, an output level is specified, at which point the third-harmonic distortion reaches a three-percent level. Beyond this point, distortion rapidly rises, effectively defining the upper limit of the analog system's dynamic range.

As described earlier, the dynamic range of the digital recording system is not a function of the tape medium, and distortion does not increase with recorded level. Instead, the distortion (or lack of it) remains constant as the maximum output level is approached. This point is defined by the number of digital bits available, and once this ceiling is reached (all bits ones), further level increases simply cause errors in the bit stream, resulting in instant and severe distortion. Error correction systems may cause mutes to occur to mask the distortion, but this solution is not much better than the distortion itself. Therefore, the transition between minimum and maximum distortion is almost instantaneous, and the engineer must take care not to let levels stray into the red. Unlike analog tape, which may forgive an occasional peak or two, digital distortion is immediately and painfully obvious.

Since the signal-to-quantizing-error ratio in a digital system remains constant until all the bits are used, it is common practice to set a "0" or system calibration point 10 to 15 dB below the maximum ceiling. Most systems use peak reading or "PPM" indicators to meter incoming analog signal, and the system level of +4 dBm is usually set at a –15 dB. Various digital metering systems will be discussed in Chapter 14.

Wow and Flutter

In the digital playback system, the serial bit stream is converted into a parallel output by the de-multiplexer as mentioned earlier in the chapter. Since each parallel output is held until the next 16-bit serial word has been received, there is—in effect—a built-in "wow-and-flutter filter" inherent in the decoding process. The start-and-stop nature of the data flow is such that any wow and flutter within the tape transport system has no effect on the decoded output.

Tape Duplication

Since the digital process is immune to the various distortion producing phenomena described above, multiple generation copies of a tape will be indistinguishable from the original master. Since only a simple series of Hi/Low logic states is being copied, there is very little that can go amiss. Because of the nature of some storage mediums, the signal may lose the transition sharpness of the leading edge of the waveform, so some reshaping of the signal prior to re-recording is often done so that the transitions between the logic states remain as instantaneous as possible.

Chapter 14

Digital Audio Recording Systems

In Chapter 13 we examined the process for converting a continuous analog waveform into a binary bit stream that accurately represents the original signal. Once this bit stream is generated, it needs to be stored so that it may later be retrieved and then converted back into an analog signal. This signal can then be sent to amplifiers and loudspeakers, mixing consoles or other analog equipment.

There exists today some equipment capable of processing the digital signal entirely in the digital domain, and there are more devices of this type on the horizon. These digital signal processors may accept the digital signal from a variety of sources. However, any digital signal must be converted back to its equivalent analog waveform, either as an electrical signal or as an acoustic wave before our ear can perceive the nature of the sound.

The accuracy of the digital storage medium is an important link in the digital recording/playback chain, and the engineer who wishes to accurately make use of this technology should understand the various storage media available for his use.

TRACKS VERSUS CHANNELS

In analog recording, the terms "tracks" and "channels" are used almost synonymously. However, it will be sometimes noted that digital specifications list two (or more) digital tracks per audio channel. To understand this distinction, we must first examine some of the specifications for a hypothetical digital tape recorder. These specifications are tabulated in Figure 14-1.

Reviewing the data tabulated at 76 cm./sec. (30 in./sec.), we find that with a 16-bit word transmitted during each sampling interval, each bit has a word length of 9.5×10^{-5} cm., and the bit stream is recorded on each tape track at a rate of 800 k-bit/sec.. If this bit stream represents an alternating 10101010.... series, the recorded frequency will be 400 kHz. At 76 cm./sec., this represents a wavelength of 1.9 μm. At 38 cm./sec. the wavelength is

Specification		TAPE SPEED		
		High	Low	Units
Sampling Rate	f_s	50	50	kHz
Tape Speed	V	76	38	cm/sec
Wavelength	λ_{f_s}	1.52×10^{-3}	0.76×10^{-3}	cm
Bit Length	$BL = \lambda/16$	9.5×10^{-5}	4.75×10^{-5}	cm/bit
Bit Rate	$BR = V/BL$	800	800	kbits/sec/track
f_{max}	$BR/2$	400	400	kHz
λ_{min}	V/f_{max}	1.9	0.95	μ m

Figure 14-1. Data specifications for a tape recorder with a sampling rate of 50 kHz.

0.95 μm. Given existing longitudinal tape recorder technology, recorded wavelengths of less than 1.5 μm are considered unreliable, and therefore the wavelength at 38 cm./sec. is unacceptable. However, if the bit stream for each audio channel is distributed across two digital tracks on the tape recorder, the bit rate per track becomes 400 kbits/sec.. Therefore, f_{max} = 200 kHz, and the minimum wavelength is once again within the acceptable limits. This will be explored further as the various types of digital recorders and track formats are discussed.

Sampling Rate Converters

For any digital signal to be decoded to its analog equivalent, the specifications of the digital bit stream must be matched to the specifications of the digital playback machine. Different sampling rates are used by several of the various systems, and in order to transfer a signal from one machine to another the sampling rates must match. The predominant sampling rates are tabulated below.

Sampling Rate	Principal Use
32 kHz	EBU (European Broadcast Union) Systems, DAT and other Broadcasting Systems.
44.056 kHz	NTSC color video based storage systems. (principally Beta and VHS recorders)
44.1 kHz	Compact Disc, DAT and NTSC monochrome video storage systems (principally U-Format recorders)
48 kHz	Professional open-reel digital recorders and DAT .
50 kHz	Older professional recording systems

Leaving aside all considerations of track layout and tape speed, the output bit stream from one recorder/player must match the sampling rate of the device to which it is being sent. If the rates are different, a sampling converter is needed to accomplish this task. The converter takes the incoming signal and, by re-clocking the signal, modifies the sampling rate to match the required configuration.

Many sampling rate converters also allow signal interchange between various digital input/output signal formats. The most commonly found formats are the AES/EBU (Audio Engineering Society/European Broadcasting Union) balanced interface format (requiring XLR connectors), the S/PDIF (Sony-Philips digital interface) unbalanced format (requiring unbalanced RCA connectors), and the SDIF-2 (Sony digital interface 2) format requiring BNC connectors. Most professional digital systems use the balanced AES/EBU interface.

ROTARY-HEAD (VIDEO) STORAGE SYSTEMS

In our previous example of a hypothetical digital recorder, bit rates of 800 kbits/sec. were being recorded and, as mentioned earlier, this represents a frequency of 400 kHz for each channel of recorded material. A stereo signal that has been converted to a digital bit stream, with additional bits added to each word for preambles and parity, can easily generate frequencies in the 1 MHz to 2 MHz range. Since most video recorders have a frequency bandwidth of around 4 MHz or better, they can be considered an ideal recorder for storing digital data streams.

A digital audio processor is used to convert the stereo signal into a digital data stream that can be recorded as video data on various types of video recorders. The stereo signal is multiplexed, that is, the channels are combined, into a continuous stream that contains both the left and right channel audio information. Vertical and horizontal synchronization pulses are also generated and added to the signal so that it will appear to be a video signal and be recorded correctly on the video recorder. However, video recording is a non-continuous process as compared with the more familiar analog recording. This is because after each video field and associated pass of the electron gun on the television screen, there is an interval of time while the beam flies back to the upper left hand corner of the screen. This is called the vertical-blanking interval. The digital audio processor contains buffer memories, which hold the signal during this interval so that the continuous serial data stream from the A/D converter can be stored in the non-continuous video fields and frames of the video system. Professional digital recorders that used a video-based storage medium usually have SMPTE time code recorded on one of the audio tracks of the video recorder (discussed in Chapter 15). This allows for synchronization and editing and will be discussed later in the chapter.

U-Format Recorders

Most of these professional video-based systems store their data on what is called U-Format video tape. U-Format tape, often called U-Matic, is a video cassette containing video tape that is three-quarters of an inch in width. The tape speed is 3.75 in./sec. and lengths can vary from 10 minutes to as long as 75 minutes. The recording system uses a technique called helical scanning where the tape is wrapped around a rotating head cylinder. The cylinder contains two video heads, and each head is responsible for recording one field of each video frame. Each head produces a track width of 3.4 mils and the tape is wrapped around the head at an angle which causes the tracks to be recorded diagonally across the tape. This yields a track length per field of 6.7 inches. Separate fixed heads record analog audio signals longitudinally along the bottom of the video tape. A CTL track, which controls when the signal switches from head to head is recorded at the top of the tape. For a further discussion on video recording and frame rates, refer to Chapter 15.

The high-frequency response necessary for video and digital audio is achieved by spinning the video head cylinder at a rate of 1800 rpm while moving the tape past the spinning heads at a relatively slow speed of 3.75 inches per second. The resulting tape speed across the heads of roughly 400 in./sec. allows data to be recorded in the megahertz range. This is often called the writing speed. U-Format recorders also place a guard band between each field of the video or pseudo-video signal. This prevents signal from one frame or field from bleeding into the next and minimizes tracking error.

The predominant frame rate for these professional digital rotary head systems is 30 frames/sec., and is the frame rate for NTSC monochrome video. The video scan rate, which determines the number of frames per second, also controls how the digital audio data is stored in the video frame. The video-scan rate of a professional U-Format video tape recorder allows a sampling rate of 44.1 kHz with 16 bit quantization when used in the NTSC monochrome mode of 30 frames per second.

Professional digital audio processors and their associated U-Format recorders are used in the mastering and manufacture of the Compact Disc.

Beta and VHS Format Recorders

Home digital audio processors, designed to be used with consumer video cassette decks, have been used successfully to record some memorable performances. However, they differ from the professional versions in several very important ways. One of the primary differences is in the width of the tape and the speed at which it travels. Helical scan recording is again employed, but at a reduced tape speed of .787 in./sec. for Beta II and 0.657 in./sec. for VHS LP. Even though the head drum rotates at 1800 rpm, as in the U-Format, the reduced speed results in equivalent tape speeds of 270 in./sec. and 225 in./sec. respectively. The track widths are also reduced to less than half the larger format and the guard bands have been eliminated to allow more frames of video information in a given tape length. Beta III and VHS EP are unsuitable for digital audio recording due to increasing dropout rates causing non-correctable errors in the digital stream. Tape width for both systems is one-half inch, and gives correspondingly smaller track lengths.

While U-Format recorders are capable of recording at a frame rate of 30 fps (frames per second) in the NTSC monochrome video mode and 29.97 fps in the NTSC color mode, Beta and VHS recorders can only record at the color frame rate. As mentioned earlier, a frame rate of 30 fps allows a sampling rate of 44.1 kHz. Sampling at the slightly slower color rate translates to a sampling rate of 44.056 kHz. This difference in sampling rate requires that, before a consumer format PCM digital audio tape can be mastered for Compact Disc or DAT release, it must be sample converted.

DAT Recorders

A relatively new type of digital storage medium is the Digital Audio Tape recorder or R-DAT. The R-DAT was developed primarily for the consumer marketplace, but because of its stability and accuracy has found its way into professional recording studios. The desire to develop small convenient digital recorders suitable for home use led to the creation of two small format digital recording systems. One used a stationary head transport system while the other used a rotating head transport similar to current video technology. They were originally called S-DAT (for stationary head) and R-DAT (for rotating head) respectively. The superiority of the R-DAT method has established it as the sole consumer digital audio recorder, and as such, the R- prefix has been dropped and the unit is simply called a DAT recorder. Tape is contained in a plastic cassette similar to a video cassette.

The tape is called a DAT cassette, and is a high coercivity metal particle tape. The actual cassette is approximately 2-7/8 inches long, 2-1/8 inches wide, and 3/8-inch tall and contains tape approximately 1/8 inch in width. The actual dimensions are 73 mm x 54 mm x 10.5 mm (W x D x H). The cassette has a completely sealed structure to prevent dirt and debris (as well as finger prints) from causing drop-outs and errors in the digital signal. The actual tape width is 3.81 mm.

The DAT recorder uses a helical scanning method of recording similar to that found in U-Format video tape recorders. However, the amount of tape that is wrapped around the drum during record and playback is considerably less than in the video formats. The tape is in contact with the head cylinder over an angle of 90 degrees which is one-fourth of the circumference of the drum. This allows the tape to be fast forwarded or rewound while still wrapped around the head drum with minimal or no tape wear or damage. Conventional video recorders remove the tape from the head cylinder prior to fast speed shuttling. The rotating cylinder has two heads on a drum 30 mm in diameter. The narrow contact angle of drum to tape means that the record or playback signal is applied to the tape only 50 percent of the time. The remaining percent of the time the signal is interrupted, and buffer memories are used once again to convert the continuous data stream to a non-continuous recording format.

The tape moves at a speed of 8.15 mm/s, which is about 1/4 in./sec. This slow longitudinal tape speed, coupled with long tape lengths in the DAT cassette, results in possible recording times of over two hours. The head drum rotates at a speed of 2000 rpm, and this gives us an equivalent writing speed of approximately 123 inches per second. The tracks are recorded on tape without

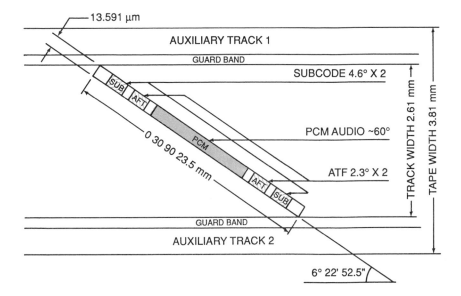

Figure 14-2. Track format for the DAT (rotary) showing positions for audio data, subcode information, and ATF (Automatic Track Finding) encoding.

guard bands. As mentioned earlier in the discussion of consumer video recorders, the lack of a guard band between tracks can create tracking problems that can produce errors in the digital bit stream. This is avoided in the DAT format by using a method called azimuth recording. The tracks are tilted away from the relative vertical of the tape by an angle of plus or minus 20 degrees. The first track has positive azimuth and the following one has negative azimuth, and this condition continues for the length of the tape. The length of each diagonal track is 23.501 mm, yet only a portion of that length contains audio data. The remaining data is for subcode and tracking information as shown in Figure 14-2. By constantly comparing the azimuth angle of the pilot and sync signals between heads, automatic track finding (ATF) is possible. This ATF azimuth type recording allows precise tracking without guard bands or CTL (tracking control head) signals that are necessary in video recorders.

The DAT recording system uses a double Reed-Solomon code for error detection and correction. The signal is also interleaved, and the data is recorded across two tracks. This makes data retrieval possible even if only one head is functioning. The DAT recorder system was designed to be able to record and playback at sampling rates of 48 kHz, 44.1 kHz and 32 kHz. However, not all DAT machines will record at all sampling rates. 16-bit quantization is used with all sampling rates. The DAT recorder will automatically select a sampling rate of 44.1 if a 44.056 digital signal is applied. This will cause a pitch discrepancy, and raise the pitch by 0.1 percent.

SUMMARY FOR ROTARY HEAD DIGITAL RECORDERS

Rotary head digital recorders have many advantages. Chief among them is that the tape is contained in an enclosed environment, and therefore protected from contamination which can cause dropouts and high error rates. Helical scan digital recorders tend to be less expensive than their reel-to-reel counterparts since their data is interleaved and recorded as a single bit stream. This requires simpler record and playback electronics and, with the exception of the DAT recorder, makes use of existing video recorders. Another financial advantage of these systems is the low tape consumption. Tape used for digital recording must be manufactured to very high standards and tolerances in terms of dropouts and uniformity. Tape of this type can be expensive, but the slow longitudinal tape speed of helical scan systems allows lengthy recordings on very little tape.

Rotary head digital recorders are limited to two-channel stereo recordings. Some experimentation has been done with a helical four-track recorder, but so far this has not proved practical. A further limitation of these systems is that razor-blade editing is not possible. Any required editing must be done electronically with the associated extra cost of editing hardware. A discussion of electronic editing methods and systems is included later in this chapter. It is not possible, in helical systems, to record on one channel while playback is accomplished on the other since the data for both channels is interleaved into one bit stream. Therefore, overdubs and other forms of synchronous recording are not possible. Figure 14-3 shows a professional DAT recorder/reproducer and a digital processor for use with a U-Matic recorder.

FIXED-HEAD DIGITAL STORAGE SYSTEMS

While helical type digital recording has become the principal method for two-channel stereo recordings, the inherent limitations of the system have precluded multi-track digital recorders. However, advances in thin film head technology have permitted

A

B

Figure 14-3. (A) a professional DAT recorder Sony PCM-2500 (Sony photo). At (B) a two-channel digital encoder designed for use with a professional U-Matic video recorder (Sony PCM-1630, Sony photo).

the design of recording heads for longitudinal recording that meet the frequency requirements of digital recording. This has led to the development of multi-channel digital tape recorders that are capable of all the synchronous recording techniques required for recording and mixdown of popular music.

Two different systems for digital multi-track recording are currently in use. These systems, DASH and PD, have replaced earlier types of digital multi-track tape recorders developed by other manufacturers. The actual uses and functions of these two systems are similar, and an engineer familiar with the operation of a conventional analog multi-track tape recorder should have no trouble adapting to these machines. However, the actual methods of data storage, error detection and correction, channel codings and track layouts are different and each format will be discussed separately. Both systems offer two-track longitudinal digital recorders as well as multi-track machines, but our investigations will be predominantly concerning the multi-channel tape recorders.

Head Configuration

In our discussions of analog recorders, reference was made to the erase, record and reproduce heads. In the digital domain, these heads are often referred to as the erase, write and read heads respectively. Because it is very difficult for a head to perform both a read and a write function simultaneously when handling high density digital data streams, there is a second read and/or write head found in the head block of a digital multi-track recorder. This extra head is necessary for the recorder to be able to perform synchronization functions.

Electronic cross-fading is used to smooth the transitions between old and new data during punch-ins and -outs. As in analog multi-track recording, the old data is erased and replaced with new data in synchronization with the material on other tracks. To keep these transitions as smooth as possible and to reduce data errors, data buffers hold the old data at the punch-in point and cross fade that with the new data before sending the signal to the write head. At the punch-out point, the reverse occurs with the new data buffered and cross faded with the old. This electronic cross fading and data buffering is as well used to prevent data errors caused by overlapping the areas of data when the tape

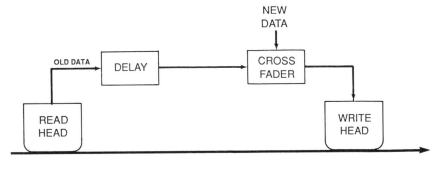

Fiigure 14-4. Shows (above) the physical head positioning required for replacing old data, (below) the actual cross-fading of old and new data.

is spliced with a razor blade. Electronic cross fading is illustrated in Figure 14-4.

THE DASH SYSTEM

The DASH (Digital Audio Stationary Head) system is one of the two professionally accepted longitudinal digital multi-track recording systems. DASH recorders are available in 2-track, 24-track and 48-track formats. The 24-track recorders have 24 channels of digital audio along with 2 analog auxiliary cue tracks, a SMPTE time code track, and a CTL or control track. This total of 28 tracks is arrayed vertically from 1 to 28 on one-half inch tape. A double-density DASH 48-track machine is also available. This machine contains 48 digital audio tracks and the same number of auxiliary tracks, also on half-inch tape. To accomplish this, the second group of 24 tracks is physically interleaved with the first 24 tracks. This allows interchangeability between the 24-track single density and the 48-track double-density formats. A 24-track DASH machine can be used to record tracks 1 through 24, and this tape can then be played back (for further overdubs) on the 48-track version. Conversely, a 24-track DASH tape recorder can play back the first 24-tracks of material that were recorded on a double-density 48-track machine.

Each digital track is 0.17 mm. wide and the gap spacing is 0.20 mm. in the single-density version and half that in the larger machine. The analog tracks are slightly separated from the digital tracks to prevent the required analog bias from affecting the digital tracks, although the double-density version uses PWM (Pulse Width Modulation) that does not require bias for the auxiliary tracks. The transport operates at 30 in./sec. and provides 60 minutes of recording time using 9000 feet of tape on 14-inch precision metal reels.

The DASH system uses 16-bit linear pulse-code modulation (PCM) and has switchable sampling frequencies of 48 kHz and 44.1 kHz. At the lower sampling rate, the tape speed is lowered to 27.56 in./sec. This keeps the recorded wavelengths the same regardless of sampling frequency. The double density DASH machine is also capable of a sampling frequency of 44.056 kHz for compatibility with CD-V projects that use a NTSC color frame rate. This lower sampling rate yields a tape speed of 27.54 in./sec.

The analog auxiliary tracks are primarily used for cueing purposes. The digital audio channels can only be listened to while the tape recorder is at the proper play speed. Yet there are times when it is advantageous for the engineer to be able to hear the signal while the tape is being slowly moved by hand. The associated analog cue inputs are fed with signal during the recording of the basic tracks. When using a typical in-line recording console, these cue inputs could be fed from say, the stereo monitor bus outs or from a spare auxiliary bus.

The control track (CTL) is used to control the speed of the transport during reproduce operations. It is recorded during the basic tracking sessions and should extend continuously all the way through the song. Because of this, the prudent engineer may pre-stripe the tape to be used prior to the beginning of the session. Most DASH multi-track recorders have a function called "Advance Record" to handle this task. The control track contains a synchronizing pattern that contains a sector identifying mark, a control word that defines the sampling rate in use, the address for data location and a CRCC (Cyclic Redundancy Check Code) word for error protection. It is possible to synchronize two multi-track DASH tape recorders together using the control tracks.

The SMPTE time code track is used to store non-drop frame longitudinal time code that is used for synchronization with other machines as well as transport control of auto-locate and cue functions.

The analog audio is converted to digital through the A to D converters and this data is used to form data blocks. Each data block contains a sync word which is used to identify the block, 12 data words which contain the audio information, 4 parity words for error checking and a Cyclic Redundancy Check code (CRC) word. These data blocks correspond to the sector identifying mark of the control track. As mentioned in Chapter 13, various modulation codes must be used with binary data for more compact high-density data storage. The DASH system makes use of a system called HDM-1 (High Density Modulation –1) for maximum packing density and to reduce the bandwidth requirements for the digital data.

As previously mentioned, it is very difficult to construct a head that will read and write data on different tracks simultaneously. However, when overdubbing new material in-sync on analog tape recorders, this is exactly what is done. To overcome this limitation inherent in digital multi-track heads, the DASH system utilizes an additional *Write* head. The first *Write* head is used for normal recording and it is followed by the *Read* head. This allows off-tape monitoring during the recording of the basic tracks. In the "sync" mode, the signal from the *Read* head is delayed and the new data is written by the second *Write* head and applied to the tape synchronous to the data on the previously recorded tracks.

THE PD SYSTEM

The other reel-to-reel stationary head digital recording system is the PRO-DIGI (Professional Digital) system that is commonly referred to as the PD format. The PD system differs from the DASH system in several ways. At this time there is no compatibility between the two systems, but data interchange between them is possible through the use of AES/EBU digital input/output ports.

On first glance, the most notable difference between the DASH format multi-track tape recorders and the largest PD format machines is the number of available recording channels and the width of the tape. Although there is a 16-channel machine available, most PD tape recorders allow 32-channels of information to be recorded and replayed. Along with the 32-channels of digital audio, there are 2 auxiliary cue tracks, 2 digital auxiliary tracks, and 1 SMPTE time code track. The SMPTE time code track is used for auto-locating functions and synchronization as well as its use as an integral part of the block locating system within the encoding/decoding process. In addition to these tracks, there are 8 additional digital tracks for a total of 45 tracks on 1-inch wide tape. The eight additional digital tracks are divided among the primary digital tracks so that for every 8 channels of information, there are 10 tracks used. These extra tracks are used to store the check words of the associated digital audio tracks for the error protection systems. Each digital track is 0.29 mm wide and the heads have a gap spacing of 0.27 mm. The tracks are not, as in the DASH single-density system, arranged numerically from top to bottom, but are shuffled so that no two consecutively numbered tracks are adjacent to each other. As in the DASH format, however, the auxiliary tracks are placed on the extreme edges of the tape where they act as guard bands, protecting the digital tracks from edge damage. Figure 14-5 shows the track layout for both the PD and DASH (24- and 48-track) formats.

The transport operates at 30 in./sec. and 60 minutes of recording time is available when using 14-inch reels. The recording system uses 16-bit PCM (Pulse Code Modulation) encoding for the digital audio tracks and Pulse Width Modulation (PWM) for the auxiliary tracks. Sampling frequencies of 48 kHz and 44.1 kHz are supported, but in the PD format the tape speed is not affected by a change in sampling frequencies. This means that at the lower sampling frequency, less data is stored on a given length of tape resulting in a change of wavelength on tape for any given input frequency. Speed control is achieved by locking the capstan to a reference frequency and so a control track is not required.

As in the DASH format, data from the A to D converters is used to assemble data blocks. Within the PD format, the data block contains a 16-bit sync word followed by 12 data words, followed by a 16-bit CRC code word for a total of 224 bits within each data block. This is slightly less than the 288 bit data block used by the DASH system which, as mentioned earlier, contains 4 16-bit check words prior to the CRC code word in each block. As previously discussed, the check words used by the PD format are stored on the dedicated additional digital tracks. It is also important to note that the check word tracks are displaced vertically from their associated audio tracks, so that the check words are not lost with the audio data in the event of a large tape dropout. The PD system uses a "Four-to-Six Modulation" (4/6M) scheme

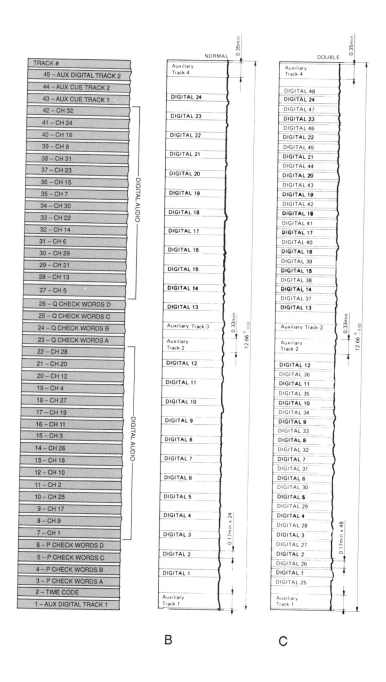

Figure 14-5. Track formats for current digital multi-track tape recorders. (A) the 32-channel ProDigi format, (B) the 24-channel DASH format, and (C) the 48-channel Double Density DASH format.

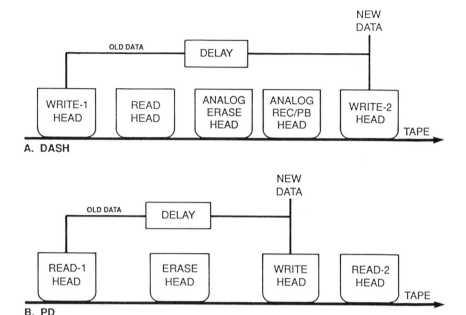

Figure 14-6. Head position for the (A) DASH multi-track system, and (B) the ProDigi multi-track system.

to achieve the high packing density necessary for digital multi-track tape recorders.

To allow overdubbing, the PD system uses two Read heads and one Write head. The basic tracks, that have already been re-corded, are played by the secondary Read head (which precedes the Write head), and delayed the appropriate amount so that the players will be "in sync" as the new data is written by the single Write head. Figure 14-6 shows the head configurations for both the PD and DASH systems.

SUMMARY OF FIXED-HEAD DIGITAL STORAGE SYSTEMS

Open-reel digital tape recorders are available in various track formats. The principal ones are 2-track (DASH & PD), 16-track (PD), 24-track (DASH), 32-track (PD) and 48-track (DASH). The major advantage of the open-reel two-track formats over the heli-cal scan recorders is the ability to edit with a razor-blade. The disadvantage of this is that no satisfactory electronic editing sys-tems have yet been devised for open-reel recorders. Helical sys-tems are better in this regard and electronic editors provide editing possibilities that far exceed what can be achieved with mechanical editing systems. However, since helical scan machines are only available in the two-channel format, multi-channel recording requires the use of one of the existing open-reel formats.

These open-reel digital tape recorders are very susceptible to errors created by tape edge damage, dirt and debris, finger prints, and tape dropouts. Tape-to-head contact is extremely critical and tape-head alignment is not possible without sophisticated test and alignment equipment. Figure 14-7 shows several typical, fixed-head digital recorders.

Other alternatives to open-reel and helical scan digital recorders are becoming increasingly more available and affordable. These will be discussed following the section on Electronic Editing.

Editing Digital Tapes

Many ways of editing digital tapes have been devised since the advent of digital recordings. The initial problem has been that while editing an analog tape means cutting a magnetic pattern that is analogous to the audio waveform, editing a digital tape requires cutting the data stream. The data stream interruptions can create havoc with the error protection and correction schemes. One of the great benefits of digital editing is the precision that is possible with electronic editing systems. These systems can be tape based or personal computer based as in the new types of digital work stations now available.

Punching-In/Out

One of the easiest ways to append or delete information from a digital tape is to either erase or replace existing data. This is done more often on multi-track recorders than on two-track recorders, but the technique is applicable to both. A discussion of the procedures for punching-in/out or insert editing for multi-track recording is included in Chapter 18.

When punching-in on an analog tape recorder, the headphone cue to the musician is played from the record head so that the new material is recorded "in sync" with the old. It is not possible to do this with a digital multi-track recorder since the write head is not capable of reading data. Digital multi-tracks utilize a second Read or Write head following the Read head as previously

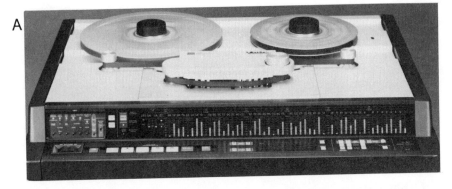

Figure 14-7. Several typical multi-track digital tape recorders. (A) Double Density DASH 48-channel (Sony PCM-3348, Sony photo), (B) Prodigi 32-channel (Mitsubishi X-850, Mitsubishi photo), and (C) DASH 24-channel (Tascam DA-800/24, Tascam photo).

C

mentioned. The data from the Read head is delayed and then sent to the second write head in synchronization with the new material or the data is taken from the extra Read head and recorded "in-sync" at the Write head. Digital cross fades are used to blend the two data streams together so that the transition from the old material to the new material will not be noticeable.

Another advantage realized when using digital multi-track recorders is that the punch-in and punch-out points can be memorized by the tape recorder. This allows the engineer to rehearse and trim the entry and exit points precisely, so that no old data is lost. Once these points are decided and programmed into the digital recording system, the punch-in and punch-out will be performed automatically at precisely the same point as many times as necessary to correct the musical slips or errors on the selected track.

Razor-Blade Editing

Traditional razor-blade editing of digital tapes presents some practical difficulties that are not encountered in the analog domain.

The first problem is that the familiar technique of rocking the tape back and forth across the head, to find the splice point, is now impossible. At the very slow speed involved, the decoding system simply doesn't function, and the operator cannot listen for the splice point. Many open-reel digital recorders get around this problem by providing a channel or two onto which analog audio information is recorded in synchronization with the digital audio tracks. The analog track(s) may then be monitored in the traditional way during editing.

The next problem is that the razor-blade edit is quite likely to interrupt the normal sequence of sync word (or preamble), audio data, CRC code and parity information. There is really no guarantee that the razor will sever the tape at precisely the right spot to preserve the proper sequence of data flow. Thus, there will surely be a momentary data discontinuity from which it may take the system a relatively long time to recover. As a result, the splice will create a noisy transition as it momentarily disrupts the orderly flow of data. This may be a disruption that can be corrected by some of the error correction schemes mentioned in Chapter 13, but if severe enough could create a momentary audio mute.

Various systems have been designed to make razor-blade editing possible. Generally, the data discontinuity is sensed and an electronic cross-fade makes a data interpolation to smooth out the transition across the splice. It is important that the ends of the tape be joined as smoothly and as evenly as possible to prevent audio mutes from occurring. One major difference in the splicing block is readily apparent when editing digital tapes with a razor-blade. That is, the cut is made perfectly vertical as opposed to the angled cut associated with analog tape. Since the flux change across the magnetic head gap is electronically cross-faded, a butt splice (90°) is perfectly acceptable and actually preferable.

As a further limiting factor, digital tape is considerably more delicate than analog tape. For comparison, Figure 14-8 lists some of the physical characteristics of several well-known analog and

	Ampex				3M			
Type	456	406	407	466*	250	206	207	265*
Base	1.92	1.42	0.88	1.00	1.30	1.42	0.85	0.79
Oxide	0.55	0.50	0.50	0.20	0.68	0.54	0.54	0.16
Backing	0.05	0.05	0.05	0.04	0.08	0.08	0.08	0.10
Total	2.02	1.97	1.43	1.24	2.06	2.04	1.47	1.05

(all dimensions in mils) * = digital tape

Figure 14-8. Physical dimensions for several representative analog and digital tapes.

digital reel-to-reel tapes. Note that the oxide and the total thickness for the digital tape is considerably less than any of the analog formulations. This thickness reduction is necessary so that the tape conforms to the head contours as completely as possible. This achieves the tape- to-head contact necessary for high packing densities and low error rates.

In other words, these digital tapes must be handled with extreme caution, and razor-blade editing must be approached with great care. Most manufacturers recommend wearing white gloves to protect the tape from fingerprints, body oils and other contaminants.

Electronic Editing

One of the more preferred formats for digital editing is based on the electronic editing techniques used in video-tape production. These techniques are used principally for two-channel audio recorded on professional U-format video cassettes. However, it is possible (but not necessarily financially feasible) to accomplish this type of editing with two (or more!) multi-track digital recorders as well.

Unlike traditional razor-blade editing, in which a collection of tapes may be played back and spliced together on a single tape recorder, the electronic editing process requires two machines: a player and a recorder.

Electronic Editing Procedures

The takes which are to be assembled into the master tape must be reproduced on the player and dubbed onto the recorder one at a time. For example, consider a final master that will be comprised of sections of three separate takes, as illustrated in Figure

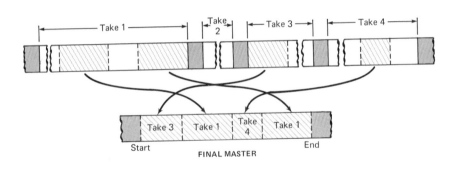

Figure 14-9. Excerpts from various takes (A) are to be assembled into a final master tape (B). The procedure begins by recording Take-3 onto the master tape recorder, and then cross-fading and dubbing Take-1 (C). The procedure continues until the entire master tape is assembled.

14-9. In the illustration, note that the master will begin with Take-3, followed by a portion of Take-1, and then a smaller segment from Take-4. Finally, the last portion of Take-1 is used to complete the master.

Briefly, there are two types of electronic editing: assembly editing and insert editing. Assembly editing is used when there is no existing control track or SMPTE time code and the material is being assembled onto a fresh video cassette. Insert editing is required when there is already continuous control track and/or SMPTE time code recorded on the tape and the new material must be placed between two segments of existing material. Assembly editing edits the video (digital material) and audio (analog material) signals simultaneously. The control track on the video cassette is edited at the same time so that the head switching lines up properly with the helical-recorded video tracks. Insert editing allows the video signal (digital) and audio track 1 and audio track 2 (SMPTE time code) to be edited independently or simultaneously, and all signals are referenced to the existing control track. Figure 14-10 shows examples of both assemble and insert editing on a U-format video cassette.

In digital editing, the assemble mode is generally used only when a song or master tape needs to be extended, as there is a possibility that there could be a break in the control track signal. Normally, the tape that is to be used for the assembled master is "pre-striped" with SMPTE time code (audio track 2) and control

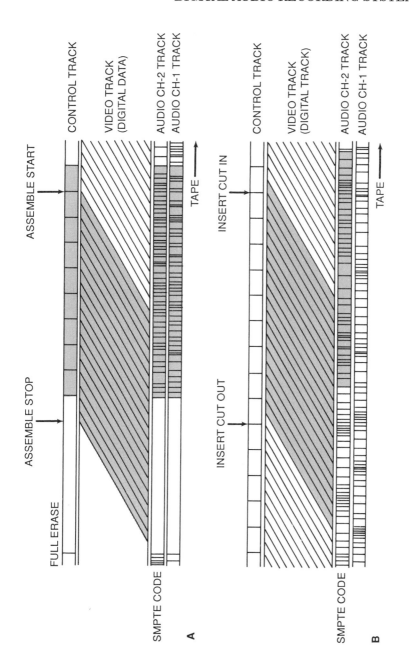

Figure 14-10 (A). Assembly Editing. Note that the control track and does not line up with the video or data track. This may cause unstable data transfer. (B) Insert Editing. Data can be edited (transferred) without interrupting the control track or time code.

track signals prior to the edit session and the insert edit mode is used. This assures continuous time code and control track which are essential for proper mastering onto CD or DAT recorder products.

We begin by dubbing the beginning of Take-3 (from our previous example) onto the recorder. The transfer should continue for several seconds beyond the actual edit-out point required. Now, Take-1 is cued up on the player and is stopped a few seconds before the edit-in point at which it is to begin replacing Take-3.

The Edit Rehearse Mode

Obviously, simply transferring Take-1 onto the end of Take-3 will not work. The odds of making an accurate and undetectable transition from one take to the other at the proper spot are too remote to be worth considering. However, all electronic editing systems have some form of a Rehearse mode, in which the edit may be simulated, rather than actually executed. Once the simulation has been perfected, the actual edit takes place electronically.

The actual editing procedure begins, after recording the first sequence, by listening to the end of Take-3 from the recorder (not the player) and executing an "edit-out" command at the appropriate moment. This command marks the selected edit point, where Take-3 ends, and transfers several seconds of audio from both sides of the edit point into a buffer memory. The contents of this memory may now be reviewed at regular or slow speeds so that the edit point may be modified or confirmed.

Next, the "edit-in" point of Take-1 (the next segment) is selected from the player. Once again, several seconds of program on either side of the proposed edit are loaded into the buffer memories in the editor system and the engineer may adjust or confirm the actual point.

Now, the actual edit is played in its entirety. Some systems do this from the buffer memories, while others actually play the previously recorded material and switch, at the edit point, to the new material. As before, the edit point(s) may be adjusted again and again until the transition is perfected. Various cross-fade intervals may be tried, similar to varying the angle of cut on a standard splicing block, in order to achieve the optimum inaudible edit. Or, if the proposed edit simply "won't work," the engineer discovers this without wasting time making the actual assembled transfer.

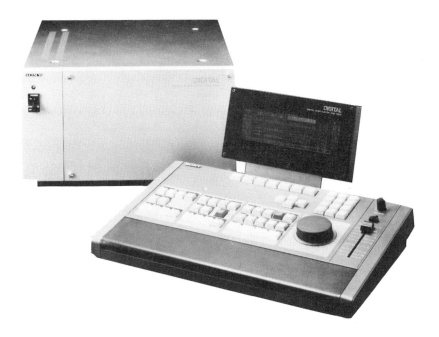

Figure 14-11. A typical digital editing controller and processor (Sony DAE-3000, Sony photo).

If it is necessary to use the traditional tape-rocking-style search for an edit point, most digital editors are able to simulate this effect. The contents of the buffer memory may be "rocked" back and forth at any convenient speed. This is usually done by manipulating a rotary knob, designed to create the illusion that a piece of analog tape is actually being moved back-and-forth across a playback head. Figure 14-11 shows a typical example of such a system.

Now that the edit points are located and confirmed, the electronic editing process begins. The master recorder rewinds to a convenient "pre-roll" location well ahead of the edit, and begins playing. As the edit point approaches, the player transport (containing Take-1) starts in synchronization with Take-3 on the recorder. SMPTE time code is used to lock the two machines together. At the appropriate moment, the recorder switches from the play mode to the record mode erasing the final moments of Take-3 (thus the importance of rehearsal!) and simultaneously replacing it with the new material from the player (Take-1). Take-1 continues to be dubbed onto the recorder through the next edit-out point, after which the recorder is stopped and the process begins again with the next take. This process continues with succeeding edits and takes until the end of the project is reached.

The electronic editing procedure just described may require some re-thinking of traditional editing techniques, especially for engineers who are long-accustomed to working with a razor-blade and some splicing tape. For example, once the electronic edit has taken place, the new material must continue to be dubbed onto the master recorder until the next edit point is reached. There can be no skipping ahead to the next edit, and the editing process takes considerably longer than the razor-blade method.

Some systems require the engineer to review the previous material up to the next edit point before proceeding. Systems with "read after write," or so-called "confidence" heads, may not require this but it is still best to verify that the material was dubbed properly before proceeding. An advantage of this assembly type edit system is that even if the edit is not correct and some data has been copied incorrectly, the edit can be recreated since the original material, that is, what is on the playback machine, is still intact.

COMPUTER RECORDING AND EDITING SYSTEMS

With the proliferation of personal computers and the attendant fast-paced developments in software, it did not take very long for the audio industry to make use of this technology. Random access memory storage systems and other disk-based storage media are appearing in the control rooms of major recording studios at a very fast rate.

The principles for recording digital audio onto disk-based systems is not so different from recording digital audio on either helical scan recorders or longitudinal digital systems. With these systems, however, the digital bit stream is written to either an optical or magnetic storage disk. The limiting factor is simply the storage capabilities of the storage disk itself. Winchester disk stacks are being successfully used by some manufacturers, while others are making use of the so-called "hard disk(s)" found in personal computers. The maximum recording time is simply limited by the storage capacity of the disk(s) divided by the sampling rate and quantization, and again divided by the number of tracks required. In many systems, the engineer can decide how many tracks are necessary for the work to be done, and apportion the disk storage system accordingly. Often a system of this type may be purchased initially with a minimum amount of storage time, and as the fortunes of the studio increase, additional blocks of storage time may be added by supplementing the number of disks in the system.

One of the limiting factors of these very flexible systems is the amount of time necessary for downloading and uploading data. If, say, a series of tracks is recorded, overdubbed and mixed down within the system, the whole system will be tied up until the material is downloaded (in real time) to some permanent storage medium. Conversely, if existing material needs to be loaded into the system for processing, editing or even further overdubs, the time required can be extensive. This can create problems in facilities where one client follows another with a minimum amount of turnaround time.

Most of these systems, as just mentioned, write the digital audio data to magnetic disks. These disks can be easily erased and prepared for new data after the wanted material is downloaded, by a simple format-type command. Other systems use Write-Once-Read-Many (WORM) optical disks. When using this Direct-Read-After-Write (DRAW) systems, once data is written it is permanently encoded into the disk. The disks are encased in a protective envelope that is inserted into the front of the recorder, not unlike a video cassette, and the disk therefore is not open to dust and debris. A benefit of this system is that the material is recorded in perpetuity and cannot be accidentally erased by an errant format command. However, a large project can use quite a few disks, and once the session is over you may not wish to ever use the material again. An optical disk can contain a substantially greater amount of data, often as much as a thousand times more, than a magnetic disk.

Editing With a Hard-Disk System

It is with electronic editing that the advantage of a hard-disk systems becomes readily apparent. Some of the editors that have recently appeared have put electronic editing within the realm of possibilities for the small studio. Using already existing personal computers, coupled with specially modified PC-type hard-disk

drives, digital audio data can be edited by specially written software just as we now edit a word file. The audio data is treated as
a file and can be moved, joined with new material, replaced or
deleted almost as easily as editing a letter on a word processor.

In most systems, the file can be called up and listened to as the
punch-in/out points are determined. The edit point can then be
brought up on a screen and visually edited with a mouse or other
pointing device. The cross fade time can be varied, and the edit
can easily be previewed and changed prior to actually performing
the edit. When the edit command is given, the computer as-
sembles a new file by copying the original material up to the
punch-in point, followed by the new material with the appropriate cross fade between the new and the old up to the marked
punch-out point. It is possible to completely pre-assemble an edit
list for an entire selection before telling the editor to proceed.
Even then, the old material is retained in the event that a change
needs to be made. The completely edited selection can then be
downloaded to a permanent storage medium such as DAT recorder or other digital storage mediums. Some systems only com-
pile an edit list (with the proper cross fades, etc.) instead of actually copying the original data to another location on the hard

Figure 14-12. A digital work station (Lexicon OPUS, Lexicon photo).

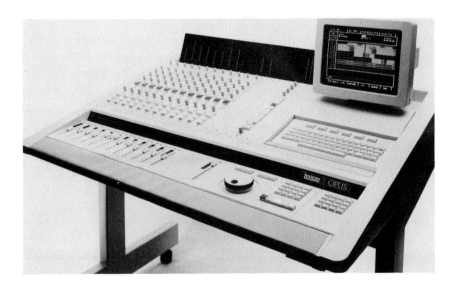

disk(s). These systems then access the original material on command, as specified by the edit list, and send the audio in the edited sequence to the system outputs. The actual edit is not accomplished until the downloading of material occurs. This way storage space is minimized, and the previous version remains available since a new edit list is made (while retaining the old) each time another modification occurs.

Most all hard-disk recorders and editors have their own digital-to- analog converters as well as the digital AES/EBU port for transferring data in and out of the system.

Further developments along these lines have created so called "Digital Work Stations" which combine recording and editing functions with digital mixing and signal processing. Figure 14-12 shows several typical systems. These digital work stations may well be the recording studios of the future.

SECTION VI

SYNCHRONIZATION SYSTEMS

Since the early days of multi-tracking, engineers have always been looking for ways to synchronize machines and accurately keep track of tape locations. Today with the strong marriage of audio and video technologies, it has become essential to have frame-accurate lock up of multiple audio and video machine systems.

Although there is only one chapter in this section, it contains much information that is important to the recording studio engineer. It explains the SMPTE/EBU time code and VITC (Vertical Interval Time Code).

Following that is a discussion of the uses for time code, including audio and video synchronization.

The chapter ends with a brief discussion of one of the newer studio phenomenons—the Musical Instrument Digital Interface, or MIDI. Even as of this writing, the MIDI standard is undergoing change and improvement, and the enterprising engineering student should attempt to keep current with the changing standards.

Chapter 15

Time Code

Since the earliest days of multi-track recording, studio engineers have had the need for an efficient and reliable means of monitoring time/music relationships. The most obvious requirement, as well as the one easiest to implement, is to establish a means of notating the playing time of the finished recording. Obviously, if this was all that was needed, a conventional stop-watch would be more than sufficient. The requirements for more sophisticated measurement methods within the time domain may have started with the introduction of overdubbing and mixdown techniques. These techniques will be described in detail in Section VI, "The Recording Process."

As these techniques developed, the engineer now needed a way to return again and again to the same location on the tape. This could occur during the artist's rehearsals, during punch-ins, and throughout the automated mixdown process. While this point was usually musically apparent, a slight change in the phrasing could carry the punch-in or overdub too far into the existing music particularly if the engineer was paying more attention to the new material than to the old. Obviously, a non-ambiguous method of noting and returning to the required points was needed.

The earliest technique, still used on many consumer tape decks, made use of a counter which generally indicated the number of revolutions of the recorder's supply reel. Directly linked to the reel motor, the system could be quite accurate. However, practical considerations prevented this system from gaining widespread acceptance.

The first drawback to a revolutions counter is that it has little or no relationship to the real-time world. Neither artist nor engineer can be comfortable with a recording that begins at say, 3473 and ends at 8136, since these numbers convey absolutely no information about starting or ending time, or about the duration of the interval between them. Worse yet, documentation for future reference is of little use, since if the tape segment gets transferred to another reel, with more or less tape on it, both the numbers and their mathematical relationship will be changed. This makes intelligent record keeping nearly impossible.

A more satisfactory system, as seen in Figure 15-1, would provide a time-based readout, typically derived from tape travel across an idler wheel placed in the tape path. Although such a system is certainly easier to read and interpret by the operator, it may be inaccurate due to tape slippage, especially if the tape is pulled away from the idler from time to time as in editing.

In either case, the systems just described will be of little practical value when tapes are exchanged between machines, or even studios, and of absolutely no value whatever in the synchronization of two or more machines.

RECORDED TIME DATA

A far more accurate and reliable system would be to record the time information as a coded signal on one of the tracks of the multi-track tape, or on a special track designed for that purpose. Once recorded, this time code would of course remain in perfect synchronization with the program material, and its future accuracy would not deteriorate due to various mechanical factors. For example, as the tape is shuttled back and forth between the reels, so is the time code. When the tape resumes playing, the time-code readout resumes as well.

Like any other "stop-watch," the code does not usually tell the actual time of day. Instead, it indicates the running time of the recorded program. This may have been keyed to the actual time

Figure 15-1. A typical tape timer displaying tape position as a function of time (Studer A820 readout panel, Studer photo).

of day at which the recording was made, or to the elapsed time since the recording began. Thus, after 2 minutes and 37 seconds, on a 9:15 AM recording session that began 31 seconds late, the time code might read 09:18:08, or simply 2:37.

The earliest and most pressing need for a longitudinal time code came from the video tape editors. Prior to 1956, when film was the only method for recording pictures, film editors used and counted sprocket holes to edit together different frames of the filmed material. However, in video recording, even though there were frames of video information on the magnetic tape, they were not directly visible as on film. Nor does the frame rate used in video match that used in film. Because of this, early editing was a hit or miss operation. Further advances in video systems, such as control tracks and timing pulses, were combined with some of NASA's (National Aeronautics and Space Administration) telemetry technology to develop a time-code technology for video tape editing. However, different manufacturers developed different systems, none of which were compatible with each other.

SMPTE TIME CODE

In 1969, the Society of Motion Pictures and Television Engineers (SMPTE) formed a committee to develop a time-code standard that would provide video-tape compatibility. Today, that time code is in universal use, and has also been adopted by The European Broadcasting Union (EBU). The complete standard is currently published as ANSI V98.12M—1981: The American National Standard Time and Control Code for Video and Audio Tape for 525 Line/60 Field Television Systems. The standard is generally referred to as the SMPTE/EBU Time Code, or more simply, SMPTE Time Code. There are actually two versions of the SMPTE time code. One is longitudinal or serial code, and the other is vertical interval code. The latter is often called VITC (Vertical Interval Time Code) and is not particularly applicable to pure audio use. Longitudinal time code is usually recorded on an available track on the multi-channel tape, while VITC is recorded in the vertical interval between the recorded frames and fields on the videotape.

The SMPTE time code provides a readout in hours, minutes, seconds, and frames, to give the operator a film-like frame editing accuracy. Thus, a readout of 23 : 59 : 32 : 21 indicates 23 hours, 59 minutes, 32 seconds and 21 frames.

Frame Rates

There are several frame rates in use today, with different rates used in film, monochrome video, color video and European television. In film, a frame is simply one visible picture on a strip of celluloid. In order to understand the video frame, a short video primer is in order.

NTSC (National Television Standards Committee) television, which is used in the United States, has 525 horizontal lines across the television screen every frame. These are called raster lines. 524 of these are full width, while one consists of two half width scans at the top and bottom of the screen. To prevent any noticeable picture flicker, interlaced scanning is used. With this scanning technique, every other line of the picture is skipped during the first half of the frame, then filled in during the second half of the frame. The scans that occur during the first half are called field 1, and the remaining are called field 2. There are therefore, 2 fields in every frame for monochrome video. Each of these fields is recorded on magnetic tape by one pass of the rotating video head(s).

At the end of each left to right scan of the screen raster, the electron beam returns to the left hand side of the screen and drops down, skipping one line, to begin the next sweep. After sweeping a complete field, the beam returns to the top left corner of the screen to begin the first line of the next field. This return to the top of the screen is referred to as flyback. Just before, and during flyback, the electron beam is switched off, or blanked. This is called the vertical blanking interval and occupies a space equivalent to 21 raster lines. The black bar visible on your television screen when the picture is rolling is the vertical blanking interval, and it is normally unseen under proper operating conditions. It is here that VITC (Vertical Interface Time Code) is recorded. This allows the time code to be read while the video machine is in pause (with the heads still rotating), a luxury that is not possible with longitudinal time code. However, since we are dealing primarily with audio, further discussions here will be about longitudinal time code. There will be a short addenda describing the differences between longitudinal and vertical interval time code at the end of this section on the make-up of longitudinal time code.

The following is a chart of the frame rates in use throughout the world.

Frame Rate	Application
frames per second)	
24	Motion Picture film work
25	EBU television standard
30	NTSC monochrome standard
29.97	NTSC color standard

Note that the EBU and original NTSC standards correspond to half the line frequency used in the respective countries. A line frequency of 50 Hz is found in EBU countries while 60 Hz is the US standard for AC power. Originally, NTSC video was broadcast with a bandwidth of 4.2 MHz, but with the addition of color in the 1960s, an additional carrier (for color) of 3.58 MHz was used. This difference caused the creation of drop-frame time code which will be explained later in the chapter.

Simply stated, the SMPTE time code is a longitudinally recorded signal, not unlike the digital data streams described in Chapter 13. The code provides an 80-bit digital word for each video frame. Unlike the coding schemes described earlier, a zero is defined whenever there is no transition within a bit cell, as shown in Figure 15-2A. In other words, there is only one transition per bit, and this occurs at the beginning of each bit. At 30 frames per second, 80 bits per frame, and 1 transition per bit, a continuous stream of digital zeroes will produce a square wave of 80 x 30 x 1 = 2400 transitions per second. This is equivalent to a frequency of 1200 Hz. A digital one is defined as a level transition occurring midway through the bit cell, as seen in Figure 15-2B. With 2 transitions per bit, a continuous stream of ones will pro-

Figure 15-2. In the SMPTE time code, a zero is defined whenever there is no transition within a bit cell (A), while a transition within the bit cell (B) defines a one.

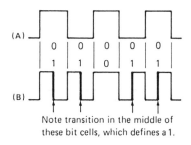

Note transition in the middle of
these bit cells, which defines a 1.

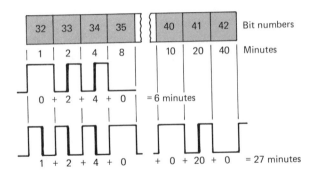

Figure 15-3. In each frame, bit groups 32, 35, and 40-42 define minutes (units + tens).

duce a square wave of 80 x 30 x 2 = 4800 transitions per second, or 2400 Hz.

The EBU standard with 25 frames per second will provide a frequency of 1000 Hz and 2000 Hz respectively for continuous streams of zeros or ones.

SMPTE Assigned Address Bits

Within the 80-bit digital word assigned to each frame, certain bit groups have been assigned to various time, sync, and user-defined functions.

Time Code Address Bits

The SMPTE time code assigns specific bit groups to indicate hours, minutes, seconds and frames. For example, Figure 15-3 illustrates bit groups 32-35, and 40-42, which indicate minutes (units) and minutes (tens) respectively. Using a binary-coded decimal (BCD) system, bits 32-35 indicate 1, 2, 4 and 8 minutes, while bits 40-42 are 10, 20 and 40 minutes. Thus, 6 minutes is defined by a one in bits 33 and 34. If bits 32, 33, 34 and 41 are one, then the time is 1 + 2 + 4 + 20 = 27 minutes. Note that the units group is used to define minutes 0-9, and the tens group defines minutes 10-59. Therefore, 12 minutes is indicated by 2 + 10, and never as 4 + 8. Similarly, 60 minutes is indicated by a one in the hours (units) group, not illustrated here, and not as 20 +40 or 2 + 8 + 10 + 40 within the bit groups presently under discussion.

A list of the bit groups assigned to time follows.

Bit Group	Time Function
0-3	Frames (units)
8-9	Frames (tens)
16-19	Seconds (units)
24-26	Seconds (tens)
32-35	Minutes (units)
40-42	Minutes (tens)
48-51	Hours (units)
56-57	Hours (tens)

Time bits can sequentially count for a full 24-hour period. After 23:59:59:29 is reached, the next number is 00:00:00:00.

Drop-Frame Time Code Bit

As described so far, we have made the assumption that the black and white video frame rate of 30 frames per second is being used. However, as mentioned earlier, the NTSC frame rate for color is 29.97 frames per second. This means that a one hour black and white program will contain 108 more frames than a one hour color program. (In video-based digital recording systems, this corresponds to a sampling rate difference between 44.1 kHz and 44.056 kHz respectively.) Therefore, if a color program is clocked by a system calibrated to the black and white standard of 30 fps, it will take an additional 3.6 seconds until the readout indicates an elapsed time of one hour (108 frames / 30 frames per second = 3.6 seconds).

To compensate for this discrepancy, a drop-frame system is used, in which certain frames are discarded, for a total of 108 frames during each hour. To accomplish this, the drop-frame time code omits the first two frame numbers (00 and 01) at the beginning of each minute, with the exception of the six minutes that start at 00, 10, 20, 30, 40 and 50 [(2 x 60) - (2 x 6) = 108 frames]. In other words, drop-frame time code omits the first two frames of every minute with the exception of the tens minutes. Thus the following sequence will be seen when in the drop-frame mode:

H: M: S: F

09:18:59:29 followed by

09:19:00:02 (not 09:19:00:00!)

-and-

09:19:59:29 followed by

09:20:00:00 (one of the six exceptions)

To implement the drop-frame code, bit 10 in each 80-bit word is defined as a drop-frame flag. When the drop-frame time code is enabled, a one is assigned to this bit. Otherwise, bit 10 remains a zero.

Color-Frame Code Bit

Due to the nature of the color video signal, edits must be made between frame pairs, rather than between any two adjacent frames. (A color frame is four fields in NTSC. Two fields for chroma and two fields for luminence.) The 1st and 3rd field are defined as color frame A, and the 2nd and 4th fields are color frame B. To prevent a horizontal shift or "H" shift in the picture, edits must preserve the AB, AB, AB sequence. Bit 11 in each frame is the color-frame flag, and is encoded as a one to indicate color frame identification. This signifies that all even-number frames are "A" frames and odd-number frames are "B" frames for electronic editing systems. Otherwise, bit 11 is recorded as a zero. Many newer systems have a built-in color framer that is set at the beginning of the editing session or when a new roll of tape is mounted on the record video tape recorder. In this case, the color-frame bit should be set to zero.

Sync-Word Bits

As with the digital bit streams described earlier, the beginning and end of each digital word must be clearly defined. In the SMPTE time code, a permanently assigned sync-word occupies bits 64-79. The word consists of 2 zeroes, 12 ones, 1 zero and 1 one (0011 1111 1111 1101). This sequence, or its mirror image, cannot possibly be duplicated by any combination of bits elsewhere within the frame word, and so it is immediately recognized by the system. This series, which will appear on an oscilloscope as a burst of digital ones, defines the beginning and end of each word and tells the reader which direction the tape is moving.

Plus-One Frame

Not all time-code readers contain this feature, but it is an important aspect if accurate absolute timing is required. Note that the 16-bit sync word just described appears at the end of the frame. When the sync word is detected, the code will be updated to display the time data contained in the word that was just completed. This means that the time data is always displayed one frame late. The Plus-One frame function automatically adds one frame to the count to correct for this built-in error.

User-Assigned Bits

Within each code word, 32 bits, in 8 groups of 4 bits each, have been reserved as "User Bits," to meet whatever unique requirements the user may have for encoding information. Some time-code generators allow the operator to enter this data from a keypad attached to or on the unit. In multiple reel situations, these bits are often used to encode the reel number and date of recording. The user bits are bit groups 4-7, 12-15, 20-23, 36-39, 44-47, 52-55 and 60-63. They are frequently referred to as binary spare bits, or binary groups.

Unassigned Address Bits

Bits 27, 43, 58 and 59 have been defined as permanent zeroes, until otherwise assigned by The Society of Motion Pictures and Television Engineers. Formerly, bits 10 and 11 were also unassigned, until being defined as drop-frame and color-frame code bits as previously described.

Bi-Phase Modulation

In the practical application of the SMPTE time code, there will never be a continuous stream of either ones or zeroes. So, although the code may superficially resemble a square wave whose frequency is continually varying between 1200 Hz and 2400 Hz, it is correctly identified as a waveform with bi-phase modulation. In other words, square wave-like in appearance, but not in name.

To sum up the SMPTE time-code format, we can say that the SMPTE time code is a bi-phase digitally encoded data stream, in which each recorded frame is identified by an 80-bit word. The word contains 26 time-code address bits, a drop-frame bit, a color-frame bit, 16 sync-word bits, 32 user-assigned bits, and 4 unassigned bits. The code is longitudinally recorded, for most audio uses, on a specially defined or unused analog audio track. Figure 15-4 illustrates the complete time-code data structure.

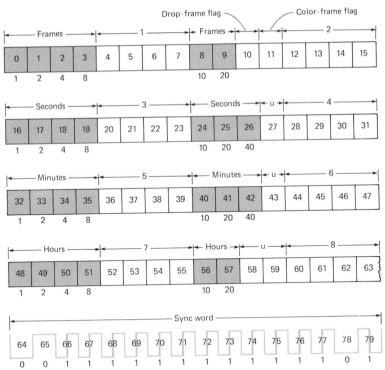

Figure 15-4. The complete SMPTE Time Code Structure. Each frame has a unique 80-bit digital word assigned to it, which identifies the frame number and the time (hours:minutes:seconds). Also included are eight binary groups (1-8) for user-assigned functions, as well as drop-frame and color-frame flags, and four unassigned bits (u). Each word is concluded with the 16-bit sync word shown here.

TIME CODE IMPLEMENTATION

In the typical operation involving time code, several pieces of hardware will be found. A typical SMPTE time-code generator is shown in Figure 15-5. This generator produces the time-code signal which is to be recorded, and also gives a front panel readout in hours, minutes, seconds and frames.

The time-code reader, shown in Figure 15-6, is a device used in playback applications. It is used to read and display time code from an external source, such as from a previously recorded program.

Much of the hardware in use today combines the functions of a generator and reader in the same chassis. Even though they often share a common power supply, one part of the device may be

Figure 15-5. A SMPTE time code generator (Cipher Model 716A, Cipher Digital photo).

generating code for a composite recording, while the reader may be switched to read the various machines providing source material.

The time-code generator/reader may have an auxiliary video character generator output which is used to display the time code on the screen of a video monitor. For optimum visibility, the time code may be displayed within a luminous window, either at the top or bottom, on the screen. On more sophisticated units, there may be controls for adjusting the size and position of the display. For applications using generators or readers which do not have this function, a separate video character generator may be employed. Video loop-through connections are frequently also found, which allow video-tape copies of the program to be made with the time-code display "burned in" or permanently recorded onto the tape copy.

Figure 15-6. A SMPTE time code reader (Cipher Model 710A, Cipher Digital photo).

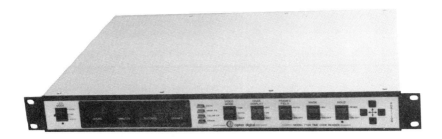

Jam Sync

Jam Sync is an important feature of any time-code system. It makes the repair or re-striping of defective or broken code possible. The jam sync function is used to synchronize, or "jam" the generator's output to an external time-code signal. This can be from a recorded source or from another generator. Jam Sync can reconstruct defective code, synchronize multiple generators to the same starting time, and generate new code to match old code. The jamming generator accepts the code from the external source and uses that data to generate the new code.

In one-time jam sync applications, activating a front panel control sets the generator output in sync with the incoming signal. When the control is released, the generator output resumes independent operation, and any subsequent discontinuities from the incoming code are ignored.

In the continuous jam sync mode, the generator continues to read the input reference signal, and if there are any discontinuities in the incoming code, these are faithfully reproduced by the generator. This is often necessary in cases where the original time-code addresses are needed.

Duplicating Time Code

In duplicating a tape, the time code should not be copied directly. This is because the bi-phase waveform often will not survive the process, and its rapid deterioration from one tape to the next will result in almost certain reader errors. For tape duplication work, the jam sync mode may be used as described above, to read the incoming time-code signal from a previously recorded program. The generator's time-code output is a regenerated replica of the incoming code, and it is this signal that is recorded on the tape copy. Assuming that the one-time jam sync mode is applied, anomalies in the incoming signal are ignored.

On the other hand, the master tape may contain time-code signal discontinuities which were intentionally introduced during the editing process. In this case, subsequent copies should retain these discontinuities, and so the continuous jam sync mode should be used instead. Now, the generator output is a restored replica of the actual input code, and retains all the addresses that are present in the input signal from the master tape.

Many time-code readers have a restored code output which may be used during copying operations. Note that the terminology introduces a possible source of confusion, since a restored code is of course a regenerated version of the original (continuous jam sync). However, the term "regenerated" is reserved for an entirely fresh code that simply used the original code once, as a reference point from which to begin (one-time jam sync).

VERTICAL INTERVAL TIME CODE (VITC)

Vertical Interval Time Code, abbreviated VITC, is very similar in composition to longitudinal time code. It is used exclusively by video tape recorders, and it does contain a few more data bits than the standard SMPTE time code. Each of the nine data bit groups, frames/units, frames/tens, seconds/units, seconds/tens, minutes/units, minutes/tens, hours/units, hours/tens and the sync word, are preceded by two additional sync bits. These sync bits replace the SMPTE time-code sync word.

In addition to this, a Cyclic Redundancy Check (CRC) 8-bit word is included. The CRC word provides a check on the accuracy of the word itself, similar to the error correction schemes used in digital audio recording. This gives us a total of 90 bits per frame for vertical interval time code.

VITC also uses one of the unassigned address bits as a field mark bit. This is bit number 27 in the longitudinal time code and bit number 35 in vertical interval time code. This makes VITC a field accurate code.

VITC is recorded in the vertical interval which, as mentioned earlier, uses 21 raster lines, and is the space between fields where the electron gun is shut off during flyback. The major advantage of using VITC for video, is that the code can be read during high speed wind and rewind functions, as well as in slow motion and freeze frame modes. This is possible because even though the longitudinal motion of the video tape has stopped while the machine is in pause, the video heads continue to spin. This allows the information stored in the vertical interval to be read. Vertical Interval Time Code is recorded using a bit rate of 1.79 MHz which is one-half the color carrier frequency.

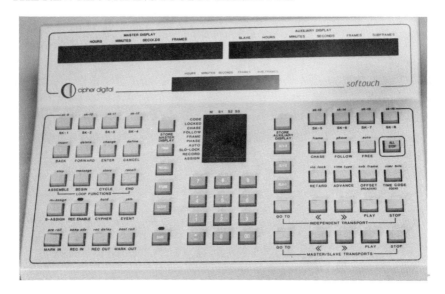

Figure 15-7. A typical time code synchronizer (Cipher Softouch, Cipher Digital photo).

SYNCHRONIZERS

As described so far, SMPTE time-code generators and readers are valuable additions to the recording engineer's arsenal of production tools. If nothing else, they make all the time-keeping chores a lot easier to perform. However, the most valuable aspect of time code may be for those applications where it is necessary to lock two or more tape transports in synchronization. An obvious application is the recording of multi-track audio "in sync" with video. The audio must be recorded to coincide with the picture, and later on mixed down (again, in sync) and transferred to the video tape's audio channels. Even in audio-only album production work, it is not uncommon to find two or more multi-track machines synchronized together for what may be called "multi-multi-track" recording sessions.

In any case, SMPTE time code, or VITC, is recorded on each machine that is to be used. During subsequent playback, one machine is designated as the master, and the other(s), the slave(s). A synchronizer, such as the one seen in Figure 15-7, reads the incoming time code from each slave, and compares it with the master code. If the codes are not identical, it is an indication that the slave machine is not properly synchronized. A control signal is sent to the slave's transport system to bring it into synchronization with the master. The procedure repeats continuously so that the transport is kept in sync with the master.

In most operations, the slave will follow the master through all modes of operation (start, stop, fast forward, rewind). It is often possible, and may even be desirable, to enter an offset so that the slave and the master will maintain a fixed time interval between them. In either case, once the master and the slave (or slaves) are locked together, the entire multi-machine system may be controlled as though it was a single machine. Figure 15-8 illustrates the interfacing requirements of a typical time-code based multi-machine system.

MULTI-MACHINE APPLICATIONS

Multi-machine synchronization capability greatly enhances the versatility of multi-track recording work. For example, the basic rhythm tracks need not be played over and over again during, say, a string overdub session. Instead of working directly with the master multi-track tape containing the rhythm tracks, a rough mix and the time code are transferred onto another machine—perhaps only an eight-track recorder. This may be played repeatedly until the string session is ready to be recorded on the remaining tracks.

Later on, the completed string tracks may be transferred "in sync" to the multi-track tape in one pass. In fact, the strings may have been recorded across town or even across the country, while the basic rhythm tracks remain safely stored away until needed for mixdown. For that matter, there may be no real need to transfer the strings to the multi-track tape at all, since the eight-track machine may be employed as a slave during the mixdown. Or, in another scenario, the strings may be transferred, and also played back from the slave during the mixdown, with an offset to create a doubling effect as discussed in Chapter 6.

Many times, even with a 24-track machine, the recording artists may feel that they need more tracks. One solution that will be discussed later in Section VI "The Recording Process," would be to combine and bounce tracks. This, however, means that the combined tracks will no longer be separately available for later

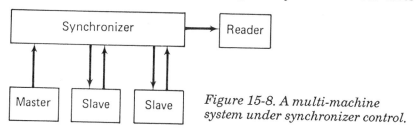

Figure 15-8. A multi-machine system under synchronizer control.

balance adjustments. Another solution is to use two 24-track machines and a synchronizing system in each room, but that can get expensive quickly. As another possible more economic advantage, the studio need not equip each of its control rooms with two synced multi-tracks, but for those sessions that do require more track capacity, additional machines may be employed as slaves. Needless to say, the slave machines do not even have to be in the same control room since they become, in effect, extensions of the master system that controls them.

Single-Machine Applications

Time code may also be used to advantage on single machine sessions. For example, with the appropriate software, the synchronizer may be programmed to automatically perform the punch-ins and punch-outs that were described at the beginning of this chapter. Once the appropriate punch-in and punch-out times are determined, this information may be entered into the synchronizer's memory. Now during recording, the synchronizer will perform the punch-in and punch-out chores without human intervention. If desired, the tape transport may also be instructed to play through the section to be recorded over and over again during the rehearsal. This would also allow the punch-in/out points to be trimmed and adjusted as necessary, prior to actually going into the record mode.

The state-of-the-art synchronizer usually duplicates the tape recorder's transport controls, as seen in Figure 15-9. With the appropriate interfacing, these controls, in conjunction with the synchronizer's memory system, may be used to perform many of the functions traditionally associated with the transport's auto-locater. Figure 15-10 shows a composite remote transport controller that combines auto-locating, synchronizer functions and time-code management, as well as transport motion control.

CONSOLE AUTOMATION

Most console automation systems, which will be discussed in Chapter 18, rely on SMPTE time code as well. A track of the multi-track tape recorder is dedicated to time code, and the time-code addresses are used to define the points where the various console adjustments need to be made. The SMPTE time-code generator and reader are usually built into the console automation

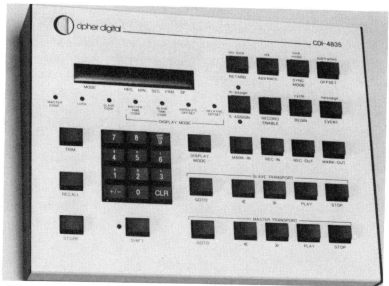

Figure 15-9. A synchronizer controller containing tape transport controls (Cipher CDI 4835, Cipher Digital photo).

system, and often the same code may be used for both automation and synchronization.

Electronic Editing Applications

Most of the electronic editing techniques described in Chapter 14 require time-code data for implementation. For example, when an edit point is located, the time-code defining that point is stored in the electronic editor. The time code also keeps the recorder and player (master and slave) in sync, and when the edit point is reached, the master goes into the record mode, based on a comparison of the edit point's stored code and the instantaneous address of the master tape. Of course, these functions are not carried out under the control of the synchronizer described in this chapter. Instead, the electronic editing hardware discussed in Chapter 14 accommodates the necessary software for this work.

The time codes from various takes to be recorded onto the final master will rarely, if ever, be usable for future production work. This is due, in part, to the inevitable gross time shifts that occur at each edit point. Worse yet, if an edited program segment is followed by a segment from an earlier take, the code will jump backwards at the edit point, making future time-code search

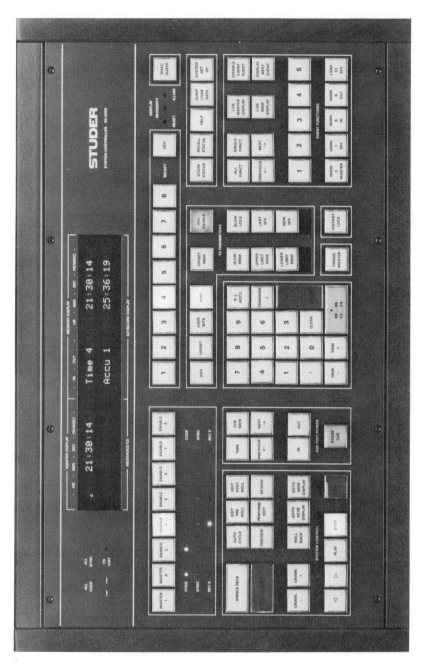

Figure 15-10. A system controller that combines synchronizer, auto-locate, time code management, and transport control (Studer SC-4008, Studer photo).

operations virtually impossible. Therefore, it is common practice to record fresh time code along the entire length of the master tape prior to the electronic editing session. This is often called pre-stripping. Now, as each new program segment is transferred to the master tape (insert edit), its original time code is discarded in favor of the new code recorded earlier.

RECORDING TIME CODE

Generally, SMPTE time code may be distributed and recorded as though it was a regular audio program signal. However, optimum performance suggests that certain precautions should be observed.

Time code is a fairly high-level signal, whose square wave-like appearance is rich in harmonic content. As such, it is apt to cause cross-talk problems, especially if routed too close to microphone-level lines. Time Code lines and microphone lines should not be bundled together or run in the same multi-pair cable or snake if the best system signal-to-noise ratio is to be maintained.

It is generally recommended that the code be recorded on an outside or edge track of the multi-track audio tape recorder, to keep inter-channel crosstalk at a minimum. If feasible, the adjacent audio track should be left vacant, or possibly used for some signal that will tolerate a moderate amount of high frequency roll-off. This may be required to filter out audible high-frequency components of the time code that bleed over from the adjacent track. This is more critical on narrow formats, such as 16 tracks on one-inch tape, than on the larger two-inch tape versions. Some experimenting may need to be done to find a recording level that is low enough to keep cross talk within reason, yet high enough to afford reliable playback of the time code. The following chart gives the generally recommended levels for recording time code on various format audio and video tape recorders.

Machine Type	Format	Where TC is recorded	Level
Multi-track ATR	2in. 16tr.	Edge Track	–3 to 0 VU
Multi-track ATR	2in. 24 tr.	Edge Track	–6 to–3 VU
Multi-track ATR	1in. 16 tr.	Edge Track	–10 to–6 VU
2-track ATR	Half-track	Channel 1	–3 to 0 VU
2-track ATR	Quarter-track	Channel 1	–10 to –6 VU
VTR	1 inch	Audio Track 3	–5 to 0 VU
VTR	¾ inch	Audio Track 2	–5 to 0 VU
VTR	Betacam	Time Code Track	–5 to 0 VU

Some two-channel tape recorders have a special track, inserted between the two standard audio tracks, just for time code. These center-track time code tape recorders may have special level requirements, and the manufacturer's recommendations should be followed.

The time code should be recorded for about 10 seconds before the musical program begins for most analog audio recordings. This allows ample margin for electronic editing or synchronization later on, in which it may be necessary to cue up to the beginning of the program, or to provide a pre-roll before the program begins. An exception to this is in the case of digital tapes prepared for Compact Disc mastering. Here, two full minutes of "digital black" on the video tracks (as discussed in Chapter 14), along with continuous time code on audio track 2 of the ¾-inch video cassette are required. The time code must start at 00:00:00:00, and the program must start at 00:02:00:00 exactly. Two minutes of digital black with time code is also recommended at the end of the last selection that is to be transferred to CD.

In order to prevent code reader confusion, each time-code address should only appear once on a reel of tape. For example, when recordings made on different sessions are later assembled onto a single reel of tape, it is quite likely that the same time-code address will appear in one or more recorded selections. In order to electronically search into the middle of such a reel of tape, it will first be necessary to record a fresh time code (jam sync) along the entire length of the tape, as previously described.

Another system for synchronizing electronic devices has recently emerged on the performance side of the control room window. This system, called MIDI, is now found in many modern recording studios.

MIDI

The Musical Instrument Digital Interface, better known as MIDI, is a relatively new tool in the recording studio. MIDI was developed as a system for creating communications links between electronic instruments such as synthesizers, electronic keyboards, and various rhythm machines. As such, MIDI is primarily used by performers, but the prudent recording engineer should be aware of the system and how it works since it is becoming more and more common in the studio.

MIDI History

In order for us to understand MIDI, it is important to see how and why it evolved. Early synthesizers were often criticized for their lack of depth or character in the sound. The instruments were monophonic, and most were only capable of providing one type of sound at a time. Many musicians solved this problem by playing on two synthesizers at once. Organ stops with the left hand and piano sounds with the right. Digital and analog delay units were often used as well to thicken and fill out the sound.

Further development with these instruments provided control voltage outputs that would allow the first synthesizer to control the second with regards to such things as note on, note off, pitch and timbre. This system was practical as long as both synthesizers used the same control signals, and provided them at the same rate, to generate or control sounds. However, manufacturers seldom agreed, and there was no standardization. MIDI was developed by an association of manufacturers as a standard so that all types of electronic instruments and devices could communicate using the same control signals and protocol.

MIDI is a digital bit stream that is very similar to the SMPTE time-code data stream in appearance. However, the information contained and the word length and transmission rates are quite different. It is a serial interface using ten-bit words at a transmission rate of 31.25 kilobaud. (There are 8 bits in a byte, and a baud is a transmission rate of 1 byte per second.) Each MIDI word contains a start-bit, eight data- or status-bits and a stop bit. The first bit in each data group determines the type of word, and the remaining 7 bits express the value. Information is sent in multi-byte groups which are usually made up of one status byte followed by two data bytes. Status bytes always start with a 1, and data bytes start with a 0.

There are two main types of messages. These are channel messages and system messages. MIDI can provide up to 16 different channels of information in the bit stream, but the more channels that are in use at one time, the slower the data rate per channel. The first four bits of the channel status word assigns the rest of the multi-byte group to a specific device or group of devices as

393

determined by the user. The remaining four bits determine voice and mode selection or status.

System messages do not carry channel assignments, but are divided into three groups called Common, Real-Time, and Exclusive. Common messages are read by all units in the system. Real-Time groups are also intended for all units, but supersede any previous instructions which may be running. Exclusive message units carry a manufacturer's identification number, and thereby are intended for only devices of that particular ID group.

As mentioned earlier, the remaining two bytes are data words. The controlled unit waits until both data bytes are received before acting on the information. The data byte contains information that controls events such as note duration, velocity (touch) and pitch.

MIDI Interconnection

The connections between MIDI devices are relatively simple. Most MIDI-capable equipment will have three jacks labeled MIDI-In, MIDI-Out, and MIDI-Thru. The MIDI specification states that 5-pin DIN connectors are to be used, but at this time only three of the pins (2, 4, and 5) are currently utilized. Some manufacturers use the specified 5-pin DIN plugs while others use XLR connectors or quarter-inch tip/ring/sleeve phone jacks and plugs. This requires the MIDI user to have on hand various types of adapters for interfacing different equipment. Cables are to be no more than 50 feet long.

MIDI-Out provides the master control signal that is sent to the various devices to be controlled. Most equipment designed for use with MIDI can be either a master or a slave. MIDI-In is where the signal from the master is accepted, while MIDI-Thru is simply a loop-through that passes the same signal on to another device. Because of losses due to cable length, no more than three devices should be chained together by the MIDI-Thru connectors. For systems requiring more than four (one master and three slaves) units, it is recommended that a MIDI distribution system be used. Figure 15-11 A&B illustrate these two conditions.

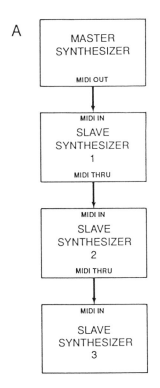

A

MASTER
SYNTHESIZER

MIDI OUT

MIDI IN
SLAVE
SYNTHESIZER
1
MIDI THRU

MIDI IN
SLAVE
SYNTHESIZER
2
MIDI THRU

MIDI IN
SLAVE
SYNTHESIZER
3

Figure 15-11. Two different methods for MIDI interconnection. (A) The MIDI "daisy chain" using MIDI Thru connecters, and (B) using a MIDI distribution system or "multi-thru" box.

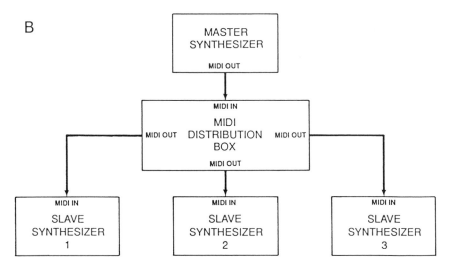

B

MASTER
SYNTHESIZER

MIDI OUT

MIDI IN
MIDI
MIDI OUT   DISTRIBUTION   MIDI OUT
BOX
MIDI OUT

MIDI IN
SLAVE
SYNTHESIZER
1

MIDI IN
SLAVE
SYNTHESIZER
2

MIDI IN
SLAVE
SYNTHESIZER
3

MIDI Equipment

Equipment designed for MIDI applications comes in many varieties. A MIDI system can include a master electronic keyboard, acoustic to MIDI converters, drum machines or electronic drum pad controllers, sequencers and signal processors such as equalizers, reverberaters and signal delay units.

The master electronic keyboard is usually the control center of the system. It is from here that the artist plays and controls the MIDI ensemble. An acoustic instrument such as a guitar, or acoustic piano may be used as a controller as well. There are also MIDI woodwinds and brass available that provide control using the instrument's keys or valves and a sensor for air intensity. Drum machines can be programmed to act as a master tempo controller, or drum control pads can be used as triggers for specific events or sounds. MIDI-controlled reverbs, limiters/compressors, noise gates, etc. are also commonly available and easily interface into the system.

MIDI Sequencers are probably the most important aspect of the MIDI system. It is here that the digital control data can be stored or recorded for later playback. This is not a music recording, but simply a recording of the digital control data. For playback, each MIDI channel must feed a MIDI instrument. In effect, the recorded performance is recreated each time the sequence is played. The way it works is this. A musician plays a melodic line into a sequencer, and the device remembers the data and assigns it to a sequencer track. Other tracks can be added (in sync) until all the available sequencer tracks are used. Some computer-based sequencers offer up to 64 tracks. Actually, the number of tracks and the length of the song is only limited by the amount of memory available in the computer. On playback, the sequencer becomes the master, and the MIDI Out is sent to the MIDI slaves. If the performance is not to the artist's liking, any sequencer track can be edited or modified until the desired performance is achieved.

MIDI in the Recording Studio

It is at this point, with the performance data stored in the sequencer, that the musician usually brings his or her MIDI system into the Recording Studio. A lot of studio time has been

Figure 15-12 (opposite page). A sophisticated studio setup using SMPTE time code and MIDI to produce a musical selection synchronized to an existing video.

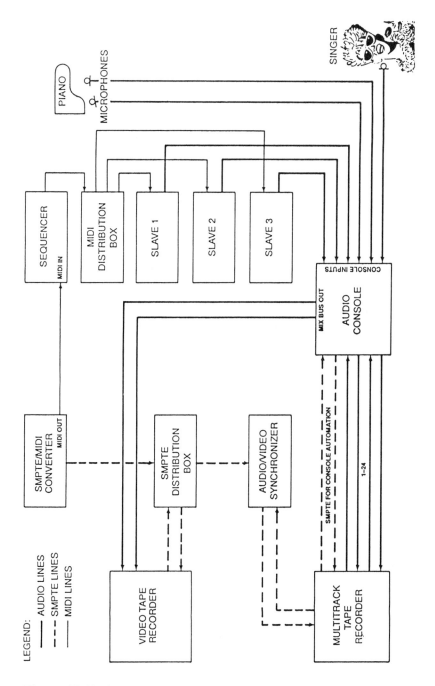

Figure 15-12. A sophisticated studio setup using SMPTE Time Code and MIDI to produce a musical selection synchronized to an existing video.

saved since the performance is essentially ready to go. Each instrument's audio output(s) are then sent to the studio console. Depending on the output level and impedance of the instruments, direct boxes may be required. When all is ready and the console input levels have been set during a rehearsal, the recording can be made either direct to two-channel stereo (if it is a complete performance), or to multi-track tape so that more parts can be added later. Often, the MIDI system is interfaced to the recording console right in the control room. This allows better communications between the engineer and the artist, and no separation problems are created since there are no microphones in use.

During this process, the engineer will make use of whatever studio processing devices are necessary to provide the best possible recording. Reverberation may be added to a direct-to-two mix, while noise gates, equalizers, compressors, etc. may be required during the multi-track recording. It is essential that the engineer make sure that the MIDI interconnection cables are routed away from the audio signal cables as interference and cross talk can occur.

THE SMPTE/MIDI INTERFACE

Using the SMPTE time code makes it easy to synchronize a MIDI sequencer to a multi-track tape. There are several SMPTE to MIDI synchronizers that will allow the studio's SMPTE output to control the rate of the MIDI sequencer. This allows the virtual tracks recorded in the MIDI sequencer to be recorded or just run along in sync with the existing multi-track tape material. This can prevent tying up too many audio tracks on the multi-track tape recorder with synthesizer information.

In mixdown, the SMPTE output from the multi-track is fed to the MIDI sequencer, and the MIDI slave outputs are fed to unused channels on the mixing console along with the output of the multi-track tape. A typical MIDI system recording session synced to time code is illustrated in Figure 15-12.

SECTION VII

THE CONSOLE

At first glance, today's modern multi-track recording console may appear to be a hopeless maze of knobs and switches cluttering the path between the microphone and the tape recorder. Yet, despite its apparent complexity, the console is essentially a collection of similar control functions that are repeated over and over again. They give the engineer a greater command over each input from the studio, and the signal output that is sent to the tape recorder. In fact, the console may be the single most important piece of equipment in the signal chain of modern recording. Nearly all systems interface with the console. It is the heart of the composite system.

Chapter 16 of this section actually discusses the recording console several times. First, briefly, to give the reader an understanding of its basic functions, and then, each section is broken down into its component parts and described in detail. Finally, various secondary signal paths are introduced, and an examination of the complete console is concluded. Many of these concepts and signal paths are common to both tracking and mixdown, but may be utilized differently in each scenario.

As more tape recorder tracks become available and used by the artist and engineer, the logistics of controlling these tracks manually in mixdown becomes a difficult job. Chapter 17 introduces console automation systems that are designed to make this task more manageable.

Chapter 16

Recording Studio Consoles

Under some circumstances, a completely satisfactory recording may be made by simply plugging a microphone into a microphone pre-amplifier and then sending that amplified signal to the input of a tape recorder. Particularly in the case of a single stereo microphone and a two-track digital tape recorder, there may be little point in inserting any type of intermediate control device in the signal path. The stereo microphone "hears" what the concert hall listener would hear, and this information is directly transferred to the storage medium. Given a well-balanced musical ensemble, playing in an acoustically satisfactory environment, an excellent recording may be made in this manner. For a longer discussion of microphone techniques, refer to Chapter 4.

However, for the majority of contemporary recording situations, somewhat more flexibility may be required and a recording console becomes a necessity. The console may be nothing more than a simple combining network where several microphone inputs are mixed together to provide two outputs to a tape recorder. At the other extreme, the console may be capable of mixing, in a seemingly endless number of combinations, the outputs of dozens of microphones, and may have perhaps 24 to 48 channels of outputs as well as separate stereo and monophonic outputs.

In either case, the console becomes a combining and routing point for microphones, line level sources, processing equipment and the tape recorder. Regardless of the apparent complexity of a modern multi-track recording console, it may be analyzed as a combination of four major control sections.

The four sections as shown in Figure 16-1 are:

1. The Input Section (inputs to the console from microphones, electronic instruments and tape recorder lines)

2. The Output Section (metered outputs from the console to the multi-track tape recorder)

3. The Master Module Section (master auxiliary sends, cue sends, reverberation returns, 2-mix outputs)

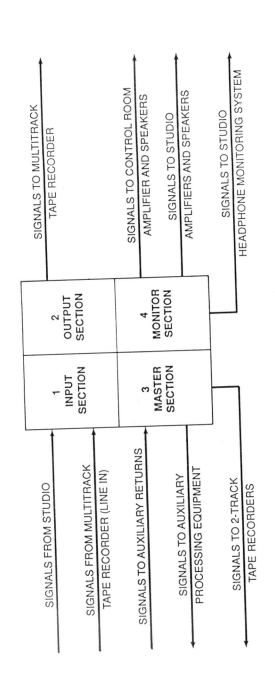

Figure 16-1. The four major sections of a multi-track recording console.

4. The Monitor Section (stereo metering, loudspeaker selection and sends, headphone monitoring, line-in/line-out switching)

Most consoles contain these four major sections, but as the complexity of popular music has increased, consoles have developed into two major types. The in-line or Input/Output Module style, and the more simple split-configuration. In the former, most of the functions for a particular input and output are merged onto one linear module. This module will also contain the monitoring functions for that I/O module, the stereo bus assignment and panning. The latter style of console maintains separate sections for the input modules and the output modules, often with the monitoring section located between the two sections. Although the basic functions and purpose of the consoles are similar, the radical difference in layout requires discussion.

Early multi-track consoles were larger versions of the split-configuration consoles developed for live recording and broadcasting. The change to the in-line style came about largely as a result of the proliferation of tracks on the multi-track tape recorder. The earlier console may have had 24 or more microphone inputs, but typically only 4, or at the most 8, outputs were required. At the time, it made sense to treat (and to locate) these outputs separately from the inputs.

The 8 outputs often represented 8 complete mixing buses, although it would be a rare occasion when even half that number were required. For example, with 16 inputs, it would be impossible to use more than 8 mixing buses, and that number could only be put to use if each bus was restricted to mixing no more than 2 inputs—a highly unlikely situation. In any case, for each additional microphone assigned to any mixing bus, the total number of buses that it is possible to use is diminished accordingly. Furthermore, as the number of recorded tracks increases, the actual requirement for mixing buses usually diminishes as well since in a one-to-one situation, the direct out, and not the mixing bus, is used.

On today's console, there are apt to be as many outputs as there are inputs. The 24-track tape recorder is an industry standard and it is not uncommon to link two such machines for even more output capability or to find 32- or 48-track digital recorders in use. Taken to its extreme, each microphone may feed its own signal to a separate track on the tape recorder with little or no mixing taking place during the actual recording session, and with no need for mixing buses at all. Consequently, it is not unheard of to find a console with a 56 input by 48 output configuration. That is, 48 inputs for multi-track returns and 8 additional for effects or other program returns. Therefore, with more and more inputs taking up valuable space in front of the operator, it makes little ergonomic sense to allocate precious space for a complex separate mixing/monitoring section. The available space may be more efficiently put to use by "folding back" the output and monitor sections so that they appear in-line with the input section. Now, module 10 will contain the controls for microphone 10 and console output 10 as well. Thus we have the I/O module as the basic block of the in-line console.

In order to optimize signal-to-noise ratio (with analog recording), the recording engineer will try to keep all recorded levels consistently at a maximum on the tape. And, with most of the balancing and mixing taking place later on, there is really little need for much more than the simplest sort of gain control device in the signal path between the microphone pre-amplifier and the tape recorder input. Furthermore, most equalization, reverberation, delay and other signal processing will be added later during the mixdown session. Certainly none of this represents a sudden departure from conventional multi-track recording techniques, but rather is the logical culmination of a practice that has been undergoing change since the earliest days of multi-track recording.

Today the equalizer, and even the familiar linear fader, may be found and put to better use within the monitor system pathway so that the engineer may hear their effects without these effects being recorded. That way, a change in the equalization or the mix of the component signals that seemed right during the recording session will not have to be undone later in the light of the mixdown session. Accordingly, the equalizer and the fader have been appropriately relocated to the monitor section. It is this monitor section that not only provides the signals for the control room monitors, but is also the source for the 2-mix bus from where the final stereo mix is sent to the 2-channel tape recorder.

On the other hand, even with the proliferation of available channels, recording is still not limited to the exclusive assignment of one microphone to one tape channel. Although such a one-on-one technique certainly allows the engineer the greatest mixing flexibility later on; there are many occasions when it will be desirable to combine two or more signals during the recording session. At these times, the equalizer or linear fader may be required within the microphone-to-tape signal path, and the appropriate signal path switching is usually provided for this purpose.

The split-configuration console is still found to some extent today, however, it is more at home in the broadcast and sound reinforcement areas than in the modern multi-track recording studio. This type of console is infinitely more practical in live reinforcement situations where the house mix may feed many banks of amplifiers while the monitor mix is directed simultaneously to the stage. The use and the architecture may be different, but the four basic sections are still the same. Our discussion will mostly deal with the I/O module style of the in-line multi-track console, but most of the functions and features are the same for the split-configuration mixer.

A brief description of the various functions within each section is given here. This will be followed by a more detailed explanation of each component part within the total signal path, from microphone to tape recorder.

THE INPUT SECTION

The first stage in each signal path is the microphone pre-amplifier, where the low-level microphone signal is amplified to the console's internal line level.

Next, assuming that the module's equalizer and linear fader will not be used at this time, the signal passes through a simple gain control. This may be nothing more than an amplifier with a rotary potentiometer.

THE OUTPUT SECTION

In electrical work, a bus is a length of copper or aluminum bar stock that is used as a central feeder line, as in a circuit breaker panel. In a recording console, a bus is a common signal path, to which the outputs of many input module signals have been routed.

After this elementary level control section just mentioned, the signal may be routed to one or more output buses. Although these are certainly capable of being used for mixing purposes, they are often referred to as Channel Buses, simply to distinguish them from Mixing Buses, which will be described later. If more than one channel bus is selected, the signal will travel through a pan-pot. Instead of using the channel buses, the signal may be directly routed to the tape recorder channel associated with each I/O module (for example, input 3 to output 3, etc.). This Direct Mode is the one that would be used most often for so-called one-on-one recording. This may be preferred because it is the shortest route from the microphone to the tape.

At this point the signal is sent to the multi-track tape recorder, usually through a buffer amplifier which may have its own rotary potentiometer or "trim" control. The channel metering signal is usually derived at this point and sent to the I/O channel meter. The channel line-out signal is also routed to the I/O modules monitor input section.

THE MONITOR SECTION

Here, the signal passes through the module's equalization section and linear fader. After equalization and level adjustments, the signal passes to a monitor pan-pot where it will be routed to the left and right mixing buses. At this point in our description, these mixing buses are being used solely for monitoring purposes. Later in the mixdown process, they will be used to feed the two-channel tape recorders used for the mixdown session.

The Master Module

Additional space must be provided for various master controls for the mixing bus outputs, cue lines, auxiliary send and effects return lines. These are commonly found on a Master Module located to the right of the I/O modules In extremely large consoles, they may be found between two large groups (24 or more) of I/O modules.

As will be noted below, the engineer/producer may wish to lower the listening level of previously recorded tracks, while concentrating on whatever is being recorded at the moment. On the other hand, the studio musicians must easily hear what was recorded before, if they are to play along in accompaniment. Accordingly, the master module section usually provides a separate set of sends for the headphone monitoring in the studio. These controls are independent of both the recording levels and the listening level in the control room. These lines are called foldback or cue send lines and large consoles may have several separate systems.

The auxiliary buses are used to send and return signals from outboard processing equipment such as reverberation systems. The returns allow the signals from these devices to be mixed into the monitor path and consequently the 2-mix bus. Since most processing of this type is done during mixdown, these returns are usually not sent to the channel outputs. The auxiliary buses often may be used for both cue and processing sends.

The Monitor Module

The recording engineer will frequently need to listen to various signals out-of-context from the level at which they are to be recorded. For example, he may want to listen to the input or output signals one at a time to verify his signal output arrangement. In the case of a tape containing some previously recorded tracks, the producer/engineer may wish to concentrate on the recording of the new material. However, during playback he will want to hear the entire program in the proper balance.

The monitor functions of the console will provide the engineer with the necessary controls to adjust the relative listening levels without affecting the channel recording levels. Of course, if the engineer adjusts his recording levels, these adjustments will be heard through the monitor bus as well. However, adjustments intended for monitoring purposes only will not find their way onto the tape. The engineer may also wish to compare the sound of the channel outputs from the console with the actual recorded tape. This comparison, or similar comparison of one program with another, is popularly known as an a/b test, and reference may be made to "a/b-ing" the tape (or other program).

Since monitor level and panning for each channel has already been established within the I/O module, the monitor module of the console may contain little more than a sophisticated switching system which is used to select the mix bus outputs, or the outputs of one of several 2-channel tape recorders that are used during mixdown. Most of the channel/tape a/b monitor switching will be found on the I/O module, but additional switches in the monitor section allow the engineer to monitor any of the auxiliary send lines which will be described later in this chapter. Master controls for the solo bus and the PFL (pre-fader listen) bus are found here also. There will be separate switching systems for both studio and control room monitor sends, as well as the associated gain controls, speaker switching and talkback systems.

Stereophonic and monophonic metering, and any phase coherency monitoring and metering are also included in this section.

Figure 16-2 identifies the console sections just described for both an in-line console and a split-type console, while Figure 16-3 pictures several console modules.

A

Figure 16-2. (A) a modern in-line console (Sony MXP-3036VF, Sony photo), (B) a typical split configuration console. Note the submasters to the right of the input modules (Soundcraft 200B, JBL photo).

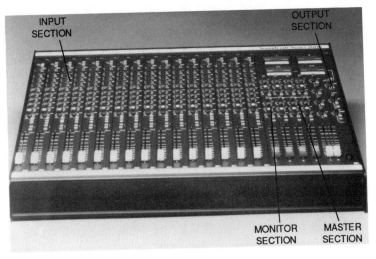

B

Figure 16-3. (A)on the opposite page,is an Input/Output module and a Master Module from an in-line recording studio console (Sony MXP-3036VF, Sony Figure), (B) shows an Input and Output Module for a split-configuration console (Sony MXP-2000, Sony Figure).

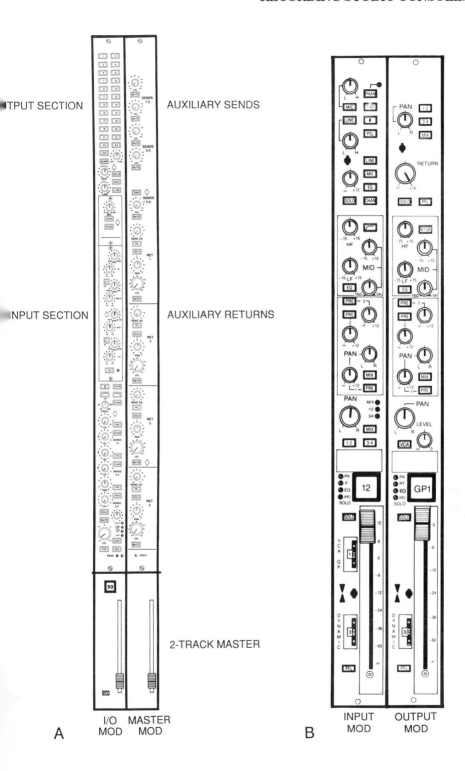

OUTPUT SECTION   AUXILIARY SENDS

INPUT SECTION   AUXILIARY RETURNS

2-TRACK MASTER

A   I/O   MASTER
     MOD   MOD

B   INPUT   OUTPUT
     MOD   MOD

THE COMPONENT PARTS OF AN IN-LINE RECORDING CONSOLE

The console to be described here is of an in-line design, with an equal number of inputs and outputs, and a two-channel monitor/mixdown system. Figure 16-4 is a simplified block diagram of the typical signal paths through the I/O module in such a console. Additional modules will be introduced as they make their first appearance within the signal path. Each important point has been assigned a letter (A-Z-CC), and a detailed description of these points follows.

Due to the nature of the in-line design, all controls and components within a certain category are not necessarily found within a single module. For example, the monitor pan pot is located on the I/O module, while the monitor (mix) bus ACN (Active Combining Network) amplifier is located in the master module. The control-room monitor level itself is found on the monitor module.

A) Microphone Input Plug

At the console, each arriving input signal line is generally assigned to a specific input, more or less permanently. In the studio, each microphone input is numbered (Figure 16-5), with each number referring to one of the console's inputs. When the console is installed, the microphone lines may be soldered in place, making later changes difficult. Another approach is to solder the microphone lines to various multi-pin connectors such as "Tuchel" or "CPC" connectors. On other consoles, designed for quick changes or portability, the connections may be made through XLR plugs (sometimes called Cannon plugs).

B) Microphone Pre-Amplifier

As discussed in Chapter 3, microphone output levels are quite low, compared to tape recorder or line levels, and therefore require amplification before any signal manipulation can take place. A microphone pre-amplifier just after the input connection boosts the signal to the console's internal line level. This is usually between –2 dBm and +4 dBm.

Just prior to the input of the microphone pre-amplifier, the phantom power bus is applied. A switch on the I/O module is used to turn the required 48 volts DC off or on as required by the

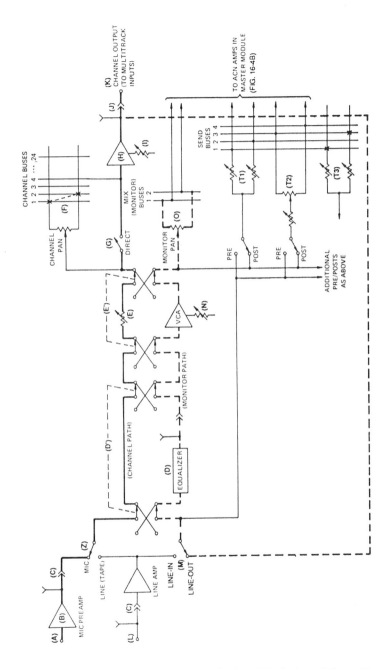

Figure 16-4. A simplified signal flow diagram through a typical I/O Module. The heavy line indicates the channel path, and the dashed line is the monitor path.

411

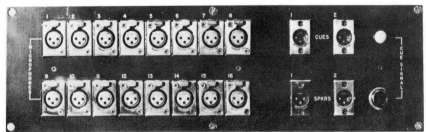

Figure 16-5. A typical microphone input panel.

microphone. The precision 6.8 k ohm dropping resistors are tied to pins two and three of the input connection and then terminated to an appropriate grounding point. See Chapter 3 for a further discussion of phantom power.

C) Patch Points

On many consoles, the microphone pre-amplifier is immediately followed by a set of patch points which are physically located in the console's jack or patch bay. These points allow the engineer to insert external (outboard) processing devices into the signal path. Or, to reroute signals for special applications.

D) Console Equalizers and Channel/Monitor Equalization Switch

The equalizers seen in Figures 16-3 are typical of the types of equalization found and built into each individual I/O module. For a detailed discussion of equalizers, refer to Chapter 7.

Note that in the simplified block diagram, Figure 16-4, a pair of ganged double throw switches (D1) on either side of the equalizer is shown. This permits the microphone signal (now raised to line level) to bypass the equalizer. Typically, switching is controlled by a single pushbutton, labelled "channel/monitor". This pushbutton switches the equalizer either into the channel signal path or into the monitor signal path depending on the preference of the engineer and the requirements at the time.

Many consoles have, just prior to the equalization block, a set of high-pass and low-pass filters. They will also have a channel/monitor pushbutton to allow them to be switched, independent of the equalization, into either the monitor path or channel path.

The phase reversal switch is also usually found here, and follows the channel/monitor switching of the equalizer. This electrically reverses the phase of the signal causing a 180° change.

E) Input Level Control and Fader Exchange Switch

In the typical multi-track recording session, fine adjustments of the channel fader are not required. Usually, the channel level is set so that the playing reaches or just slightly exceeds 0 VU on the analog multi-track tape recorder. This produces maximum signal-to-noise ratios on all tracks, thereby minimizing the cumulative effects of tape noise in mixdown. When digital systems are in use, the levels are set more conservatively since a zero reading may well be the absolute maximum signal level allowed. Whichever storage system is used, after the initial level is set, there is little need for change. Consequently, another pair of double-throw switches (E1) routes the input signal through a simple gain-adjust device. As noted earlier, this may be a simple rotary potentiometer, or perhaps a linear fader with a shorter throw than the customary fader which will be described later on. As with the equalizer section, a single control performs the necessary switching, allowing either the monitor fader or the rotary or shorter fader to be placed in the channel path while the other is placed in the monitor path.

F) Channel Assignment Switches (Output Bus Selector Switches)

After each input signal has been suitably processed, it may be routed to one or more outputs by depressing the appropriate bus selector switches. Or, several input signals may be combined and sent to one output. For example, the engineer may wish to use a microphone and a direct box on an electric guitar, mixing their outputs together to form one composite signal which will be routed to, say track number 2 on the tape recorder. By depressing the channel 2 selector switch on both input modules, the two signals are sent to channel 2's ACN where the signals are summed.

As a space-saving consideration, channel assignment numbers are usually laid out in two vertical rows. Depending on the particular design, there may be a single button for each odd-even channel pair, or a separate button for each channel. Various examples of channel assignment switches are shown in Figure 16-6. In each case, a nearby pan-pot usually allows for panning the signal between the selected channels.

G) Direct Assignment Switch

In the typical one-on-one recording setup, there is little need for the traditional mixing bus since each microphone input will be directly routed to a separate channel on the multi-track tape recorder. Therefore, rather than going through the exercise of assigning, say, input 3 to channel bus 3, etc., a single direct-assignment switch on each module accomplishes the same thing. The direct switch usually bypasses the channel assignment switches and their respective ACN amplifiers. This reduces the length and complexity of the signal path and thereby reduces the channel noise level.

H) Channel Active Combining Network Amplifier

At this amplifier, all the input signals that have been assigned to the channel output bus are combined into one composite output signal. There is a similar amplifier for each output channel on the console.

I) Channel Trim (Output Bus Level Control)

It used to be customary (and still is in split-type designed consoles) for each output channel to have its own linear fader for over-all gain riding of the signals which had previously been combined. Given the nature of present multi-track recording practice, a full-scale fader at this point in the signal path may now be quite unnecessary. Therefore, a simple rotary channel trim potentiometer may be commonly found instead. This is certainly adequate for making coarse adjustments in channel gain, and may even be used for a certain amount of simple gain riding during the recording session. However, when more demanding gain riding is required, a grouping function may be used, and this will be discussed later in the chapter. On many modern consoles, the direct assignment switch bypasses the channel trim control as well.

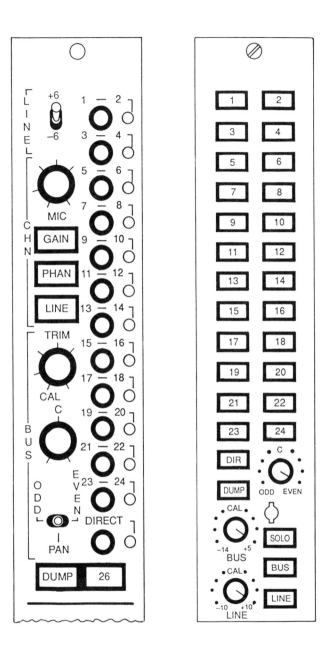

Figure 16-6. Channel assignment switches are usually found at the top of the input/output module. Typical arrangements may be as in (A) a single row of switches for odd/even pairs of channels, or as in (B) where each channel has its own individual switch.

J) Channel Out (Output Bus) Patch Points

Prior to the output plug where the signal is sent to the multi-track tape recorder, there may be a set of patch points similar to those described at C). An external signal processing device inserted here will affect all of the individual signals that were assigned to that channel bus.

K) Channel Output Plugs

At this point, the signal path leaves the console and goes to a specific track on the multi-track tape recorder. Once again, a variety of output plug configurations are available.

L) Line Input Plug

Here, the tape recorder output is returned to the console. Although this signal will actually be routed to several points within the console, at this time only the monitoring path is shown in Figure 16-4.

Master Line-In/Line-Out Monitor Switch

Depending on the position of this switch, the engineer may monitor either the console line-out (channel out), or the line-in signal from the tape recorder. This single control will act as a master line-in/line-out switch so that the entire console monitor system can be switched between the two. There are also usually line-in/line-out switches on the individual I/O modules, but the master switch always takes precedence.

M) Master Line-In/Line-Out Switch

The line-in/line-out switch just described is a master control typically found on the monitor module, since it selects the mode which is to be monitored. When activated, it switches all I/O modules simultaneously. However, it is often desirable to be able to switch one or more individual modules to the opposite mode. That is, when the console is monitoring the multi-track tape recorder outputs, a few selected modules will monitor the channel outputs, and vice versa. A line-in/line-out reverse switch on the I/O module is usually provided for this purpose, as seen in the detailed drawing in Figure 16-15 found later in the chapter.

Note that when the switch is in the normal position (as shown), the module mode agrees with the master Line-In/Line-Out status that was selected on the monitor module. However, when the switch is in the reverse position, the individual module mode is always the opposite of the master status. This function may be a convenience when overdubbing in the sel-sync mode on a multi-track tape recorder that is not set up for automatic input/output (monitor) switching.

With the console monitoring the tape recorder outputs, those I/O modules that are being used as microphone inputs for the overdub parts of the song are put into the reverse mode so that the operator can hear the microphone outputs as well as the previously-recorded material.

N) Monitor VCA Fader

As already noted, the familiar linear fader is now more often found within the monitor lines, as indicated in Figure 16-4. Furthermore, the actual gain-riding action is frequently regulated by a VCA (Voltage Controlled Amplifier) within the audio signal path. As before, the gain is determined by the fader position, but now the signal passing through the fader is a direct-current control voltage whose amplitude determines the gain of an amplifier. This VCA control allows great flexibility in mixing and is the basis for automated mixdown which will be discussed in detail in Chapter 17.

As described earlier, the function of this linear fader can be interchanged with that of the rotary or shorter channel fader by means of a fader reverse switch.

O) Monitor Pan Pot

In the earliest days of multi-track recording, it was not uncommon to find four monitor loudspeakers at the front of the control room. This was a more or less reasonable culmination of a practice that began still earlier as mono gave way to stereo pan. As the number of available recorder channels doubled, so did the number of speakers. As three- and, very soon thereafter, four-track recording was introduced, the number of loudspeakers kept pace. Fortunately, common sense prevailed as the industry progressed from 4 to 8 and then to 24 or more channels, and the number of speakers was held at four. Now, recent control room design favors the return to a two-channel monitor system, which is of course a more accurate representation of what the consumer will eventually hear at home.

Accordingly, on an in-line console, a monitor pan pot will be found. This pan pot sends the monitor signal from its respective I/O module to either the left or right monitor bus, or any proportion in between. The phrase *pan pot* actually stands for panoramic potentiometer, and is simply a control made up of two concentric rotary potentiometers, with opposite tapers, mounted on one shaft. As the level is raised on one, it is lowered by the same amount on the other. When the control is placed in the center, equal signal is sent to both the left and right buses. Since the monitor bus is providing the signal for the 2-mix as well as for the monitor system, the monitor pan pot assigns the signal to the respective channels of the stereo mixdown tape recorder as well.

P) Left and Right ACN Amplifiers

It is at this point that all signals to be routed to the monitor buses are combined. As mentioned previously, the ACN amplifier outputs feed the various mixdown tape recorders as well as the monitor system (Figure 16-6).

Q) Speaker Level Control

This potentiometer functions as a master gain control for the combined signal fed to the loudspeaker systems. As discussed before, there will be separate controls for control room and studio loudspeaker systems.

R) Master Audio Fader

The Master Audio Fader at the outputs of the monitor mix bus ACN amplifiers regulates the signal level that is fed to all mixdown recorders, as well as to the speaker level control just described.

S) Monitor Output Plugs

At this point, the monitor signal leaves the console and goes to the power amplifier(s), and then to the monitor loudspeaker systems.

T) Auxiliary Send Controls

These controls (Figure 16-4), usually rotary potentiometers, are found in the I/O module. They allow the engineer to feed some portion of any input signal to an auxiliary bus that is summed at the master module. These buses are then sent to various outboard devices such as reverberation systems or other processing equipment. The auxiliary bus outputs are also often used to feed the headphone cue system. As in earlier designs, where these buses may have been called Echo Sends, these lines may be fed from before (pre) or after (post) either the channel fader or the monitor fader. These auxiliary buses are often used for multiple purposes. For example, the same send line can be used with the cue system during recording and as a reverberation send during mixdown. Or, it may be used at any time to feed some external device such as a digital delay line.

In Figure 16-4, the *pre position* picks up the signal before the equalizer. Also, several alternative send systems are shown. In the first (T1), separate send-level controls are permanently assigned to send buses 1 and 2. Or, there may be a master send level plus a pan pot (T2). As another method (T3), there may be separate send levels plus pushbutton (or toggle) switches to select any of the available send buses. Depending on the specific console design, between four and eight of these systems may be found.

A detailed drawing of a typical auxiliary send system for an in-line console is shown in Figure 16-7. Note that the signal can be picked up from a point before or after the channel rotary fader (E) or before or after the monitor linear fader (N) depending on the position of the pre/post switch and the channel/monitor switch. As shown, the signal to be sent to the auxiliary bus must first pass through the channel fader. Consequently, the fader's position influences the auxiliary send signal level. On the other hand, if the selector switch were in the pre-fader position, the signal level to the auxiliary bus becomes independent of the position of the channel fader.

There are at least two applications for a pre-fader send position. If the channel fader is brought way down to attenuate a signal going to the output bus ACN and assignment switches, there may not be sufficient level after the fader to provide the send level that is required. In the pre-fader position, a full level signal is available at the auxiliary send line, regardless of the input fader.

As a second application, when the auxiliary bus is being used as a reverberation send, a satisfactory blend of direct and artificial reverberant sound may be established with the monitor fader at some average level position. Now, as the fader is raised, the

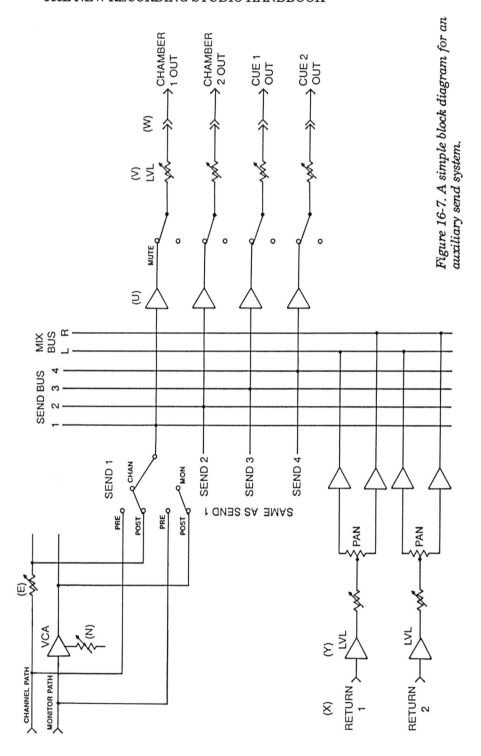

Figure 16-7. A simple block diagram for an auxiliary send system.

direct sound level increases, while the reverberant sound remains, and as the direct sound becomes louder, the signal seems to move forward in the stereo image. On the other hand, as the fader is brought down, the direct signal will fade out, leaving only the reverberation, so the signal seems to recede into the distance.

Often, one or several pair of auxiliary buses will be normalled to the reverberation devices(s) while others are reserved for alternate uses.

U) Auxiliary Send ACN Amplifier

This amplifier (Figure 16-6) combines all the signals that are routed to that particular auxiliary send bus. Provisions are also often made to send the monitor mix bus to the auxiliary send ACN combining amplifier that is normally used to feed the headphone cue system. This allows the engineer to quickly send what is being heard in the control room to the musicians' headphones.

V) Master Auxiliary Send Level

Usually a rotary potentiometer that regulates the level of the combined auxiliary send bus may be found next. Any auxiliary bus metering is usually derived directly after this control.

W) Auxiliary Send Plug

Here the auxiliary send signal leaves the console, going by way of the patch bay, to the input of the selected reverb or other device.

X) Auxiliary Return Plug

A series of auxiliary inputs, designed to accept the return signal from the external reverberation system or other processing equipment.

Y) Auxiliary Return Level

Since the external system is not necessarily a unity gain device, this potentiometer and associated pan pot give the engineer control over the output level of the device and the image placement of the signal returned to the console.

As will be discussed in Chapter 17, it is generally best to record the basic tracks "dry," that is, without any artificial reverberation. Reverberation will be added later on during the mixdown.

Consequently, the auxiliary return buses are fed to the monitor/2-mix bus only. It is possible to return effects or reverberation to the channel outputs—that go to the multi-track tape recorder—if necessary, by patching the effects return to a spare I/O module and assigning that module to the desired channel ACN bus. However, precautions must be taken to prevent a feedback loop when recording reverberation on the same channel with the direct signal that is feeding the reverberation device.

It is often possible and desirable, however, to return reverberation to the auxiliary sends that are being used to feed the headphone cue system. This way, the musicians in the studio can hear the headphone mix with or without reverberation as needed. Often, reverberation is required so that the musicians can hear the proper blending of instruments that they are accompanying.

SUMMARY OF THE SIMPLIFIED SIGNAL FLOW PATH THROUGH THE IN-LINE CONSOLE

The microphone input signal is boosted to line level, after which a pair of patch points permit the insertion of external signal processing devices. The signal follows the channel path through the console and directly out to the associated channel on the multi-track tape recorder. Alternatively, the signal may be sent to one or more of the channel buses for routing/mixing to any channel out.

The signal is also returned to the front end of the console where it is routed along the monitor path through the equalizer and linear fader and then to the monitor loudspeakers and the 2-mix bus. Pre (equalizer) and Post (fader) lines route the signal to one or more of the auxiliary send buses, as desired.

SIGNAL FLOW PATHS IN THE CONSOLE—ADDITIONAL DETAILS

L) Line Inputs, Z) Mic/Line Selector Switch

So far, the recording console has been discussed as a routing and processing point between microphones and a tape recorder. A secondary, yet no less important function, is as a control point between one tape recorder and another. For example, after a multi-track tape has been completely recorded, it must be mixed down to two tracks if a stereo master tape is needed, as is usually the case.

Instead of the console ACN channel outputs, the multi-track tape recorder outputs are routed to the input of the console monitor section at point (M) in Figure 16-4. The multi-track tape recorder is normalled to these (L) line input plugs that may be found near to or adjacent to the microphone input plugs.

The line-in/line-out switch determines the input to the console monitor section, and will be discussed in greater detail later on. The mic/line switch (Z) on the I/O module determines whether a line level source or the output of the microphone pre-amplifier is applied to the channel input. When in mixdown, the mic/line switch may also allow the channel paths to be used as additional auxiliary sends.

C) Patch Points

A detailed drawing of the signal path through some of the patch points in the recording console patch bay is shown in Figure 16-8. Note that the act of inserting a patch cord into patch point (1) allows this signal to be routed elsewhere without interrupting the normal signal flow. However, insertion of a jack at patch point (2) does interrupt the circuit, allowing the path through some external device to take the place of the normal signal flow. This wiring convention, although by no means standard practice, allows the engineer considerable flexibility in changing signal routing paths to meet the needs of the recording session.

Foldback (Cue) System

When the studio musicians are acoustically isolated from each other, the engineer must be able to feed a well-balanced program into a headphone system so that each musician will be able to hear what the others are doing. Previously recorded tracks must also be sent to the headphone lines so that the musicians may play along in accompaniment. The auxiliary send buses are used for this purpose, with usually one particular pair normalled to the cue system. Often the dedicated cue send buses mentioned earlier can access the monitor mix as well.

Mute (Channel Cut Switch)

The mute or channel cut switch is a simple on/off switch that allows the engineer to remove the signal flow entirely without disturbing any of the level or auxiliary controls. This facility is

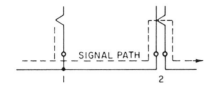

A

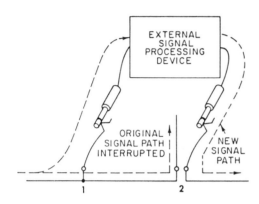

B

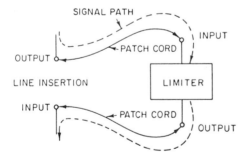

C

Figure 16-8. (A) patch points not in use—no interruption of regular signal path, (B) patch points in use—the regular signal path is interrupted, at patch point 2. Note that a meter could be inserted at patch point 1 without affecting the normal signal path, and (C) a detail of the flow path through the patch bay when an external device is inserted in a signal path.

particularly useful for briefly shutting off a microphone or tape track that must later be turned back on again at the same relative setting. When the channel is grouped (discussed later), the mute may mute all signals assigned to that group.

Solo Function

At times, it may be desirable to listen briefly to the output of one microphone only, in order to check its performance or placement. The solo function is one of the methods available that allows the engineer to do this without affecting the recording in any way. From each I/O module, a solo send line is permanently routed through the solo switch to the solo combining amplifiers. When the switch is depressed, the input signals reach the combining amplifiers. Another set of contacts on the same switch energizes a relay which routes the output of the solo combining amplifiers to one of the control room amplifiers in place of the signal regularly assigned to it. At the same time, as shown in Figure 16-9, the signal paths to any other control room speakers

Figure 16-9. The solo function. When any solo button is depressed, a relay interrupts the normal signal path to the monitor switches and the solo signal only is sent to one path of the control room speakers.

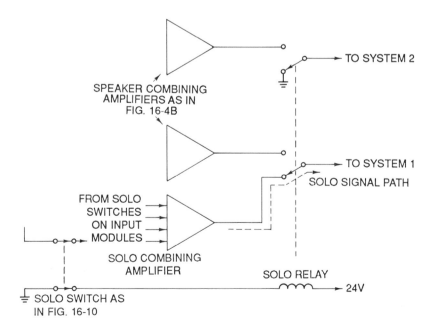

SPEAKER COMBINING
AMPLIFIERS AS IN
FIG. 16-4B

TO SYSTEM 2

TO SYSTEM 1
SOLO SIGNAL PATH

FROM SOLO
SWITCHES
ON INPUT
MODULES

SOLO COMBINING
AMPLIFIER

SOLO RELAY

24V

SOLO SWITCH AS
IN FIG. 16-10

are interrupted so that the solo signal alone is heard. Two or more solo buttons may be depressed at once, and the appropriate inputs will be combined and routed to the solo circuit.

Many of today's modern in-line consoles furnish the engineer with a stereo non-destructive solo bus. The solo signal is derived post-fader, post-pan but pre-mute switch. This allows the engineer to monitor the signal at the selected level with proper panning and with equalization and effects if selected. Earlier consoles made use of a mono solo bus only with the solo signal going equally to both control room monitor speakers. There is usually a solo switch for both the channel path and the monitor path on each I/O module. This allows the engineer to solo the channel ACN bus out, or to just hear the individual channel signal.

Before stereo non-destructive solo became common place, an earlier version used the VCA controls in the monitor path to achieve this effect. Depressing the solo-in-place switch for any channel would mute the VCAs for the remaining channels, allowing the operator to solo the input signal with proper panning and equalization, along with its reverberation return, if any. (Other sends to the reverberation lines were muted along with the channels themselves.) Note that the solo-in-place function could not be used during recording since it performs its function by muting all other channels. For solo during recording the regular solo button on each I/O module would be used. This solo-in-place function is still retained in many consoles, and its implementation is relegated to the automation software, and as such will be discussed in Chapter 17.

Pre-Fade Listen

Another way for the engineer to listen briefly to an incoming signal is with the pre-fade listen circuit. It is similar in operation to the solo circuit, except that the signal is derived just after the mic/line switch. This allows the engineer to hear the quality of the incoming signal prior to any level control, equalization or processing. The pre-fade listen circuit is strictly a monophonic bus, and often the signal is sent to a small monitor speaker built into the console meter bridge or, to just the left or right control room monitor while the other speakers are muted.

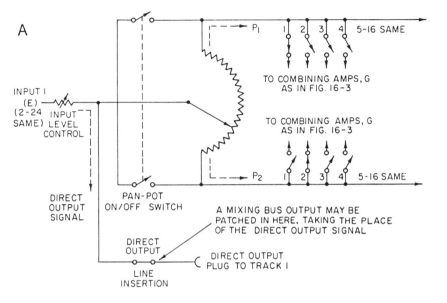

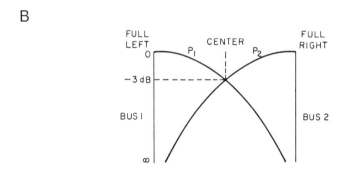

Figure 16-10. (A) detail of a flexible bus selector/pan pot switching system, showing additional direct output facility, while (B) is a graph of relative power delivered to buses 1 and 2 by pan pot. At any position, $P_1 + P_2 = 0$ dB.

Output Bus Selector Switches and Pan Pots

As described earlier, the bus selector switches allow the engineer to route an input signal to one or more of the channel output buses. A somewhat more involved switching system will permit the input signal to be routed to two or more buses in unequal proportions. A pan pot (panoramic potentiometer) is

427

used, and is shown in Figure 16-10. Note that there are now two sets of bus selector switches, and that bus number 1 has been selected in one set and bus number 2 in the other. The pan pot wiper arm is closer to the lower set of switches, so although the signal is routed to both buses 1 and 2, the power distribution is unequal, with bus number 2 being favored somewhat. Assuming that these buses are monitored on separate speakers, say number 1 on the left, and number 2 on the right, the position of the pan pot will determine the apparent location of the signal. As shown, the signal would appear to be slightly right-of-center.

As mentioned earlier, the pan pot is really two concentric but reverse gain controls. The pan pot is designed so that at its midway position, the signal to both sides is attenuated by 3 dB, as compared to the level if the signal were routed to one side only. Since a 3 dB drop represents a halving of power, both buses add up to the same amount of power as when the signal is routed to one side only. Thus, if the signal is gradually panned from one bus to another, there is no change in apparent level as the sound source moves from one loudspeaker to another. Without the 3 dB drop feature, a signal would get louder as it was panned to the center.

When only one output bus is selected, the pan pot is usually bypassed in the circuit regardless of its position. Only when two or more buses are selected does it enter the circuit.

Direct Outs

As just described, the bus selector switching system with pan pots offers great flexibility in mixing input signals to one or more channel ACN amplifiers. However, when a single microphone is to be routed to one track on a tape recorder, there is little point in going through such a switching system if a more direct route to the tape recorder is available.

On perhaps the majority of recording sessions, very few mixing buses are required at one time. For example, although the drums, string section, and chorus may be recorded using several microphones each, perhaps everything else is done with just one microphone per recorded track. Therefore, a complete mixing bus for each track is not necessary, in fact, the extra circuitry lowers the signal-to-noise ratio of that channel.

As shown in Figure 16-10, there may be a direct out plug after every channel fader. By way of these plugs, input 1 is routed directly to tape recorder track 1, and so on. A single microphone, to be routed to say, track number 7, is simply plugged into console input number 7 at the microphone panel in the studio. In this case, the mixing bus assignments are simply not used. The buses are only used when several microphones are to be combined onto one track. Then, a convenient output bus is selected and the output of its combining amplifier is routed to the appropriate track on the tape recorder. When the direct switch on an I/O module is selected, that channel's ACN is disconnected from the output plug and the direct out is substituted.

Combining Amplifiers

As so far illustrated (Figure 16-11), the combining amplifier must have many inputs, one for each I/O module in the console. And, each auxiliary circuit, solo circuit, pfl circuit and monitor channel require one as well. These multiple inputs are usually in the form of a large number of resistors, as shown in Figure 16-11A. The resistors prevent a group of inputs that are routed to one output from shorting each other out and, in the case of inputs routed to more than one output, keep the outputs isolated from each other.

In many consoles, these resistors are found in the input section of the various I/O modules, as seen in Figure 16-11B. The resistors are wired to the output bus lines as shown, and each bus is routed to a separate combining amplifier, which in this application may be called a line amplifier.

Broadcast Mode

From time to time, it may be necessary to record a multi-channel program and a stereo version simultaneously. This can certainly be done without any modification to the console as presently described. Of course, gain adjustments made in the channel path will alter the stereo mix as well, as is desirable during the typical multi-channel-only recording.

However, in the case of, say, a simulcast stereo broadcast/multi-track recording, the integrity of the stereo mixdown (now being broadcast as well) must not be compromised by multi-track recording gain adjustments made while the broadcast is in progress.

429

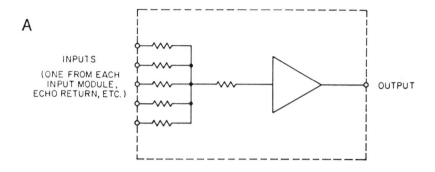

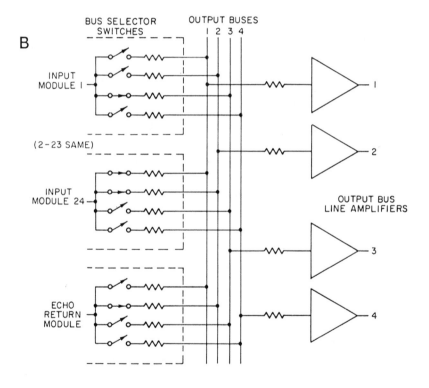

Figure 16-11. At (A) a typical combining amplifier, at (B) in many consoles, each input module is connected to each output bus as shown here.

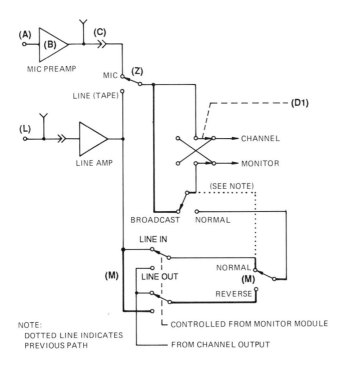

Figure 16-12. Detail drawing, showing channel-reverse and broadcast-mode switches. In actual practice, the line, channel, and reverse modes are usually accomplished by FET switching. New circuit details are indicated by heavy lines.

The *broadcast* switch seen in Figure 16-12 permits the operation just described. Note that when the switch is in the *broadcast* position, both the channel and the monitor paths are directly fed from a common point (the mic/line switch), regardless of the position of the channel/monitor switch (D). However, the channel and monitor paths are now completely independent of each other so that adjustment to the multi-channel buses will have no effect on the stereo mix. Note, that while in the *broadcast* mode, it is not possible to monitor the channel outputs.

The *broadcast* mode is also extremely useful when recording direct to two. This is when any number of microphones are mixed directly to a two-channel tape recorder. This is often the way that classical music is recorded due to the nature of the music. The

431

ensemble required for this music is best maintained by recording all parts simultaneously, with subtle balance changes made by the engineer as the music is recorded directly onto the two-channel tape recorder.

The *broadcast* mode permits the engineer the full use of the filters, equalization, auxiliary buses, etc. while mixing the signals from the microphones onto the monitor bus. The channel buses are not used during this process.

Grouping

When signal levels are under VCA control, it is relatively easy to use a single fader to control the levels of a group of several signals. Simply stated, the direct-current control voltage from the fader is used to control all the VCAs within a selected group. With the exception of this group control of levels, the signals remain completely isolated from each other. Thus, the signals passing through, for example, modules 3, 5 and 23 may be controlled with (if you like) fader 24. If it happens that these signals are to be combined onto a single channel, then fader 24 may be considered as a temporary group master channel control, removing the need for a permanently assigned channel level control to perform this function. In other words, for simple level adjustments to the channel, the regular channel trim pot may be used. When more extensive control is required, the grouping mode may be used.

Of course, the modules just mentioned may just as easily feed separate channels, with fader 24 continuing to serve as a master level control for the group. The aforementioned situation actually parallels the function of the channel submaster on a split-type console. However, when the inputs are assigned to varying output channels, VCA grouping would still be required.

Group-Select Switch

In a typical implementation of grouping, a multi-position thumb wheel or set of individual group-select switches will be located near each channel fader, as seen in Figure 16-13. To assign several faders to Group 3, for instance, simply select Group 3 on the appropriate thumb wheel or pushbutton switch. Next, determine which of these faders is to be the group master by depressing the master switch usually found quite near the group assign-

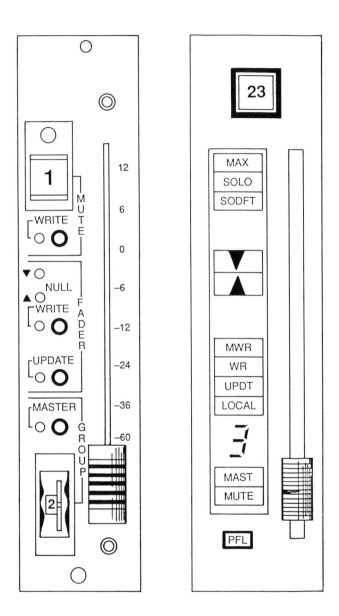

Figure 16-13. Monitor fader modules showing (A) rotary switch and (B) software assignable grouping. Also seen are some automation controls and indicators.

ment switch. The fader so designated will function as a group level control for all faders assigned to Group 3. Each of the faders within the group may also be independently adjusted as well. In many applications, the group master may be any fader that is conveniently located and otherwise un-assigned. Or, it may actually be one of the faders within the group, thereby controlling its own signal and the group's as well.

Some consoles have a separate set of faders (typically three to eight) permanently assigned as group masters. In this case, there may be no master buttons near each channel's group select switch.

A third option places the grouping function under the control of the console's automation software, thereby doing away with all switches, thumb wheels, separate group masters and the like. This function will be discussed in detail in Chapter 17 on console automation.

AA) Monitor Pan to Channel Buses (Dump)

From time to time, the engineer may want to record a microphone group as an equalized stereo mix on two of the multi-channel buses, while simultaneously recording each microphone separately on other individual channels. For example, consider a five-microphone drum pickup. The five microphones are to be recorded on, say, tracks 7, 8, 9, 10 and 11, with a stereo mix of the drums going to channels 3 and 4. In this case, the microphones must be plugged into the correspondingly numbered inputs, and routed directly (G) to the corresponding channel outputs, thus freeing the channel buses (for the moment).

Each microphone is monitored in the usual manner, as described earlier. In addition, the monitor pan-to-channel or Dump switch (AA) on each I/O module allows this monitor feed to also be routed to the channel bus selector, as shown by the drawing in Figure 16-14. Now, by selecting channel buses 3 and 4 on each of the five I/O modules, a stereo mix of the drum microphones is recorded on these two channels. Of course, the stereo mix-only could be recorded simply by not assigning the five inputs directly (G) to any channel outputs. Or, the five previously recorded tracks could be combined or "bounced" to channels 3 and 4 at a later time by using the dump switch.

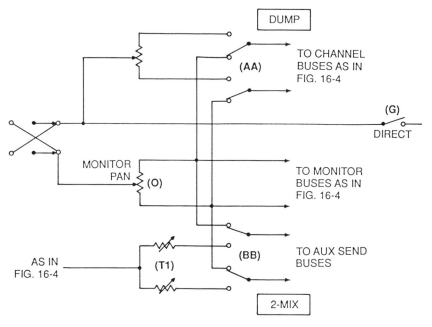

Figure 16-14. Detail drawing showing monitor pan-to-channel buses and monitor pan-to-auxiliary send buses.

BB) Monitor Pan to Auxiliary Send Buses

A similar switching system, seen in Figure 16-6, allows each I/O module's monitor feed to be sent to the (cue) send buses as well. This may prove to be convenient during particularly complicated recording sessions, since it removes the need to take the time to establish a separate cue mix.

CC) Monitor Mix (2-Mix) to Cue

A similar function may be available just after the master fader (R) as seen in Figure 16-5. This allows the entire stereo mix to be routed into the cue system. In this case, the cue system might also contain more (but never less) of a certain signal by continuing to feed the appropriate I/O module to the cue lines (as described earlier), in addition to the stereo mix cue feed.

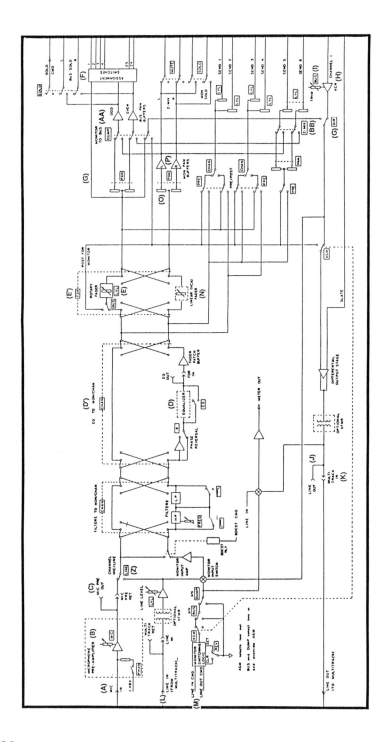

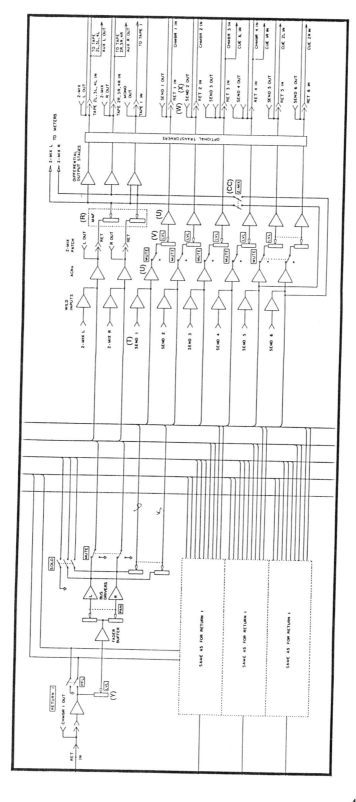

437

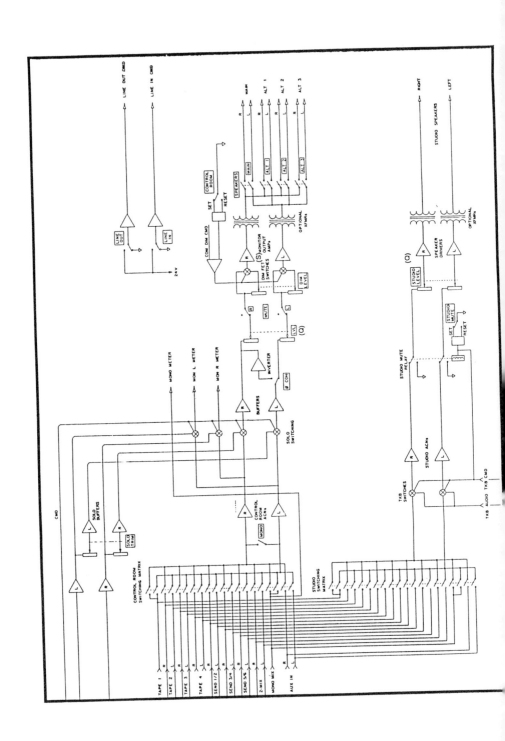

Figure 16-15 (A-C). On the preceding three pages have been actual block diagrams or flow charts for a typical I/O Module, Master Module, and Monitor Module. Compare with the simplified diagram as seen in Figure 16-4. The console is a modern professional in-line multi-track recording console with VCA automation, vacuum fluorescent metering and wild faders and was previously pictured in Figure 16-2A (Sony MXP-3036VF, Sony photo).

SUMMARY

The console described in this chapter is representative of a typical in-line multi-track recording console. It is important to remember that the specific nomenclature, physical appearance and relative position of each function will vary from one manufacturer to another, and even among different models from the same manufacturer. Furthermore, not every function described here will appear on every console.

For the less experienced engineer who may have learned on the simpler split-configuration type of console, the in-line design will take at least a little "getting used to." The primary difficulty may be in becoming familiar with the monitor path system. For example, although I/O module 3 always represents microphone 3 in the studio and tape track 3 in the control room, the two may not otherwise be related. If the channel bus selectors are in use, perhaps microphone 3 is being routed to, for example, track 7, while microphone 18 feeds track 3. In this case, I/O monitor fader 3 is used to monitor microphone 18, while microphone 3 may be heard over I/O module 7. Even when one remembers that the monitor linear fader is controlling its respective channel signal and not necessarily the microphone plugged into that I/O module, the situation can be challenging.

Such potentially confusing situations may be minimized, if not eliminated completely, by a judicious mixture of pre-session planning of microphone assignments and some re-routing at the patch bay, as required.

Figures 16-15 (A), (B), and (C) on the preceding pages show the actual signal flow charts of a modern in-line multi-track console. The actual console is pictured in Figure 16-2A.

Chapter 17

Console Automation Systems

From our previous chapter on audio recording consoles, it may be noted that an engineer working alone will have a difficult job manipulating all of the controls required for a complex mixdown of 24 or more tracks. As is often the case, a "second" engineer or assistant may be required to help mix large and complicated orchestrations and arrangements. As will be explained in Chapter 19 (on the mixdown procedure), controlling fader levels, channel mutes, reverberation and effects returns, equalization and other outboard or inboard processing equipment can be a difficult process indeed. These problems can be compounded by the design of the modern in-line console. What makes great ergonomic sense for recording basic tracks and for unassisted mixdown operations doesn't necessarily allow a lot of elbow room for two engineers working together on a closely spaced in-line design. In fact, in some of the larger film and video studios, the audio console is physically split into three in-line sections. With a section for music, one for dialogue, and one for sound effects. This type of design allows three engineers to work as a team without getting in each other's way.

It is also often desirable to set the levels on a group of faders, such as the drum tracks returning from the multi-track, and then to be able to control that group with a single fader without affecting the groups internal balance. Split-configuration consoles allow this, in a way, by using the sub-group masters. However, all inputs assigned to a particular sub-master will be summed in mono. To maintain the left-to-right orientation of the drum kit, the multi-track returns of the drum tracks would have to be assigned between two different sub-masters. The two sub-masters could then be moved together to vary the overall stereo level of the entire drum set. This approach can work very well, but if there are many such sub-groups required, such as a drum mix, a back-up vocal mix, a keyboard mix, etc., the available number of sub-masters would soon be exceeded.

Recording console automation systems solve these problems and many more. By automating certain functions within the console, the engineer's hands are free for other functions during the actual transfer of the multi-track signals to the two-channel mixdown tape recorder. The functions that are most often automated are the individual mixdown fader levels and the respective channel "mute," or off and on status. Some consoles allow for automating other functions as well, such as equalization, panning, and effects returns.

The data that is generated by and for these automated functions can be stored for later retrieval. This allows the engineer to work on small sections of the mix one part at a time. It is possible to establish the rhythm mix for the first verse alone, and to then store that data and hear the results while adjusting the lead solo levels and equalization. This complete mix of the first verse can then be stored while work proceeds on the second verse, bridge, and chorus. In fact, since the data is stored and can be retrieved at will, it is possible to create two different balances of the same section (such as the rhythm instruments) and to then compare them within the context of the remaining tracks.

When the entire song has been mixed to everyone's satisfaction, the multi-track tape recorder is rewound to the beginning of the selection and played. The console automation system takes control and operates the various automated functions as the tape is played, and the resulting mix is transferred to the two-track mixdown recorder.

The Voltage-Controlled Amplifier

These functions would not be possible without a way to encode the various fader positions. This is accomplished by using a fader as a simple voltage attenuator. A known voltage level is sent through the fader, and its output, when measured (relative to the reference voltage), will represent the fader position. This changing voltage is used to control the gain of a voltage-controlled amplifier, more commonly referred to as simply a "VCA."

In earlier chapters, it was stated that many amplifier circuits were passive; i.e., a fixed gain amplifier was preceded by a variable attenuator or "fader." An exception to this was in the case of an active microphone pre-amplifier where the actual gain of the amplifier was adjusted by the microphone trim control. These active circuits allow greater flexibility and lower noise than the equivalent passive design. The gain of the amplifier is adjusted by turning a potentiometer that varies a DC voltage that controls the bias and negative feedback on a transistor or integrated circuit. The greater the applied DC voltage, the greater the attenuation of the amplifier. This technique gives a gain range of 100 dB or greater—a very wide range indeed.

In a typical VCA-equipped console, the monitor path faders vary a DC control voltage that changes the gain of the VCA proportional to the movement of the fader. These faders are linear potentiometers rather than the more familiar logarithmic or audio taper. The audio signal is routed through the voltage-controlled amplifier and not through the fader itself. This method of level change is transparent to the engineer, since the signal behaves exactly the same as if the audio were going through the fader. This control voltage is often then digitized and stored in binary form for later retrieval. It is possible, with this technology, to automate any function involving an amplifier. This includes channel mutes, grouping, group mutes, and solo functions as well as fader levels. It is even possible, in some cases, to automate functions such as compression and gating if desired.

Another form of fader automation is possible by using similar DC control voltages. Instead of controlling the gain of a VCA, the resultant voltage drives a servo-motor. These small servo-motors are attached to the actual audio taper fader, and the control voltages (when regenerated) energize the motor and move the fader. In these so-called "moving fader" systems, the audio signal does go through the actual fader. This was often the preferred method with early automation systems, since many engineers felt that the VCA lacked the quality of a passive fader. Today, however, it is the preference of the engineer that determines which system is selected. Figure 17-1 shows a simplified signal path for a split configuration console submix bus, a VCA-controlled group, and a moving fader system.

Several manufacturers offer VCAs for in-console installation, and the specifications for some typical examples are shown in Figure 17-2. The specifications for a typical active transformerless microphone pre-amplifier are shown for comparison.

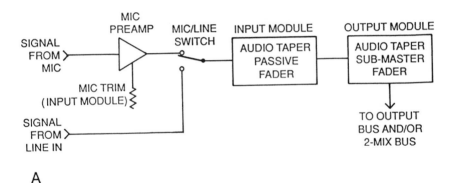

A

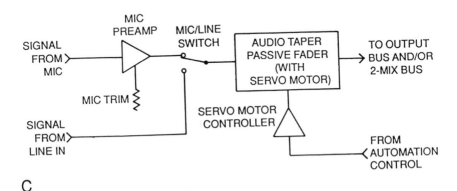

B

C

Figure 17-1. (A) a simplified signal path for a split configuration console submix bus, (B) is a simplified automation signal path for a VCA-controlled console group, and (C) is a simplified automation signal path for a moving fader console group.

	VCA 1	VCA 2	Microphone Preamp
Gain Range	−90 to +12 dB	−90 to +12 dB	15 dB to 65 dB
Distortion			
nominal gain	.0042%	0.0074%	0.010%
+12 dB gain	.0135%	0.0044%	0.019%
Intermodulation			
nominal gain	.0105%	0.0130%	0.015%
+12 dB gain	.0495%	0.0100%	0.019%
Noise Level			
0 dB gain	−95.1 dB	−85.2 dB	−89 dB (+65 dB)
−30 dB gain	−101.4 dB	−99.7 dB	−125 dB (+20dB)

Figure 17-2. Chart comparing two typical VCAs with a high-quality transformerless microphone pre-amplifier.

AUTOMATION DATA STORAGE

For the automation system to be of use, the representative data must be stored and then retrieved in synchronization with the music material. One way of doing this is to record the data on a track of the analog or digital tape along with the music. This vertical alignment will assure that the automation data is synchronized with the program material. To prevent distortions of the recorded control voltages, distortions that can be caused by analog tape recording systems (see Chapter 10), the control voltage for each VCA is periodically sampled and quantized. For a further discussion on digitizing a signal, refer to Chapter 13, "Digital Audio." The controls to be automated are sampled and quantized in a pre-specified sequence called scanning. The scanning rates of different automation systems vary, but generally in the 10 Hz to 100 Hz range. This means that the amplitude of the control voltage for every VCA is measured every one-tenth to one-hundreth of a second depending on the system. Between samples, the value is held in a buffer memory similar in nature to the sample-and-hold circuit of digital recording systems. This stream of binary code, generated by the automation computer or digitizer circuit, is then sent to the storage medium. Of course, there can be a delay between the time of the last scan and the movement of a fader or control particularly if the fader continues to move between scanning samples. Obviously, the higher the scanning rate, the less noticeable this effect is. In fact, when in the automated mode, the engineer hears exactly what the automation system has recognized as valid data since the fader sends its signal to the automation computer which in turn controls the VCA. When the automation computer is turned off, control of the VCA is then accomplished by the voltage change generated by the fader itself. Most systems have a smoothing filter at the output of the D/A converter to remove as much of the step functions as possible from the control voltage.

Some systems have a bypass mode that allows the engineer to switch the audio signal to a second logarithmic onductive element within the fader pack, thereby bypassing the VCA altogether for non-automated requirements. This will allow the audio taper linear fader to be used for basic tracks or direct-to-two recording without the VCA in the signal path, yet giving the engineer the flexibility of automation for the mixdown of multi-track masters. A separate element is needed since audio faders use a logarithmic taper, while DC controllers use a linear one. Moving fader systems use a similar principal in that there is a logarithmic taper for the audio signal, while a linear track is used for voltage control of the servo motor.

Some current (and many older) systems use two tracks on the multi-track tape for storage of the automation information. The signal is recorded and played back "in-sync" with the existing material in a manner similar to the way that an overdub is accomplished. In this case, however, the musical material is monitored from the playback head while the automation data is recorded on a separate track by the record head. This records the automation data slightly non-vertically aligned, that is, offset by the spacing between the record head and the play head on the multi-track tape. To ensure that the intended level changes of say, the keyboards, are accomplished in time with the music, the automation data is played "in-sync" from the record head to maintain the proper time relationships. Changes to these stored levels are accomplished by generating new data based on the original data along with any further changes or by generating new data, and recording this information on a second track. By alternating between these two data tracks, the mix can be continually revised until the desired mix is attained.

A disadvantage of this type of storage system is that as more and more revisions are made, the automation data lags further and further behind the musical material. During the process of getting the perfect mix, the data is continuously read from one track of the tape recorder, revised and re-recorded on the other data track and vice versa. There is an approximate delay of 0.5 ms. to 1 ms. between the two events depending on the speed of the computer in use. This delay is cumulative, and can become a problem with multiple revisions.

This problem and others related to tape-based data storage, such as drop-outs, edge damage, etc. have been solved by the use of computer based non-tape storage systems. These automation systems store their data on a hard disk like those that are found in current personal computers. A 20-megabyte hard disk can hold up to two hours of mix data, and when it is full, the desired mixes can be down-loaded onto conventional mini-floppy disks. These can then be stored with the multi-track master tape for future reference or updates. Synchronization between the multi-track tape and the hard disk is accomplished with SMPTE time code (refer to Chapter 15). The code is provided by the built-in time code generator and reader found in the automation system. The code is usually recorded on track number 24 of the multi-track tape prior to the beginning of the mixdown session. When the tape is running, the multi-track tape recorder becomes the master and the hard disk is locked in synchronization by the time-code comparison circuit. This makes sure that the automation data is synchronous with the program material. These systems are said to be frame accurate or better, and there is no cumulative lag time with multiple revisions since each revision is referenced to the original time code track. Most systems will support standard and drop-frame time-code as well as film and EBU standards.

Hard-disk storage systems require only one track on the multi-track master tape recorder and can be used with either VCA or moving fader systems. A bonus provided by this type of system is that the output of the multi-track time code channel can be sent to synchronizers and SMPTE/MIDI converters as well as to the automation system. This can provide multi-machine lockup, audio/video synchronization and other post-production techniques that also require SMPTE time code.

PRIMARY AUTOMATION FUNCTIONS

There are four primary modes of operation for automation control in most systems. These are the *Write* mode, the *Read* mode, the *Update* mode, and the *Mute-Write* mode. these functions may often be combined, such as say, *Write* and *Mute-Write*, and all functions can be used independently on any or all channels. Some of the moving fader systems do not specifically delineate these functions, but the system function modes are similar. Transitions from one mode to another are initiated whenever a fader is moved or a mute button is pressed, whereas in the VCA systems, the engineer must manually select the mode for the function desired.

Write Mode

The *Write* function is the initial mode that is selected at the beginning of the automated mixdown procedure. In this mode, the scanned voltage levels are digitized and stored in synchronization with the program material. All revisions will be based on these initial *write* levels. A "master" or "global" write mode is used to place the entire console in *Write* and *Mute-Write* simultaneously for this initial pass. The *Write* mode is the only function where information is generated for each fader without regard to previous data.

Mute-Write Mode

The *Mute-Write* data is written as a separate signal from the fader level data. It is important to note that even though a channel is muted, its fader level data is still written to the storage medium. This mode, usually used on the initial automation pass in conjunction with the *Write* mode, is used to program whether the channel is off or on at any given time. When the channel is muted, its signal is removed from the monitor path, and therefore from the mix that goes to the two-track mixdown tape recorder. If there are auxiliary sends derived from the channel that is muted, they will also be muted. *Mute-write* is a separate function, even though a global *Write* command will usually cause the system to enter *Mute-Write* also. As such, it can be used on individual channels or all channels alone or in conjunction with other modes (except *Read*).

Update Mode

The *Update* mode is used to revise existing fader level data. Update uses the existing automation data and adds to or subtracts from those levels. Most systems automatically "null" the fader when the *Update* mode is entered. That is to say, the current physical position of the fader is the position that becomes the starting point for additions or subtractions of level. It is important not to enter the *Update* mode with the fader in either the fully-open or fully-closed position since movement in one or the other direction would be impossible. The engineer should always make sure that there is enough fader movement available for the planned change prior to entering the *Update* mode.

Consoles with VCA automation systems have arrows or plus and minus LEDs (light-emitting diodes) to indicate the null point relative to the fader. This indicates which direction the fader needs to be moved to reach the null point. This allows the engineer to return the fader to the null after making an update, so that the transition from the new data back to the old is as smooth as possible.

Many engineers prefer to record a base line mix on the initial pass of the automation system and to then make all further revisions in *Update*. Other engineers would rather write fader data for a few channels at a time and create mix revisions by "re-*Writing*" the remaining faders singly or in small groups. Both methods have their proponents, and both methods will achieve a similar result.

Read Mode

When the *Read* mode is selected, operation of the console VCA levels and *Mute* status is under the total control of the automation computer. That is to say, operation of the mute functions, automation solos, fader movements, etc. will have no effect on the signals being sent to the mixdown bus. However, the engineer can make changes in the non-automated functions of the console, such as equalization, panning or filters. If a console has a separate post-fader solo or solo-in-place system, individual channel equalization, panning, etc. can often be adjusted while in the *Read* mode.

There are buffer memories in the *Read* circuit that hold the current level until new data is received. These buffers make sure that there are no unwanted level changes between scans, or level changes caused by tape drop-outs on the data track or data discontinuities from the hard-disk system.

In actuality, the *Read* mode is probably the most frequently used function in the system since, when updating a mix, only the channels that are to be changed are switched into *Update* while the majority remain in *Read*.

Group Functions

VCA grouping is an important and useful function of the automation system. Although automation is not necessary for VCA grouping, they are usually found together. It is possible, however, to have VCA grouping without automation.

As discussed in the opening paragraphs of this chapter, it is often desirable to control the balance of an entire group of faders with one single master control. Most consoles that contain VCA grouping provide for up to 8 or 9 different groups. Group selection can be assigned by a mechanical thumb-wheel or by software controls through the automation system. Either way, the faders that are to be assigned to a specific group are selected to a group number. Any number of faders can be assigned to the selected group, and a group master is selected. This is usually a fader that is a member of the group. The relative balances between all the members of the group should be determined prior to selecting a group master. Once the group master is selected, moving that fader up or down will cause the entire group to mimic this action while maintaining their relative relationship with each other. With moving fader systems, the actual faders in the group will move as the master is adjusted, while with VCA-equipped systems the gain of the VCAs in the group will follow the gain changes of the master VCA. The group's balance should be set prior to selecting a group master since it is impossible to change the individual VCA level on a channel that has been selected as a group master without affecting the other members of the group. If a group master is selected first, that individual channel cannot be adjusted independently unless the master is de-selected, adjusted, and then re-selected as a master.

For instance, let us say that we wish to group a number of channels, such as 1 through 8. These 8 channels represent 8 drum tracks that were recorded from microphones placed on the kick drum, the overhead cymbals (left and right), the hi hat, the snare, and the three tom-toms. We can pan the drums, in the stereo monitor mix, between 9 o'clock and 3 o'clock and assign all 8 of these channels to a group, such as say, group 5. The relative levels between the 8 channels are now adjusted to achieve the desired drum mix within the stereo image. We can now assign one fader, say fader number 1 (the kick drum track), to be the master for the entire group. Later in the mix, when it is desired to raise or lower the level of the entire drum mix, this can be accomplished by moving fader number 1. The levels of the 8 drum tracks will follow the gain adjustments made to fader number 1 without losing their internal balance or panning. And, as long as all members of the group are in either Update or Write mode together, the automation system will store the changes for the entire group.

Any number of groups, such as for the vocals, the keyboards, or for the entire string section tracks, can be assigned, thus, allowing the engineer to change the relative balances between large instrumental and vocal ensembles as a block while maintaining the internal ensemble balances.

The Solo and Mute System

As mentioned earlier, channel mutes can be written separately from the fader VCA data. Once again, this means that even though a channel is muted, its VCA level is being recorded and stored whenever the channel is in *Write* or *Update*. This fact may be useful if a previously muted channel needs to be retrieved, such as when the producer changes his mind, or a new version of the song is required.

The fact that mutes are part of the automation system allow several other helpful functions to be used. They are the group mutes, solo-in-place with effects, and group solos.

Group mutes are simply the system's ability to mute any number of channels simultaneously with the push of one button. This is accomplished by using the previously mentioned group assignment system. Any member of a group may be muted independently but, if the assigned group master fader is muted, the entire group will be muted also. For instance, if we desired to mute the tom-tom tracks from our previous example, the mutes on channels 6, 7, and 8 would be depressed individually. However, if it was desired to mute the entire drum mix (channels 1 through 8), the engineer would depress the mute button on the group master (fader number 1) to mute the entire group.

Another function of the automation Mute system is the so-called "automation solo-in-place." When solo is enabled on the automation system, any channel that is selected will cause all of the remaining channels to mute. This condition may or may not be written to the automation storage system depending on the console's *Mute-Write* status. However, care must be taken since all channels, except those that are soloed, will be muted to the monitor path and therefore to the two-track mixdown bus. This is often called a "destructive solo." The advantage of this type of solo is that, by muting all channels except the ones selected, these channels can be heard by themselves in the stereo image along with any effects returns. For instance, if the engineer desires to hear the solo guitar with its associated reverberation (derived from the auxiliary sends and returned to the mix bus), the only way to do so is by muting all the other channels. This is accomplished by depressing the automation solo button for that monitor path channel. The channel's track solo button (on the I/O module) will place only the guitar in one or both monitor loudspeakers, while the monitor path's solo button will only place the guitar in the monitor loudspeakers in stereo (in place based on the monitor pan pot). Only the automation solo will, by muting all the other inputs, allow the engineer to hear the individual track with its derived effects returns.

Any number of channels can be automation soloed at once, and by storing this data in the automation system, a quick change from say, a large string section of 8 or 10 tracks to a string quartet (the section principals) of only 4 tracks, can be accomplished on cue. Group soloing is accomplished the same way, and is an inverse function of group muting. By soloing the group master, the entire group is soloed and all other channels are muted.

OTHER AUTOMATION FUNCTIONS

Depending on the system, some other useful functions are available to an engineer working with an automation-equipped console.

The Automation Master

The automation master allows the engineer to "fade-out" the entire console if required and to have this fade recalled for later playback. In effect, the automation master is a group master for all of the console VCAs. Lowering or raising the level on the automation master causes the gain of all the channel VCAs to vary accordingly, whether they are grouped or not. Only those channels that have been completely removed from automation control (local only mode) will be unaffected by the automation master. The automation master differs from the two-track or mixdown master in that the mixdown fader only attenuates the output of the stereo 2-mix bus and does not affect the gain of any VCAs.

Merges

It is possible, with hard-disk storage systems, to combine sections from various versions of the automated mix. These so-called "merges" allow the engineer to take a section of say, revision 1 and place it within the confines of revision 3. For instance, if it is desired to have the same mix each time the chorus section of a song is repeated, the automation levels for that section can be merged into another revision of the mix whenever the chorus appears. This means that the engineer only has to mix the chorus once, and then that data can be plugged in or merged into the final mix whenever the chorus is repeated. The location or beginning and end of a merge are defined by the SMPTE time code values on the master tape. Automatic merges are created by the system each time an update is performed on a part of the mix. For instance, if an update is made of a small section of the second verse, when tape is stopped, data from the previous revision is filled onto either end of the revised section to form a complete version of the song. It is therefore extremely important to null the faders that have been updated before stopping tape. If this is not done, level jumps between the new data and the old may occur.

Cues

Often, various cue points within a song can be stored for later recall. These can be the points required for merges, or simply defined points for roll-back to the beginning of a particular section. These points are defined in terms of their SMPTE time code values, so no two points can be the same and confusion is avoided. These points can often be defined "on the fly" (while the tape is running) with the push of a button. When the tape is stopped, the point can then be labelled or listed for later use.

Rehearsal Modes

There is usually some type of rehearsal or practice mode available on most hard-disk systems. This allows the engineer to rehearse or practice fader moves without actually storing the auto-

Figure 17-3. A moving fader automated console (Neve Flying Fader System, Neve photo).

mation data. This prevents the storage device from becoming full too quickly. If this were not the case, the hard disk would fill up very quickly since a new complete mix version is generated each time the tape is played.

Figure 17-3 shows an automated console with a moving fader system.

AN AUTOMATION SESSION

In summary, we can list the steps involved in an automated mixdown session as follows. The reader is also advised to refer to Chapter 19 on mixdown to supplement this list.

1. The tape is stripped with SMPTE time code, or the two data tracks on the multi-track tape recorder that are to be used are defined and patched into the proper locations in the automation system.

2. In a hard-disk system, the tape is played for a 30 second period to calibrate the time code reader to the type of code in use (standard, drop-frame, EBU, etc.)

3. The faders are positioned, either in the rehearse mode or to some approximate mix position and the system is placed in the *Write* (and *Mute-Write*) mode. Groupings can be selected at this time after the rough mix is ready to be stored.

4. The song is played from beginning to end to define the beginning and ending point for the selection. The automation system "writes" the fader levels and mute status in synchronization with the program material.

5. The system is put in the *read* mode and the tape is played, while the engineer determines what panning, equalization and effects are desired. These decisions may be partially made prior to the initial *Write* mode as well.

6. The entire system or individual channels are put into the *Update* mode, and the balances for the song are revised until everyone is satisfied. Mutes may be updated independently of fader levels by selecting *Mute-Write*. If a particular channel or number of channels has so many wrong level changes that an update is impossible, those channels can be placed in *Write* (re-*Write*) mode and new data can be written.

7. The system is placed in the *Read* mode and the resulting mix is recorded on the two-track mastering tape recorder.

8. With a hard-disk system, the data is down-loaded to a floppy disk or other storage medium, and stored with the multi-track master tape.

SECTION VIII

THE RECORDING PROCESS

In this final section of the book, various aspects of both the recording and mixdown sessions are described.

In Chapter 18, overdubbing and the selective synchronization or Sel-Sync sessions are discussed, along with the techniques of "bouncing tracks," "punching-in," and the remote control of the tape recorder. Later, pre-session preparation of the control room and the studio is covered, along with a discussion of the use of signal processing devices while recording.

Chapter 19 concludes the book with a discussion of the final step in the recording process: the mixdown session. The mixdown session is actually a form of recording. However, in place of microphones, a previously recorded multi-track tape is routed back through the console, mixed down to a stereo program, and recorded onto another tape recorder. Both automated and non-automated functions will be discussed.

Chapter 18

The Recording Session

Before the introduction of the multi-track tape recorder, recording studio procedures were reasonably standardized. A song or symphony would be recorded in its entirety in one sitting. All the musicians would be present, and they would play—and replay—the music to be recorded until the engineer and producer were satisfied with the balance, the performance, the room acoustics, the soloist's interpretation, and so on.

Longer works might be recorded in sections, which would later be spliced together to create the complete performance. Chances were the musicians would make several recordings or "takes" of each section, and often the best segments from several takes would be edited together to form the ideal composite recorded performance. The editing process will be discussed in greater detail in the next chapter.

Beyond the editing process, little could be done to modify the recorded music. Nevertheless, the luxury of tape editing represented a major advance over earlier recordings made directly to disk. Here, the performance was permanently cut into the groove at the moment of recording, and there was no practical way of making even a simple edit later on.

OVERDUBBING

Once magnetic tape became the standard studio recording medium, it was only a matter of time before musicians began adding accompaniments to their recordings by playing along with a previously-recorded tape. Both the new and the previously taped performance would be mixed together and recorded onto a second tape recorder. This technique became known as overdubbing. At about the time that it came into wide use, studio tape recorders with three or four separate tracks were pretty much the industry standard.

During the initial session, all the tracks would be used. Then, the tape would be rewound and played while the musicians added additional parts, by listening over earphones to the first machine, and playing along in accompaniment. The engineer would mix the original recording from the first tape recorder with the new material from the microphones in the studio to the record head of the second machine. A typical example of the overdub process is illustrated in Figure 18-1A. Earlier, the orchestra was recorded on a four-track tape recorder, and the soloist now listens to the four-track recording and sings along with it. The engineer mixes the four tracks-plus-soloist down to a mono or stereo master tape. If, on playback, the balance is judged unsatisfactory, the soloist will have to be recorded again, while the engineer makes the necessary adjustments.

In many cases, the orchestra might be originally recorded on only two or three tracks, which would be directly transferred to the second tape recorder while the soloist is recorded on the third and/or fourth tracks during the overdub session. Later, these will be "mixed down" to produce the final mono or stereo master tape, as seen in Figure 18-1B. Although this development allowed more flexibility in arriving at an ideal balance later on, it added an additional generation of tape noise to the final product.

The overdub process brought a measure of efficiency and economy to the recording session. As the orchestral background was being recorded, complete attention could be given to the instrumental balance. Later, the solo could be added without the time and expense of having the orchestra make repeated takes while the vocalist searched for the perfect interpretation. And, the ideal instrumental accompaniment could be assembled, by editing from several takes, before the solo was added. In either case, since the accompaniment was recorded first, the soloist became in effect the accompanist, as he or she would be forced to follow the tempi and phrasing of the previously-recorded material. However, at the cost of some spontaneity, a technically superior recording could be made, since unsatisfactory balances of soloist-to-accompaniment could be redone at only the loss of the engineer's time.

In the vocabulary of the recording studio, the instrumental background became known as the basic tracks or simply, the tracks.

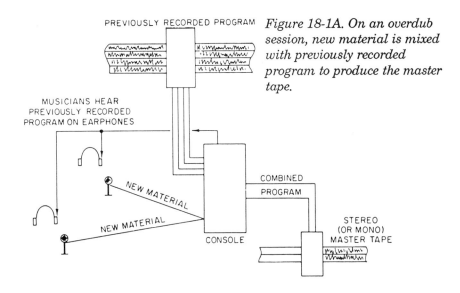

Figure 18-1A. On an overdub session, new material is mixed with previously recorded program to produce the master tape.

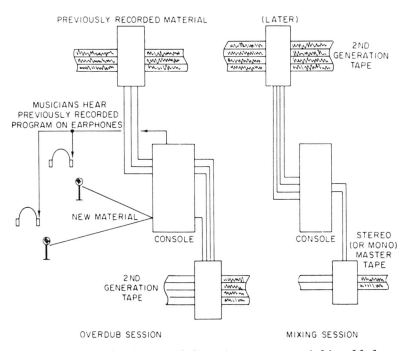

Figure 18-1B. On this overdub session, new material is added on a second generation tape, which is later mixed down to produce the master tape.

Although the overdub process expanded the capabilities of the recording medium, each successive overdub required an additional generation of tape. This presented no real problem on a single overdub, however, multiple overdubs could be troublesome since each would add another generation of tape noise. And in the case of old material being mixed with new, the only possible balancing that could be done was between the part being recorded at the moment and everything that had gone before. In the case of a recording consisting of many tracks, recorded sequentially, it is difficult or impossible to predict the ideal balance until the recording is complete. On a tape that is a product of multiple overdubs, there would be no way to correct the balance of, say, the third overdub, without scrapping everything that was recorded subsequently, and beginning again with a new version of the third overdub.

The Sel-Sync Process (Selective Synchronization)

The Sel-Sync process overcomes this very serious limitation of the overdub process. Sel-Sync, a term copyrighted by The Ampex Corporation, really became popular with the introduction of 8-track tape recorders. The recording begins in the usual manner, using as many tracks as are required, but leaving at least one track—and usually more—unused, or open. After recording the basic tracks, the tape is rewound, and the new material is recorded on the open tracks while the musicians listen to what was previously recorded. In many cases, the rhythm section (drums, bass, rhythm guitars, keyboards, etc.) is recorded first, and these instruments comprise the basic tracks. Later on, perhaps strings and/or back-up vocals or keyboards may be added. These additional sessions are popularly called sweetening sessions. Last, but not least, the solo lines can be added.

Of course, if the basic tracks are monitored in the usual manner, from the playback head, the new material will be recorded on the tape out-of-sync with the old. This is illustrated in Figure 18-2. Imagine a simple two-track tape, with a basic track already recorded on track No. 1. If the musicians listen to the tape, by way of the playback head of track No. 1, the new material recorded on track No. 2 will be out-of-sync later on playback, since it is being recorded about two inches behind the original material. The actual distance is the spacing between the record and play-

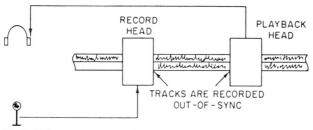

Figure 18-2. When a previously-recorded program is monitored from the playback head, new material is recorded out-of-sync.

back head, and the amount of signal delay depends on that distance and the speed of the tape.

To prevent the out-of-sync effect, the previously-recorded track, or tracks as the case may be, is monitored from the record head while the same record head is adding the new material to the tape. Of course, no individual track within the record head is performing both the record and the playback function at the same time. Rather, as in this particular example, track No. 1 of the record head is acting as a temporary playback head, while track No. 2 is functioning in the normal record mode. Since the musicians are now listening to the tape at the precise point at which the new material is being recorded, new and old tracks will be in perfect sync. Later on, after the recording is completed, the tape will be monitored from the regular playback head in the normal manner. The Sel-Sync process is illustrated in Figure 18-3.

Figure 18-3. The Sel-Sync process. (The term Sel-Sync is an Ampex trademark, therefore other manufacturers use a slightly different term to describe the same process such as sync, self-sync, etc.) Previously-recorded material is monitored from the record head while new material is being recorded, using the same record head.

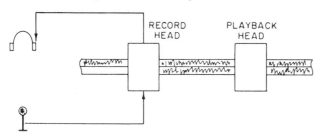

On a machine equipped for Sel-Sync, the finished recording could be monitored in its entirety from the record head. This is, after all, the way an inexpensive home machine functions, with one head performing the dual function of record, and later on, playback. However, since the design parameters for playback and record heads are not identical, the optimum record head leaves something to be desired as a playback head, and the playback head cannot make an optimum recording.

Although on recent machines the record head performs quite well as a playback device, such was not always the case. On the earliest machines, playback from the record head was conspicuously inferior, particularly at high frequencies. At the time, this was not considered to be a significant limitation given the obvious advantages of Sel-Sync over previous overdubbing techniques. Record head monitoring was merely a production convenience. Critical listening and mixdown would come later on, after the recording work was completed. At that time, the regular playback head would be used, and so the poor playback response of the record head was of no consequence. Many current machines now have separate equalization circuits to optimize the frequency response and signal-to-noise ratio of the record head when in the Sel-Sync mode.

Transferring, or "Bouncing" Tracks

Of course, there inevitably comes a time when the number of available tracks is not enough, no matter what that number is. In a typical situation, with 23 out of 24 tracks recorded, it may become desirable to have three more tracks available.

Theoretically, this presents no problem. Instead of recording new material on track No. 24, three of the previously-recorded tracks (5, 6, and 7, for example) can be monitored from the record head, mixed together, and re-recorded onto track No. 24, as shown in Figure 18-4. Now, track No. 24 contains a mono mix of tracks 5, 6, and 7, and these three tracks may be erased and reused for new material.

Any imperfections in the record head's behavior as a playback device will show up in the mixdown of tracks 5, 6, and 7. So, when bouncing tracks becomes necessary, the playback response of the record head can no longer be ignored. The frequency response and level must be as close to that of the regular playback head as is possible. This requirement becomes even more impor-

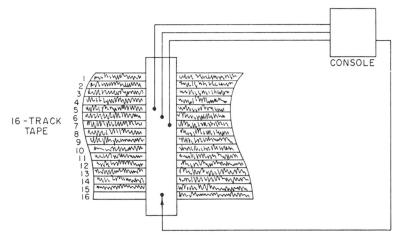

Figure 18-4. Transferring, or "bouncing" tracks. At the console, tracks 5, 6, and 7 are mixed together and routed to track 16.

tant when a noise-reduction system is being used. Refer to Chapter 9 on noise reduction for a discussion of tracking error due to level differences.

As just mentioned, most state-of-the-art tape recorders have separate circuitry for use with the record head. Thus, during alignment, the record head playback output and frequency response should be adjusted using the standard alignment tape.

Transferring Onto Adjacent Tracks

In planning a session that may require transferring tracks, it is important to remember that material from any track may not be bounced to an adjacent track. For example, although tracks 5, 6, and 7 may be bounced to track No. 24, as just described, they may not be bounced to either track No. 4 or No. 8, since No. 4 is adjacent to No. 5 and No. 8 is adjacent to No. 7.

The reason for this restriction is that the inter-channel cross talk and separation within the record head is by no means infinite. Consequently, while recording onto track No. 8, the track No. 7 section of the record head "hears" some slight portion of what is being recorded (as does track No. 9). This has no particular significance unless track No. 8 is being fed some mixture that includes track No. 7 (or No. 9). Now, if track No. 7 is being fed to track No. 8, and track No. 7 is also picking up some of track No.

465

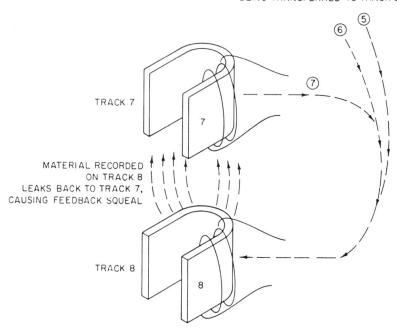

PREVIOUSLY RECORDED TRACKS
BEING TRANSFERRED TO TRACK 8

TRACK 7

MATERIAL RECORDED
ON TRACK 8
LEAKS BACK TO TRACK 7,
CAUSING FEEDBACK SQUEAL

TRACK 8

Figure 18-5. Recorded material cannot be transferred to an adjacent track.

8 internally through the head stack, the feedback squeal thus created will be recorded on track No. 8, preventing the use of the track. This condition is illustrated in Figure 18-5.

"Punching In"

In conventional recording, a series of takes are made until a satisfactory recording is achieved. Or, by editing, the definitive performance may be assembled by splicing together sections from two or more takes. However, when recording tracks on a tape that already contains previously-recorded material, the manner of doing retakes is quite different.

To illustrate, assume that the instrumental background has been recorded and a chorus is now being added to the master tape. The chorus sings the first verse properly, but a mistake is made within the second verse. A new take of the second verse cannot be started on a fresh piece of tape, since the chorus must, of course, fit in with the previously-recorded material on the master tape. So, the master tape is rewound to a point before the beginning of the second verse. The tape is played, and just before the point at which the second verse begins, the chorus track is placed in the record mode, while the chorus sings the second verse again. The new performance takes the place of the old, while the previously satisfactory first verse remains as is. The process may be repeated again and again until a complete performance has been recorded, perhaps, even phrase by phrase.

The practice of inserting the new material in this manner is popularly known as punching in, since the engineer spends much of his time punching the record button.

While awaiting the punch-in point, the musicians may wish to listen to the earlier performance, and perhaps play along with it so that the new material may closely match the previously-recorded parts that are to be saved. If the playback response of the record head sync output has been properly aligned, there should be no distracting differences in sound quality as the musicians hear first the performance which is being saved, and then the new performance of the sections being redone.

Remote Control of Record/Playback Mode

On any session involving the Sel-Sync process, it is important that the record/safe and input/sync/playback mode of each track be independently controllable. For example, it may be necessary to record on, say, tracks Nos. 9 through 12, while the material previously-recorded on tracks Nos. 1 through 7 is monitored in the sync mode. The remaining tracks are reserved for future use. Obviously, a single record button that puts all tracks into the record mode at one time would be useless. On the other hand, 24 or more separate record buttons would be very difficult to operate and would make it very easy to accidentally erase a wanted track.

Figure 18-6 shows a typical multi-track remote control unit, providing individual control over the mode of each track. When the single record button is depressed, the machine will record only on those tracks whose safe/ready switches were previously put in the ready position. These switches are, in effect, standby switches, readying the appropriate tracks for recording while protecting the other tracks from accidental erasure. Previously-recorded tracks may be monitored from the record or the playback

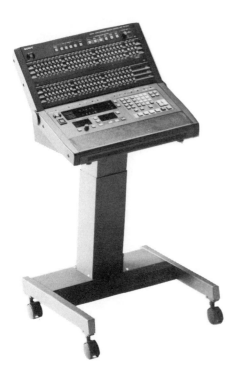

Figure 18-6. A remote-control unit allowing individual control over each track along with monitor switching, locate memories and transport control (Sony PCM-3348, Sony photo).

head, depending on the position of the input/Sel-Sync/reproduce (i.e., record head/playback head) switch, also seen in Figure 18-6.

Most multi-track tape machines also provide automatic switching so that when the record circuit is energized, the channel in ready goes into the record mode and the input/Sel-Sync/reproduce switch changes from the Sel-Sync mode (record head playback) to input monitoring on the selected channels. This allows the musicians to hear from the record head on the selected track until record is selected, and when record is depressed, the signal in the headphones switches from the previously-recorded material to the new material being played and recorded.

The Console in the Sel-Sync Mode

As described earlier, in Chapter 16, the multi-track recording console will contain monitoring facilities which enable the musicians in the studio to hear previously-recorded tracks. In Figure 16-10, the tape recorder outputs, returned to the console through the multi-track tape returns or line inputs, are routed to the cue system as shown. These previously-recorded tracks are also routed to the monitor path and control room monitor system so that the engineer/producer may likewise hear them. In the detailed drawing of the console monitor section (Figure 16-4) the line-in/line-out switch (M), would be in the line-in position for each previously-recorded track.

If the multi-track machine in use has a standby monitor setting, the entire console can be put in the line-in mode. Positioning the standby monitor to the input monitoring position on the input/sync/ reproduce switch of the tape recorder and the master monitor switch to Sel-Sync will cause the tape recorder to enter the input monitoring mode when stopped. The machine will automatically be switched to sync mode when the record mode is entered, with the exception of any channel that has "ready" already selected. These selected channels will remain in input mode as previously discussed.

Figure 18-7 is a simplified description of the signal routing through the console in the Sel-Sync mode. Note that the engineer must provide the musicians with a balance of previously-recorded

Figure 18-7. Simplified signal flow paths during a Sel-Sync recording session.

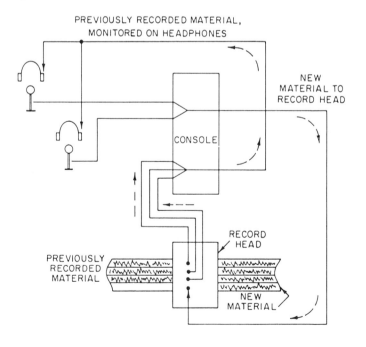

and new program material, while at the same time the new material is being added to the tape.

The controls for the control room monitor system and the auxiliary send headphone monitor system are usually independent of each other so that the engineer may route a suitable headphone mix to the musicians, while in the control room he may listen to, perhaps, just the new material to make sure that it is being recorded and added to the tape properly.

Headphone Monitoring

Depending on the acoustic isolation between the instruments in the studio, the engineer will probably have to set up a well-balanced headphone cue mix of the program being recorded so that the musicians may hear each other in addition to what was previously recorded. In fact, even when no material has been previously recorded, headphones may be required as the isolation between instruments prevent the musicians from adequately hearing each other without them.

Often, several different headphone balances will be required to suit the needs of various musicians. The drummer, for instance, may not need to hear himself in the headphones, yet the guitarist in an isolation booth will certainly need to hear the drums in his headphones if he is to play along in time. In short, a flexible headphone monitoring system is a very important part of any modern recording studio console, and the engineer must be prepared to establish quickly one or more headphone balances in addition to the basic recording balance heard through the console's monitor section.

Selection of Headphones

Headphones with open cell foam ear pieces should be avoided in most studio applications, despite their wearing comfort and frequently excellent reproduction capabilities. Although the headphones allow the musicians to hear each other directly, they also permit a considerable amount of headphone monitor mix in the studio to be heard in the studio. Consequently, the microphones in the studio pick up a lot of this headphone leakage which then gets recorded on the tape again, along with the new material. In severe cases, a feedback squeal may be produced if the microphone picks up too much of a headphone feed that already contains a portion of the microphone's output. And, for the same reason, inexperienced musicians should be cautioned against hanging their headphones across an active microphone between takes.

When a large number of headphones are in use, the engineer should periodically listen to just the program being recorded at the moment, over the control room monitor system. Very often, some musicians will remove their headphones without unplugging them. The headphone program is then heard in the studio and picked up by the microphones again. If a musician decides not to wear headphones, they should be unplugged before any recording is done. A periodic check of the material being recorded will verify that headphone leakage is being kept to a minimum. A very quick check can usually be made by depressing one or more of the solo buttons, and listening for headphone leakage during a pause in the part being recorded.

Loudspeaker Monitoring of Cue System During Rehearsals

When strings and/or brass are to be added to a basic track, the conductor may wish to rehearse without headphones in order to better communicate with the musicians. At this time, the musicians may listen to the basic tracks over loudspeakers as they rehearse their parts. Although this is certainly no technical problem, the producer should understand that the engineer will probably need some additional rehearsal time, once the loudspeakers are shut off and the musicians are wearing headphones again. As long as the loudspeaker is active, all the microphones in the studio will hear the cue feed, making it difficult or impossible to establish a meaningful balance of the program about to be recorded. In addition, if the microphones themselves are being routed to the cue system, their output will have to be kept at a minimum so long as the loudspeakers are on, to prevent feedback.

Track Assignment

Beyond operator convenience, there are few precautions to be observed in assigning instruments to the various tracks of the modern multi-track tape recorder. Whenever possible, it is a good idea to assign the same instrument to the same track on each successive recording session so that later recording and mixdown work may proceed with a minimum of switching changes. For example, if strings and brass overdubs are to be added to several songs, a great deal of time will be saved if the same tracks are available on each song. In addition, once a basic cue mix has been achieved, it will probably suffice for much of the session, providing that the track assignment has remained constant during the earlier sessions.

The mixdown session will be discussed in detail in the next chapter, but here it should be noted that mixdown work will proceed a lot more efficiently if the tracks are arranged in some logical order prior to recording. For example, rhythm instruments may be recorded consecutively from track No. 1, while sweetening tracks begin at track No. 22 and work backwards towards the center of the tape. (Track No. 23 and 24 are usually reserved for time code and/or automation data.) This leaves the center tracks open until last, so that additional instruments may be recorded towards the rhythm or sweetening sides as appropriate. The lead vocal can then be recorded in the middle.

In the early days of multi-track recording, the outside tracks were often reserved for the least important instruments, since there was apt to be some problem with tape-to-head contact. However, this should no longer be a problem, providing the tape recorder is in proper mechanical alignment.

PREPARING FOR THE MULTI-TRACK SESSION

Seating Plan

In preparing the studio for the recording session, a little pre-planning will go a long way towards improving the efficiency with which the recording work progresses. The first step is to work out a seating arrangement that will be most comfortable for the musicians. Often, they are spaced as far apart as possible under the mistaken impression that this will keep leakage at a minimum. In a very dead studio this may in fact be true, but in most cases the wide spacing creates more problems than it solves. In the average studio, there is not that much attenuation as the distance between instruments is increased. The further away one musician moves from another, the more reflections each one hears, and the resultant signal delay makes it much more difficult for the musicians to play together. The performance probably suffers far out of proportion to any improvement in the recorded sound.

If leakage is that much of a problem, a far greater improvement might be made by moving the microphone a few inches closer, rather than moving the other musicians a few more feet away. For example, if two musicians, A and B, are 1 and 3 feet away from a microphone (3 to 1 rule—see Chapter 4), this ratio can be doubled by moving musician A 6 inches closer to the microphone, or by moving musician B back an additional 3 feet. The first alternative will usually be the most satisfactory.

Microphone Setup

Once the seating plan has been worked out and set up, the microphones may be placed in position. When running microphone cables across the studio, a great deal of confusion may be avoided if the cable is plugged into the microphone input panel first and then brought to the microphone, rather than the other way around. The cable slack is laid near the base of the microphone stand so that if the microphone has to be moved during the session, it will be possible to do so without too much difficulty. This also prevents the slack from every cable in the studio accumulating in front of the microphone input panel making it difficult to make quick changes or trace problems later on.

Console Preparation

It is a good idea to neutralize or normal all console controls before beginning any session. That is, make sure that all signal routing switches are off, and that the equalizers are in their zero position. With in-line console designs, it is also important to make sure that all switches relating to the monitor and channels paths are in their monitor path position. By following this precaution, signals will not be routed to the wrong place due to a depressed switch that went unnoticed, and unwanted equalization will not be applied to any channel path.

When an automated console is in use, it is sometimes a good idea to ready the automation system for a write pass sometime before the end of the overdub session. Since with the in-line console design the VCA faders are feeding the monitor system, a basic mix that can be used as the starting point for the mixdown session can be stored during the last overdub.

Using Artificial Reverberation During Recording

Generally, artificial reverberation is best applied after the recording session, during the mixdown session. As noted earlier, stereo reverberation requires two outputs, which are fed left and right. If stereo reverberation were added during the recording session, two tracks would have to be used. This of course wastes tracks needlessly, adds tape noise, and besides, a more suitable reverberant field can probably be created during the later mixdown session when the individual tracks are heard and processed in context.

Of course, if it is necessary to add reverberation to one or more signals which are being combined during the recording session with other unprocessed signals, this must be done as recording is taking place. For example, the rhythm guitar may be being taken direct, and through a microphone with the combined signal sent to one track. A slight amount of reverberation added to the dry direct signal may enhance the sound, yet no reverberation may be desired on the microphone signal. So, during recording, the direct sound feeds the reverberation device while the microphone does not. In this case, if the reverberation was added later, during the mixdown session, it would affect the total guitar sound rather than just the sound that came from the direct box.

Often musicians will want to hear some reverberation in their headphone cue auxiliary mix. The producer may also wish to hear the control room mix with reverberation. It is important to make sure that the required reverberation only goes to the monitor and auxiliary paths, and not to the channel paths. Reverberation added to the tracks of a multi-track recorder becomes additive in mixdown. This may result in a muddy or distorted sound. For this reason, any reverberation added to the multi-channel tape during the recording of basic tracks and overdubs should be done with extreme caution.

Other Signal-Processing Devices

As with echo and reverberation, other types of signal processing should be used with some caution during the recording session. Equalization, phasing, or compression effects that may sound just right during the recording session often turn out to be unsuitable later on, after all the succeeding tracks have been recorded. Most of these effects can and should be added during the mixdown session. An exception to this rule is noise gating, which is often used to help keep the individual tracks as noise free as possible during recording.It is difficult and often impossible to remove the effects of signal processing devices that were applied during the recording session.

Of course, as before, when several inputs are combined during the recording session, it is necessary to process each one as desired before they are mixed together.

RECORDED LEVELS

In analog multi-track recording, it is a common practice to record each track at as high a level as possible. The desired control room monitor balance is achieved by adjusting the monitor fader of each track. In this way, each individual signal is recorded as high above the noise floor as possible. As mentioned earlier (Chapter 1), the engineer should realize that VU meters are not an accurate indication of the program's peak levels, and meters with peak ballistics should be used, or at least checked periodically, especially on percussive instruments, if available.

Conversely, when a digital multi-track is in use, the prudent engineer will make sure that the recorded level does not exceed the maximum quantization levels as discussed in Chapter 13. In general, digital recording levels should be more conservative since signal-to-noise ratio is not dependent on recording level.

Slating

Prior to each take, the tape is usually slated. The term is taken from the film industry, where a slate board with the take number is held in front of the camera before each shooting. In the recording studio, the slate consists of a spoken announcement, such as "take 3," usually made from the control room. Some consoles feed a low frequency tone to the tape recorder, along with the voice, during the slate announcement. Later on, when the tape is rewound at high speed, the tones are heard as high-pitched beeps which identify the beginning of each take. By counting these beeps, the engineer may quickly locate the beginning of a desired take.

Takes are numbered consecutively, and sometimes each new song begins with "take 1." However, it is often a good idea to continue the count for the duration of the session. Thus, if one song ends after take 10, the next one will begin with take 11. This is a great help when recording unfamiliar music, or for tapes that will be sent to other studios for additional recording, editing, or mixing. If there is only one "take 17" on the entire collection of master tapes, there can be no question as to the identity of a take.

Count-Offs

When it is known that additional material will be added to the tape, beginning at the first beat, a lot of trial-and-error time may be saved by recording a spoken count-off during the first session. On subsequent overdub sessions, the musicians will hear the count-off and be able to enter on the proper beat without resorting to guess work or complicated visual cues from the control room.

When there are to be long pauses during the recording of the basic tracks, during which additional instruments will enter later on, it is a little more difficult to provide satisfactory entrance cues. If someone in the studio counts time, it will be heard over most of the microphones, especially since there will be no music masking it. This will make it very difficult to remove the count later on. In such cases, it is better to have someone in the control room or in an isolation booth count time onto just one track. Later on this track may be erased with little difficulty before the mixing session. This track may often be called the cue track.

Tuning

If any sort of tuned instruments are to be added later on, it is a good idea to record a reference tone (e.g. A-440) during the recording of the basic tracks. This will enable the musicians on later sessions to tune to the basic track in case there is a slight pitch variation between one session and/or tape recorder and another. Or, if the tape recorder in use has variable speed, the machines's speed may be tuned as required.

End of Recording

Many contemporary popular recordings eventually fade out rather than coming to a definite musical ending. The fade-out is usually made during the mixdown session as described in the next chapter. During the recording, the musicians usually play the final phrase over and over again, giving the engineer sufficient material to use during the fade later on. At the recording session, it is often advisable to simulate the eventual fade-out by bring down the monitor path master fader or control room monitor gain, thus verifying that the music continues long enough to make a suitable fade during the mixdown session.

For those songs that do not end in a fade-out, it is important to maintain a few seconds of silence at the end of the recording so that the reverberation (natural) will have a chance to die away.

End of Session

It is equally as important to return the studio and control room to their original state upon the completion of recording as it is to properly set up before the recording session begins. The console should be returned to its normal state (all switches in their proper positions), microphones should be put away and cables returned to their normal storage place in readiness for the next recording session.

Chapter 19

The Mixdown Session

During the mixdown session, the completed multi-track tape is played back through the console. Each track takes the place of a microphone input, and is routed, processed and combined with the other tracks to form a stereo program which is then recorded onto another analog or digital tape recorder.

EDITING

After the recording session, the takes that are to be used for the mixdown session are usually removed from their various reels and placed on one or more separate reels. The "out takes" may then be filed or discarded so that the engineer does not have to be encumbered with them while mixing. Often, this type of editing work is done just after the basic tracks are recorded, and before the overdub or "sweetening" sessions. It is important to remember not to remove any of the count-offs at the beginning of each master take, and to leave enough extra tape at the end for any string, brass or effect parts recorded as overdubs that may last longer than the basic tracks. If the tape has been "striped" with SMPTE time code during the basic sessions, the editing engineer should remember to leave at least 10 or 15 seconds of uninterrupted code prior to the beginning or "punch-in" point of the musical selection. If the tape is to have time code added after all tracks are recorded, enough blank tape should be left at the beginning of the selection to accomplish this. As mentioned in Chapter 17, some automation systems may require up to 25 or 30 seconds of time code to calibrate the system.

For easy identification, the master takes may be separated from each other by a length of white leader tape. This type of editing is quite simple. The engineer listens to the beginning of the desired take, stops the tape, rewinds it to an appropriate point before the beginning of the music and physically cuts it. A length of white leader tape is wound around an empty reel, and the beginning of the master tape is spliced to the end of the leader. The take is then wound onto the master reel. At the end of the take, the tape is again cut and leader tape is spliced in. The master reel is put aside and the editing engineer locates the next desired take and repeats the process, splicing the take onto the master reel. The procedure is illustrated in Figure 19-1.

Musical Editing

When the master take is to be a composite of segments of several takes, the editing process is somewhat more complex, although the principle remains as described. However, great precision of editing may be required, as the beginning of one segment is spliced directly to the end of another. Since the segments come from different takes, the engineer must listen carefully to the proposed splice point before cutting the tape. Slight differences in phrasing, tempo, level, pitch, etc., that are not objectionable in themselves may become extremely noticeable if the takes are spliced together. Careful listening will usually reveal whether the splice can be made. However, if an attempted splice turns out to be unacceptable, the segments can be restored to their normal position and a new splice point sought.

In the event that a master tape containing a track of continuous SMPTE time code must be edited, the code must be replaced after the editing is completed as any discontinuities or discrepancies in the code will cause the automation system to provide false data to the mixdown monitor bus VCAs. Previously-stored automation data may be lost in some systems, while in others the data

Figure 19-1. The editing process. The takes that are to be used for mixdown work are removed and stored on a separate reel.

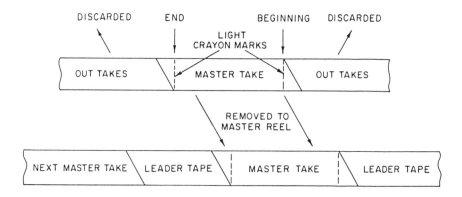

Figure 19-2. Commercially available splicing blocks. The vertical cuts are used for cutting digital tape and the angle cuts are used for splicing analog tapes.

can be reconstructed through merges or by starting the replacement code at the original SMPTE time-code address.

Splicing Blocks

Figure 19-2 shows several commercially available splicing blocks. Note that the analog splicing blocks pictured on the right allow the tape to be cut at an angle. This is done to distribute the cut over a short segment of the tape. A 90 degree or "butt" splice will usually make an audible "thump" as it passes the playback head. This occurs because the change or shift in magnetic flux density strikes the playback head gap space simultaneously for the full width of the tape. An angle cut allows the splice to slide across the playback head, thus distributing the flux change gradually across the gap space. The time before and after the center of the splice is known as the "lead" and "lag" time respectively. The digital tape splicing blocks pictured at the left of Figure 19-2 have the vertical cut that is necessary to prevent digital data discontinuity.

Although a 45-degree cut may be used and is desired on analog narrow width monaural tapes, it should be remembered that this angle distributes the cut over a length of tape that is equal to the width of the tape. Thus a 45-degree angle cut on a 2-inch tape takes up 2 inches of tape travel. This means that at a speed of 15

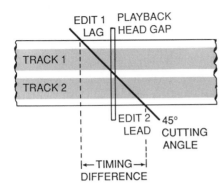

Figure 19-3. A two-track tape with a 45-degree angle edit. Note the timing difference between the beginning of the cut on track 1 and the end of the cut on track 2.

in./sec,, the splice will take $\frac{2}{15}$ of a second (133 milliseconds) to pass through all the tracks. This means that the edit on track No. 1 will occur 133 ms. prior to the edit on track No. 24. This length of time could make the splice quite noticeable, and so a narrow angle cut is usually used. Narrow editing angles take advantage of the psychoacoustic fact that the ear is unable to distinguish signal transitions that occur for less than 10 ms. Figure 19-3 shows a 2-track tape with a 45-degree angle cut, illustrating the lead and lag between the two tracks.

The preferred angles for splicing tape are:

¼-inch monaural	45 degrees
¼-inch two track or quarter-track stereo	30 degrees
1-inch multi-track tape	22 degrees
2-inch multi-track tape	15 degrees

The above angles will result in splices with signal transitions below the 10 ms. threshold.

Track Editing

On a multi-track tape that is a product of many overdub sessions, it is very easy to wind up with unwanted material on small segments of various tracks. For example, there may be studio noises on some of the tracks during long pauses. Or a verse or instrumental solo may no longer be wanted once the complete recording has been reviewed.

It is obviously impossible to physically edit a track on a multi-track tape without affecting all the remaining tracks, so electronic editing measures are necessary. One method entails removing some of these segments by simply switching the appropriate tracks on and off on cue. In non-automated mixdown situations this must be done manually. If there are several such segments, it may be difficult to coordinate all the channel-on/channel-off cues while also concentrating on the mixdown itself. In this case, it may be wiser to review each track carefully and to erase the unwanted segments before beginning the mixdown work. Before doing any erasing, the engineer should make certain that there is sufficient clearance before and after the segment to be erased so that wanted material is not accidentally lost. When this tape "housekeeping" is properly accomplished, only wanted usable material remains on the tape.

With an automation assisted mixdown system, this track editing can be programmed with the *Mute-Write* function of the system. Any number of channels can be switched on or off throughout the duration of the musical selection. Once programmed, the channel-on/channel-off status will be repeated automatically on each successive mixdown pass. One of the advantages of this method over the former "housekeeping" method is that in the former system, although the track is empty of unwanted material, it is still contributing noise to the monitor/mixdown bus. The latter system maintains a quieter mixdown by keeping the unwanted channels muted when not required.

TRACK ASSIGNMENT AND PANNING

In many cases, during recording, instruments are assigned to various console channel ACN outputs without regard to their eventual left-to-right orientation. Each track may be heard on the left, center, or right simply by panning the signal sent to the console's monitor path. However, during the mixdown session, the monitor path is used to feed the two-track mix bus, and the monitor pans are used to send the various multi-track signals to these two console outputs. One represents the left track and the other the right track. Signals that are to be heard in the center are routed equally to both left and right tracks, or the pan-pot may be used for intermediate positions between left and right. The action of the pan-pot was described in Chapter 16, and illustrated in Figure 16-12B.

Preparing for Mixdown

Before beginning the mixdown work, the tracks may be reviewed individually, while equalization, reverberation, and other types of signal processing are tried. Although there is nothing wrong with spending a little time verifying the contents of each track, there is little point to spending a lot of time evaluating each track out of context with the total program. By the time of the mixdown session, it really makes no difference what each isolated track sounds like. The signal processing that sounds right when the track is heard by itself will rarely remain effective once the track is mixed with others. What really matters is the contribution of each track to the total recording.

For example, two guitar tracks heard individually might be processed at great length, only to find that when they are combined together, they are noticeably out of synchronization with each other. It makes better sense to spend some time listening to groups of tracks to hear the effect of one instrument against another. The basic tracks may be monitored first, to work out position and balance. Then, rhythm instruments that were added during overdub sessions may be added and mixed in.

Later, strings, brass and synthesizer parts may be reviewed as an ensemble. Once a basic balance for this group is worked out, they are mixed in with the rhythm section. The solo vocal performance is often added last; however, it is a good idea to carefully listen to the vocalist before spending too much time working out the ideal instrumental balance. Depending on the performance, the instrumental balance may have to be substantially modified once the vocalist is added.

During these mixdown preparations, decisions as to VCA grouping, as mentioned in Chapter 16 and 17, can be made. For example, once the initial balance adjustments and panning for the drum kit are decided, the entire set of drum tracks can be grouped to Group No. 1. A group master can be assigned and then whenever a balance decision affecting the entire drum set is made, moving the group master will raise or lower the level of the entire drum mix without affecting the drum kit's internal balance or panning.

When an automation system is in use, these initial adjustments concerning balance, equalization and other processing are usually done in what is called the rehearsal or monitor mode. This allows the engineer to set up all the signals returning from the multi-track tape recorder and the external processing equipment before the initial *Write* pass is made. With tape-based automation systems this prevents cumulative offsets between the data and the music, and with disk-based systems (hard or floppy) this prevents filling up the storage space with multiple revisions. Refer to Chapter 17 for a more detailed discussion on this subject.

Assistance During Mixdown

On a complex non-automated mixdown session, there may be more changes to be made than can be handled by one engineer. However, the role of the assistant must be carefully spelled out in advance, to keep confusion at a minimum. One person must remain in complete charge of the mixdown, while the other makes whatever changes have been assigned to him. If the two engineers attempt to function independently of each other, each will be confused by the action of the other, and little or nothing constructive will be accomplished. Mixing is pretty much like sailing: there can be only one captain at a time.

It is at this stage in the mixdown process that automated mixdown systems justify their existence. After initial console adjustments are made, the first *Write* (a global *Write*) pass is made. This stores the fader VCA level and the *Mute* status for each channel in the monitor path contributing to the stereo mix. After a *Read* pass to verify that the initial data was stored properly, the system is then switched to the *Update* mode. This allows the engineer to make changes to individual track levels and mutes that are remembered by the automation system during subsequent passes of the master tape.

When the engineer is satisfied with the final mixed version of the selection, the system is once again placed in the *Read* mode, and upon playback, all the stored levels, level changes and mutes are executed by the automation system. This makes it possible for a single engineer to handle the mixdown of as many tracks as necessary. By routing the reverberation and effects returns to automated channels in the monitor path, these effects can be automated as well.

Recording and Monitor Levels

As the mixdown session begins, the engineer establishes a comfortable listening level in the control room. But, as more and more tracks are added, the monitor level rises accordingly, and may have to be turned down to maintain a reasonable sound level. However, the two-track recorded level also rises with each additional track and may become excessive once all the tracks have been added to the monitor path and sent to the two-track tape recorder.

The two-track master fader can of course be brought down somewhat. However, this does nothing to protect the amplifier stages just before it from high level overload. In most cases, the individual input faders should each be brought down to maintain a safe recording level. This can be inconvenient, since it means that as each group of tracks is brought into the mix, all the monitor faders must be readjusted—an awkward procedure at best. Some automation systems allow the automation master fader (different from the two-track master fader) to be brought down prior to nulling (refer to Chapter 17) all the faders for another update pass. This automation master lowers all of the VCA gains simultaneously. This is a stopgap measure at best since at some point the maximum travel point on the individual linear faders is going to be reached.

As a practical alternative, the mixdown session may begin with the monitor loudspeaker levels at a higher than normal setting. With the monitor level up, the engineer will not be tempted to raise the monitor path faders quite so high, thus keeping the recording level down. As more and more tracks are added, the control room monitor level may be brought down, and as the recording level gradually increases, it should remain within safe limits. A little practice will determine the optimum starting setting for the monitor control level.

As the mixdown continues, listening levels have a way of creeping gradually upward. (Some engineers say that they can tell how long they have been mixing by looking at the position of the control room monitor level potentiometer.) But, as the listening level increases, the engineer should keep in mind the implication of the equal loudness curves discussed in Chapter 2. Music mixed at high listening levels will sound quite differently when played back later at a lower level. The engineer who disregards this important fact does so at his or her own risk.

Monitor Loudspeakers for the Mixdown Session

Presumably, the well-equipped recording studio will have the best monitor system possible within its budget limitations. At this point in the book, the advantages of a well-designed, wide range monitor system should require no further discussion. However, a valid argument may be made for using a reasonably inexpensive monitor speaker at various times during the mixdown session. Despite the impressive technology discussed in the preceding chapters, it is unlikely that the majority of the recorded music buying public will be listening over state-of-the-art professional playback equipment. There are more portable radios in this world than can be counted, and their sound quality is—to put it politely—not up to professional standards. Yet, this is where much of the final product will be heard. The question is: what does it sound like on the beach, or in the car? One doesn't have to be an expert to realize that many mixing subtleties will be lost on a two-inch speaker in a plastic case.

And so, it is good to have an inexpensive speaker system available in the control room, to get some idea of what the ultimate mixdown will sound like in the hands of the consumer. Some ambitious studios even rig up a feed through a small radio receiver so that the engineer and the producer may get some impression of what the CD or Compact Cassette buyer will hear when he brings the final product home, or hears it in his car.

It is an exercise in futility to attempt a mixdown that will sound ideal on all systems. A review of Chapter 5 should clear up any misconceptions on that point. However, the engineer should have at least some idea of what the master tape may sound like once it leaves the studio.

THE TWO-TRACK MASTER

Now that the two-track master has been mixed from the composite multi-track master, any additional musical editing that could not be done earlier can be accomplished. Since the whole take has been mixed to provide a continuity of style and rhythm, it is often better to edit out extra verses, choruses, etc., after the mixdown has been completed.

Next, white leader tape of the appropriate length should be placed between succeeding selections. The timing of this may vary, depending whether the product is going to be produced at the manufacturing facility into a vinyl record, a Compact Disc, a Compact Cassette, or a DAT (Digital Audio Tape).

Most mastering facilities will require reference tones at the head of the tape, whether it is a two-track digital master or an analog master. It is important that the reference tones be recorded on the same machine that produced the two-track master. This allows the mastering engineer to adjust the frequency balance, operating level, tape head azimuth, and overall response of his playback equipment to match that of the two-track mixdown tape recorder. This way, what was heard in the mixdown studio will be accurately transferred to the appropriate final playback medium. Reference tones should include a 1 kHz signal for level purposes, a high-frequency tone of 10 kHz or 15 kHz for azimuth and frequency-response adjustments, and a low-frequency tone of 50 Hz or 100 Hz so that the low- frequency response of the system can be adjusted. If noise reduction is used on the reel, these calibration tones should be included also. All of these tones should be separated from the first selection by a length of white leader tape.

Finally, an analog tape should be wound at low speed onto a reel and stored "tails out" with the end of the final tail of white leader secured to the reel with adhesive tape to prevent the tape unwinding during transport. Digital reel-to-reel tapes should be handled similarly, while in-cassette digital tapes should be stored "heads out."

It is also important to label the box containing the tape, and the reel or the cassette itself with the appropriate recording information. This information should include the tape speed, operating level, track format, order of tones, and timings for the listed selections. Sampling rates, quantizing rates, and digital system type should be included with the digital format (DASH, PD, etc.)

MIXDOWN SUMMARY

Following is a brief summary of the steps required to produce a finished two-track master tape from a completed multi-track master.

Non-Automated

1. Prepare the mixdown machine. The machine to be used should be cleaned, de-magnetized and loaded with the selected type of magnetic tape. The record and playback alignment should be checked and any discrepancies corrected.

2. Record the calibration and alignment tones onto the mixdown machine.

3. Prepare the console for mixdown. Place the console in the "mix" or line-in mode so that the output of the multi-track recorder is routed to the monitor path on the console. Make sure that all console adjustments entered during the tracking sessions have been returned to their normal positions.

4. Assign monitor channel path inputs to groups (and select group masters) and set pan pots for the desired instrumental placement in the stereo image.

5. Play the multi-track tape as many times as necessary to achieve the desired basic mix.

6. Add equalization, reverberation and effects while monitoring the playback of the entire mix, making adjustments as necessary.

7. Changes that are to be made during the actual recording of the two-track mixdown master are noted in the score or on the lead sheet, so that the engineer will be reminded to make these adjustments as the mixdown progresses.

8. The two-track mixdown machine is placed in the record mode and the mixdown of the multi-track tape and any effects are committed to tape.

9. The mixdown tape is rewound and played while the engineer and producer follow the score or leadsheet to verify that the mix is correct. The tape is edited, leadered, and labeled. Often, a safety copy of the mixdown master is made and stored or kept in a separate location.

Automated

The process for an automated mixdown is very similar to the steps listed above. The following steps would be added.

2a. Prepare the multi-track master to receive and send automation data or SMPTE time code, either by preparing two channels for record and playback with tape based systems, or by stripping a selected channel on the multi-track recorder with SMPTE time code for use with disk-based systems.

4a. Assign the automation system to the rehearsal or monitor mode.

6a. Place the console in the global *Write* mode and record the control settings of the basic mix with equalization and effects to the automation storage system.

7a. Place the console in the *Update* mode. Make and store any changes made during the mix as revisions of the basic storage *Write* pass. The multi-track may be rewound and played as many times as necessary until all fader VCAs and mutes are updated. Reverberation and effects returns may be automated and stored at this point also.

7b. When all changes and updates have been made, the console is placed in the *Read* mode. When the multi-track tape is played, the various monitor path fader VCAs and channel mutes will be controlled by the automation system.

Bibliography of Selected Reference Works

Backus, J. The Acoustical Foundations of Music, W.W. Norton Co. Inc., 1969

Badmaieff, A. and Davis, D. How to Build Speaker Enclosures, Howard Sams, 1966

Benade, A. Fundamentals of Musical Acoustics, Oxford University Press, 1976

Beranek, L. Acoustics, McGraw-Hill, 1954

Beranek, L. Music, Acoustics and Architecture, John Wiley and Sons, 1962

Bore, G. Microphones, Georg Neumann GMBH, 1978

Borwick, J. (ed). Sound Recording Practice, Oxford University Press, 2nd Edition 1980

Camras, M. Magnetic Recording Handbook, Van Nostrand Reinhold, 1988

Davis, D. and C. Sound System Engineering, Howard Sams, 2nd Edition 1987

Eargle, J. Sound Recording, Van Nostrand Reinhold, 2nd Edition 1980

Eargle, J. The Microphone Handbook, ELAR Publishing, 1982

Everest, F.A. Acoustic Techniques for Home and Studio, TAB Books, 1973

Everest, F.A. The Master Handbook of Acoustics, TAB Books, 1981

Hickman, W. Time Code Handbook, Cipher Digital, 1984

Nakajima, H. Digital Audio, TAB Books, 1983

Olson, H. Music, Physics and Engineering, Dover Publications, 1967

Pohlmann, K. Principals of Digital Audio, Howard Sams, 1985

Tremaine, H. The Audio Cyclopedia, Howard Sams, 1978

Various Authors, Digital Audio, Collected Papers from the AES Conference, Rye, NY, 1982

Various Authors, Digital Audio Basics, Professional Audio Training Group, Sony Professional Products Co., 1987

Various Authors, Loudspeakers, an anthology published by the Journal of the Audio Engineering Society, 1980

Various Authors, Stereophonic Techniques, an anthology published by the Journal of the Audio Engineering Society, 1980

INDEX

-T-